You're reading the
WRONG WAY

MAGI reads from right to left, starting in the upper-right corner. Japanese is read from **right** to **left**, meaning that action, sound effects, and word-balloon order are completely reversed from English order.

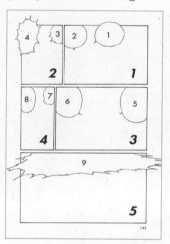

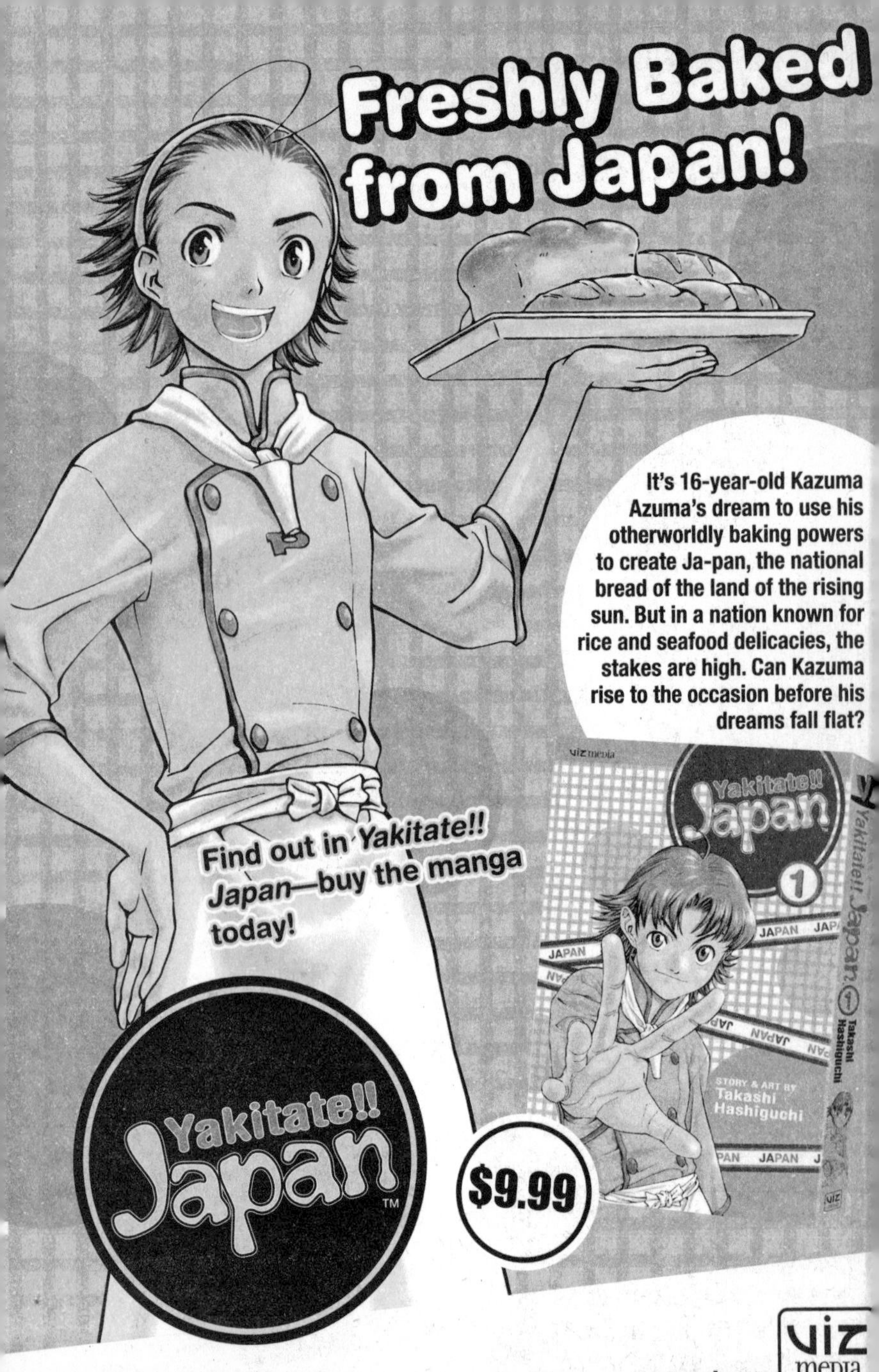
Freshly Baked from Japan!
It's 16-year-old Kazuma Azuma's dream to use his otherworldly baking powers to create Ja-pan, the national bread of the land of the rising sun. But in a nation known for rice and seafood delicacies, the stakes are high. Can Kazuma rise to the occasion before his dreams fall flat?
Find out in Yakitate!! Japan—buy the manga today!
Yakitate!! Japan™
$9.99
viz media
Yakitate!! Japan 1
STORY & ART BY Takashi Hashiguchi
viz media

MAGI

The labyrinth of magic

29

Story & Art by
SHINOBU OHTAKA

MAGI
The labyrinth of magic

29

CONTENTS

Night 279: Victor and Vanquished

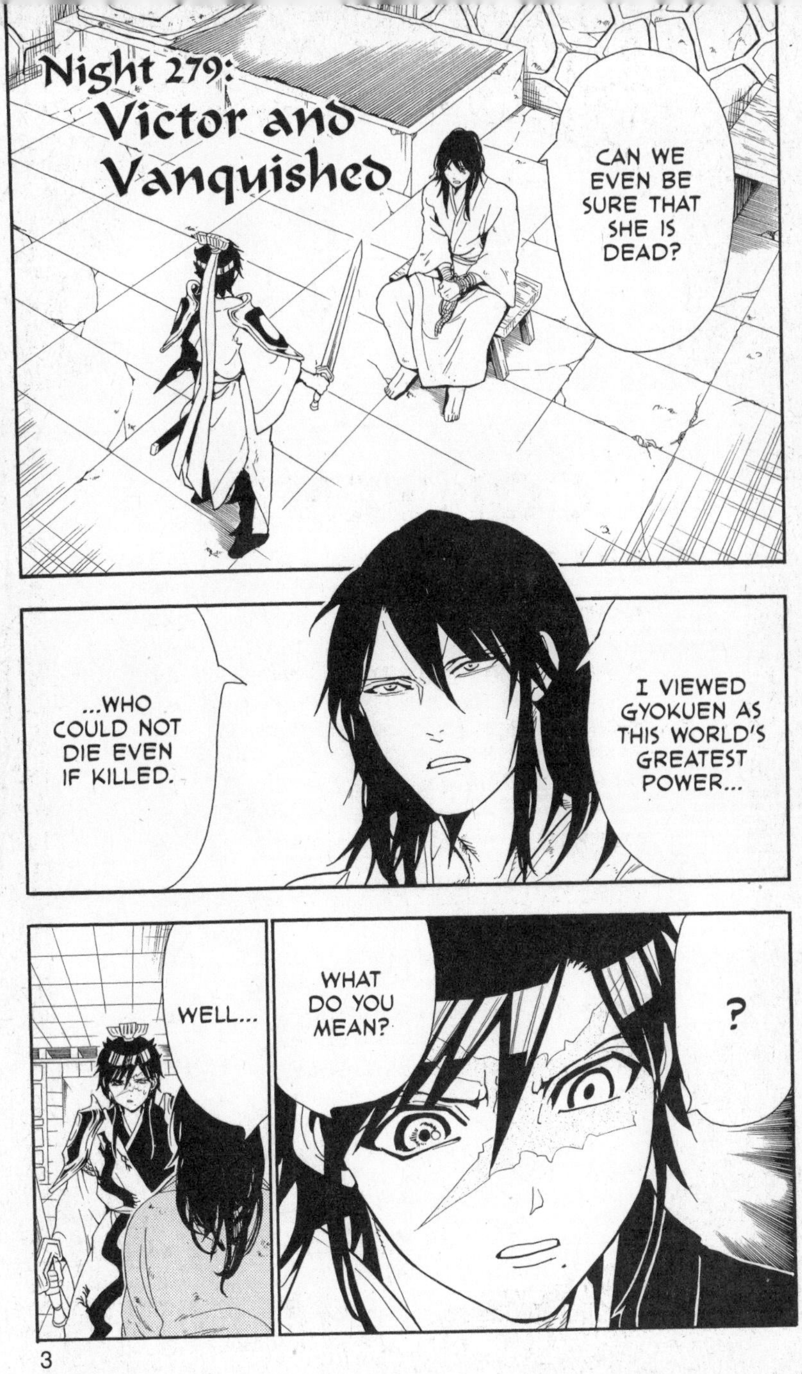
CAN WE EVEN BE SURE THAT SHE IS DEAD?
I VIEWED GYOKUEN AS THIS WORLD'S GREATEST POWER...
...WHO COULD NOT DIE EVEN IF KILLED.
?
WHAT DO YOU MEAN?
WELL...

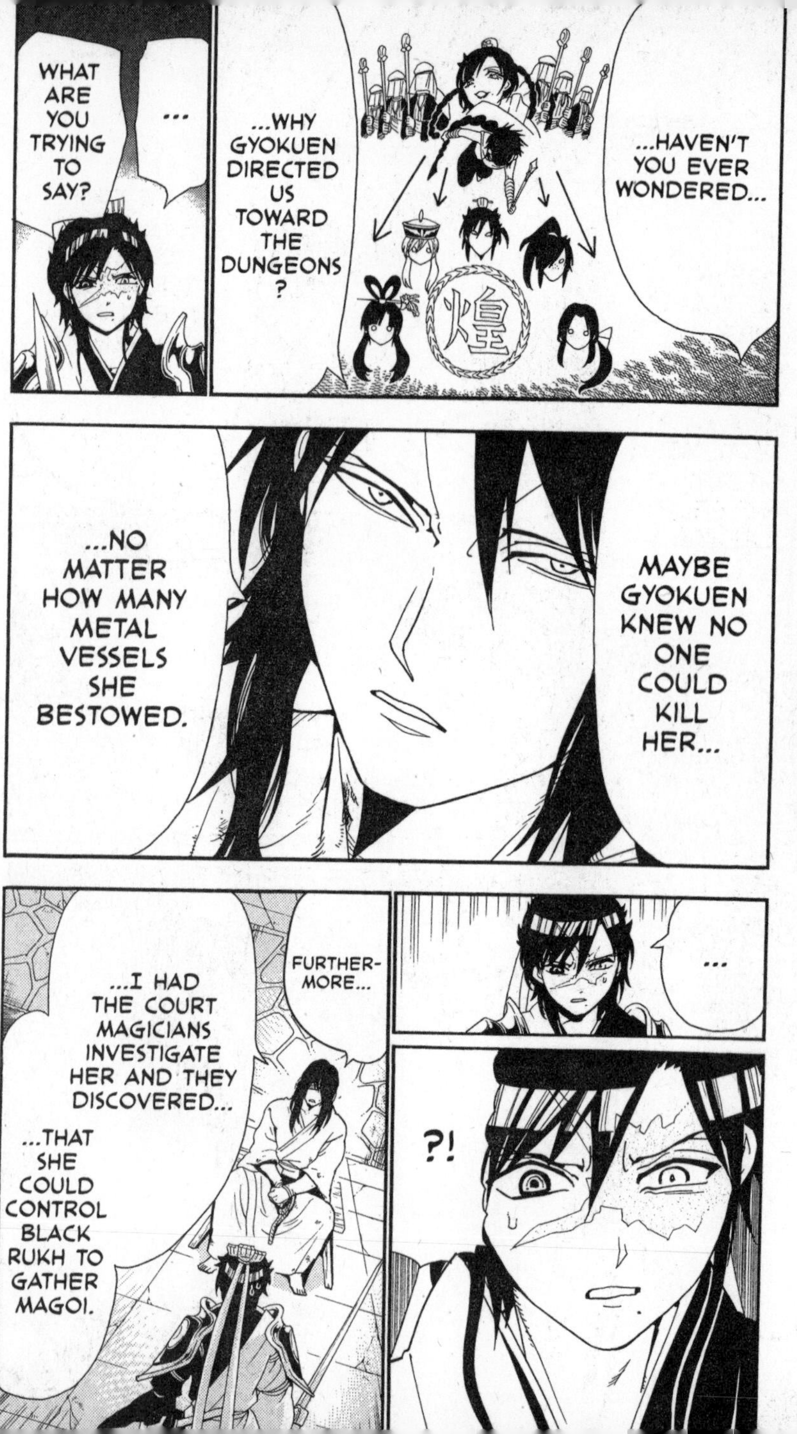
...HAVEN'T YOU EVER WONDERED...
...WHY GYOKUEN DIRECTED US TOWARD THE DUNGEONS?
...
WHAT ARE YOU TRYING TO SAY?
MAYBE GYOKUEN KNEW NO ONE COULD KILL HER...
...NO MATTER HOW MANY METAL VESSELS SHE BESTOWED.
...
?!
FURTHER-MORE...
...I HAD THE COURT MAGICIANS INVESTIGATE HER AND THEY DISCOVERED...
...THAT SHE COULD CONTROL BLACK RUKH TO GATHER MAGOI.

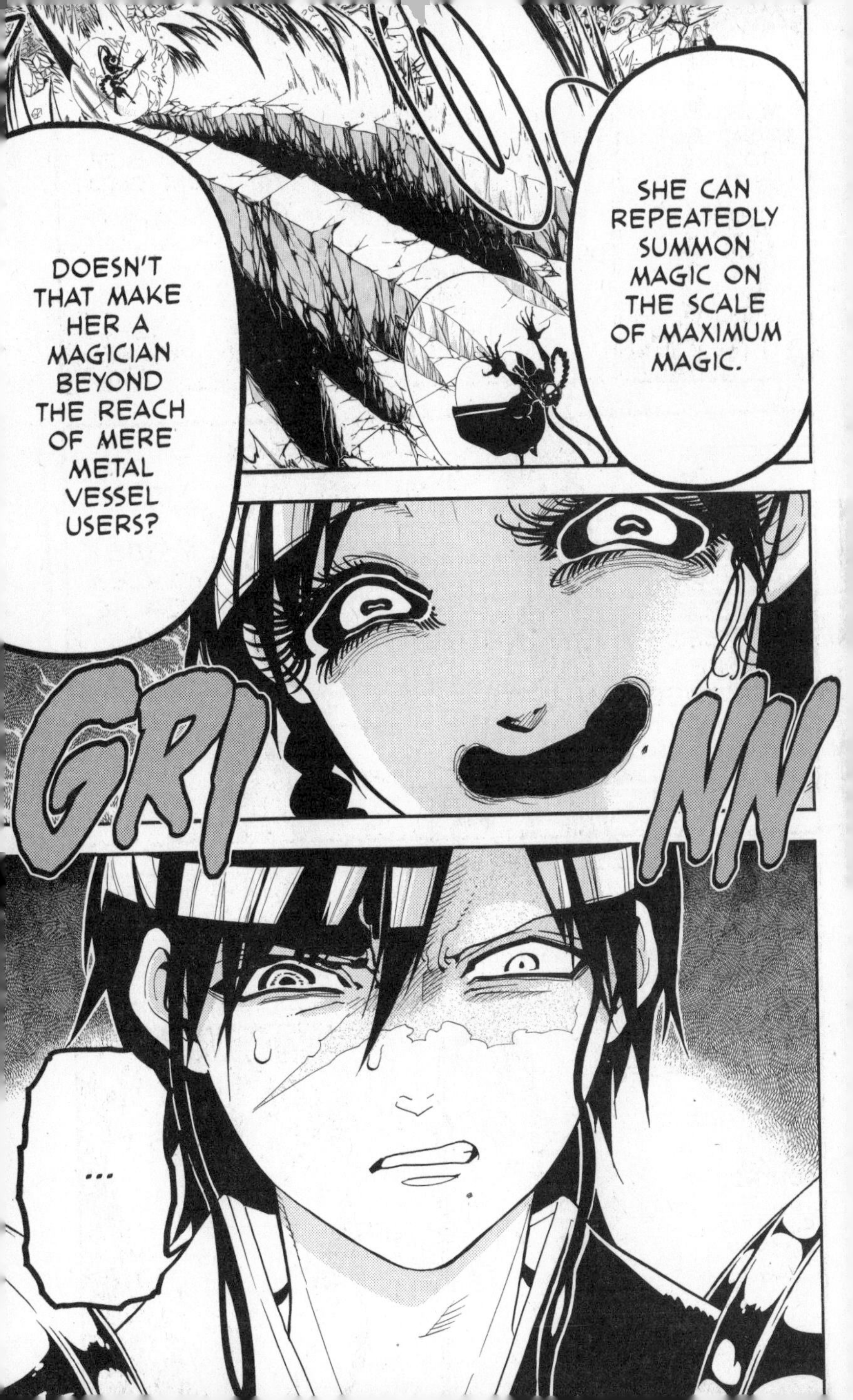
SHE CAN REPEATEDLY SUMMON MAGIC ON THE SCALE OF MAXIMUM MAGIC.
DOESN'T THAT MAKE HER A MAGICIAN BEYOND THE REACH OF MERE METAL VESSEL USERS?
GRINN
...

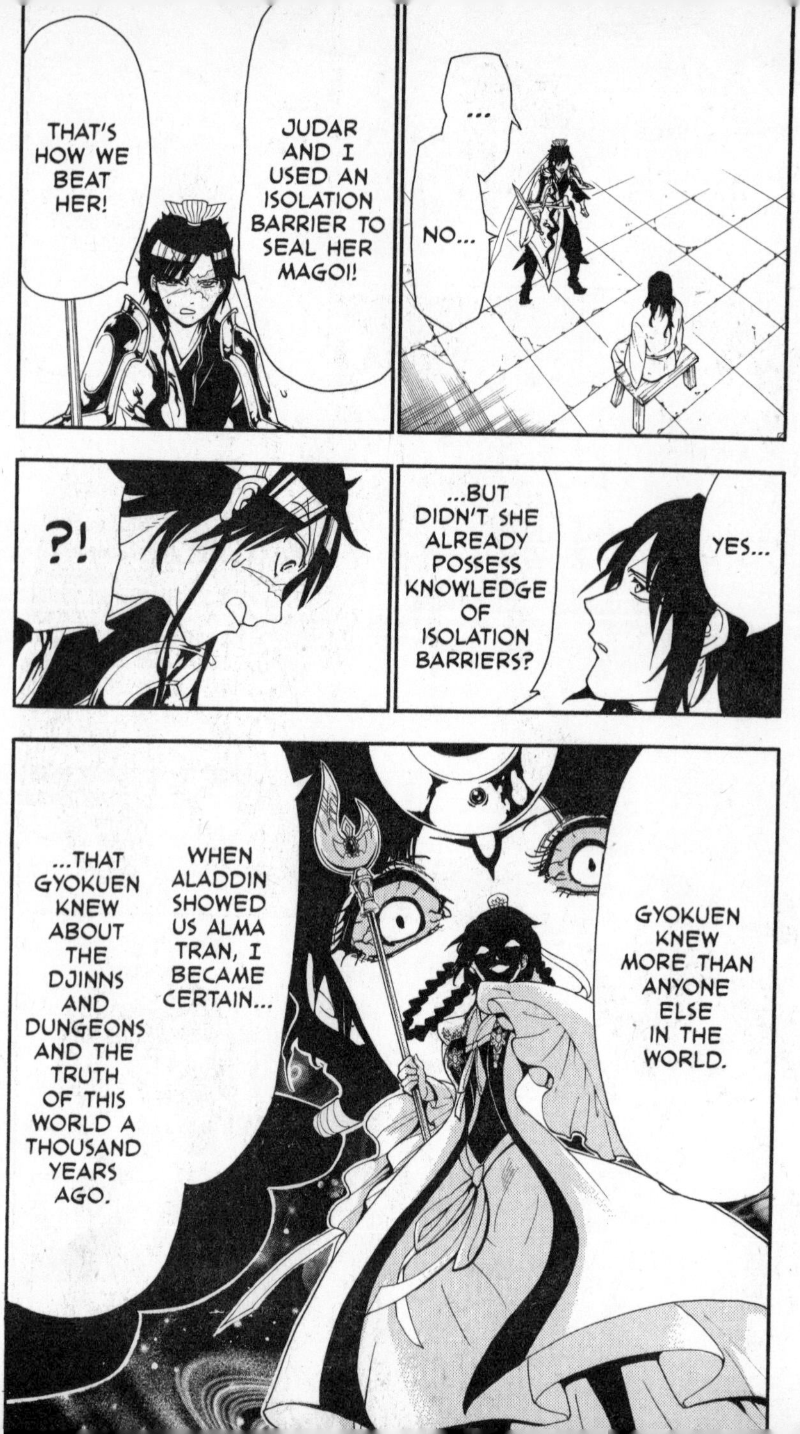
...
NO...
JUDAR AND I USED AN ISOLATION BARRIER TO SEAL HER MAGOI!
THAT'S HOW WE BEAT HER!
YES...
...BUT DIDN'T SHE ALREADY POSSESS KNOWLEDGE OF ISOLATION BARRIERS?
?!
GYOKUEN KNEW MORE THAN ANYONE ELSE IN THE WORLD.
WHEN ALADDIN SHOWED US ALMA TRAN, I BECAME CERTAIN...
...THAT GYOKUEN KNEW ABOUT THE DJINNS AND DUNGEONS AND THE TRUTH OF THIS WORLD A THOUSAND YEARS AGO.

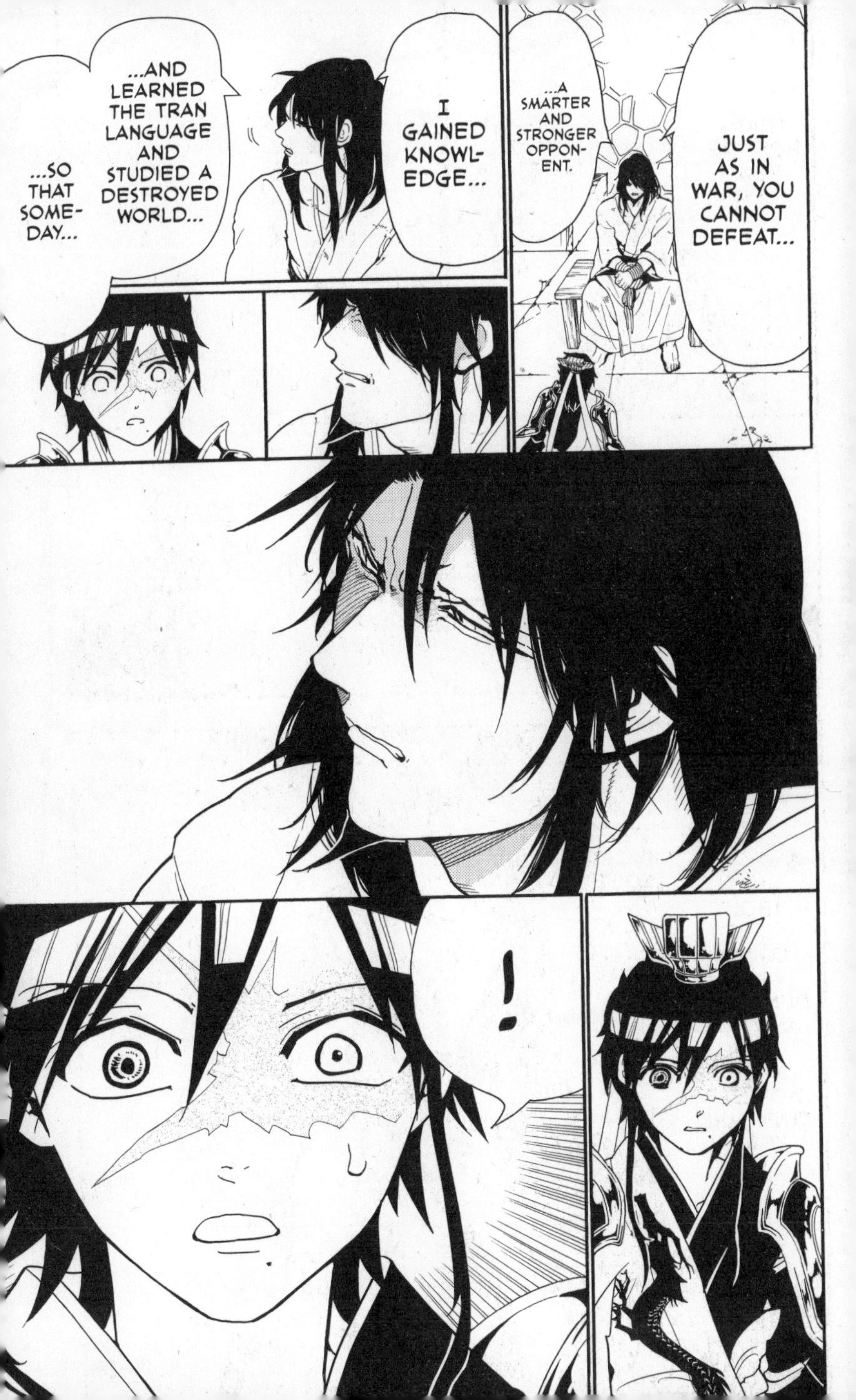
JUST AS IN WAR, YOU CANNOT DEFEAT...
...A SMARTER AND STRONGER OPPONENT.
I GAINED KNOWLEDGE...
...AND LEARNED THE TRAN LANGUAGE AND STUDIED A DESTROYED WORLD...
...SO THAT SOMEDAY...
!

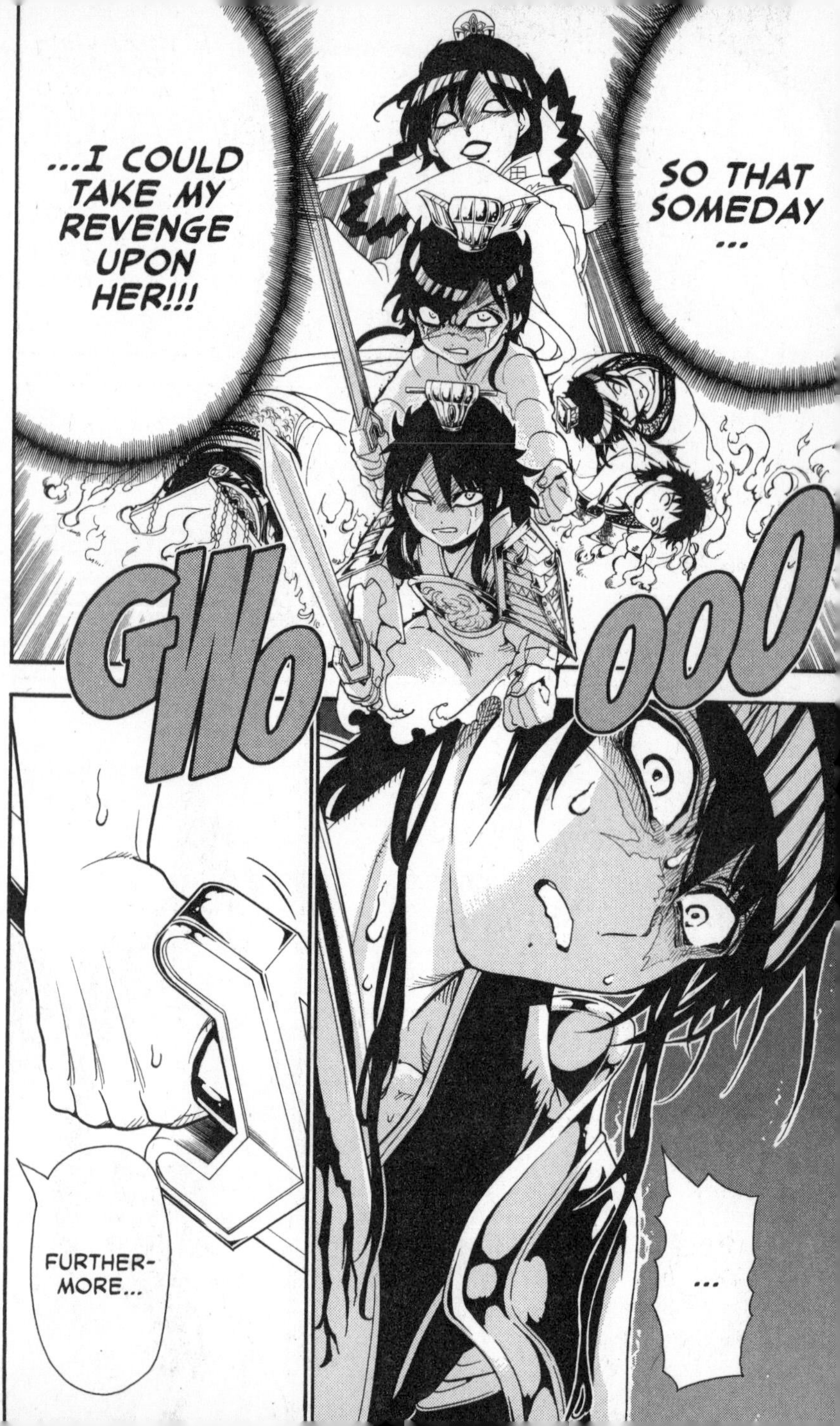
SO THAT SOMEDAY...
...I COULD TAKE MY REVENGE UPON HER!!!
GWOOOO
...
FURTHER-MORE...

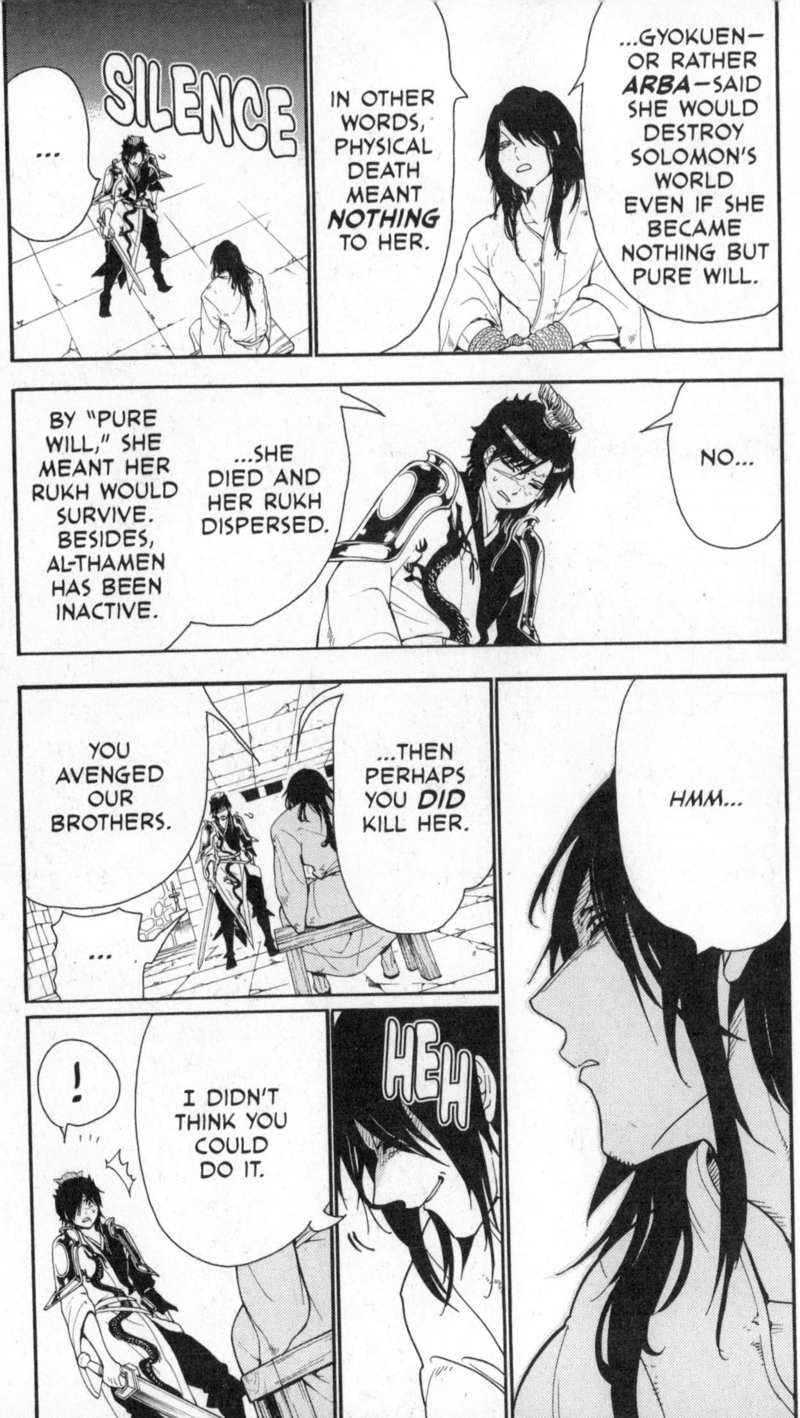
...GYOKUEN—OR RATHER ARBA—SAID SHE WOULD DESTROY SOLOMON'S WORLD EVEN IF SHE BECAME NOTHING BUT PURE WILL.
IN OTHER WORDS, PHYSICAL DEATH MEANT NOTHING TO HER.
SILENCE
...
NO...
...SHE DIED AND HER RUKH DISPERSED.
BY "PURE WILL," SHE MEANT HER RUKH WOULD SURVIVE. BESIDES, AL-THAMEN HAS BEEN INACTIVE.
HMM...
...THEN PERHAPS YOU DID KILL HER.
YOU AVENGED OUR BROTHERS.
...
HEH
I DIDN'T THINK YOU COULD DO IT.
!

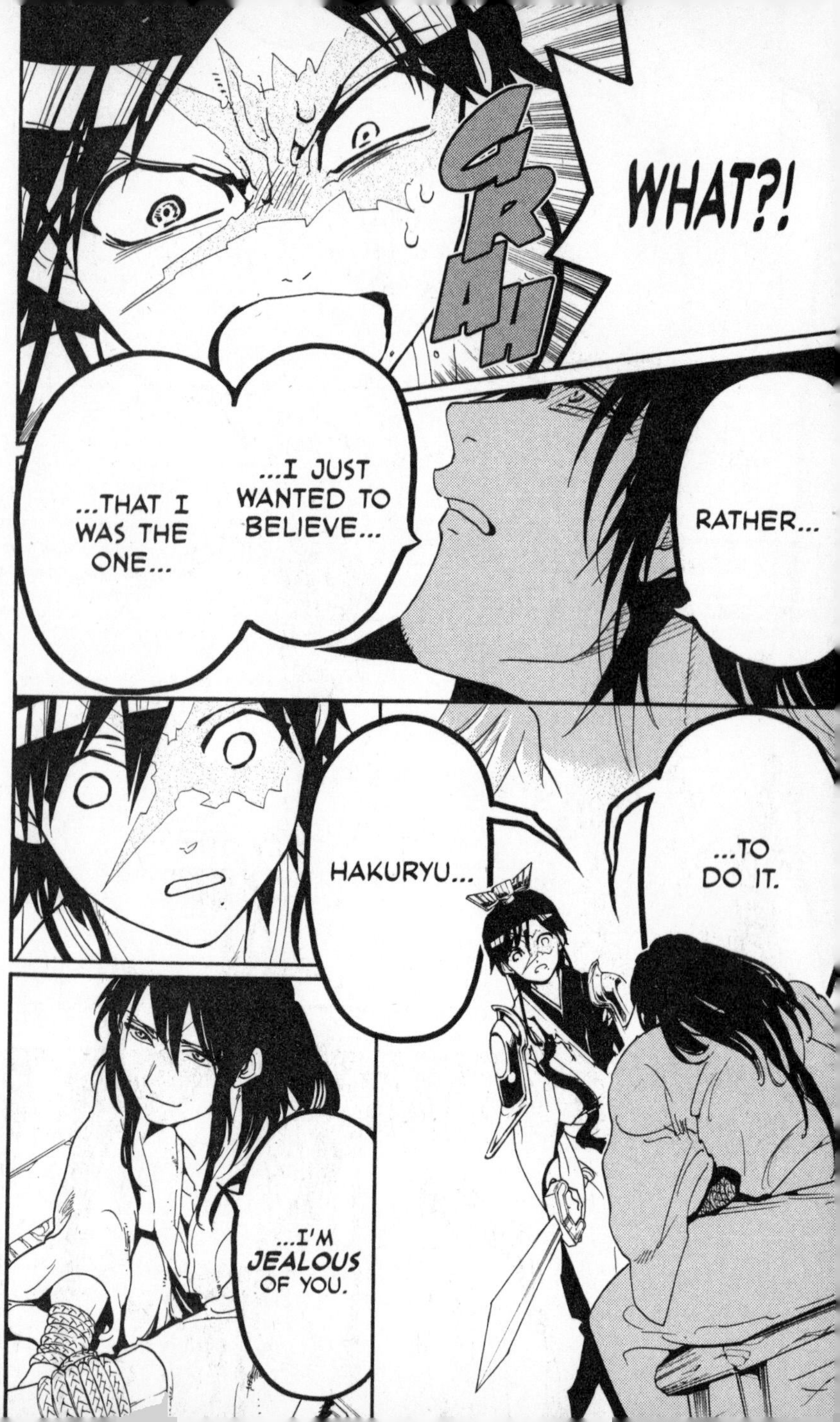
WHAT?!
GRAH
RATHER...
...I JUST WANTED TO BELIEVE...
...THAT I WAS THE ONE...
...TO DO IT.
HAKURYU...
...I'M JEALOUS OF YOU.

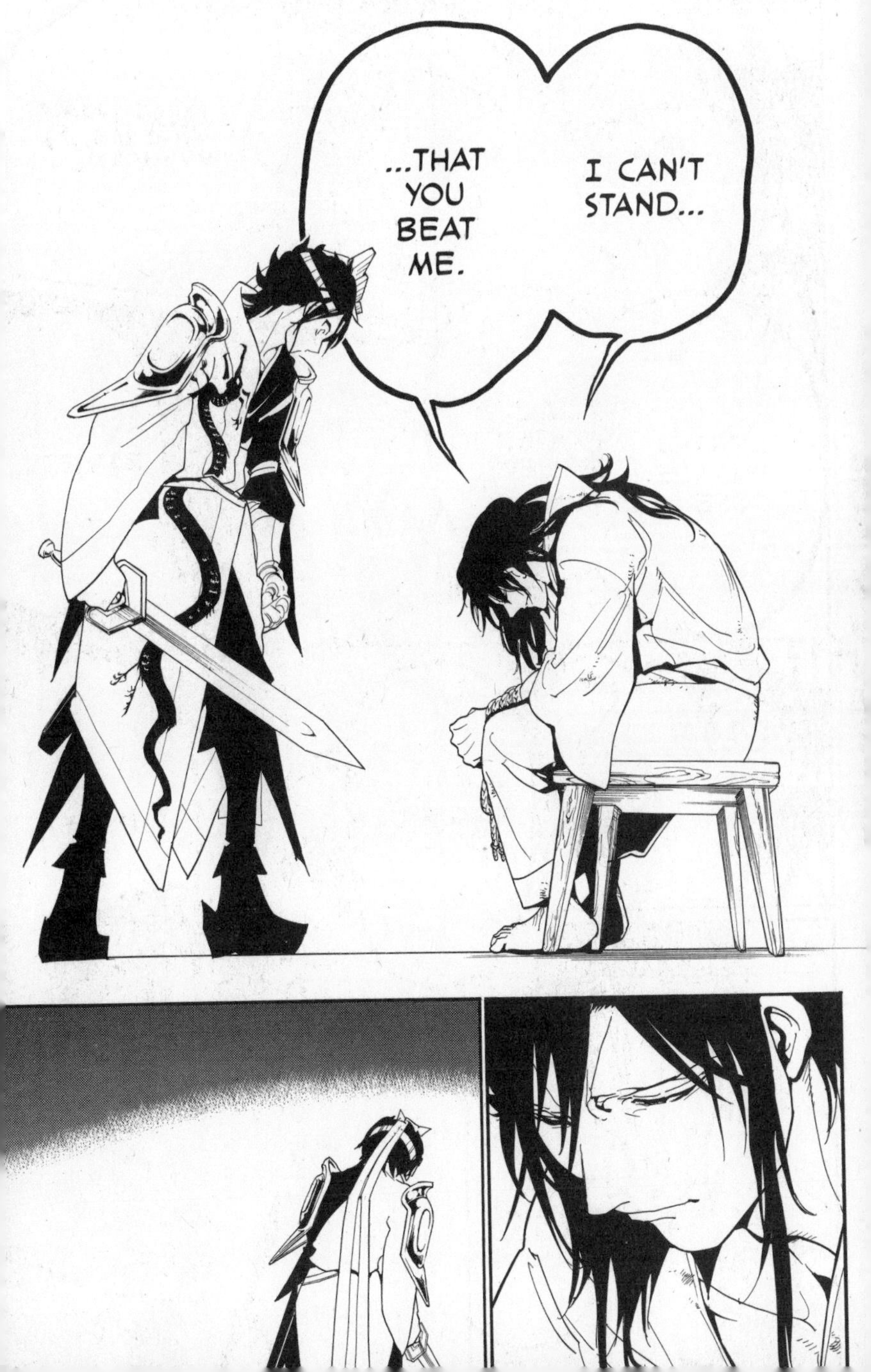
I CAN'T STAND...
...THAT YOU BEAT ME.

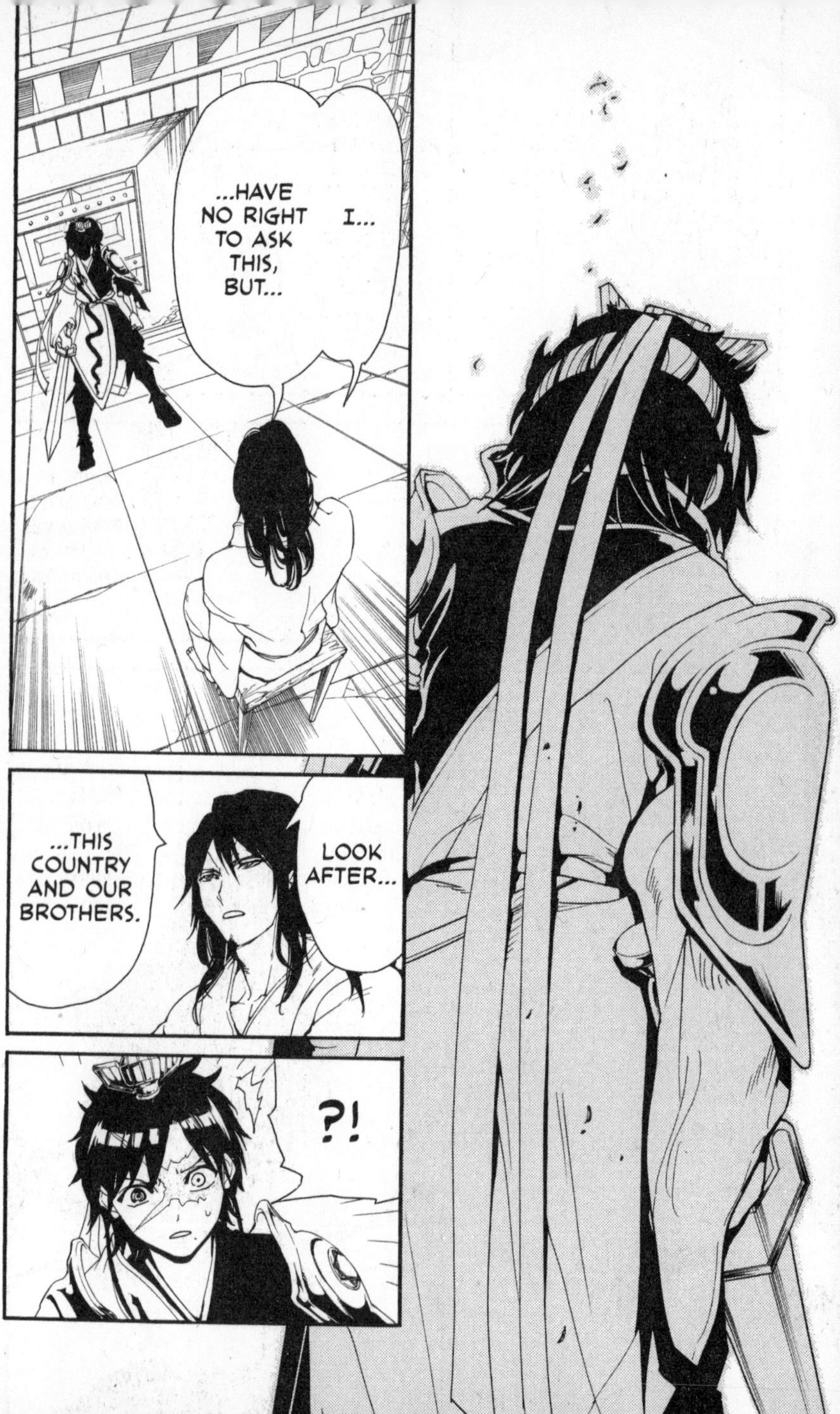
I...
...HAVE NO RIGHT TO ASK THIS, BUT...
LOOK AFTER...
...THIS COUNTRY AND OUR BROTHERS.
?!

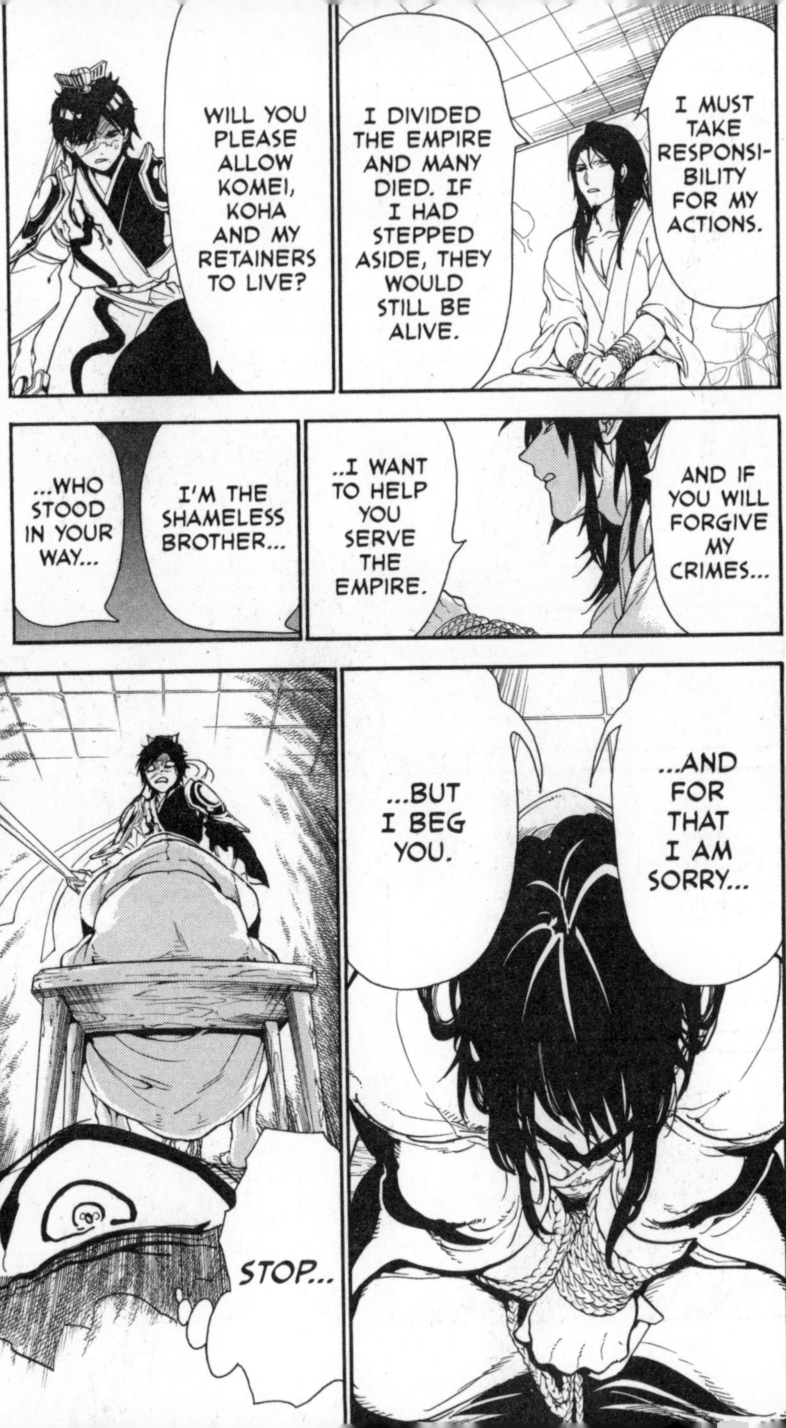
I MUST TAKE RESPONSI-BILITY FOR MY ACTIONS.
I DIVIDED THE EMPIRE AND MANY DIED. IF I HAD STEPPED ASIDE, THEY WOULD STILL BE ALIVE.
WILL YOU PLEASE ALLOW KOMEI, KOHA AND MY RETAINERS TO LIVE?
AND IF YOU WILL FORGIVE MY CRIMES...
..I WANT TO HELP YOU SERVE THE EMPIRE.
I'M THE SHAMELESS BROTHER...
...WHO STOOD IN YOUR WAY...
...AND FOR THAT I AM SORRY...
...BUT I BEG YOU.
STOP...

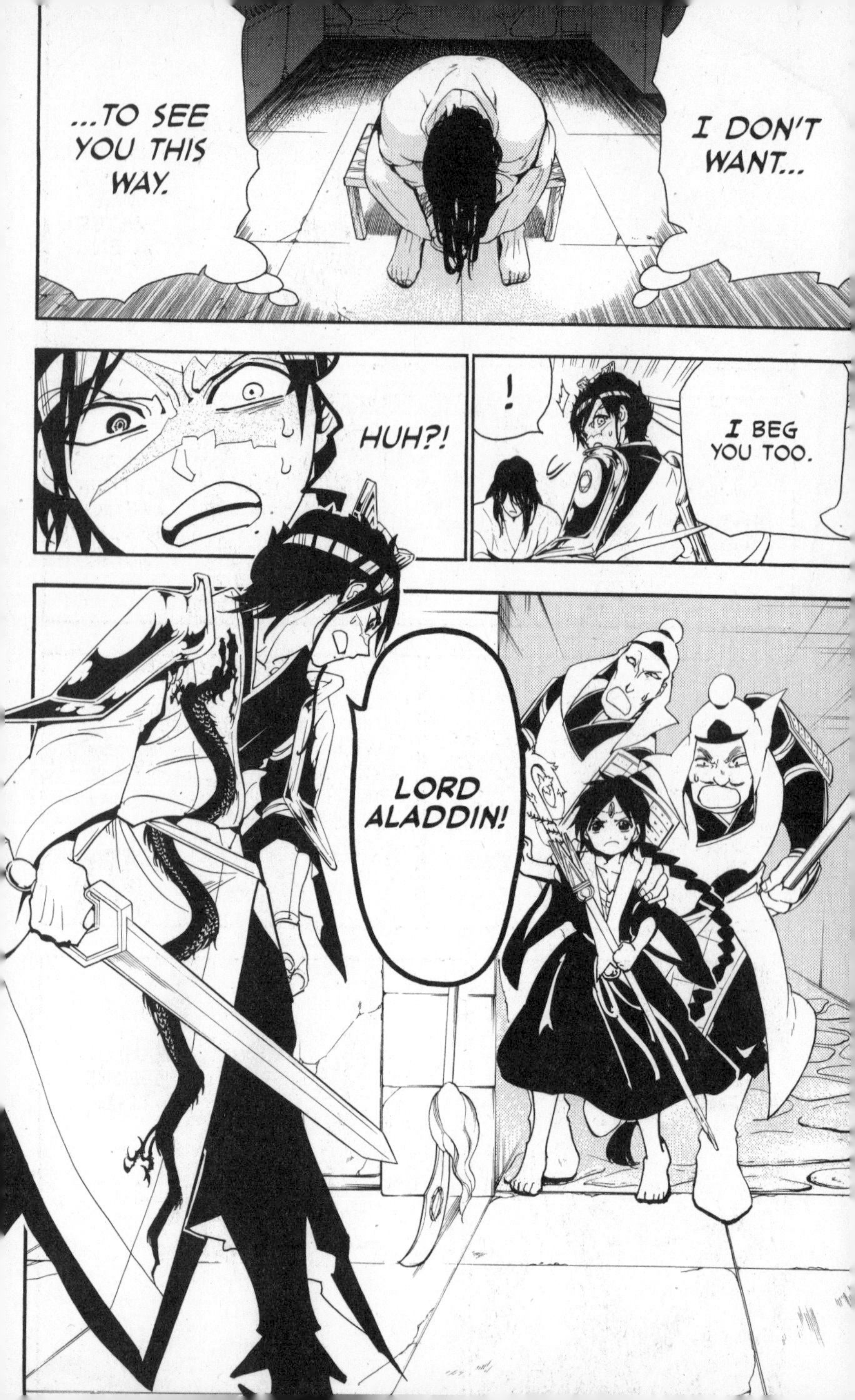
I DON'T WANT...
...TO SEE YOU THIS WAY.
I BEG YOU TOO.
!
HUH?!
LORD ALADDIN!

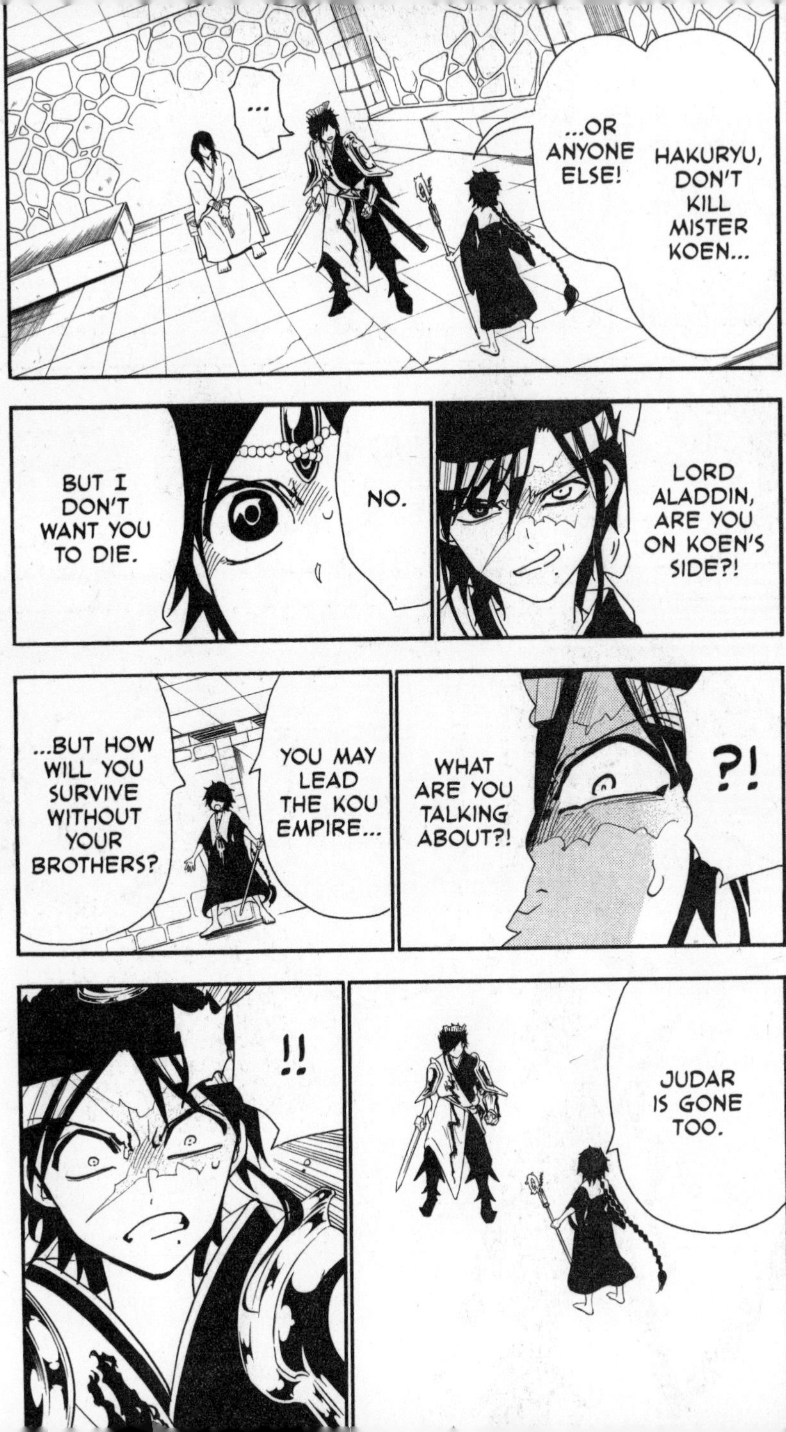
HAKURYU, DON'T KILL MISTER KOEN...
...OR ANYONE ELSE!
...
LORD ALADDIN, ARE YOU ON KOEN'S SIDE?!
NO.
BUT I DON'T WANT YOU TO DIE.
?!
WHAT ARE YOU TALKING ABOUT?!
YOU MAY LEAD THE KOU EMPIRE...
...BUT HOW WILL YOU SURVIVE WITHOUT YOUR BROTHERS?
JUDAR IS GONE TOO.
!!

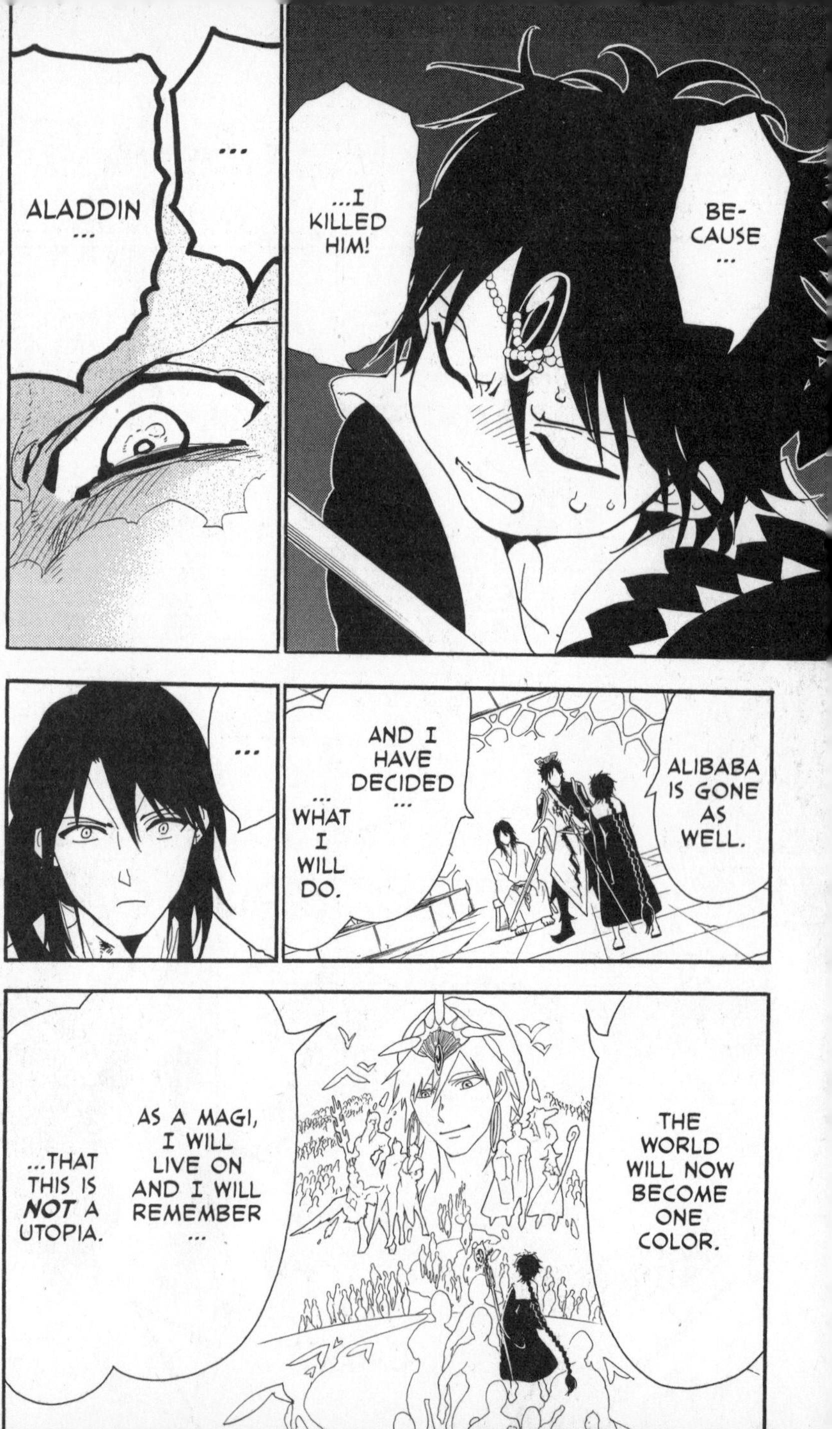
BE-CAUSE ...
...I KILLED HIM!
...
ALADDIN ...
ALIBABA IS GONE AS WELL.
AND I HAVE DECIDED ...
... WHAT I WILL DO.
...
THE WORLD WILL NOW BECOME ONE COLOR.
AS A MAGI, I WILL LIVE ON AND I WILL REMEMBER ...
...THAT THIS IS *NOT* A UTOPIA.

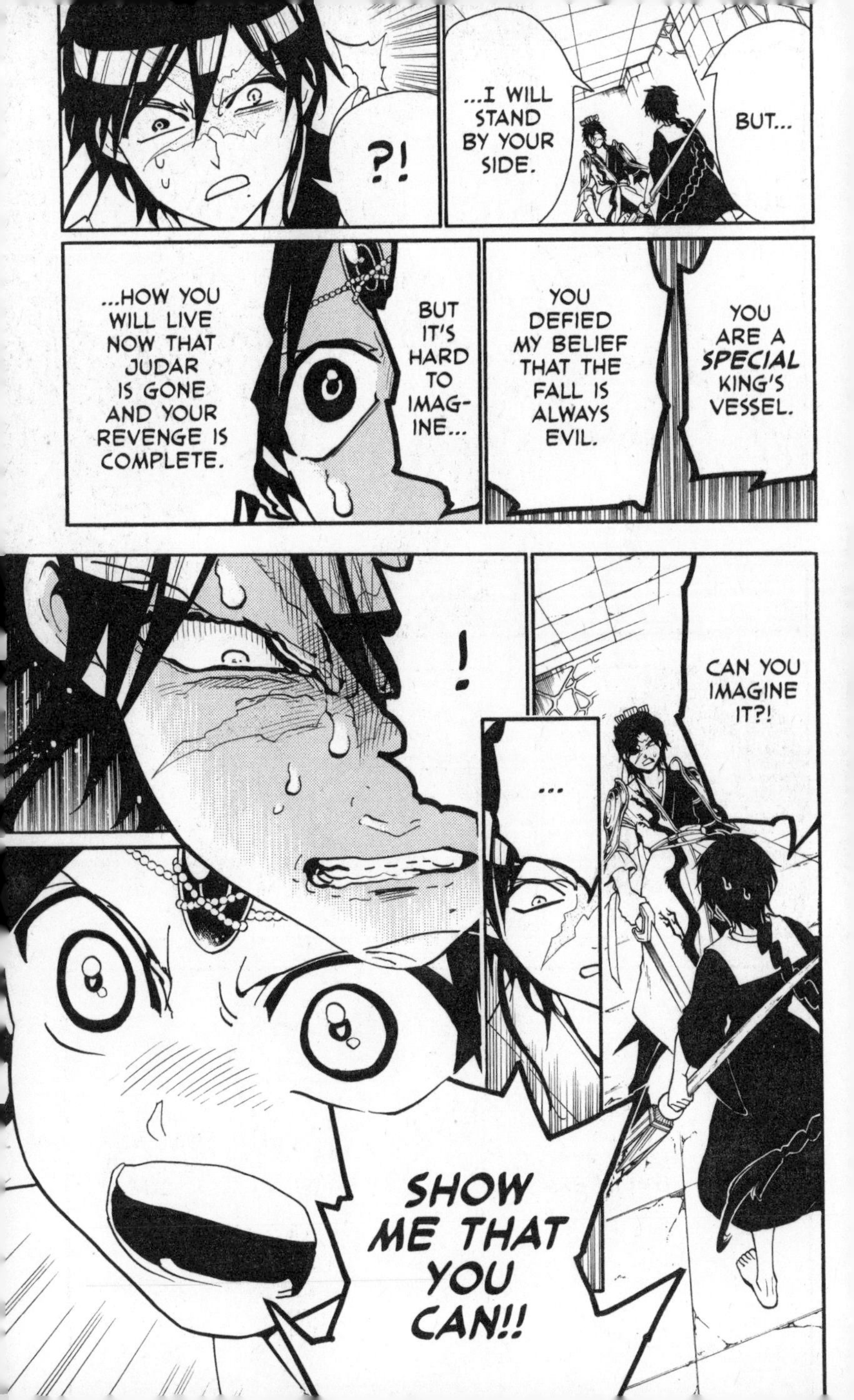
BUT...
...I WILL STAND BY YOUR SIDE.
?!
YOU ARE A *SPECIAL* KING'S VESSEL.
YOU DEFIED MY BELIEF THAT THE FALL IS ALWAYS EVIL.
BUT IT'S HARD TO IMAGINE...
...HOW YOU WILL LIVE NOW THAT JUDAR IS GONE AND YOUR REVENGE IS COMPLETE.
CAN YOU IMAGINE IT?!
...
!
SHOW ME THAT YOU CAN!!

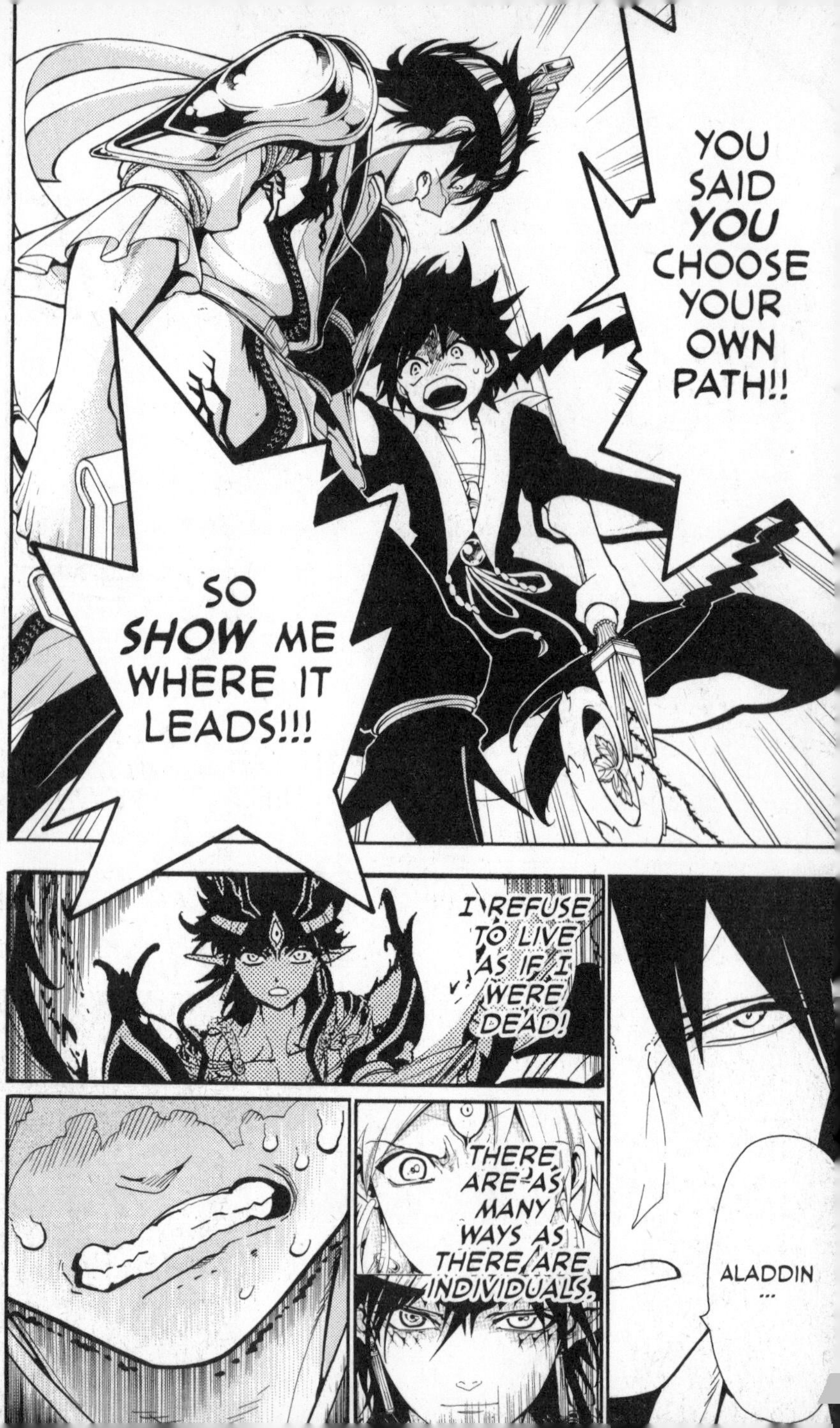
YOU SAID YOU CHOOSE YOUR OWN PATH!!
SO SHOW ME WHERE IT LEADS!!!
I REFUSE TO LIVE AS IF I WERE DEAD!
ALADDIN ...
THERE ARE AS MANY WAYS AS THERE ARE INDIVIDUALS.

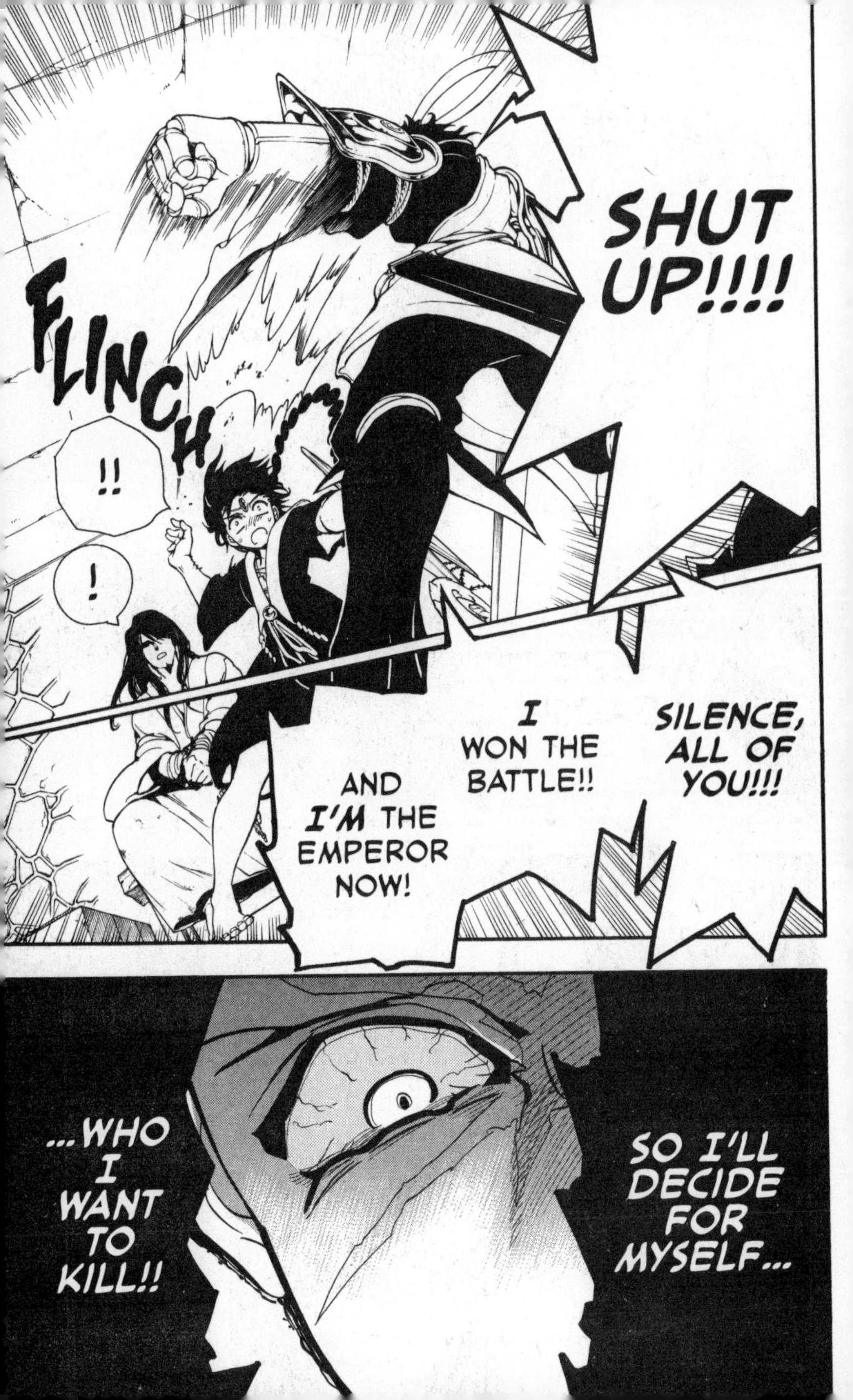
SHUT UP!!!!
FLINCH
!!
!
SILENCE, ALL OF YOU!!!
I WON THE BATTLE!!
AND I'M THE EMPEROR NOW!
SO I'LL DECIDE FOR MYSELF...
...WHO I WANT TO KILL!!

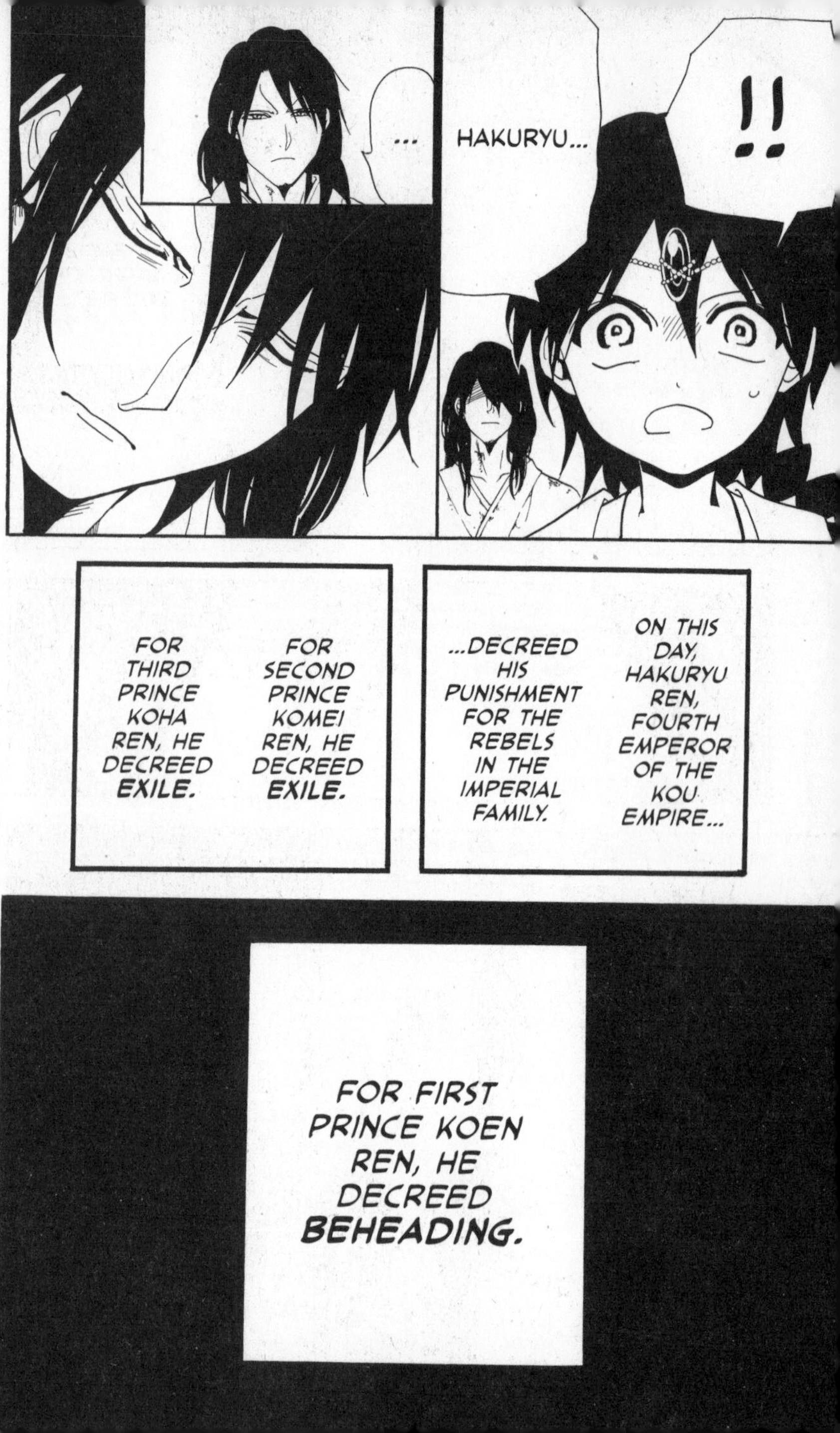
!!
HAKURYU...
...
ON THIS DAY, HAKURYU REN, FOURTH EMPEROR OF THE KOU EMPIRE...
...DECREED HIS PUNISHMENT FOR THE REBELS IN THE IMPERIAL FAMILY.
FOR SECOND PRINCE KOMEI REN, HE DECREED EXILE.
FOR THIRD PRINCE KOHA REN, HE DECREED EXILE.
FOR FIRST PRINCE KOEN REN, HE DECREED BEHEADING.

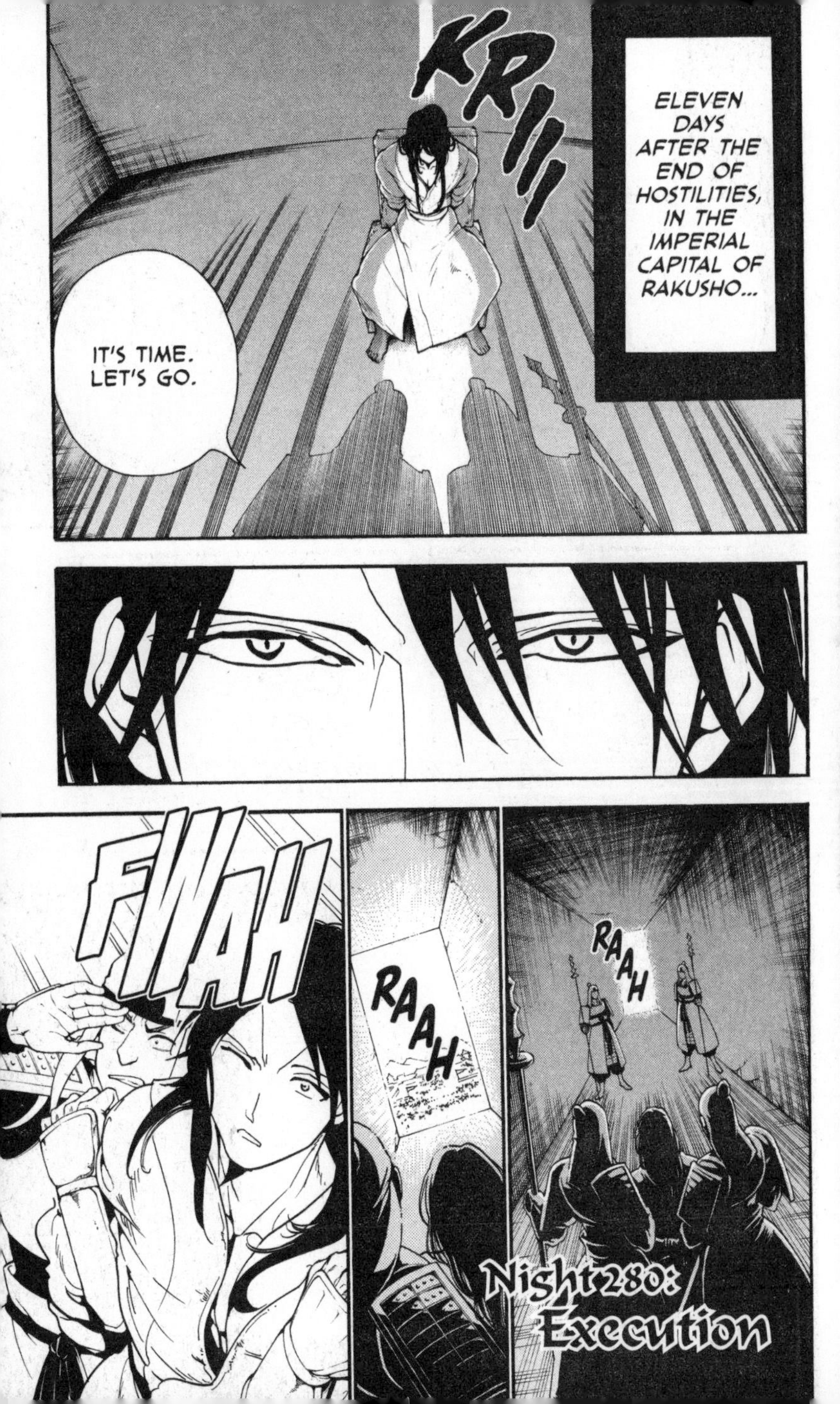
ELEVEN DAYS AFTER THE END OF HOSTILITIES, IN THE IMPERIAL CAPITAL OF RAKUSHO...
KRIII
IT'S TIME. LET'S GO.
RAAH
Night 280: Execution
RAAH
FWAH

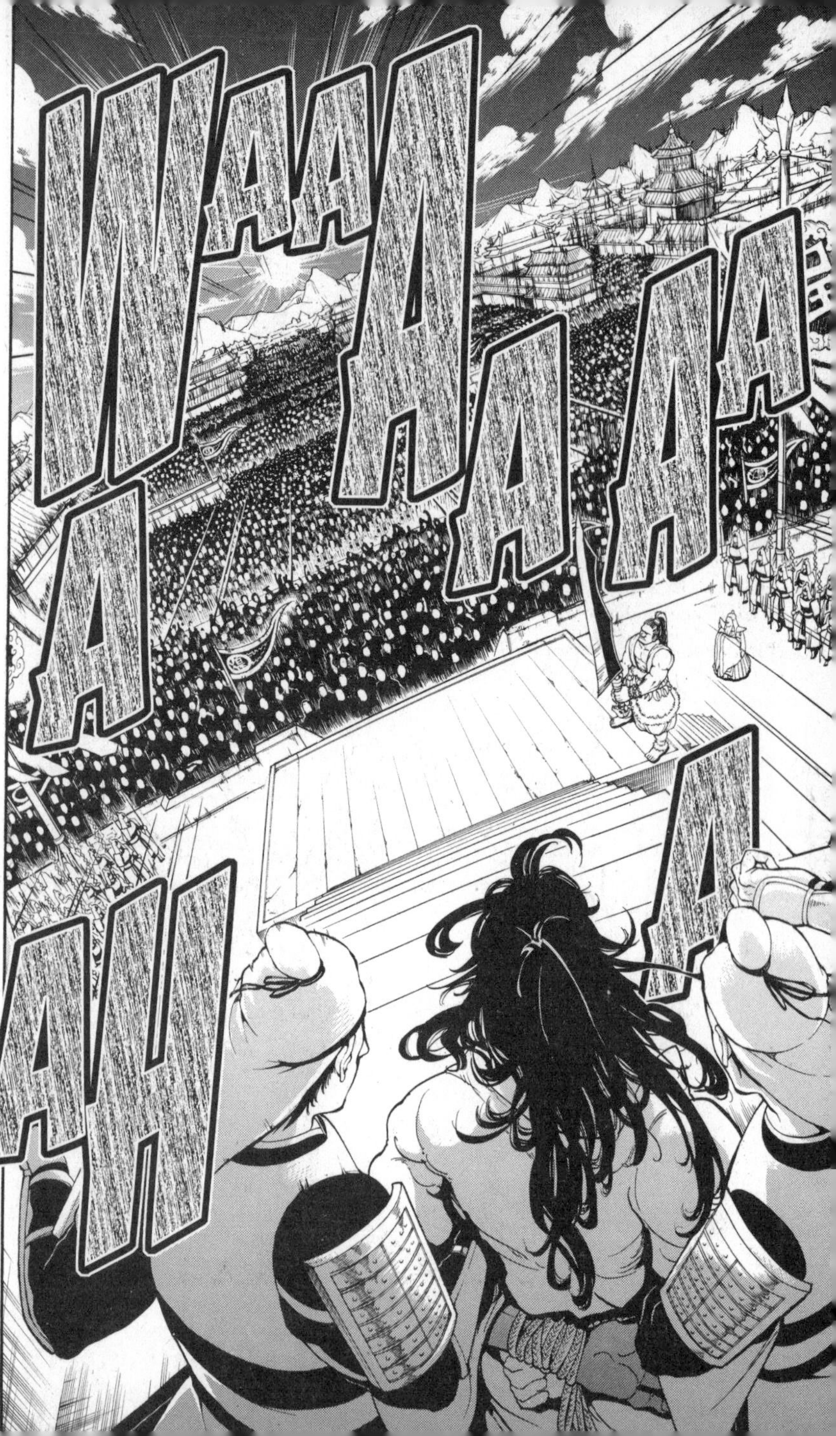
WAAAAAAAAAAAAH

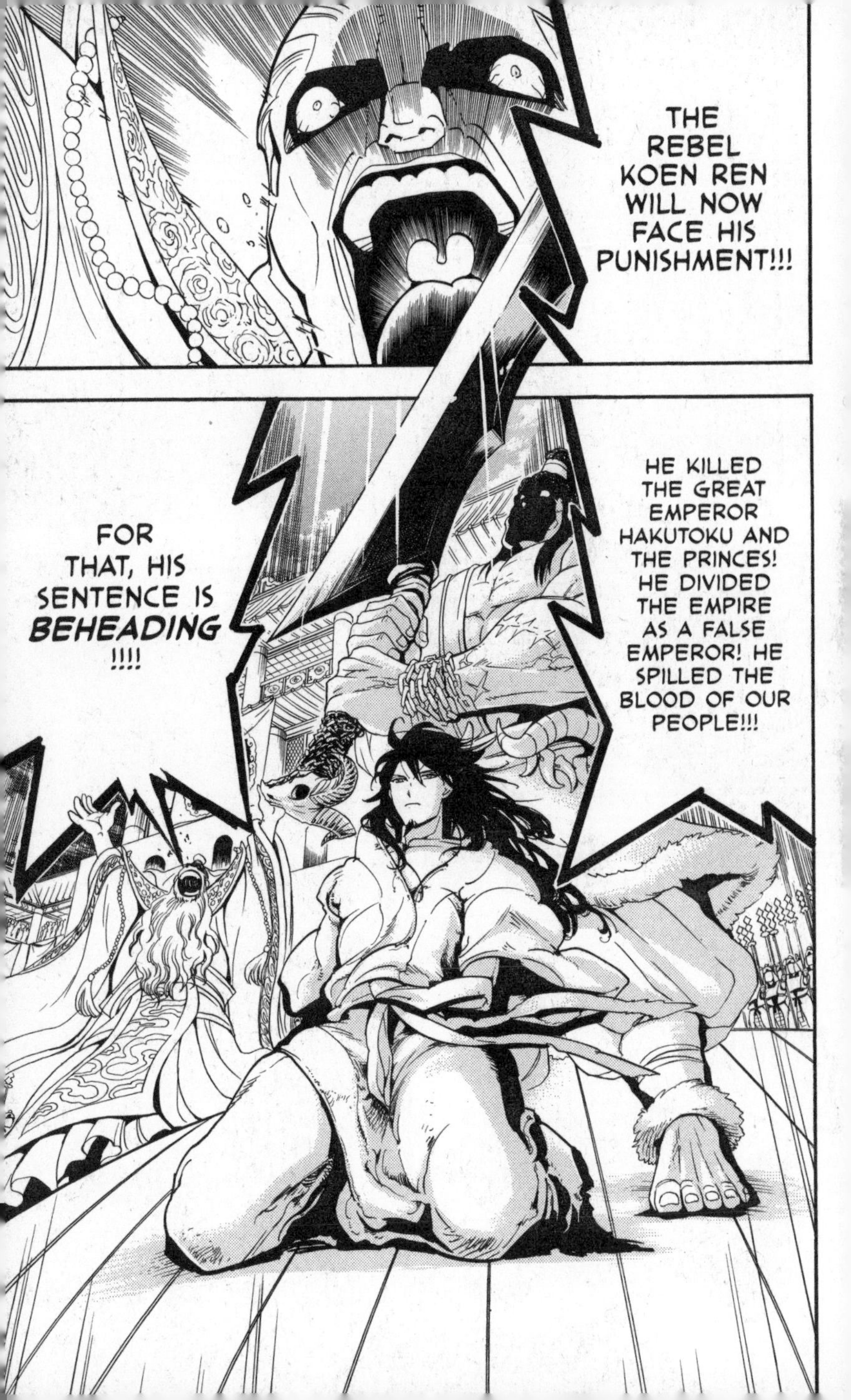
THE REBEL KOEN REN WILL NOW FACE HIS PUNISHMENT!!!
HE KILLED THE GREAT EMPEROR HAKUTOKU AND THE PRINCES! HE DIVIDED THE EMPIRE AS A FALSE EMPEROR! HE SPILLED THE BLOOD OF OUR PEOPLE!!!
FOR THAT, HIS SENTENCE IS *BEHEADING* !!!!

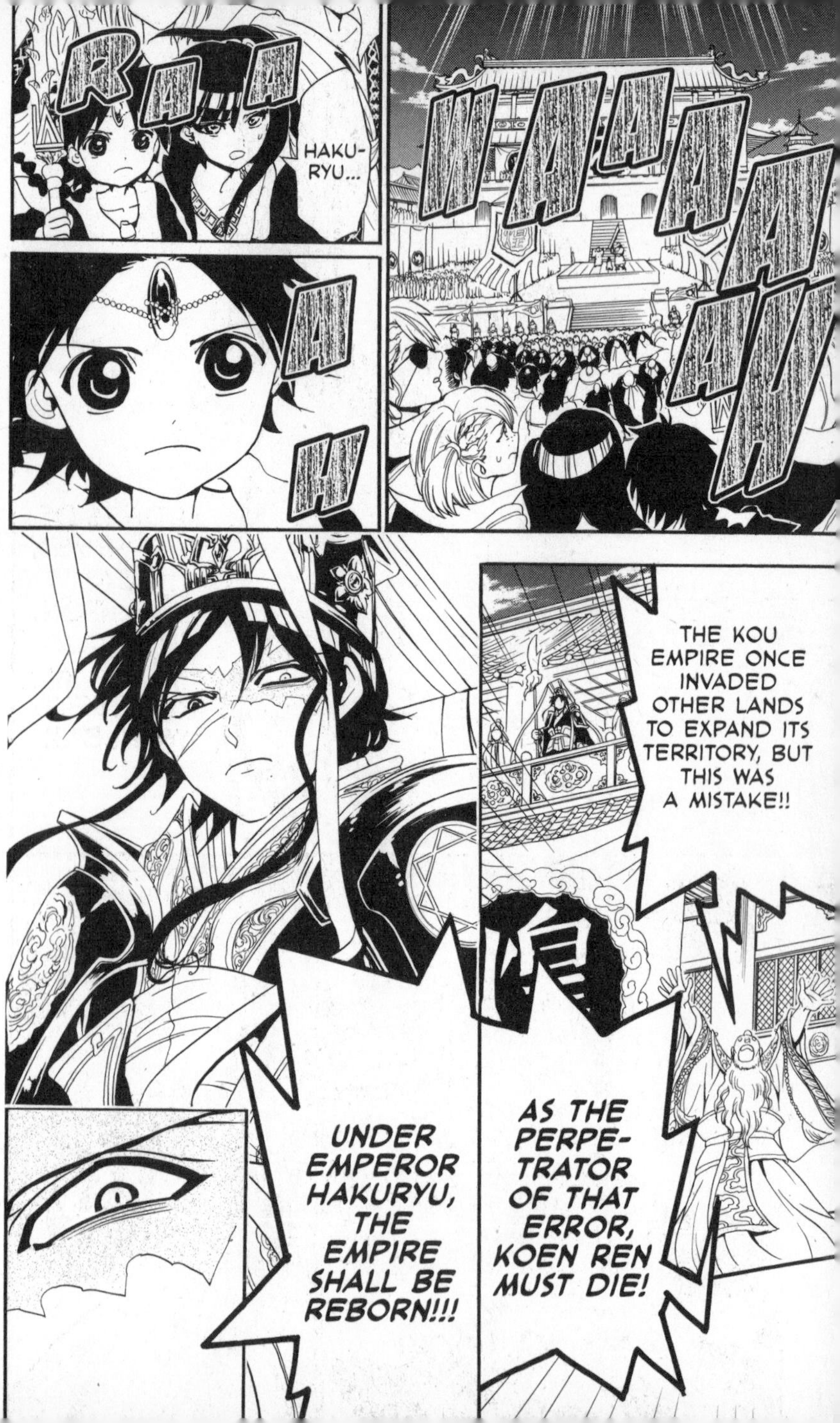
WAAAAAAAAH!!
RAAA
HAKU-RYU...
AAH
THE KOU EMPIRE ONCE INVADED OTHER LANDS TO EXPAND ITS TERRITORY, BUT THIS WAS A MISTAKE!!
AS THE PERPE-TRATOR OF THAT ERROR, KOEN REN MUST DIE!
UNDER EMPEROR HAKURYU, THE EMPIRE SHALL BE REBORN!!!

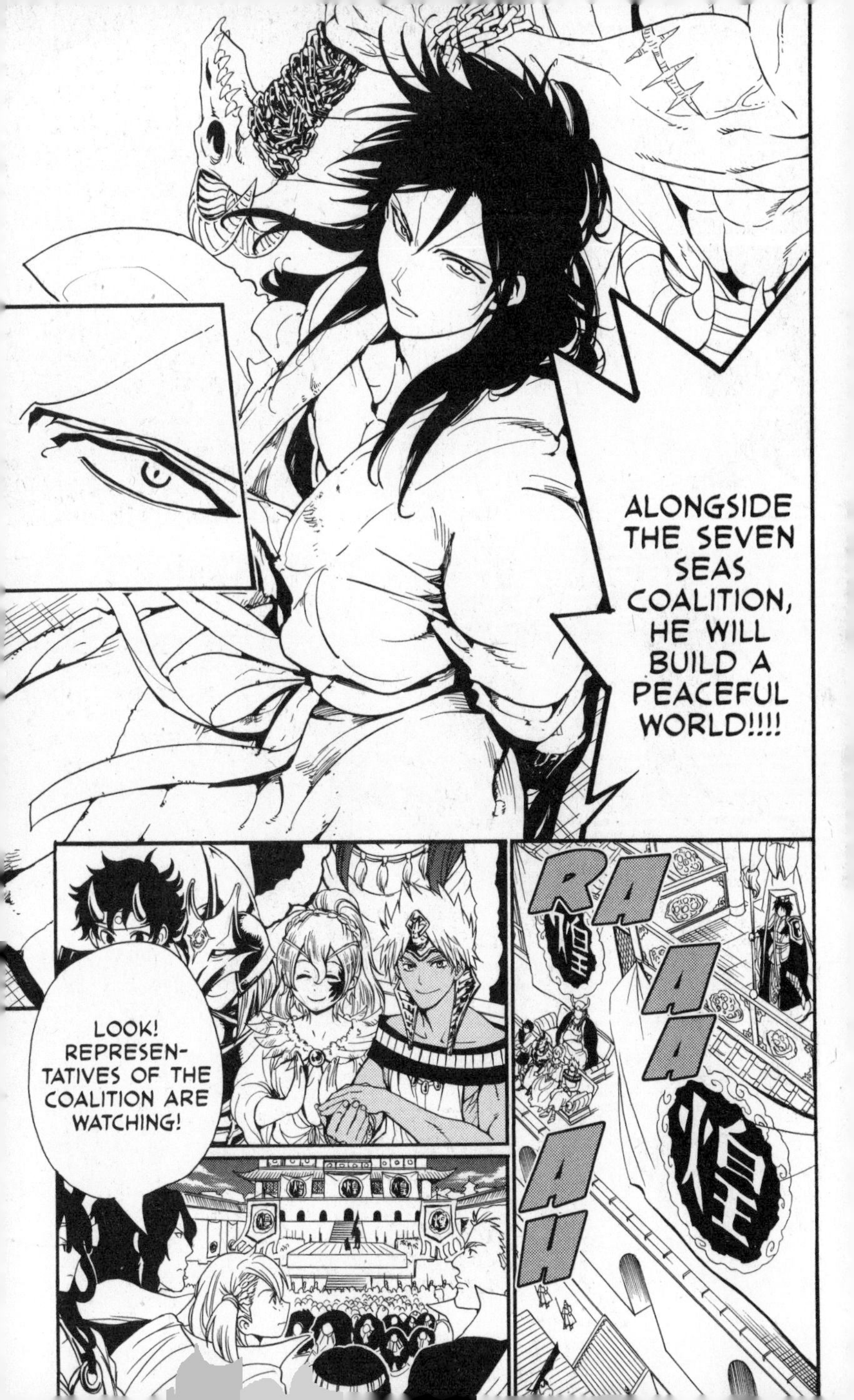
ALONGSIDE THE SEVEN SEAS COALITION, HE WILL BUILD A PEACEFUL WORLD!!!!
RAAAAAH
煌
煌
LOOK! REPRESEN-TATIVES OF THE COALITION ARE WATCHING!

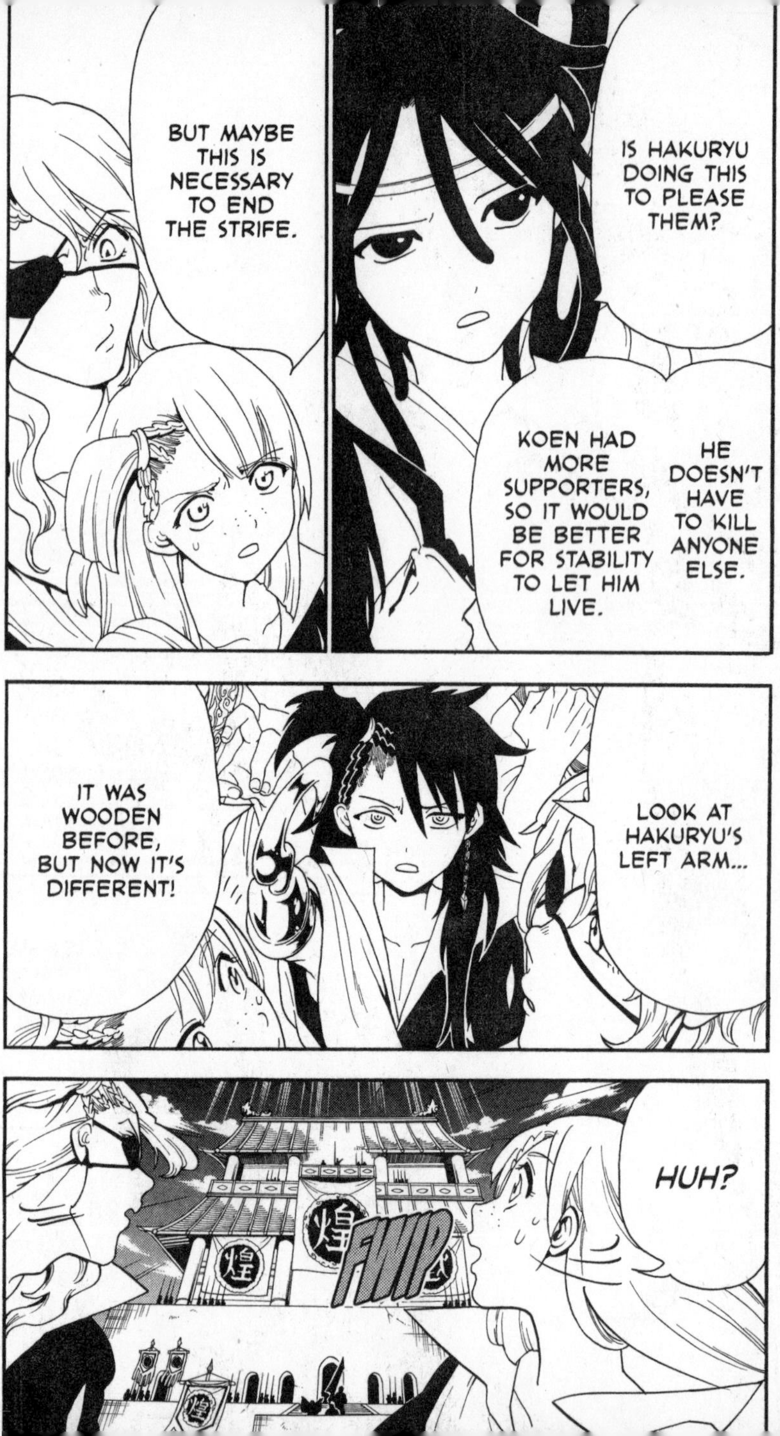
IS HAKURYU DOING THIS TO PLEASE THEM?
HE DOESN'T HAVE TO KILL ANYONE ELSE.
KOEN HAD MORE SUPPORTERS, SO IT WOULD BE BETTER FOR STABILITY TO LET HIM LIVE.
BUT MAYBE THIS IS NECESSARY TO END THE STRIFE.
LOOK AT HAKURYU'S LEFT ARM...
IT WAS WOODEN BEFORE, BUT NOW IT'S DIFFERENT!
HUH?
FWIP

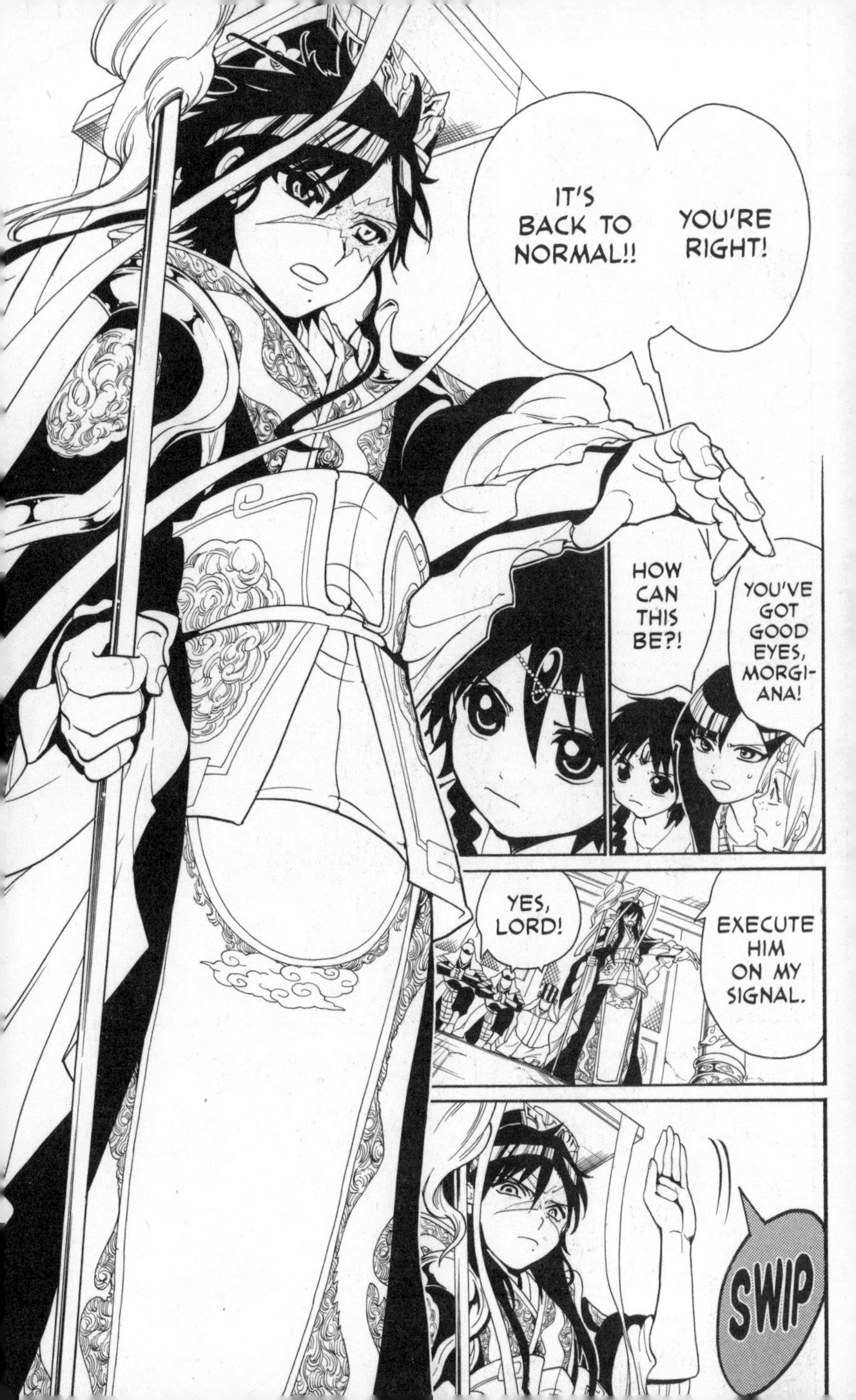
YOU'RE RIGHT!
IT'S BACK TO NORMAL!!
YOU'VE GOT GOOD EYES, MORGI-ANA!
HOW CAN THIS BE?!
EXECUTE HIM ON MY SIGNAL.
YES, LORD!
SWIP

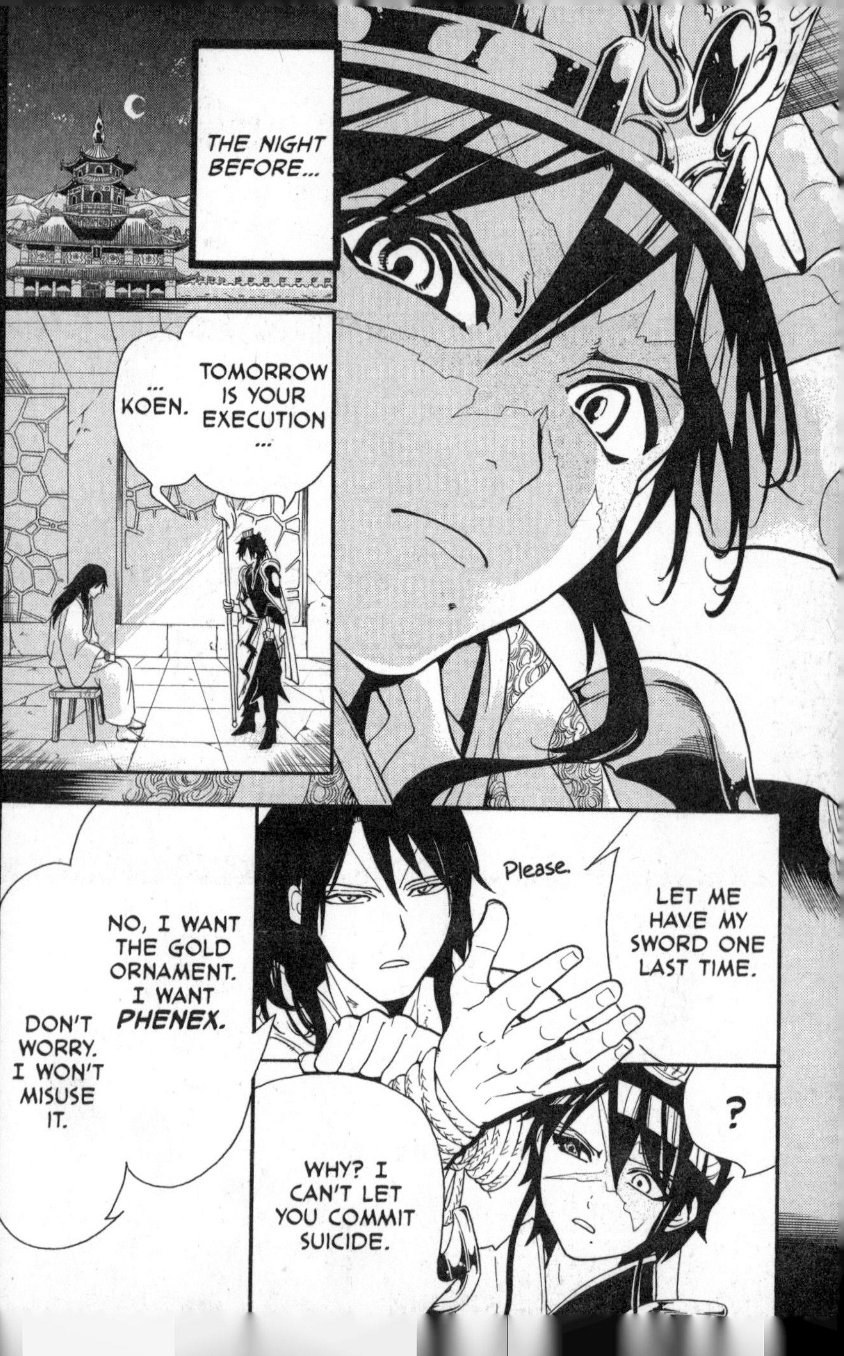
THE NIGHT BEFORE...
...KOËN. TOMORROW IS YOUR EXECUTION...
LET ME HAVE MY SWORD ONE LAST TIME.
Please.
?
WHY? I CAN'T LET YOU COMMIT SUICIDE.
NO, I WANT THE GOLD ORNAMENT. I WANT PHENEX.
DON'T WORRY. I WON'T MISUSE IT.

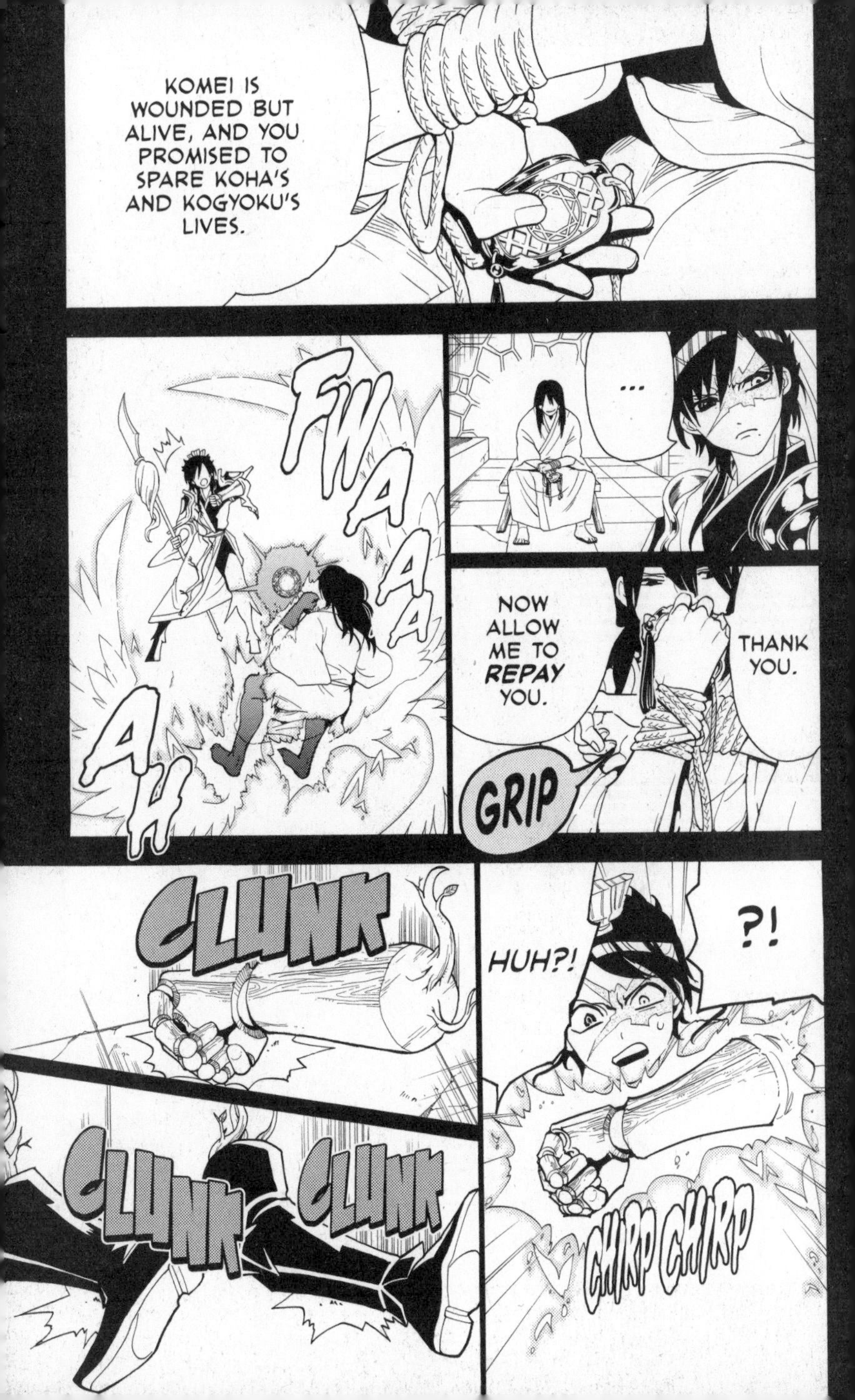
KOMEI IS WOUNDED BUT ALIVE, AND YOU PROMISED TO SPARE KOHA'S AND KOGYOKU'S LIVES.
...
THANK YOU.
NOW ALLOW ME TO REPAY YOU.
GRIP
FWAAA
AH
?!
HUH?!
CHIRP CHIRP
CLUNK
CLUNK
CLUNK

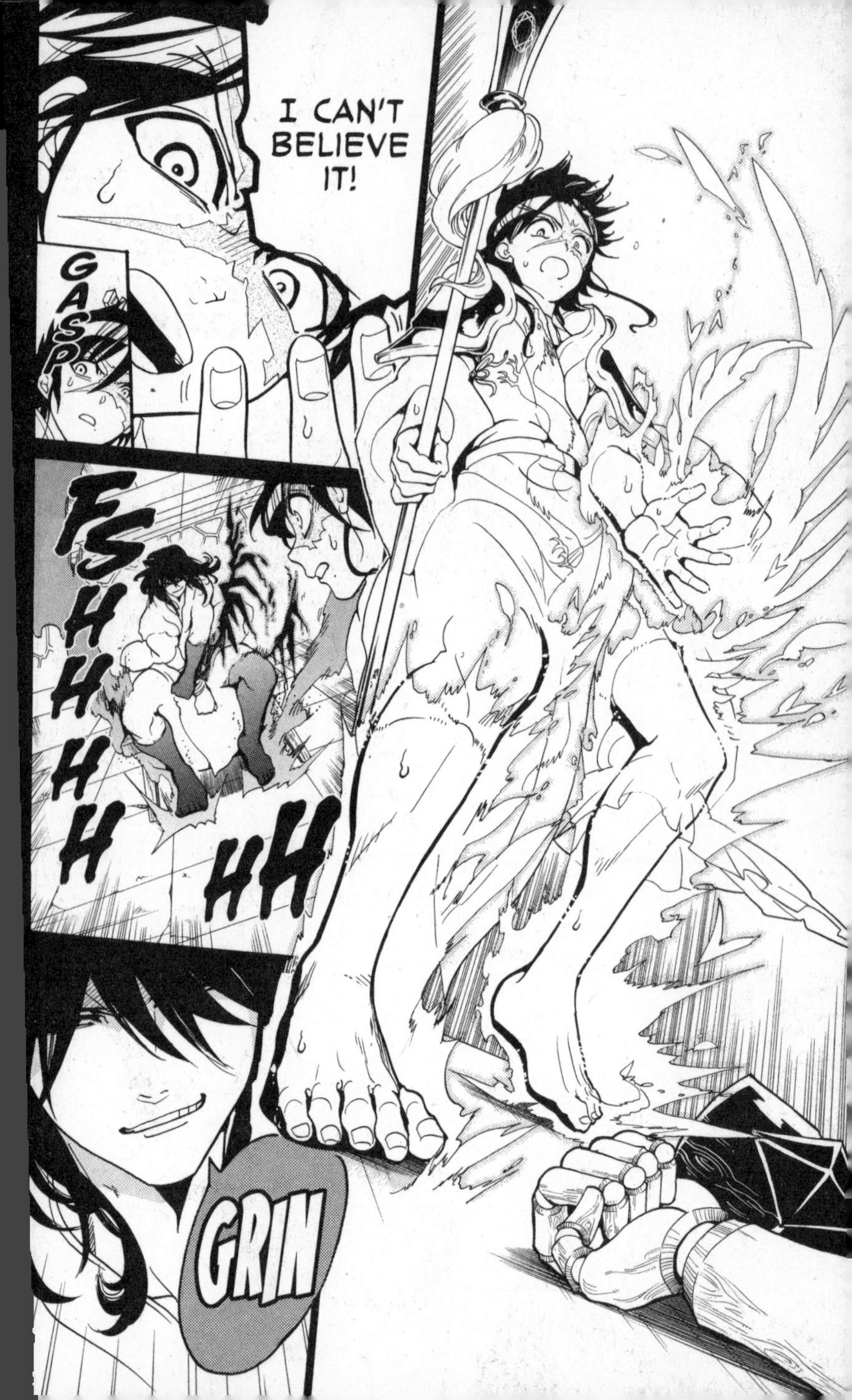
I CAN'T BELIEVE IT!
GASP
FSHHHHHH HH
GRIN

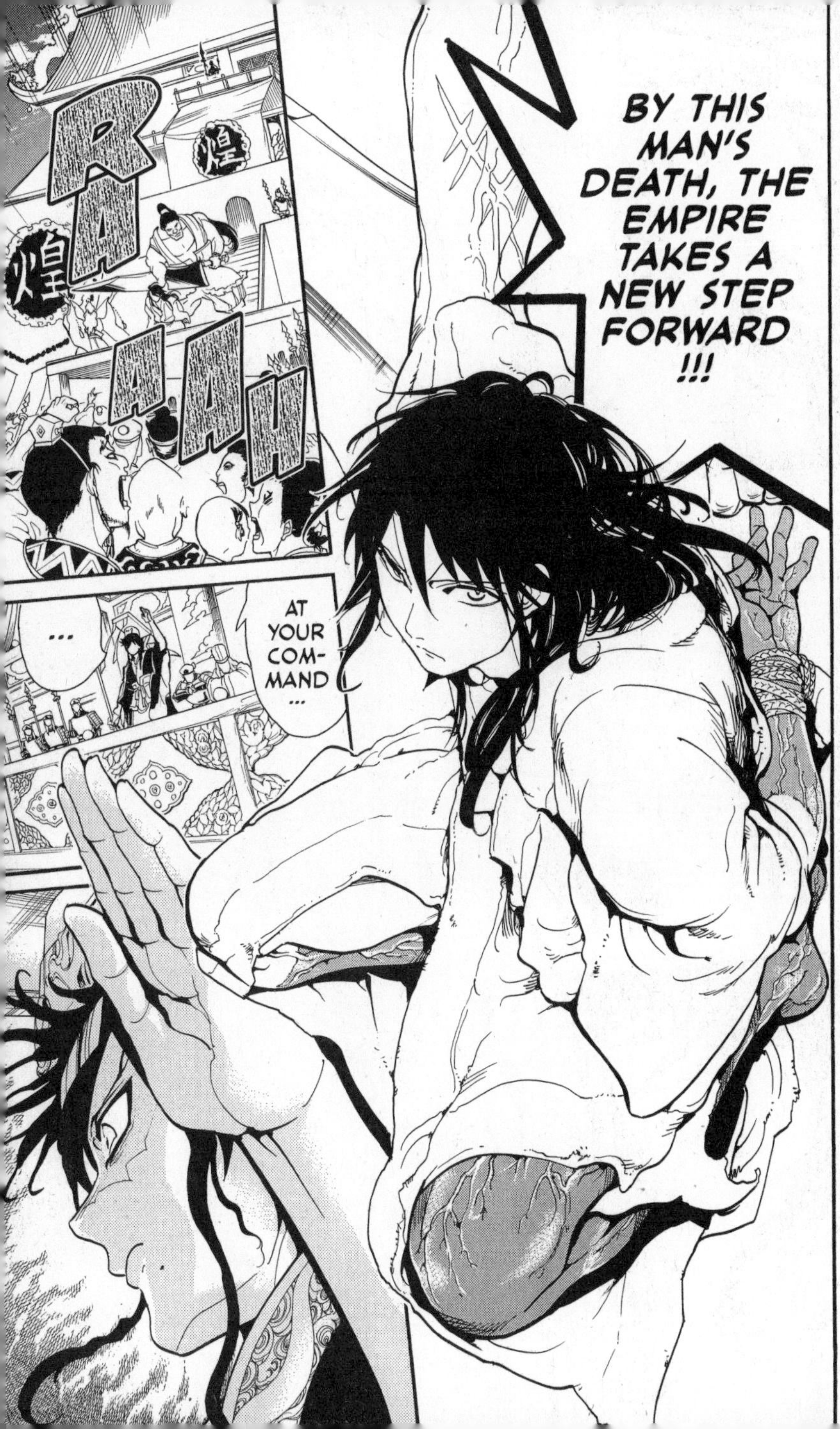
BY THIS MAN'S DEATH, THE EMPIRE TAKES A NEW STEP FORWARD !!!
RAAAH
AT YOUR COM-MAND ...
...

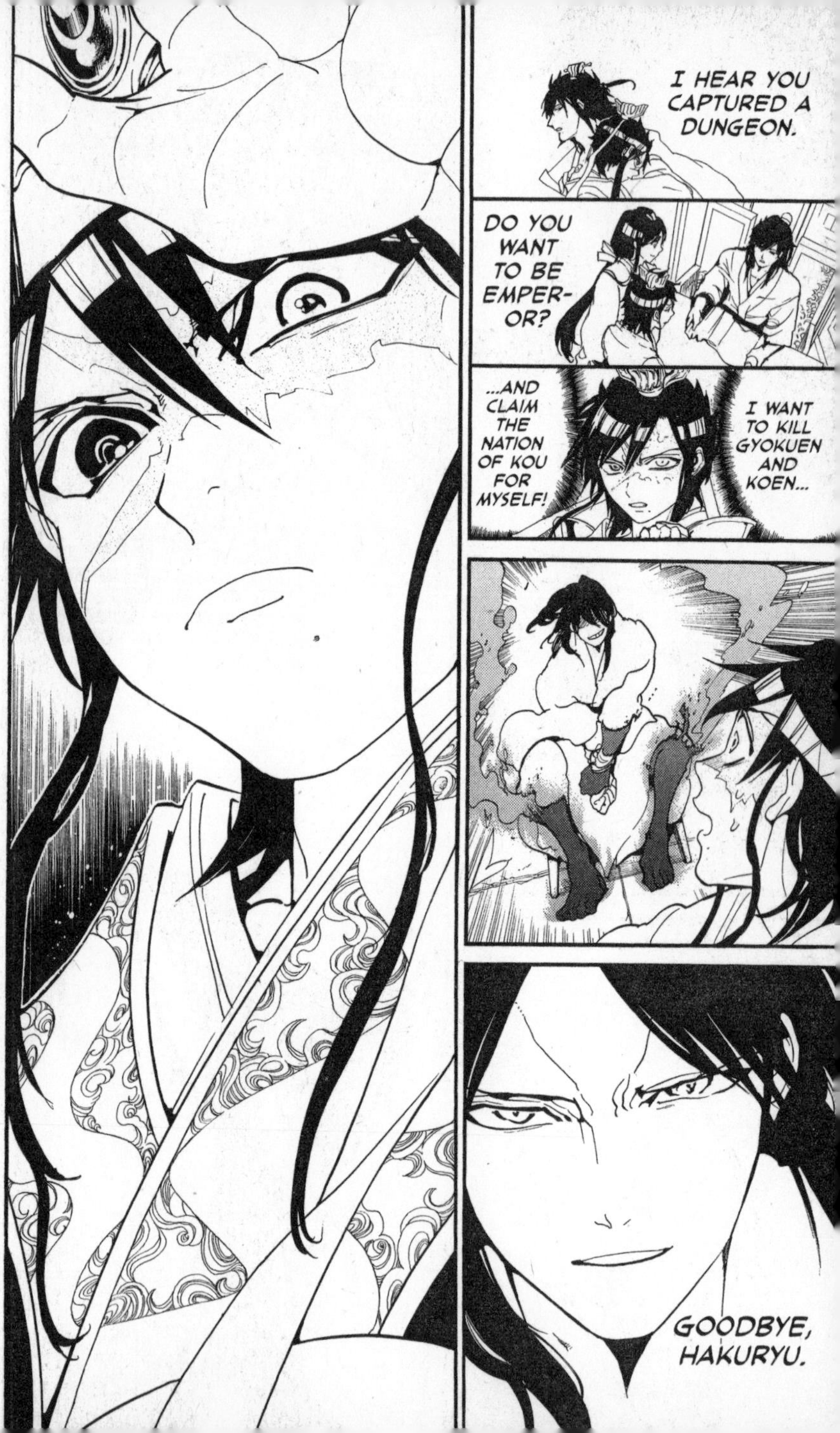
I HEAR YOU CAPTURED A DUNGEON.
DO YOU WANT TO BE EMPER-OR?
I WANT TO KILL GYOKUEN AND KOEN...
...AND CLAIM THE NATION OF KOU FOR MYSELF!
GOODBYE, HAKURYU.

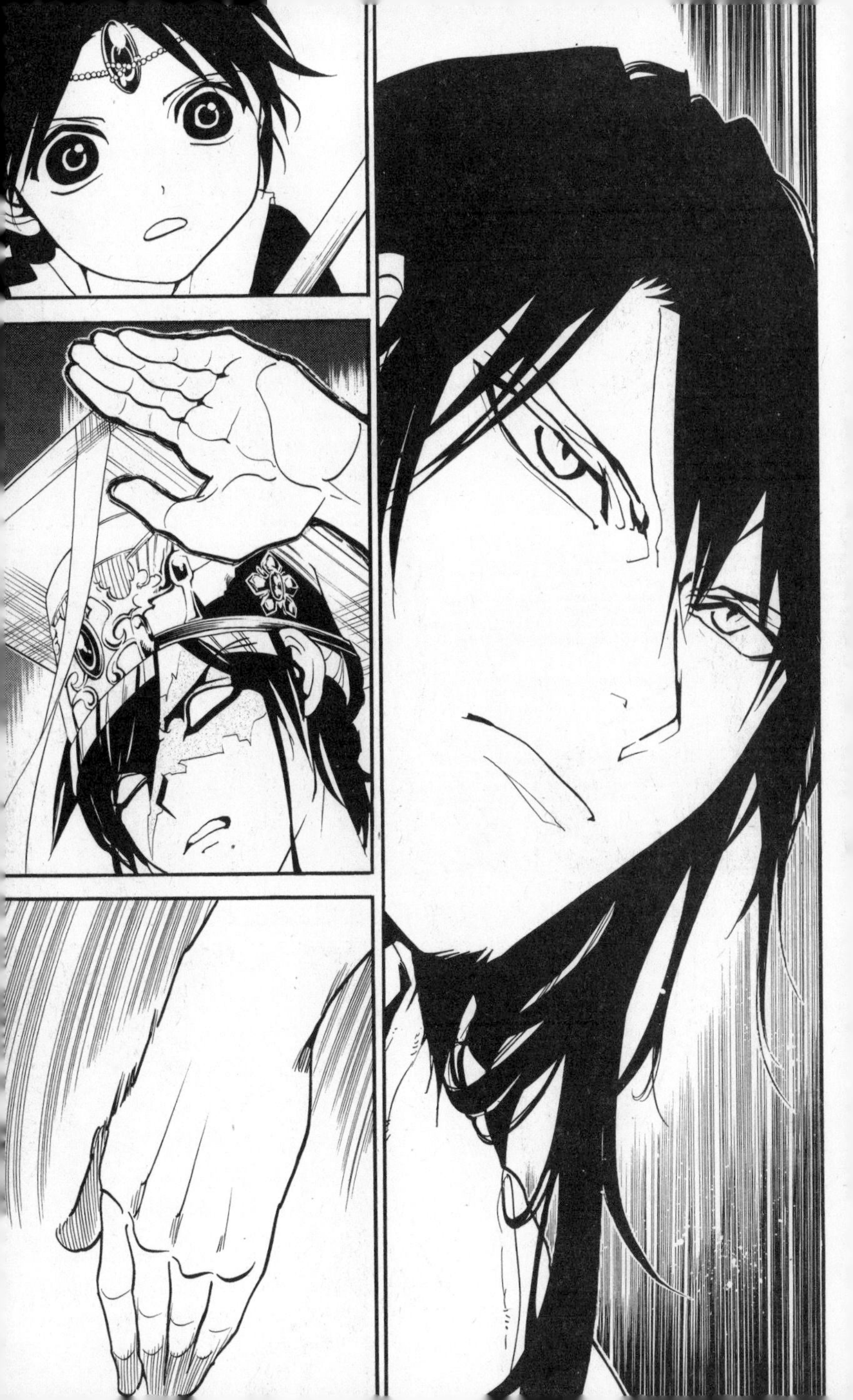

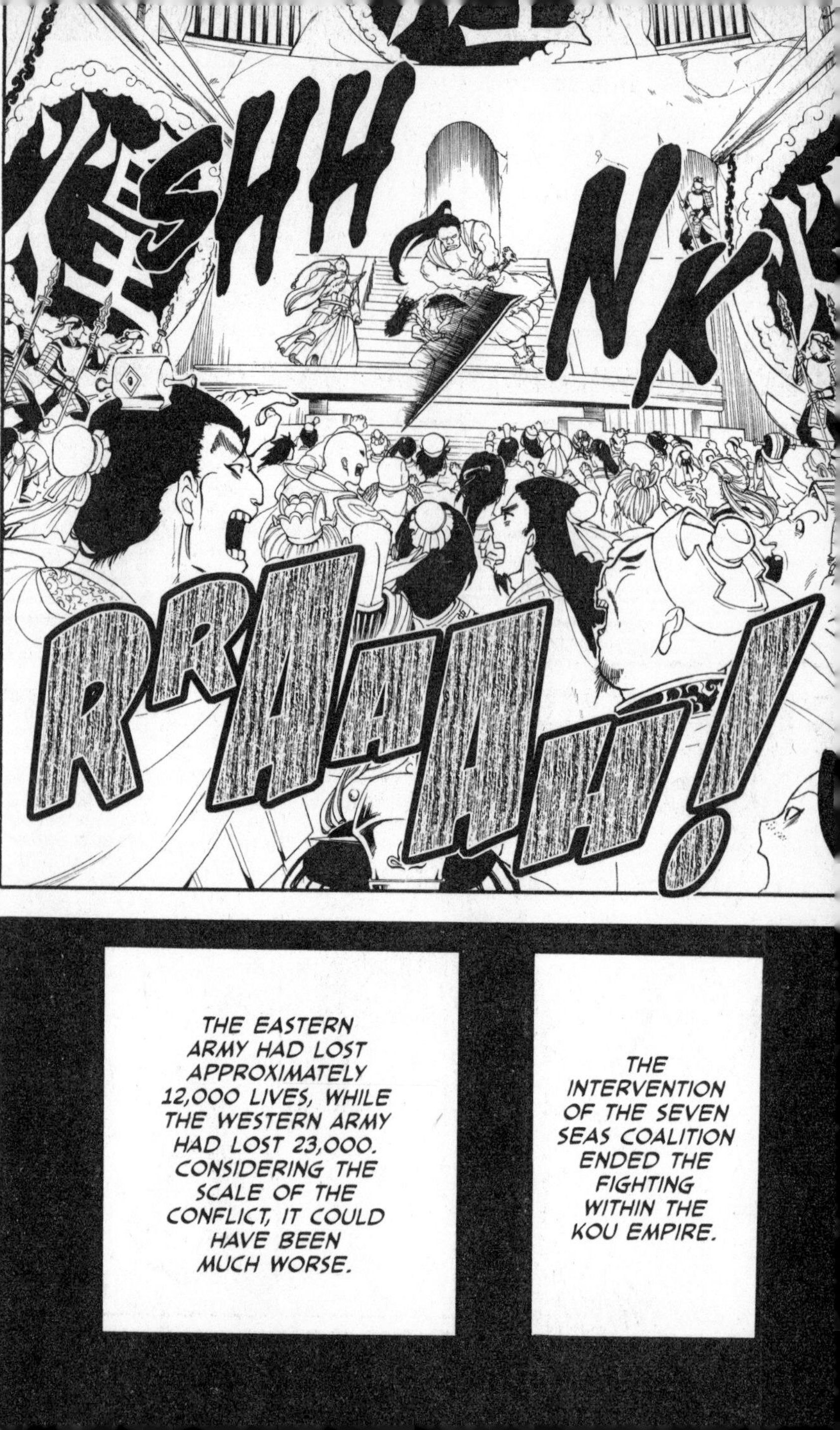
SHHNK
RRAAAAH!
THE INTERVENTION OF THE SEVEN SEAS COALITION ENDED THE FIGHTING WITHIN THE KOU EMPIRE.
THE EASTERN ARMY HAD LOST APPROXIMATELY 12,000 LIVES, WHILE THE WESTERN ARMY HAD LOST 23,000. CONSIDERING THE SCALE OF THE CONFLICT, IT COULD HAVE BEEN MUCH WORSE.

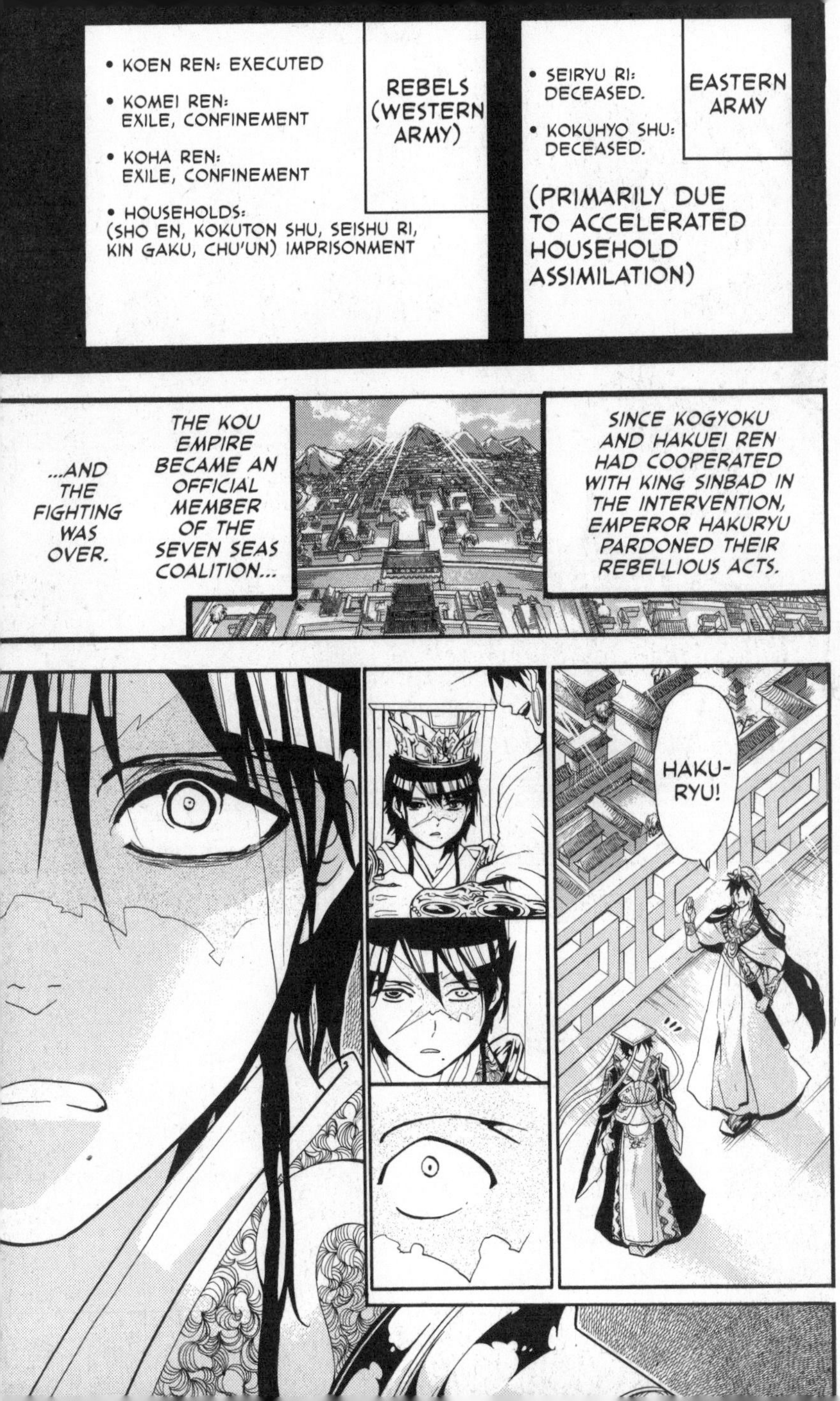
EASTERN ARMY
• SEIRYU RI: DECEASED.
• KOKUHYO SHU: DECEASED.
(PRIMARILY DUE TO ACCELERATED HOUSEHOLD ASSIMILATION)
REBELS (WESTERN ARMY)
• KOEN REN: EXECUTED
• KOMEI REN: EXILE, CONFINEMENT
• KOHA REN: EXILE, CONFINEMENT
• HOUSEHOLDS: (SHO EN, KOKUTON SHU, SEISHU RI, KIN GAKU, CHU'UN) IMPRISONMENT
SINCE KOGYOKU AND HAKUEI REN HAD COOPERATED WITH KING SINBAD IN THE INTERVENTION, EMPEROR HAKURYU PARDONED THEIR REBELLIOUS ACTS.
THE KOU EMPIRE BECAME AN OFFICIAL MEMBER OF THE SEVEN SEAS COALITION...
...AND THE FIGHTING WAS OVER.
HAKU-RYU!

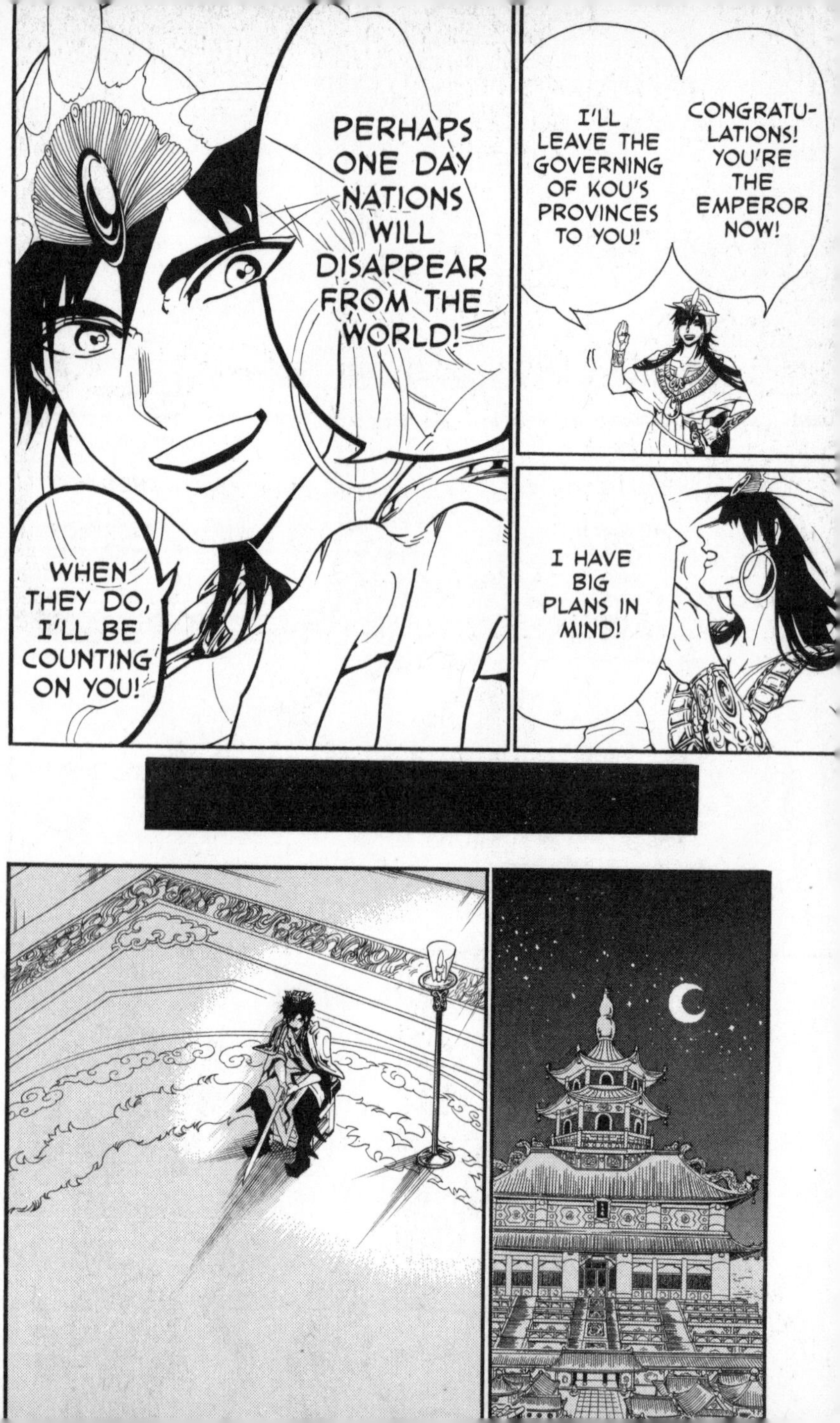
CONGRATULATIONS! YOU'RE THE EMPEROR NOW!
I'LL LEAVE THE GOVERNING OF KOU'S PROVINCES TO YOU!
I HAVE BIG PLANS IN MIND!
PERHAPS ONE DAY NATIONS WILL DISAPPEAR FROM THE WORLD!
WHEN THEY DO, I'LL BE COUNTING ON YOU!

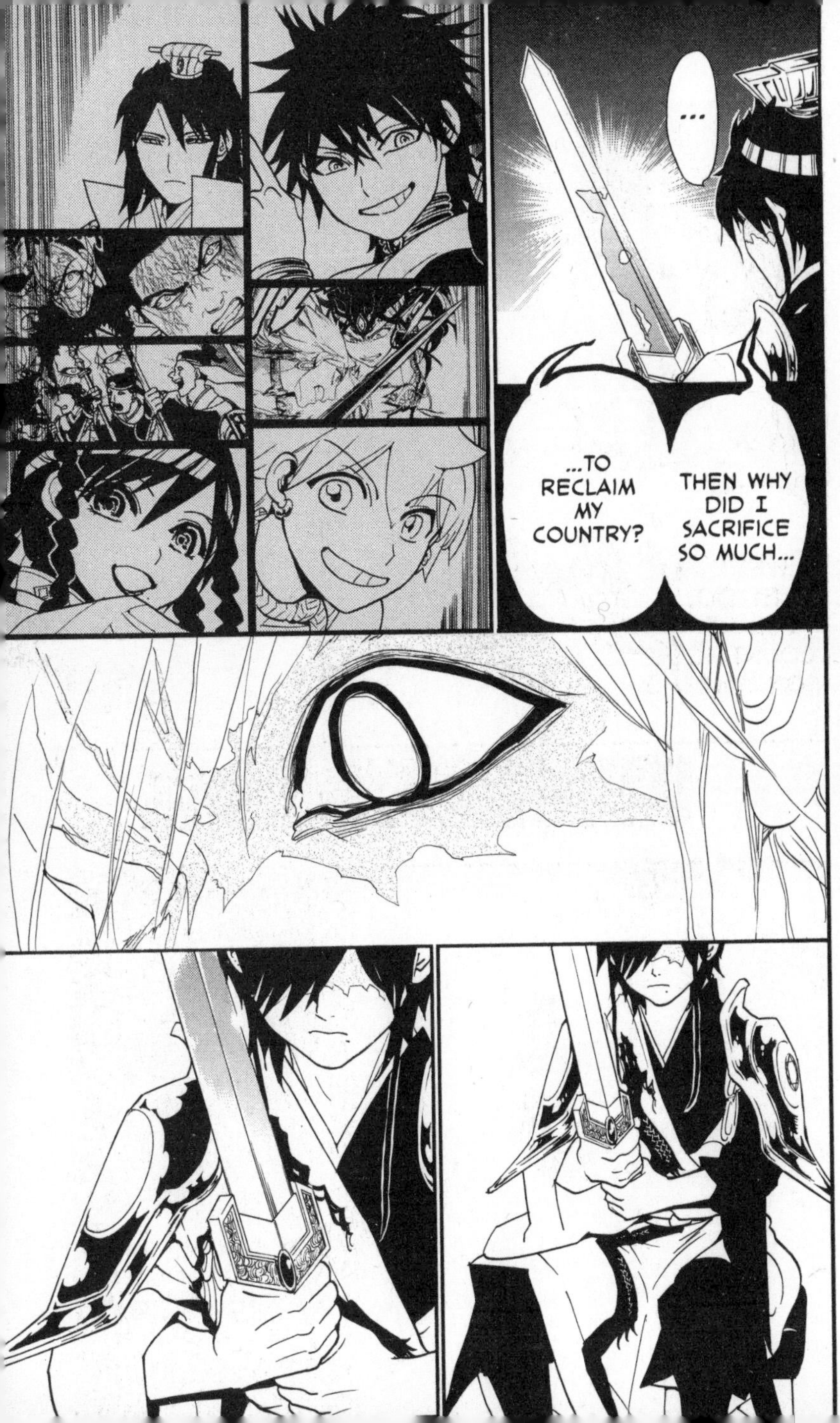
...
THEN WHY DID I SACRIFICE SO MUCH...
...TO RECLAIM MY COUNTRY?

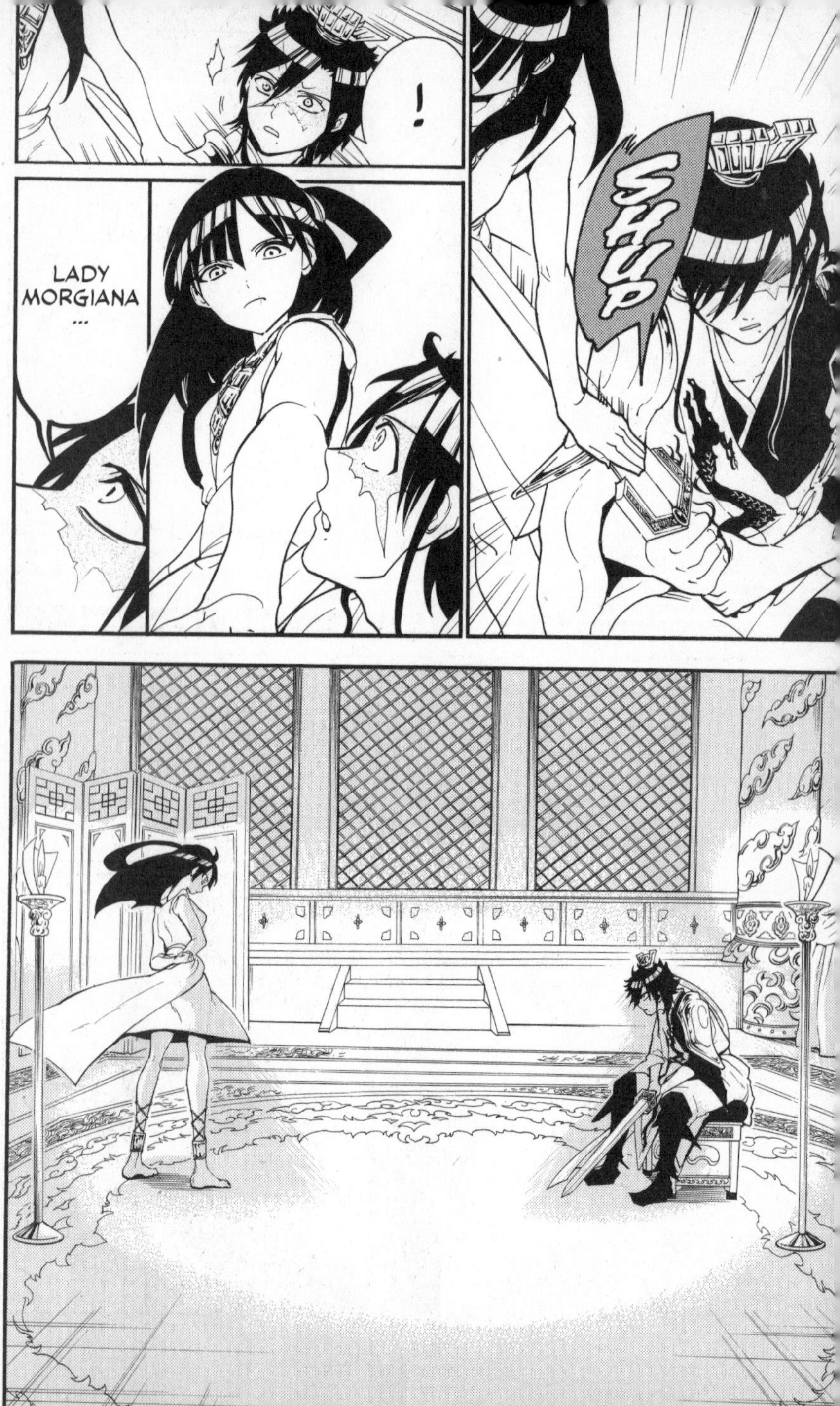
SHUP
!
LADY MORGIANA
...

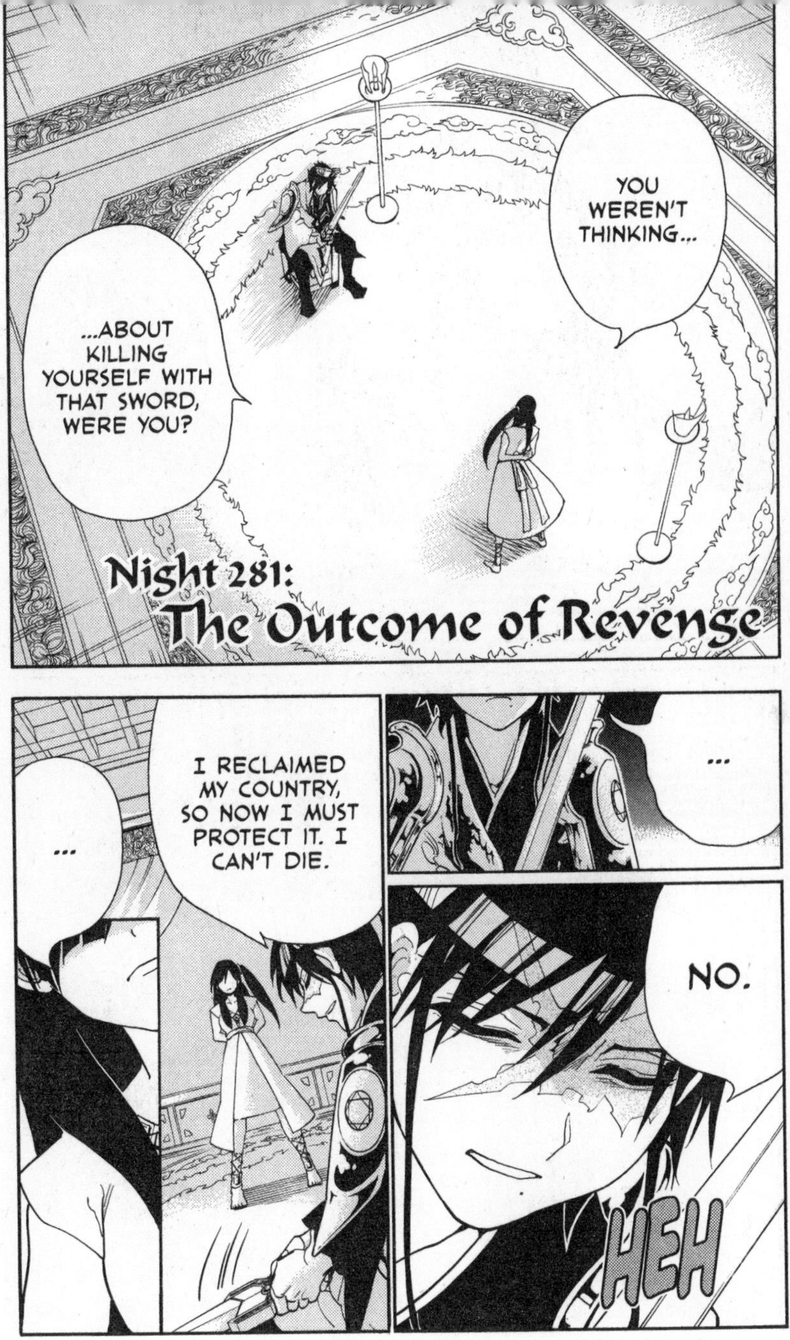
YOU WEREN'T THINKING...
...ABOUT KILLING YOURSELF WITH THAT SWORD, WERE YOU?
Night 281: The Outcome of Revenge
...
NO.
HEH
I RECLAIMED MY COUNTRY, SO NOW I MUST PROTECT IT. I CAN'T DIE.
...

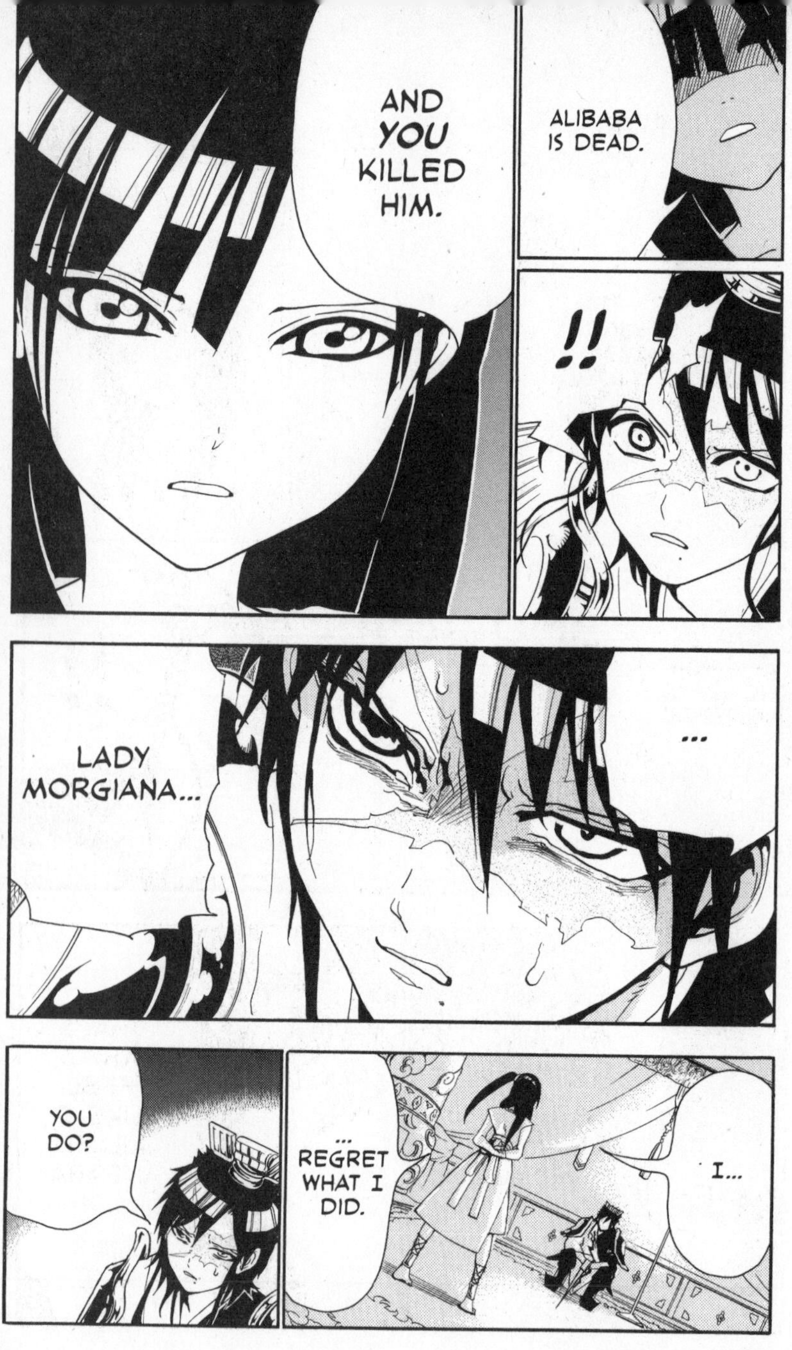
ALIBABA IS DEAD.
!!
AND YOU KILLED HIM.
...
LADY MORGIANA...
I...
... REGRET WHAT I DID.
YOU DO?

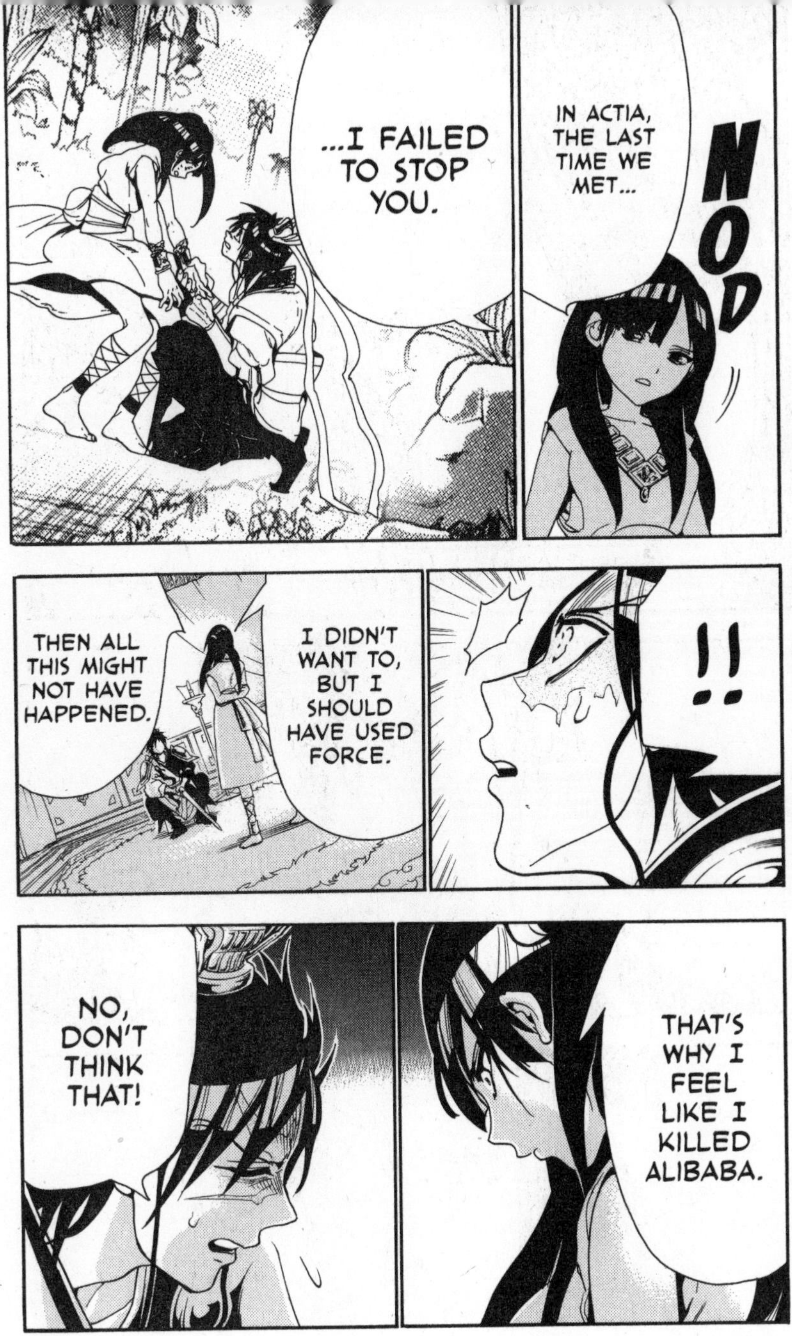
IN ACTIA, THE LAST TIME WE MET...
NOD
...I FAILED TO STOP YOU.
!!
I DIDN'T WANT TO, BUT I SHOULD HAVE USED FORCE.
THEN ALL THIS MIGHT NOT HAVE HAPPENED.
THAT'S WHY I FEEL LIKE I KILLED ALIBABA.
NO, DON'T THINK THAT!

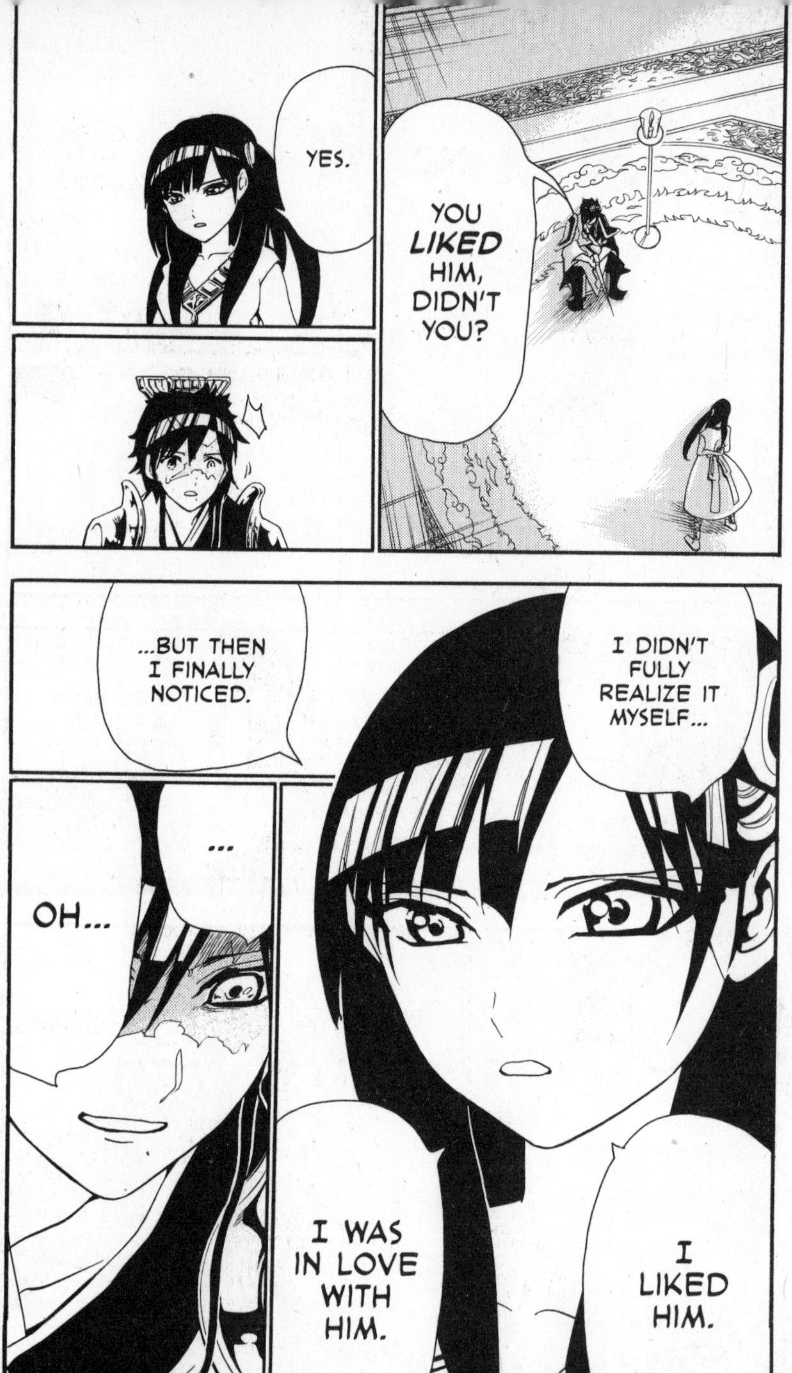
YOU *LIKED* HIM, DIDN'T YOU?
YES.
I DIDN'T FULLY REALIZE IT MYSELF...
I LIKED HIM.
I WAS IN LOVE WITH HIM.
...BUT THEN I FINALLY NOTICED.
...
OH...

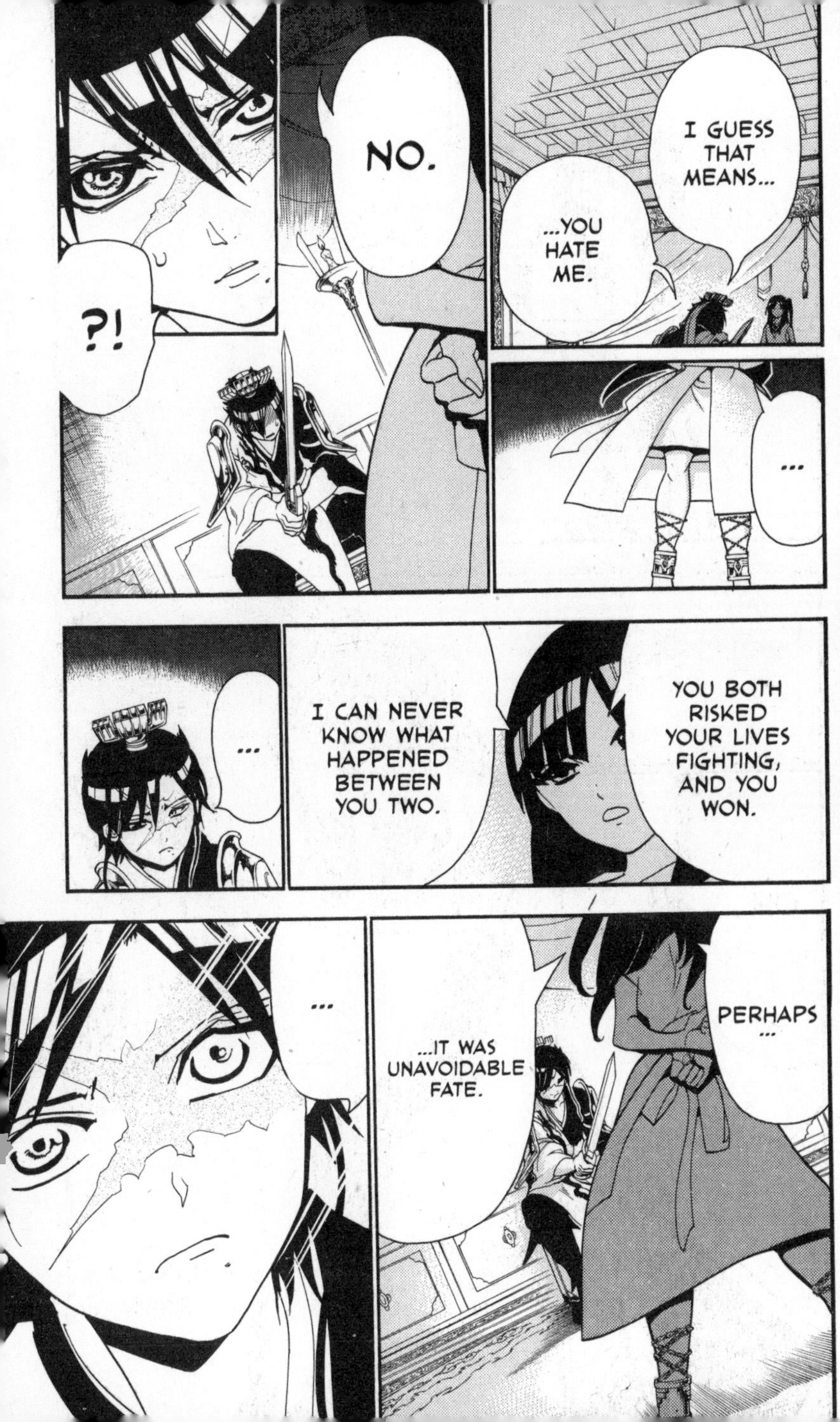
I GUESS THAT MEANS...
...YOU HATE ME.
...
NO.
?!
YOU BOTH RISKED YOUR LIVES FIGHTING, AND YOU WON.
I CAN NEVER KNOW WHAT HAPPENED BETWEEN YOU TWO.
...
PERHAPS...
...IT WAS UNAVOIDABLE FATE.
...

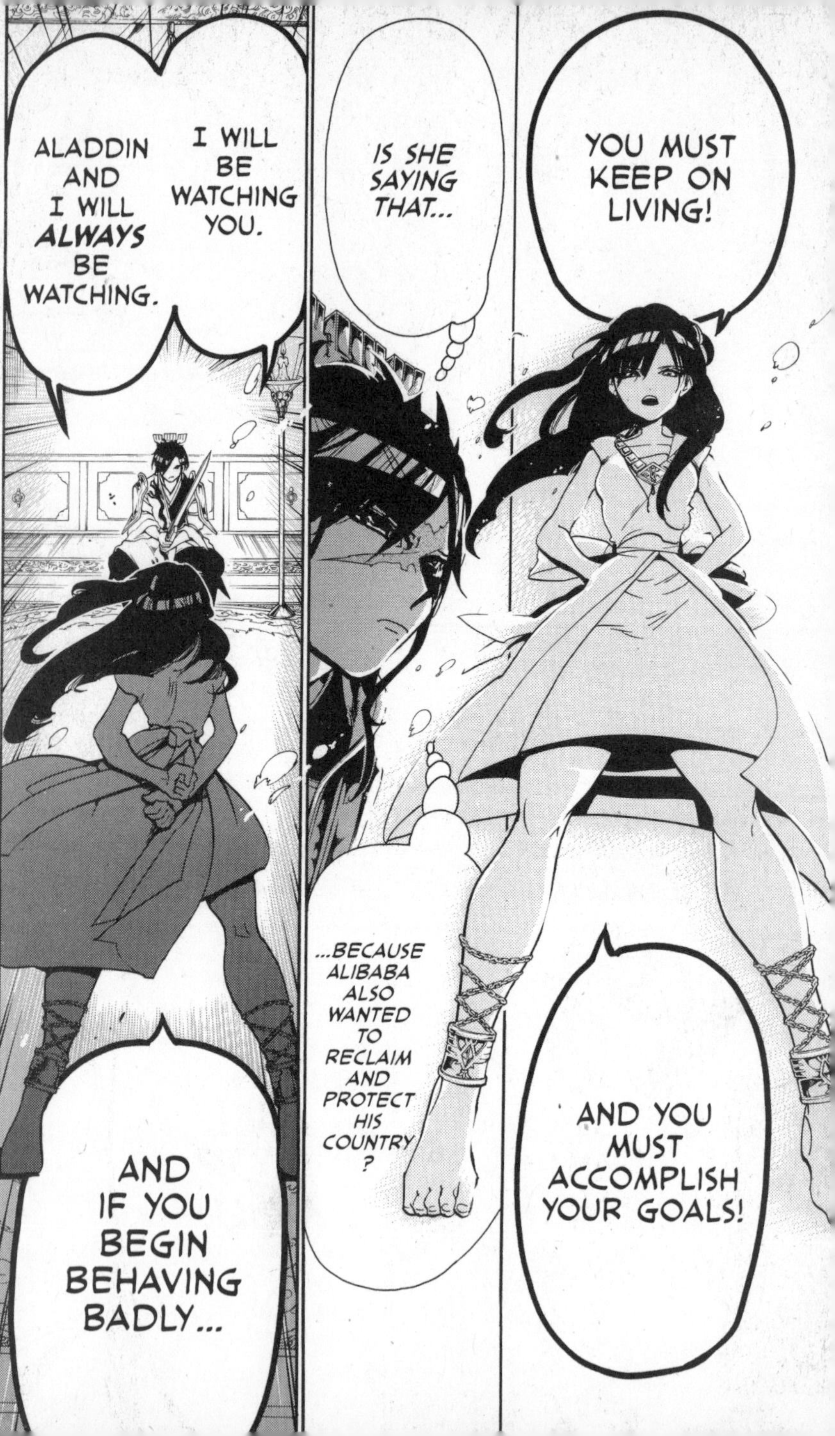
YOU MUST KEEP ON LIVING!
AND YOU MUST ACCOMPLISH YOUR GOALS!
IS SHE SAYING THAT...
...BECAUSE ALIBABA ALSO WANTED TO RECLAIM AND PROTECT HIS COUNTRY?
I WILL BE WATCHING YOU.
ALADDIN AND I WILL *ALWAYS* BE WATCHING.
AND IF YOU BEGIN BEHAVING BADLY...

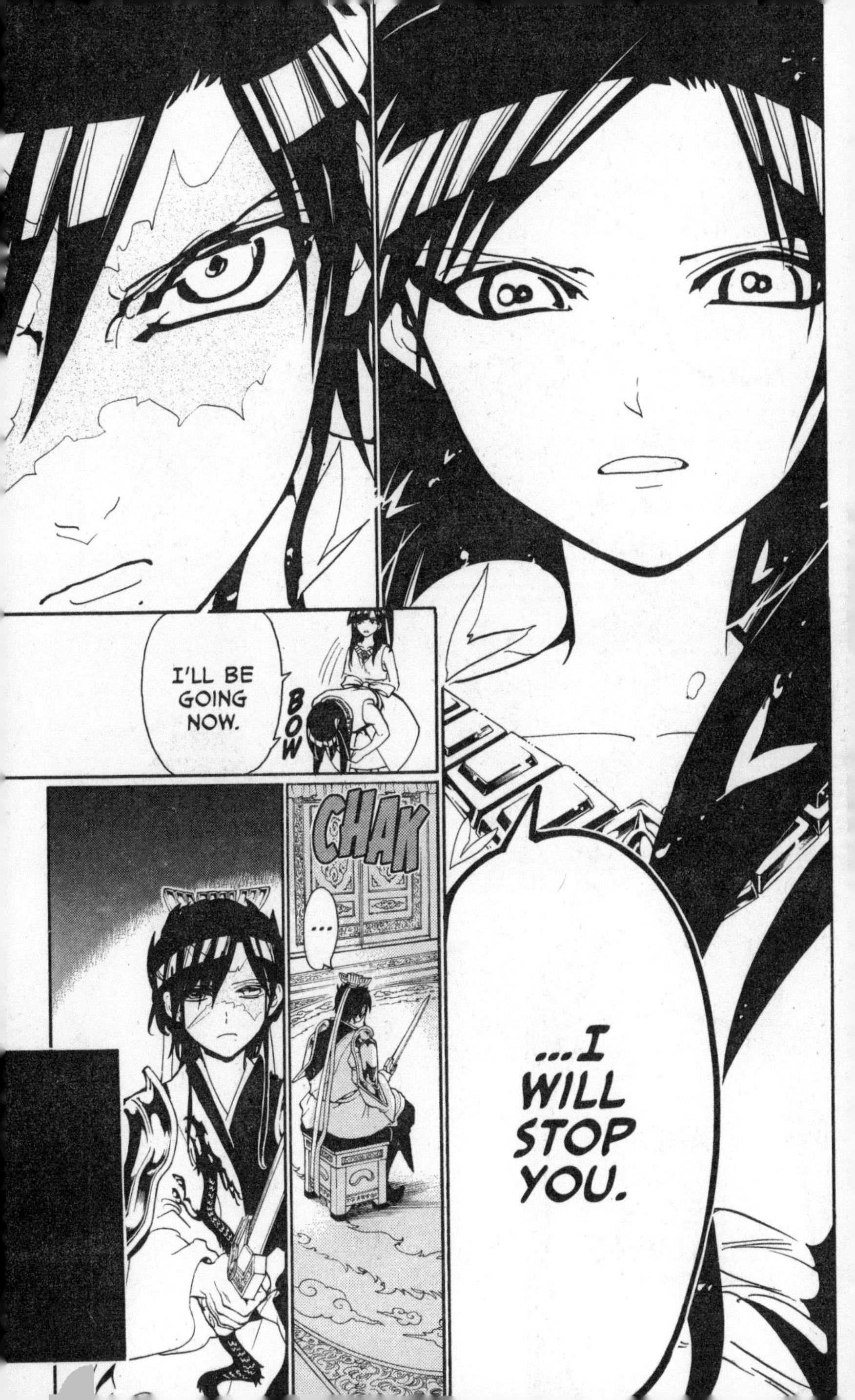
...I WILL STOP YOU.
I'LL BE GOING NOW.
BOW
CHAK
...

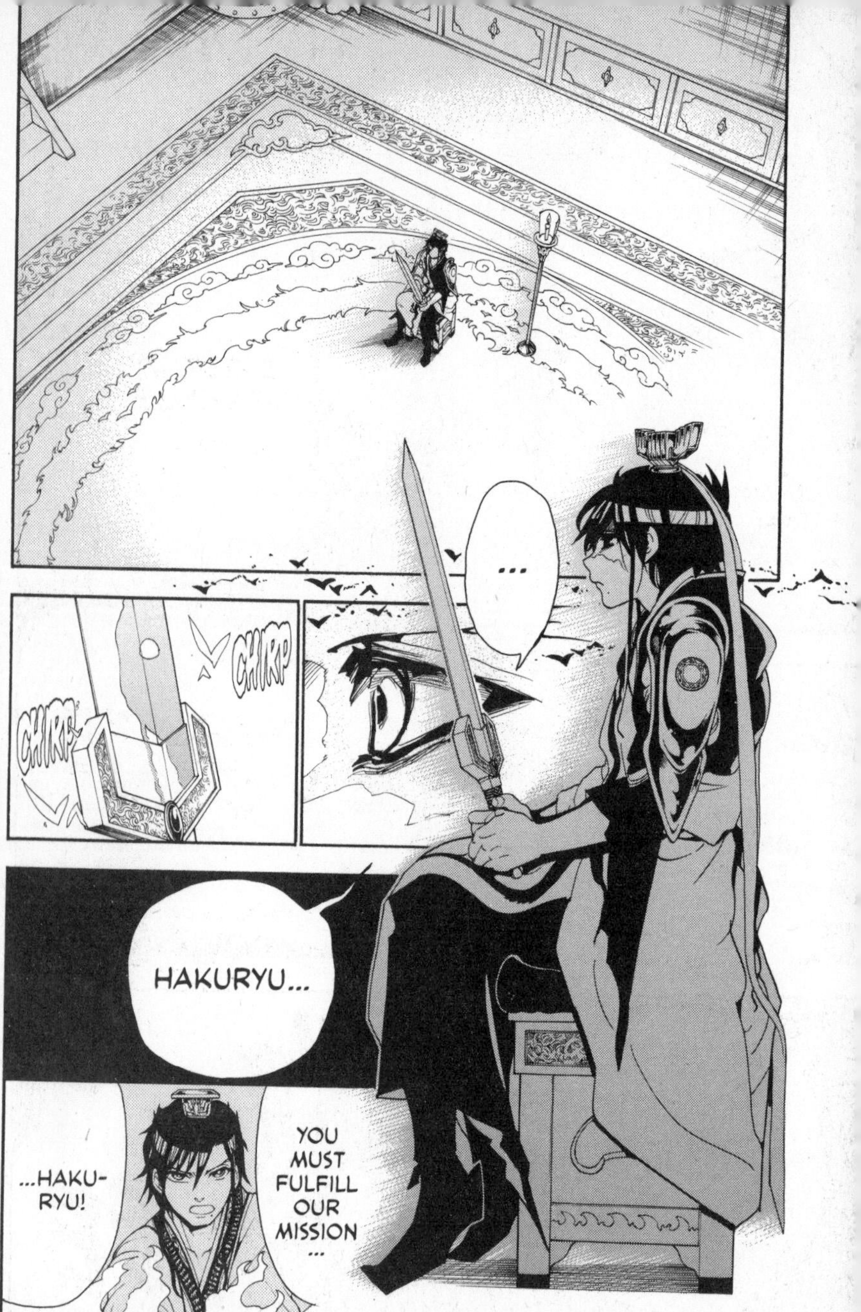
...
CHIRP
CHIRP
HAKURYU...
YOU MUST FULFILL OUR MISSION ...
...HAKU-RYU!

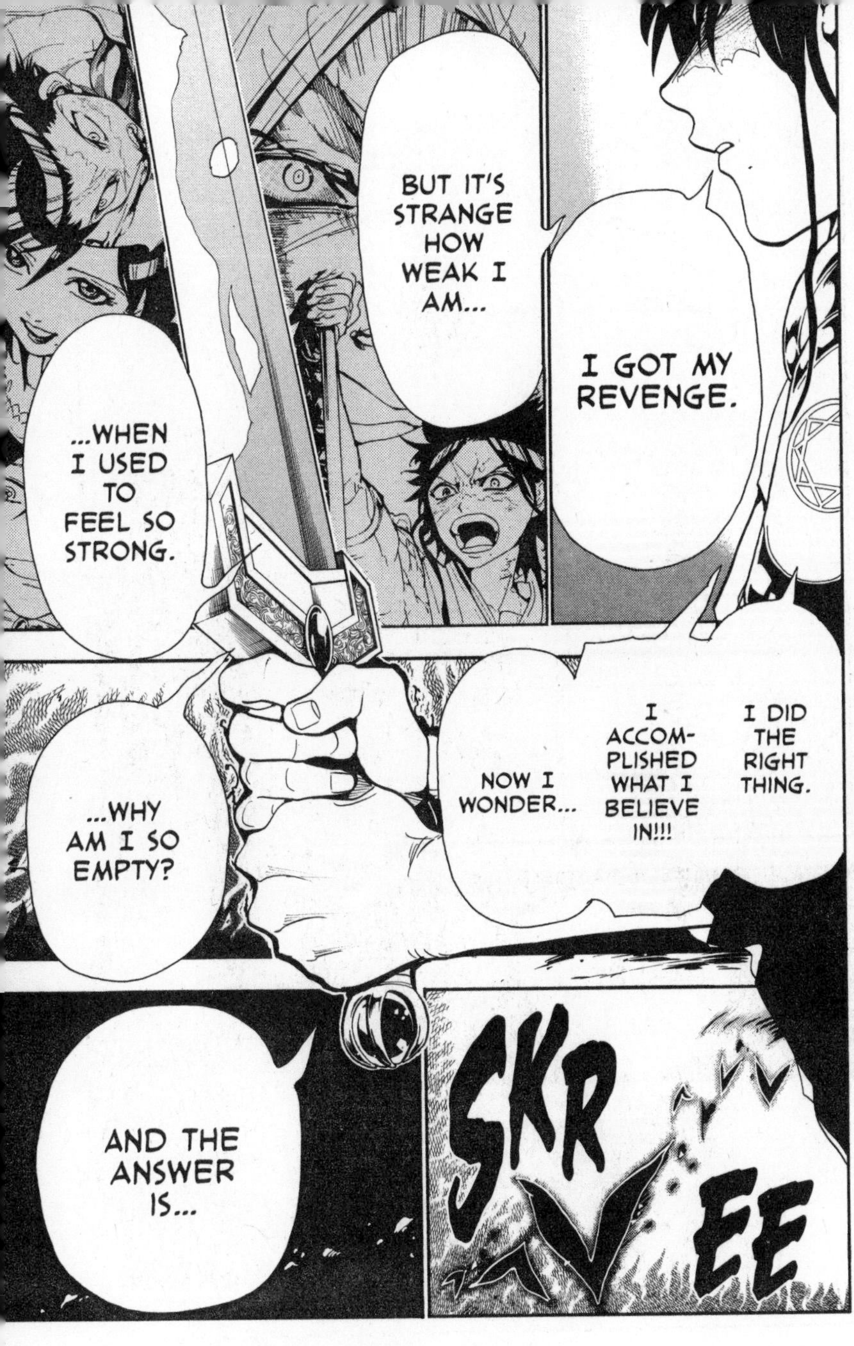
I GOT MY REVENGE.
BUT IT'S STRANGE HOW WEAK I AM...
...WHEN I USED TO FEEL SO STRONG.
I DID THE RIGHT THING.
I ACCOMPLISHED WHAT I BELIEVE IN!!!
NOW I WONDER...
...WHY AM I SO EMPTY?
SKRVEE
AND THE ANSWER IS...

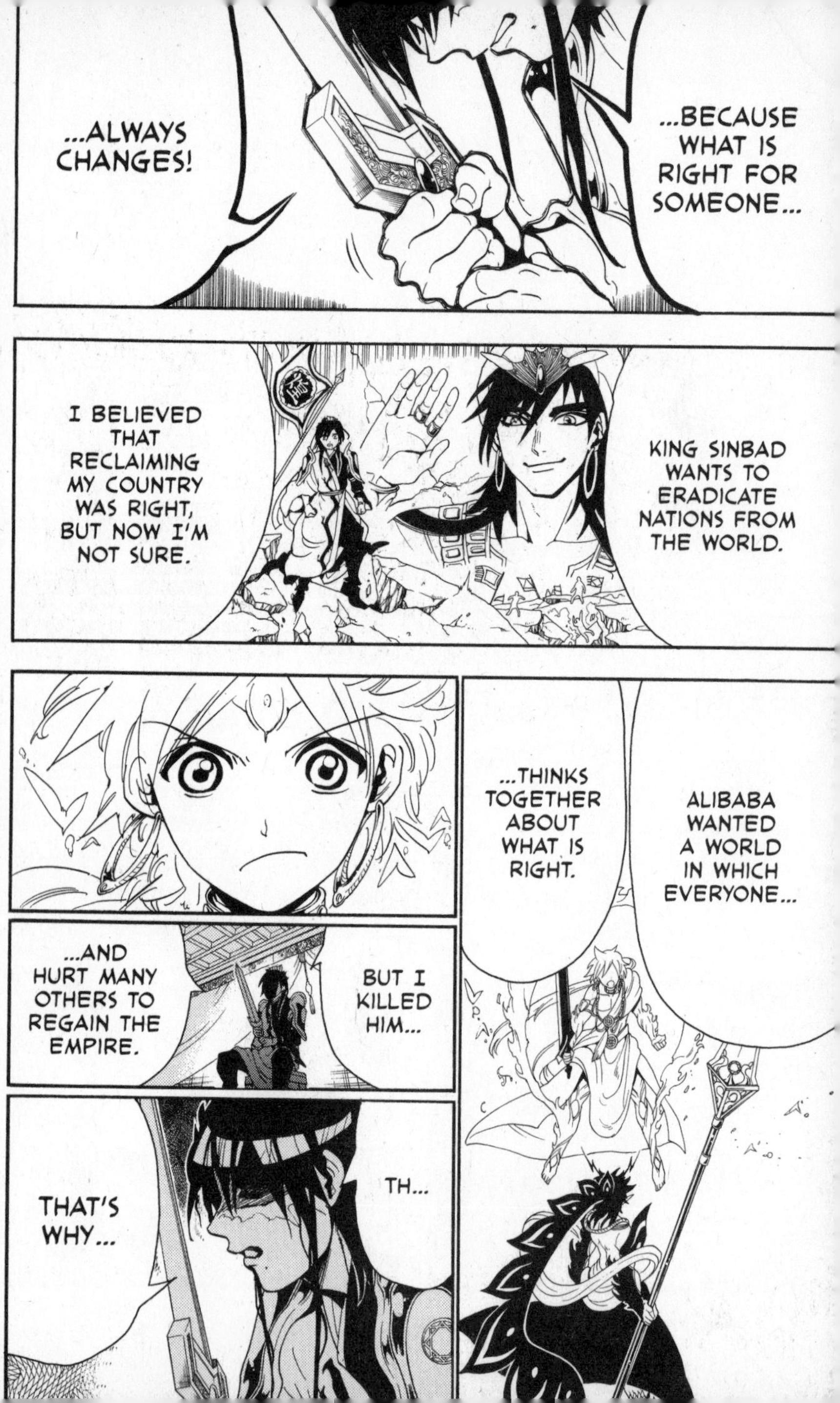
...BECAUSE WHAT IS RIGHT FOR SOMEONE...
...ALWAYS CHANGES!
KING SINBAD WANTS TO ERADICATE NATIONS FROM THE WORLD.
I BELIEVED THAT RECLAIMING MY COUNTRY WAS RIGHT, BUT NOW I'M NOT SURE.
ALIBABA WANTED A WORLD IN WHICH EVERYONE...
...THINKS TOGETHER ABOUT WHAT IS RIGHT.
BUT I KILLED HIM...
...AND HURT MANY OTHERS TO REGAIN THE EMPIRE.
TH...
THAT'S WHY...

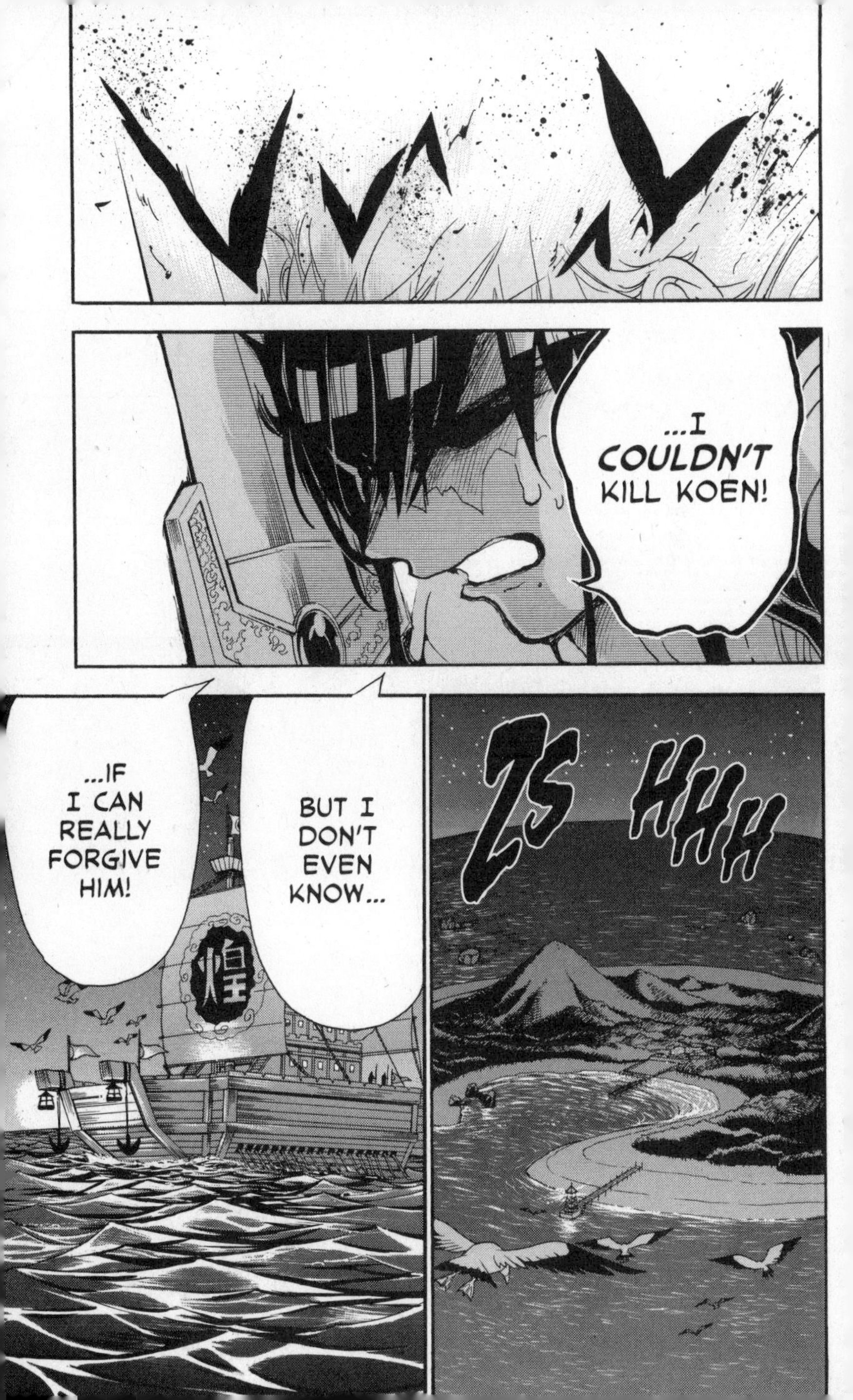
...I COULDN'T KILL KOEN!
ZSHHH
BUT I DON'T EVEN KNOW...
...IF I CAN REALLY FORGIVE HIM!
煌

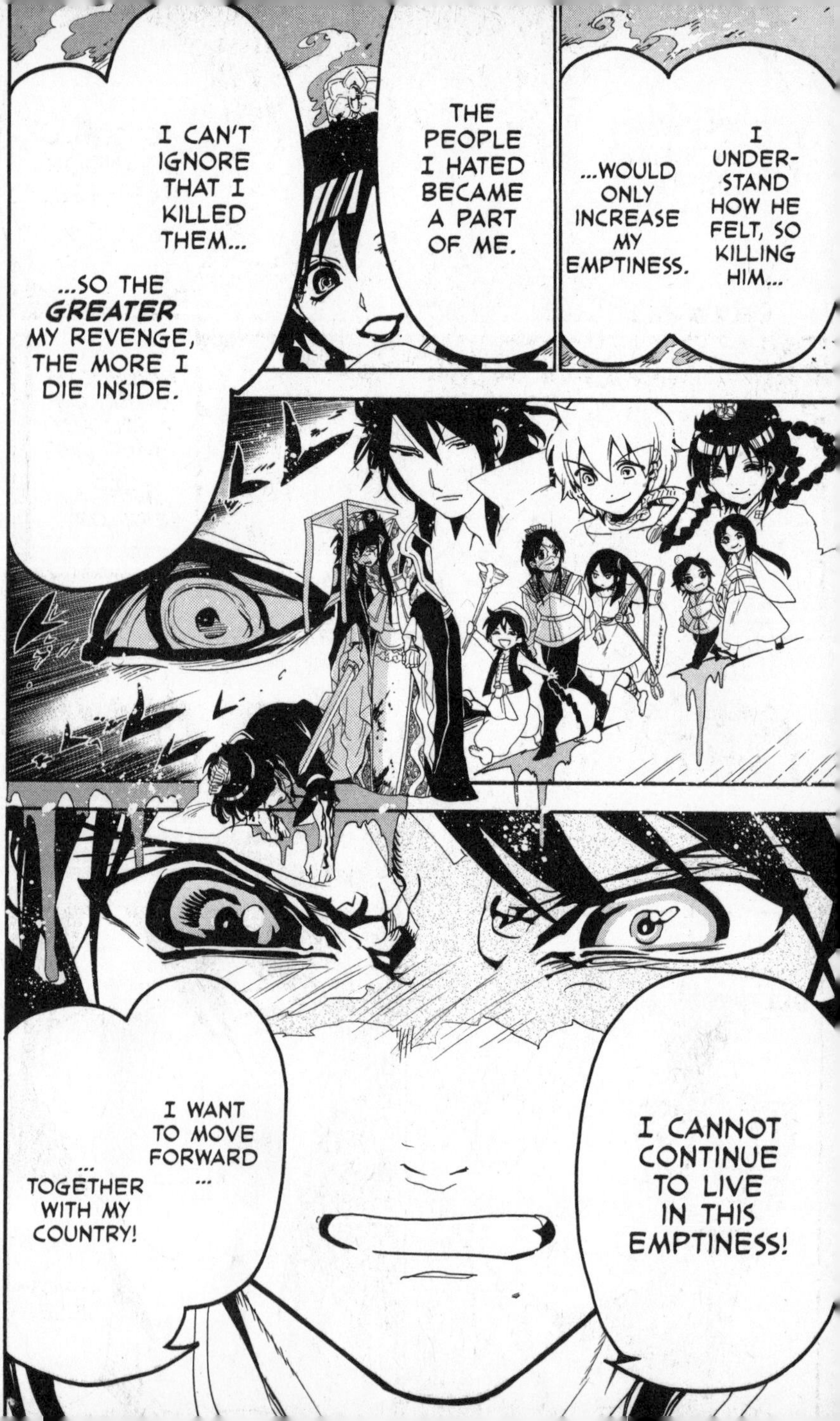
I UNDERSTAND HOW HE FELT, SO KILLING HIM...
...WOULD ONLY INCREASE MY EMPTINESS.
THE PEOPLE I HATED BECAME A PART OF ME.
I CAN'T IGNORE THAT I KILLED THEM...
...SO THE GREATER MY REVENGE, THE MORE I DIE INSIDE.
I CANNOT CONTINUE TO LIVE IN THIS EMPTINESS!
I WANT TO MOVE FORWARD ...
... TOGETHER WITH MY COUNTRY!

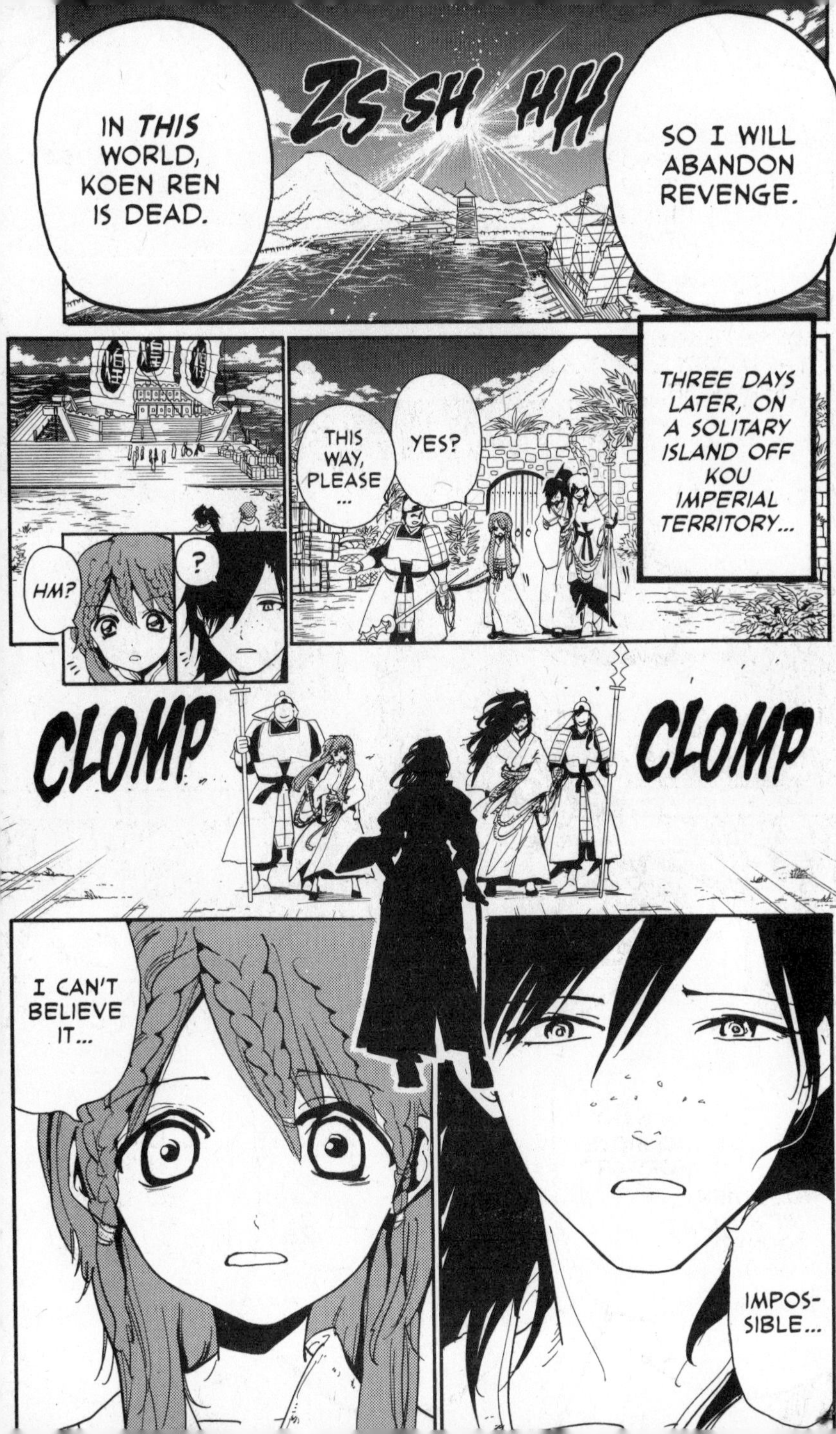
SO I WILL ABANDON REVENGE.
ZS SH HH
IN THIS WORLD, KOEN REN IS DEAD.
THREE DAYS LATER, ON A SOLITARY ISLAND OFF KOU IMPERIAL TERRITORY...
YES?
THIS WAY, PLEASE...
?
HM?
CLOMP
CLOMP
IMPOSSIBLE...
I CAN'T BELIEVE IT...

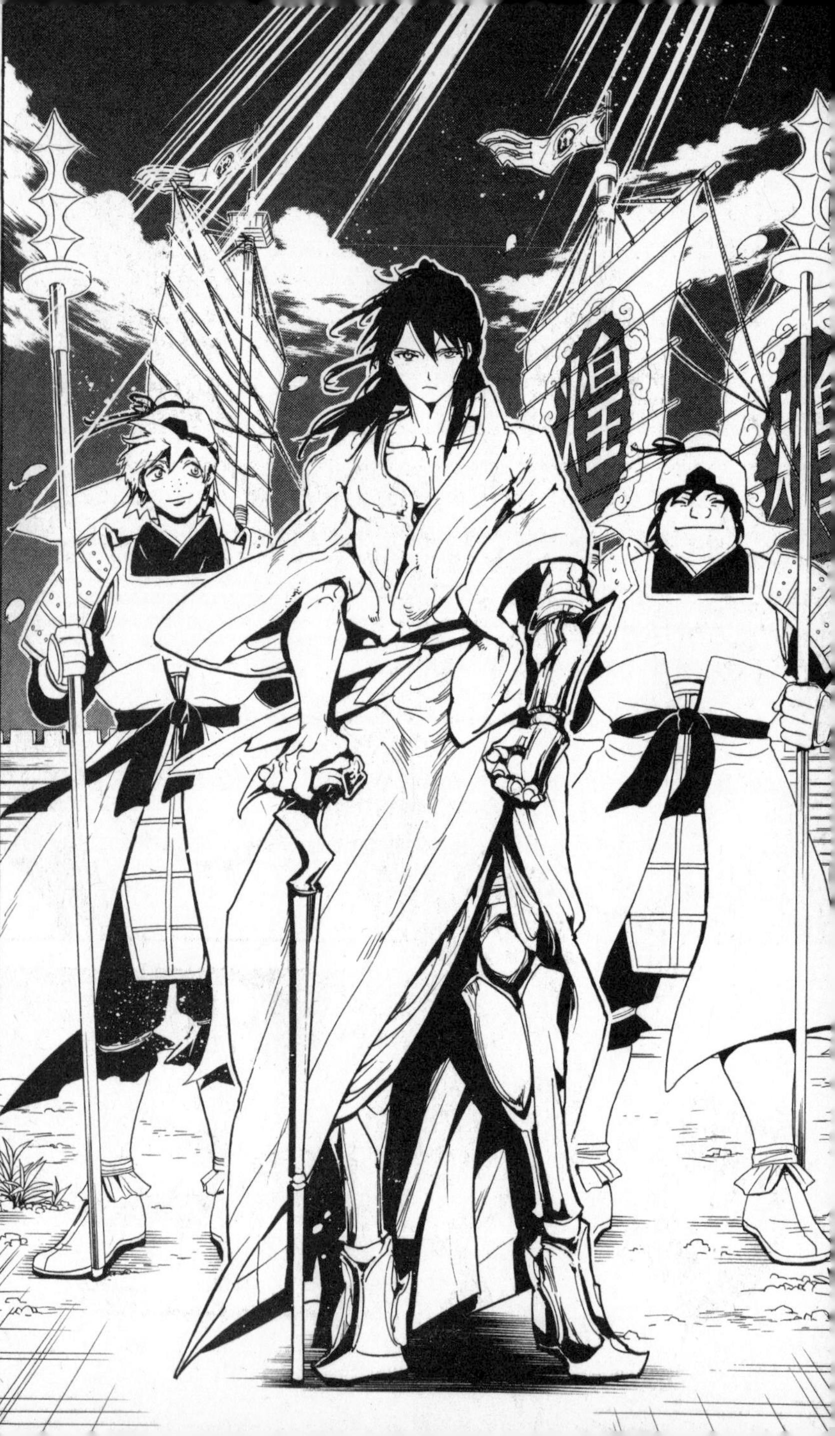
煌

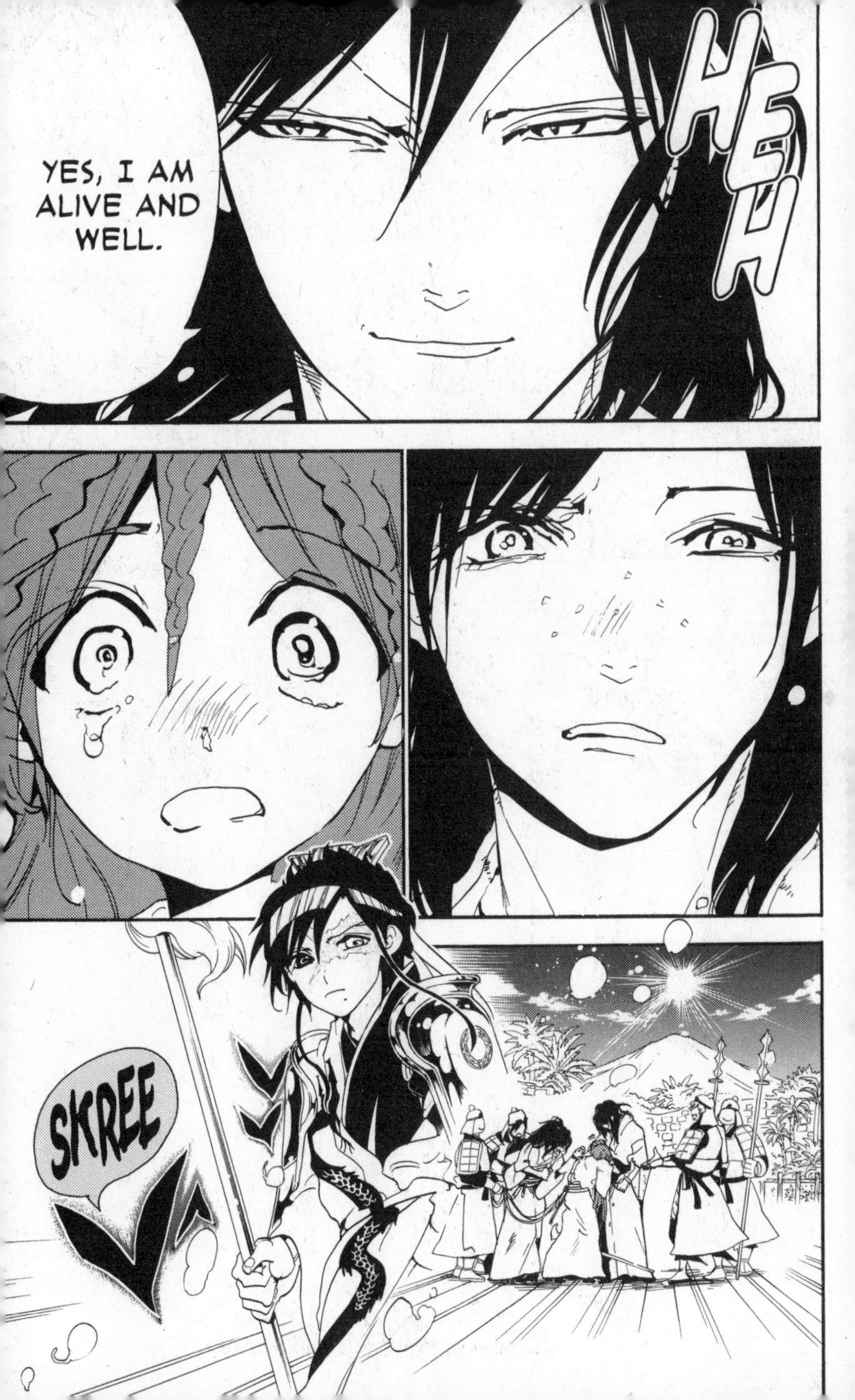
HEH
YES, I AM ALIVE AND WELL.
SKREE

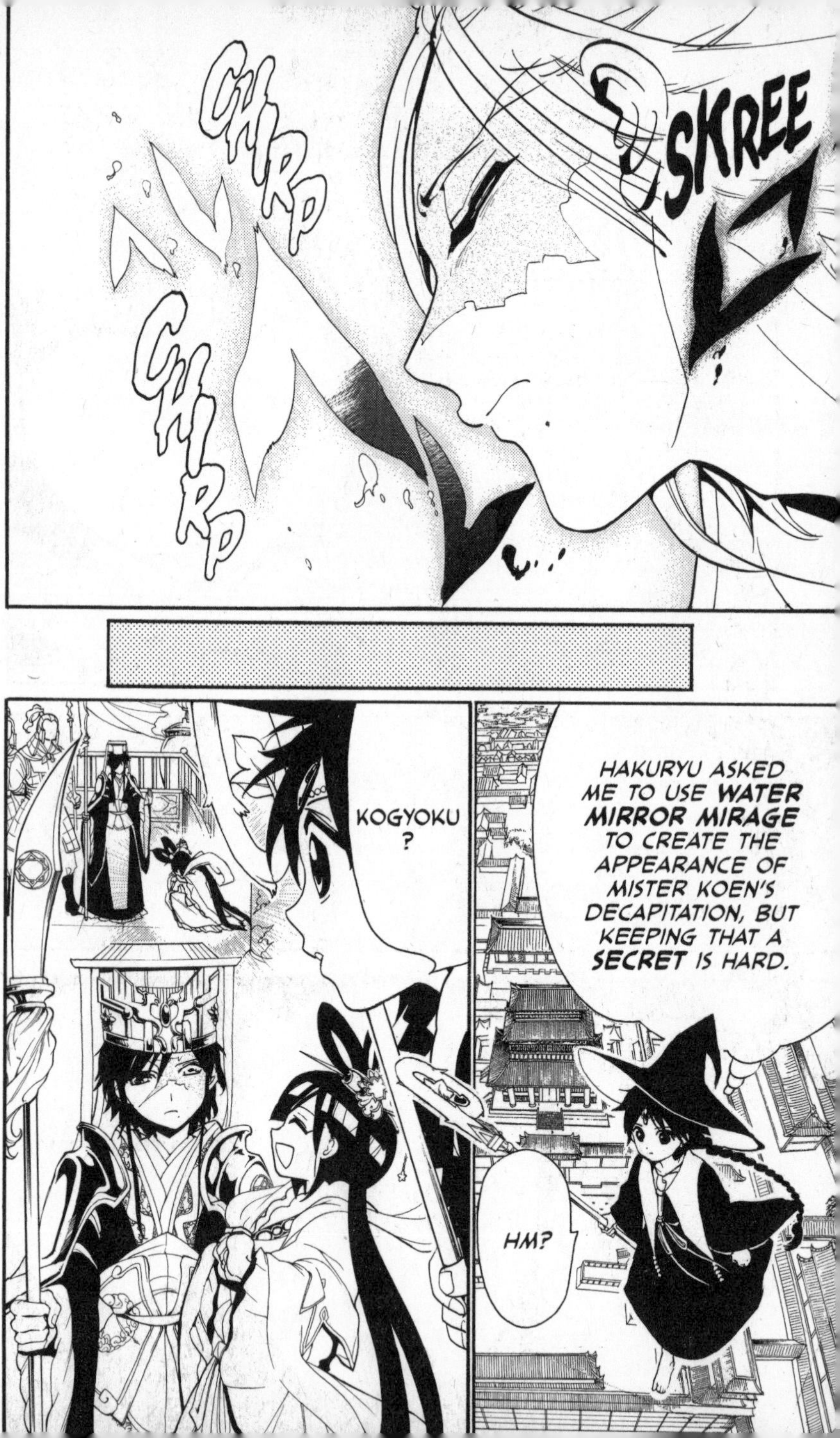
SKREE
CHIRP CHIRP
HAKURYU ASKED ME TO USE WATER MIRROR MIRAGE TO CREATE THE APPEARANCE OF MISTER KOEN'S DECAPITATION, BUT KEEPING THAT A SECRET IS HARD.
HM?
KOGYOKU ?

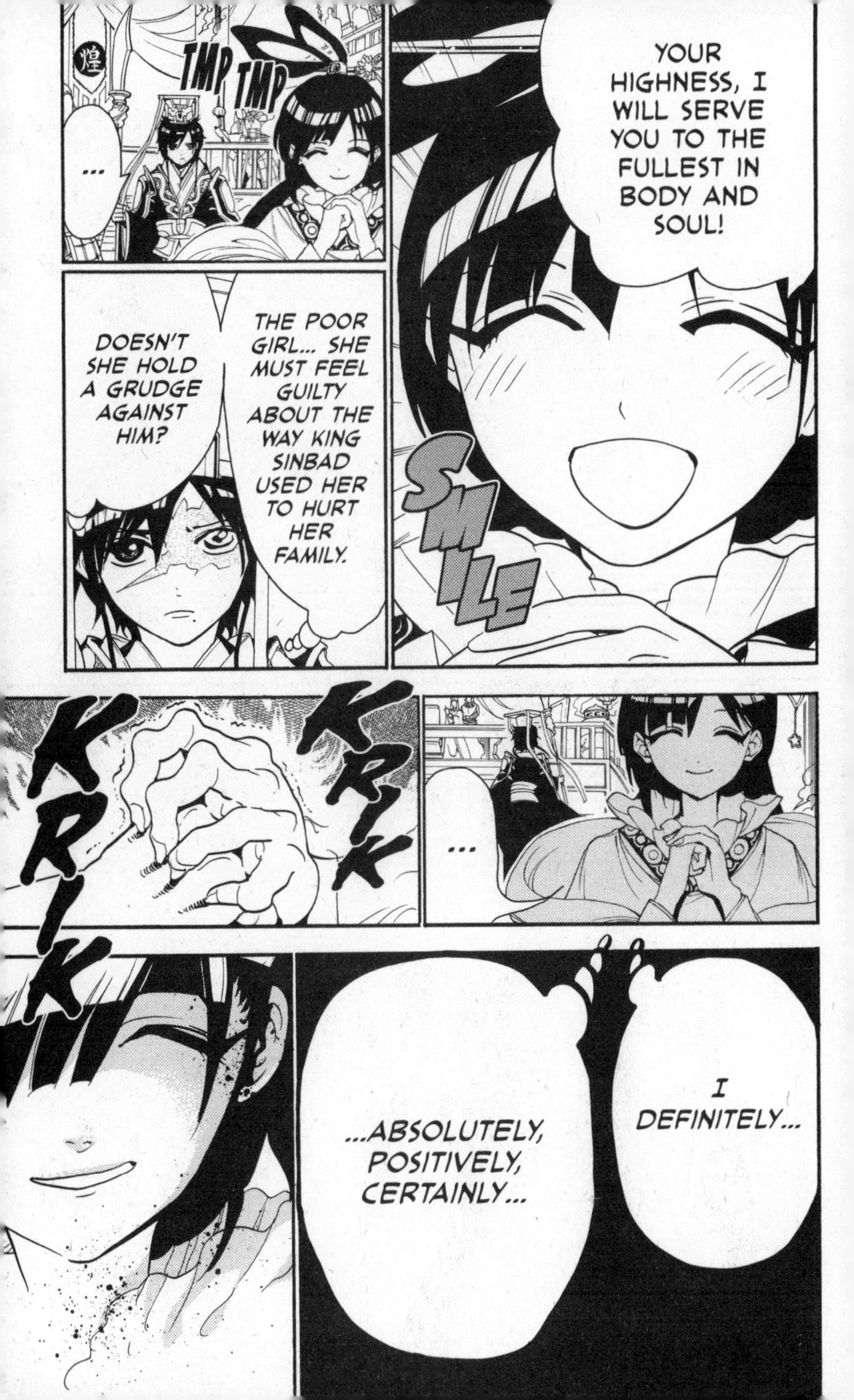
YOUR HIGHNESS, I WILL SERVE YOU TO THE FULLEST IN BODY AND SOUL!
SMILE
TMP TMP
...
THE POOR GIRL... SHE MUST FEEL GUILTY ABOUT THE WAY KING SINBAD USED HER TO HURT HER FAMILY.
DOESN'T SHE HOLD A GRUDGE AGAINST HIM?
...
KRRK
KRRK
I DEFINITELY...
...ABSOLUTELY, POSITIVELY, CERTAINLY...

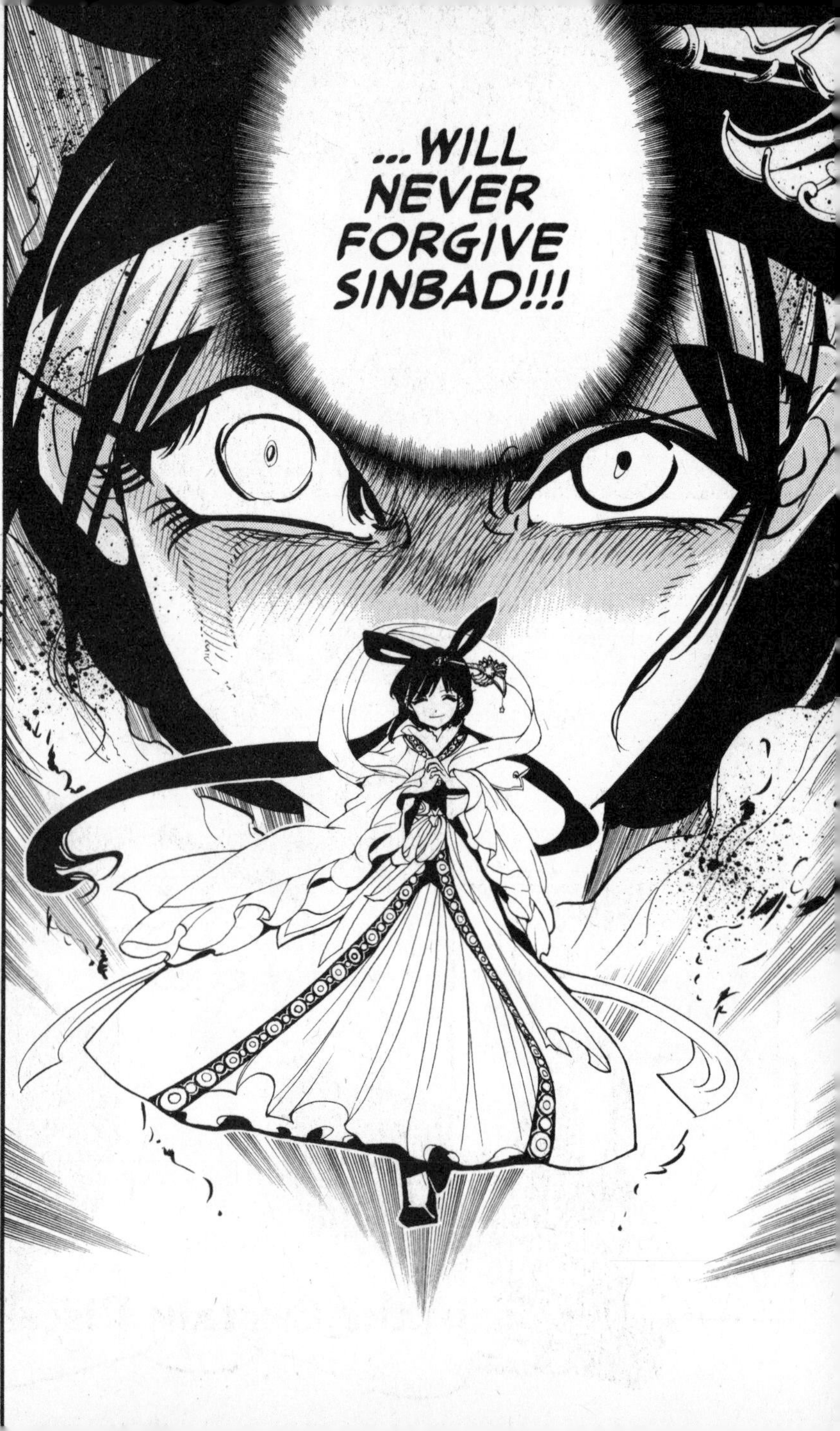
...WILL NEVER FORGIVE SINBAD!!!

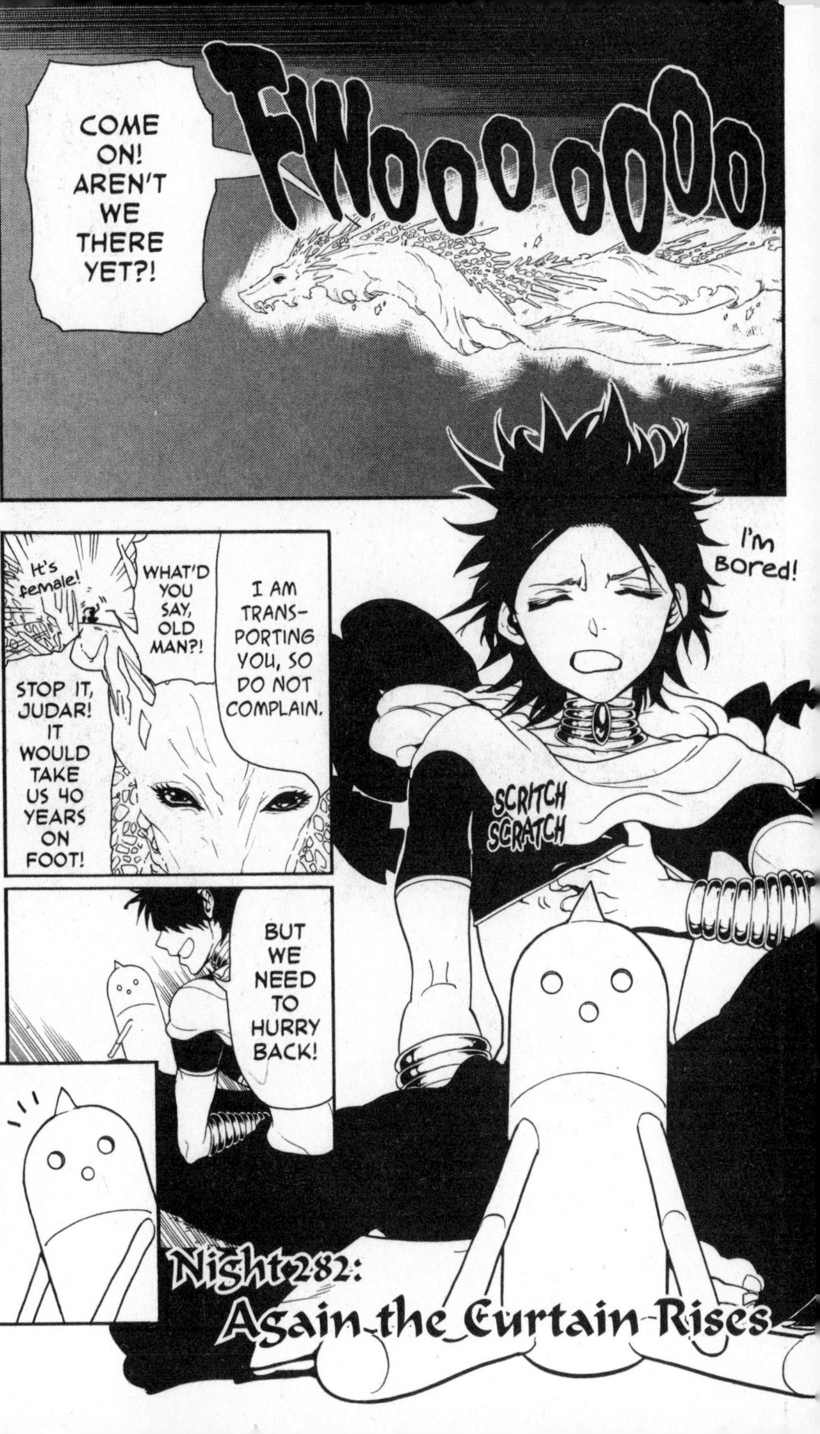

FWOOOOOOOO
COME ON! AREN'T WE THERE YET?!
I'm Bored!
SCRITCH SCRATCH
Night 282:
Again the Curtain Rises
I AM TRANS-PORTING YOU, SO DO NOT COMPLAIN.
WHAT'D YOU SAY, OLD MAN?!
It's female!
STOP IT, JUDAR! IT WOULD TAKE US 40 YEARS ON FOOT!
BUT WE NEED TO HURRY BACK!

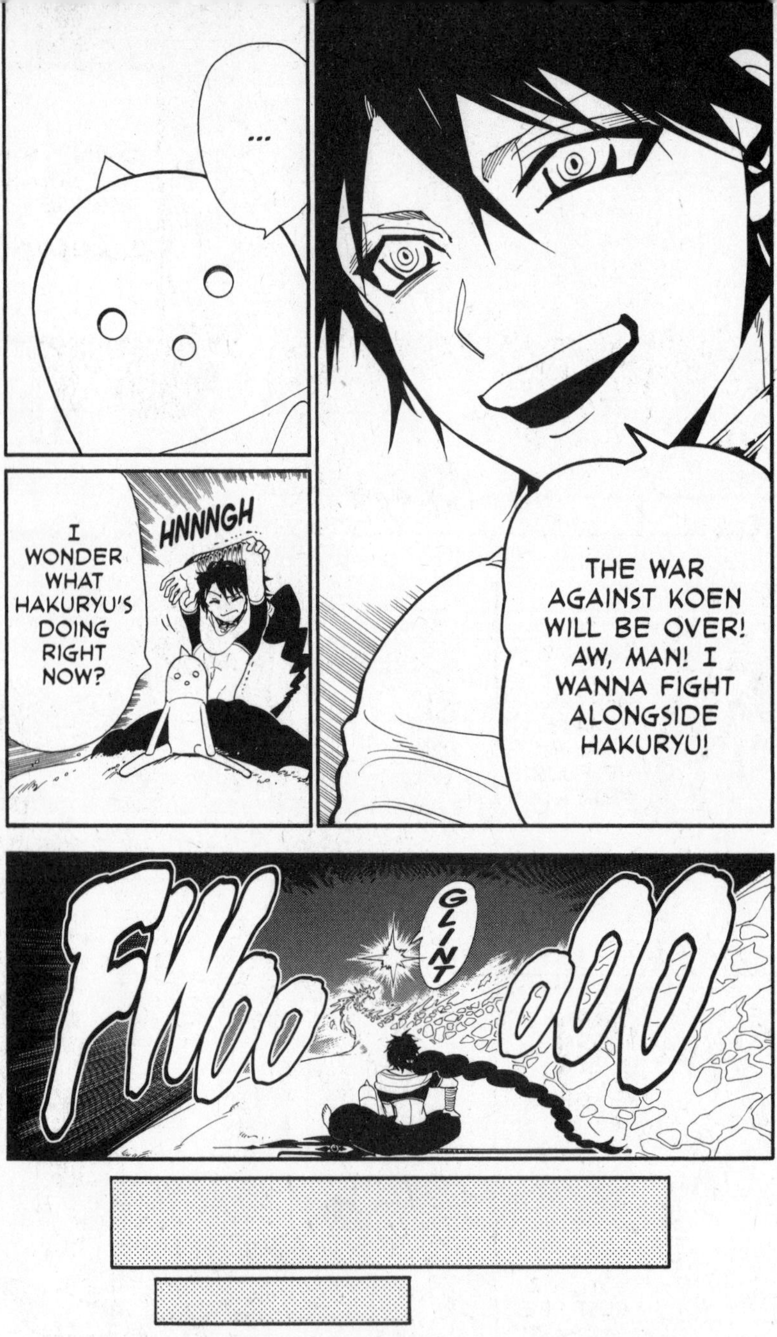
THE WAR AGAINST KOEN WILL BE OVER! AW, MAN! I WANNA FIGHT ALONGSIDE HAKURYU!
...
HNNNGH
I WONDER WHAT HAKURYU'S DOING RIGHT NOW?
FWOOOOO
GLINT

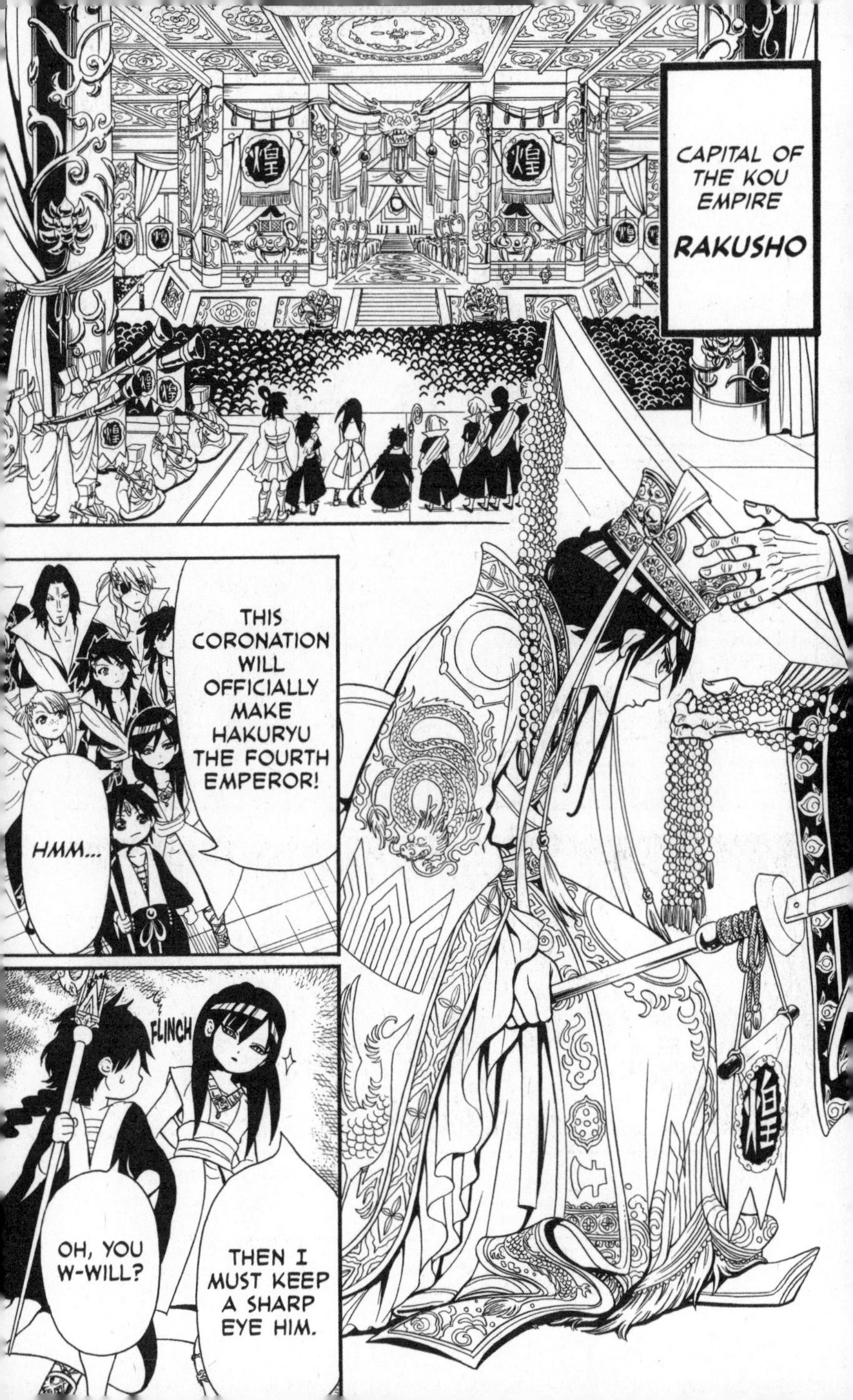
CAPITAL OF THE KOU EMPIRE
RAKUSHO
THIS CORONATION WILL OFFICIALLY MAKE HAKURYU THE FOURTH EMPEROR!
HMM...
FLINCH
THEN I MUST KEEP A SHARP EYE HIM.
OH, YOU W-WILL?

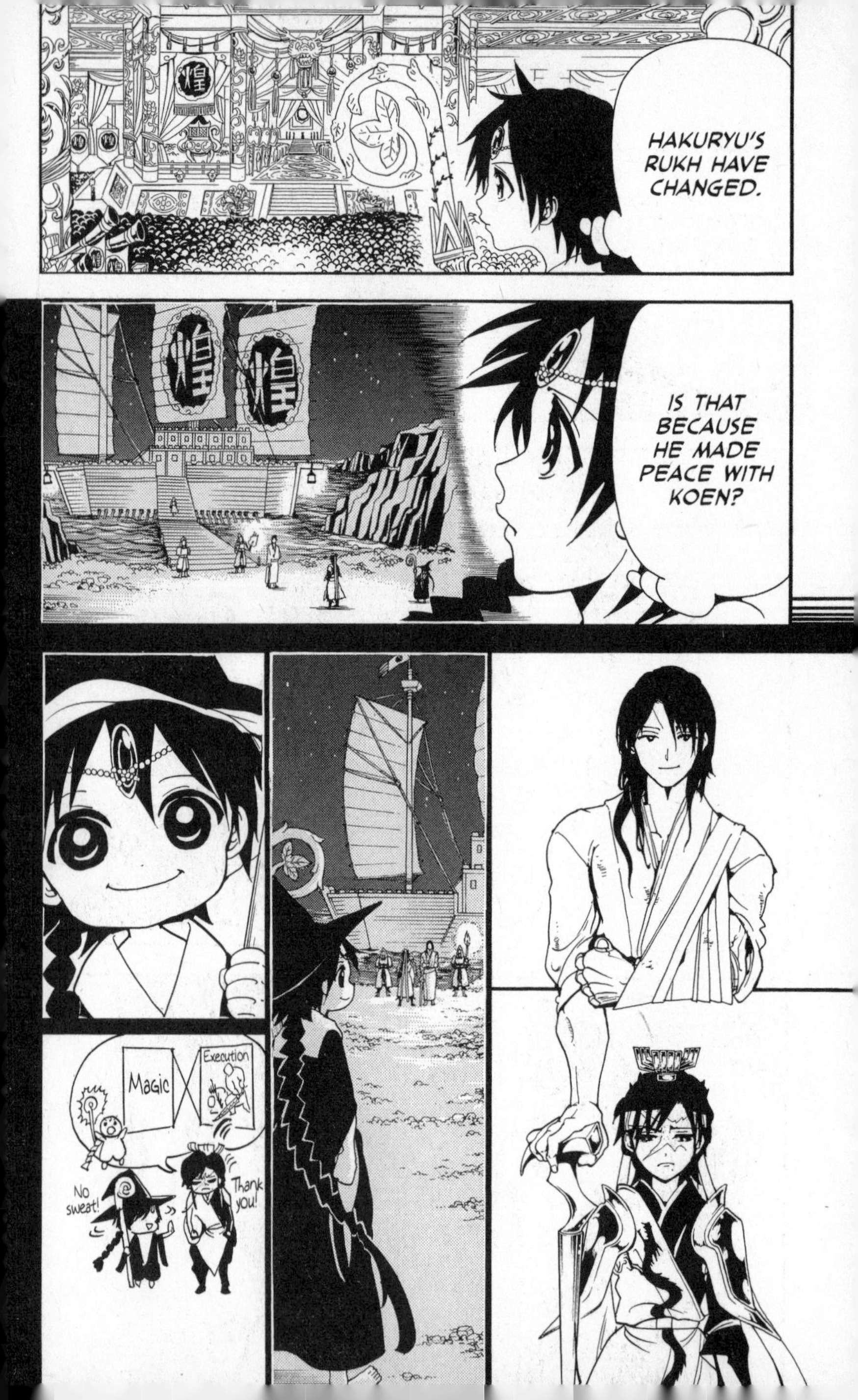
HAKURYU'S RUKH HAVE CHANGED.
IS THAT BECAUSE HE MADE PEACE WITH KOEN?
Magic
Execution
Thank you!
No sweat!

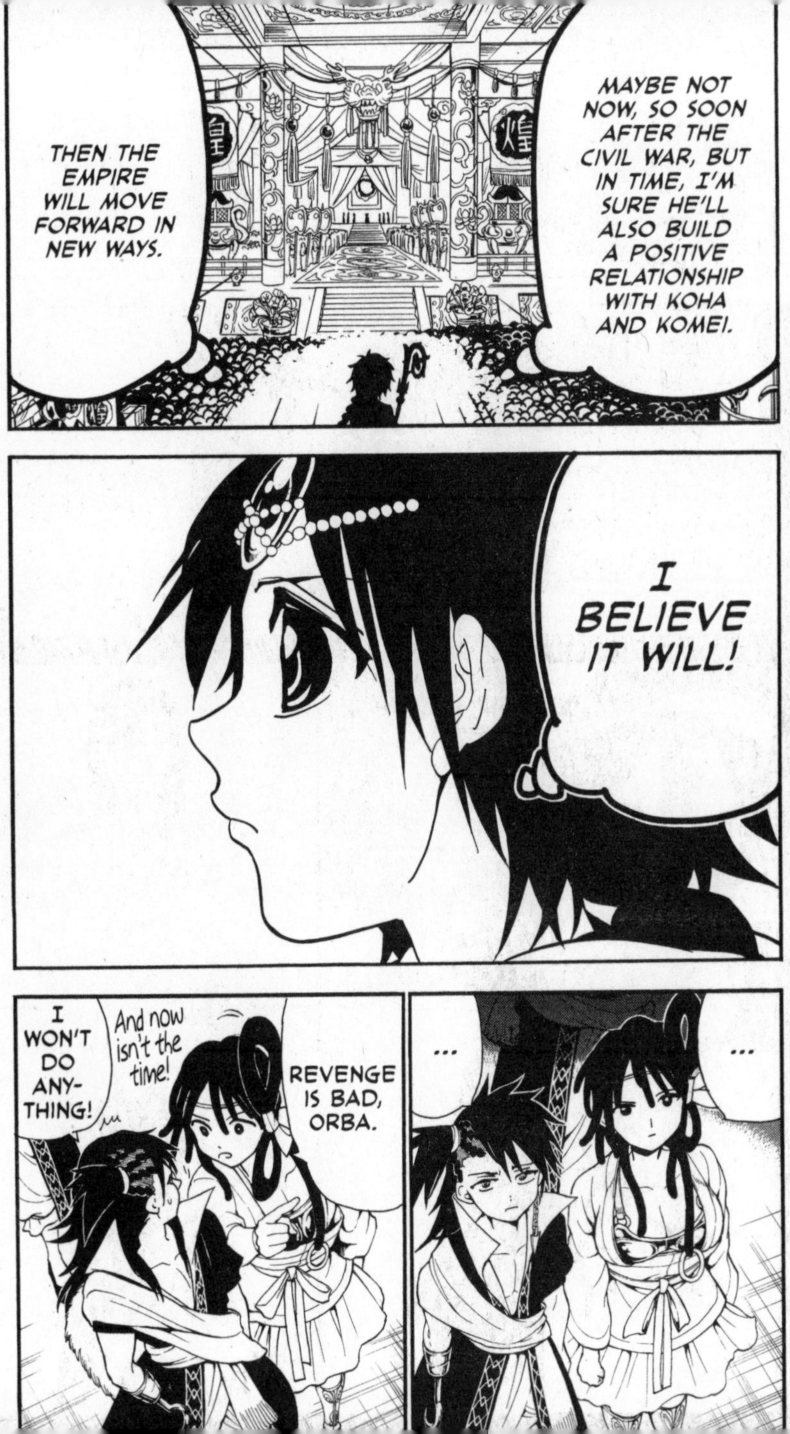
MAYBE NOT NOW, SO SOON AFTER THE CIVIL WAR, BUT IN TIME, I'M SURE HE'LL ALSO BUILD A POSITIVE RELATIONSHIP WITH KOHA AND KOMEI.
THEN THE EMPIRE WILL MOVE FORWARD IN NEW WAYS.
I BELIEVE IT WILL!
...
...
REVENGE IS BAD, ORBA.
I WON'T DO ANYTHING!
And now isn't the time!

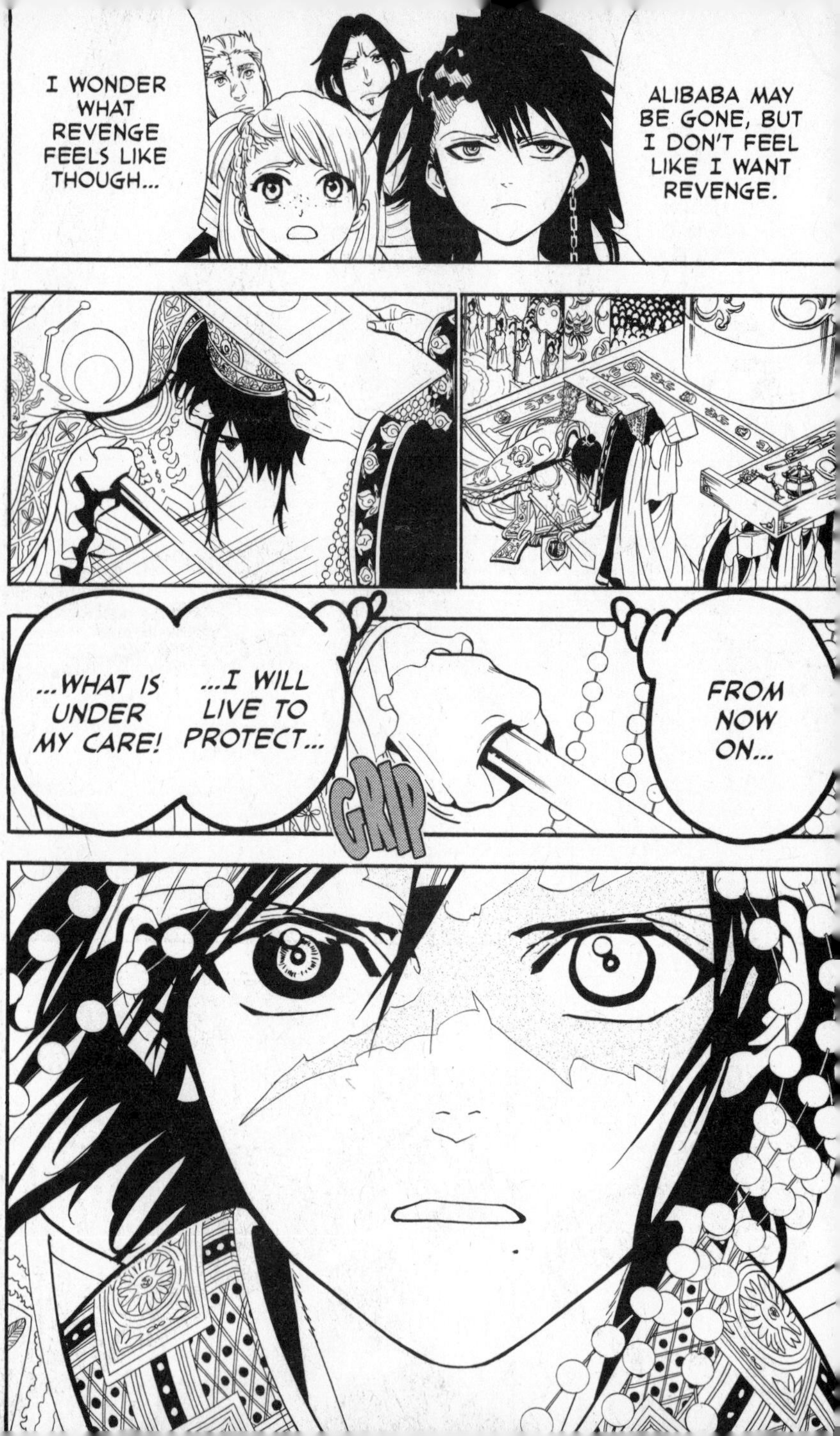
ALIBABA MAY BE GONE, BUT I DON'T FEEL LIKE I WANT REVENGE.
I WONDER WHAT REVENGE FEELS LIKE THOUGH...
FROM NOW ON...
...I WILL LIVE TO PROTECT...
...WHAT IS UNDER MY CARE!
GRIP

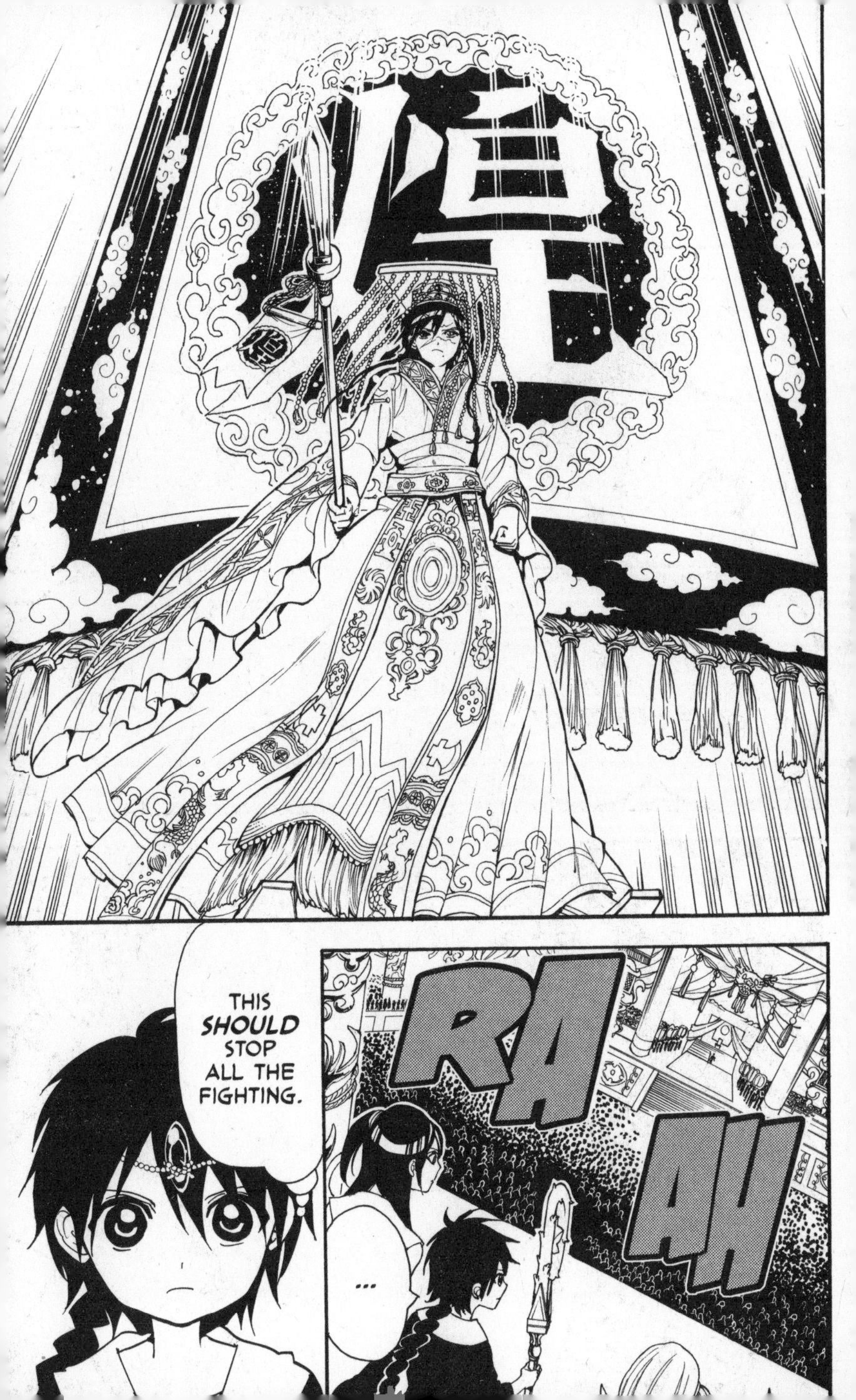
RA AH
...
THIS SHOULD STOP ALL THE FIGHTING.

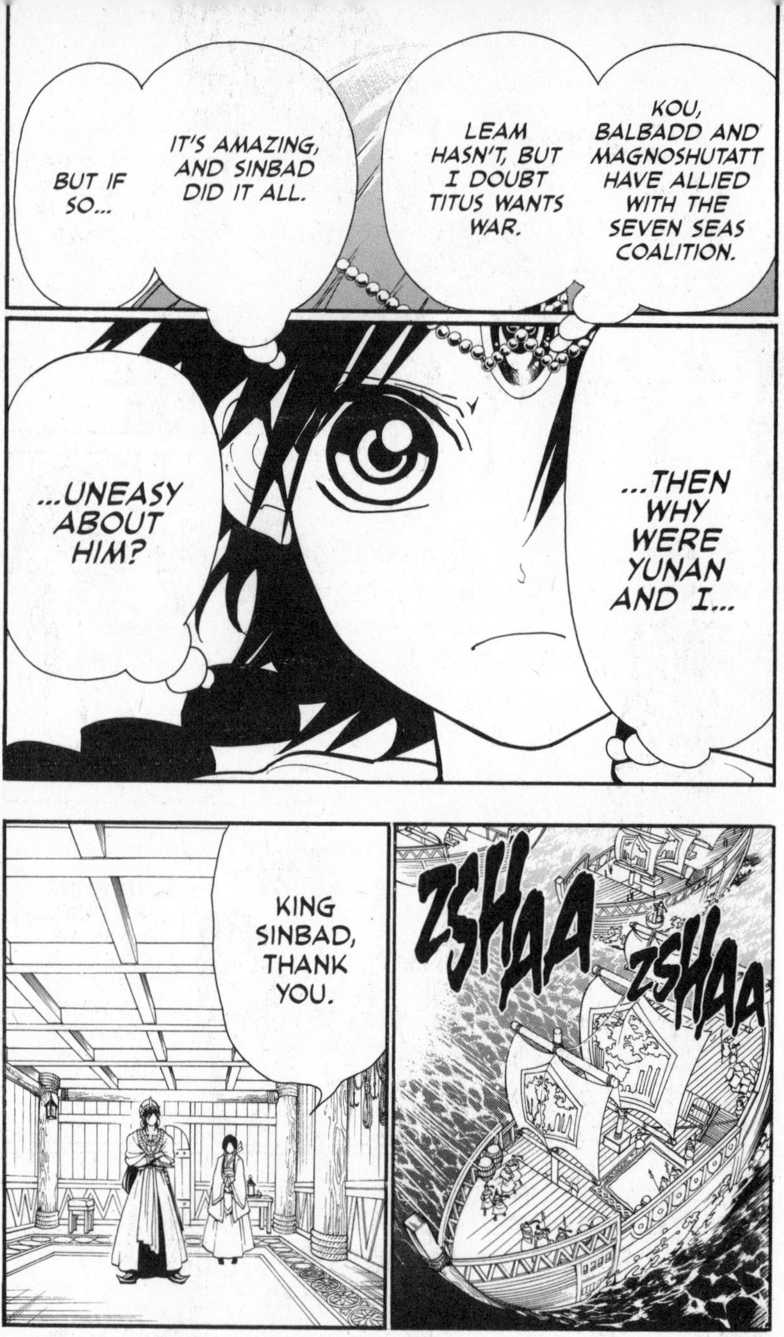
KOU, BALBADD AND MAGNOSHUTATT HAVE ALLIED WITH THE SEVEN SEAS COALITION.
LEAM HASN'T, BUT I DOUBT TITUS WANTS WAR.
IT'S AMAZING, AND SINBAD DID IT ALL.
BUT IF SO...
...THEN WHY WERE YUNAN AND I...
...UNEASY ABOUT HIM?
ZSHAA
ZSHAA
KING SINBAD, THANK YOU.

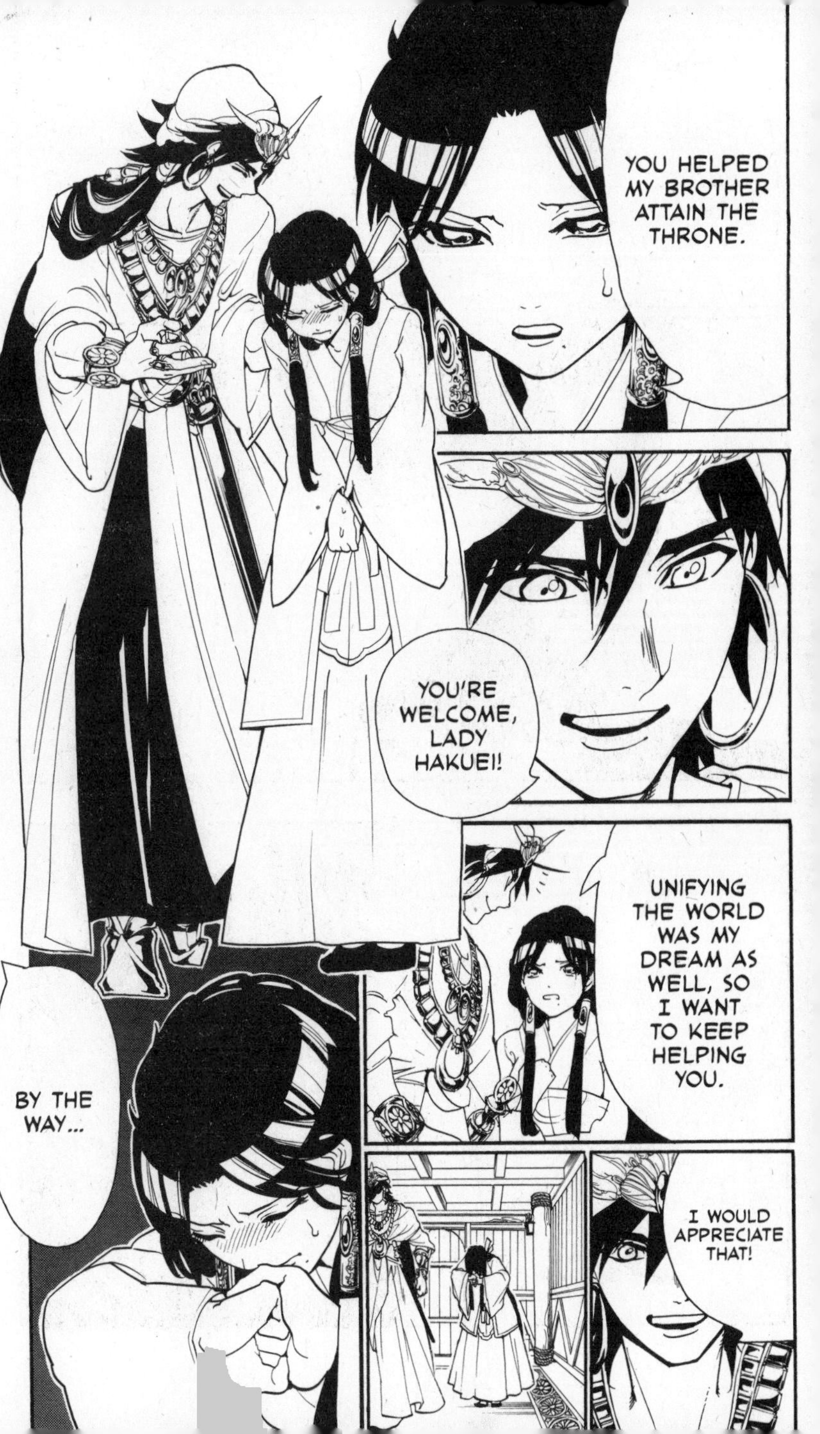
YOU HELPED MY BROTHER ATTAIN THE THRONE.
YOU'RE WELCOME, LADY HAKUEI!
UNIFYING THE WORLD WAS MY DREAM AS WELL, SO I WANT TO KEEP HELPING YOU.
I WOULD APPRECIATE THAT!
BY THE WAY...

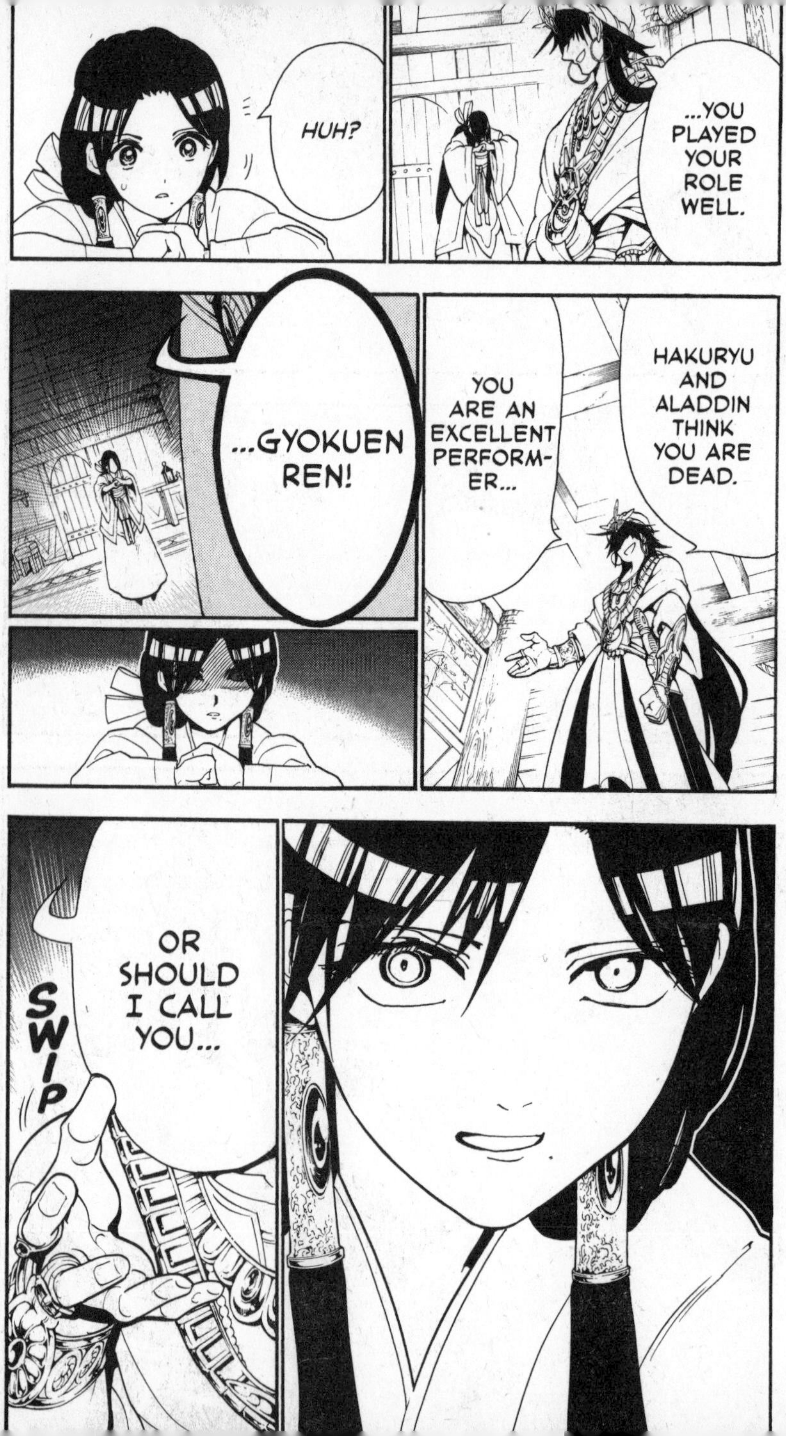
...YOU PLAYED YOUR ROLE WELL.
HUH?
HAKURYU AND ALADDIN THINK YOU ARE DEAD.
YOU ARE AN EXCELLENT PERFORM-ER...
...GYOKUEN REN!
OR SHOULD I CALL YOU...
SWIP

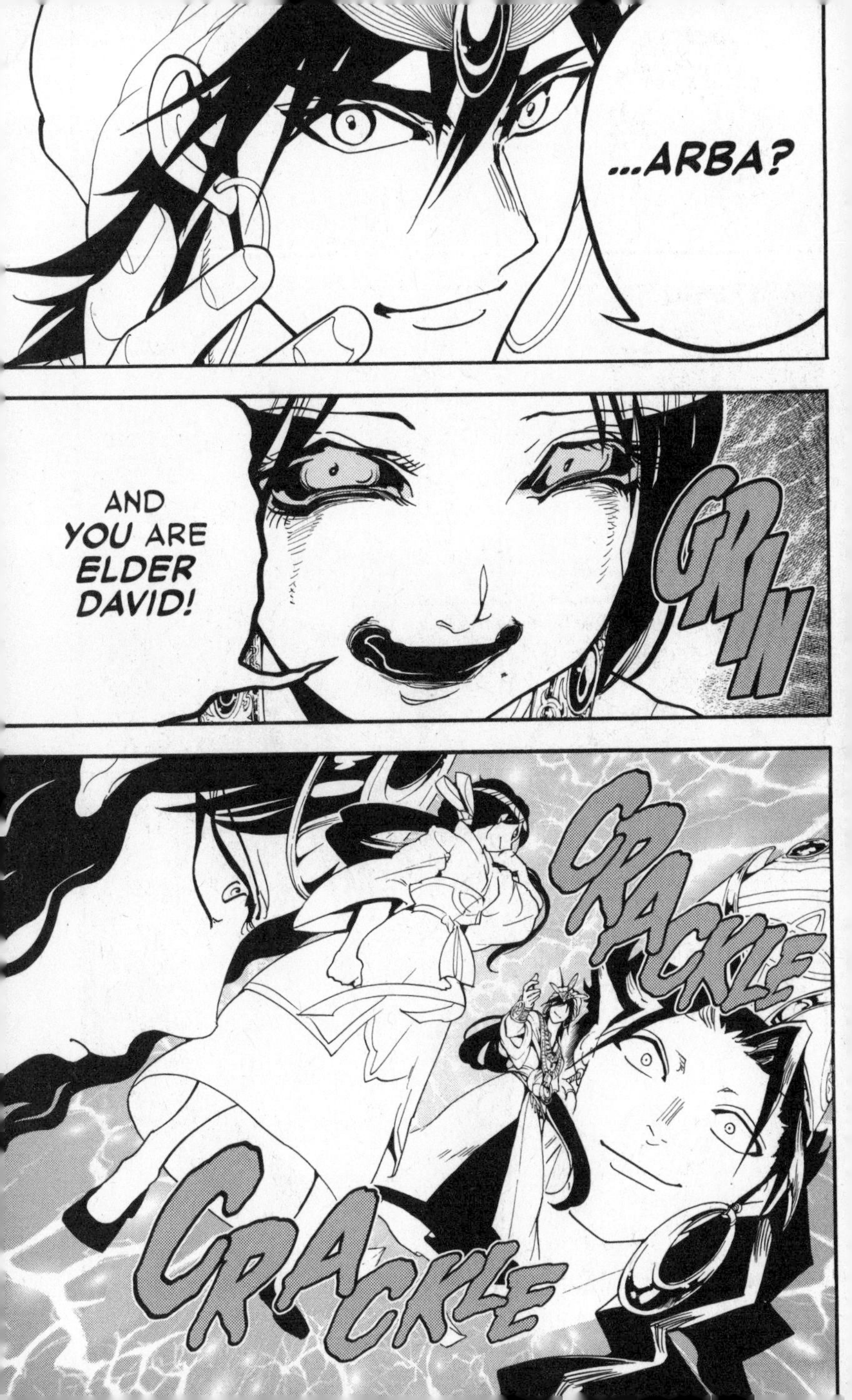
...ARBA?
GRIN
AND YOU ARE ELDER DAVID!
CRACKLE
CRACKLE

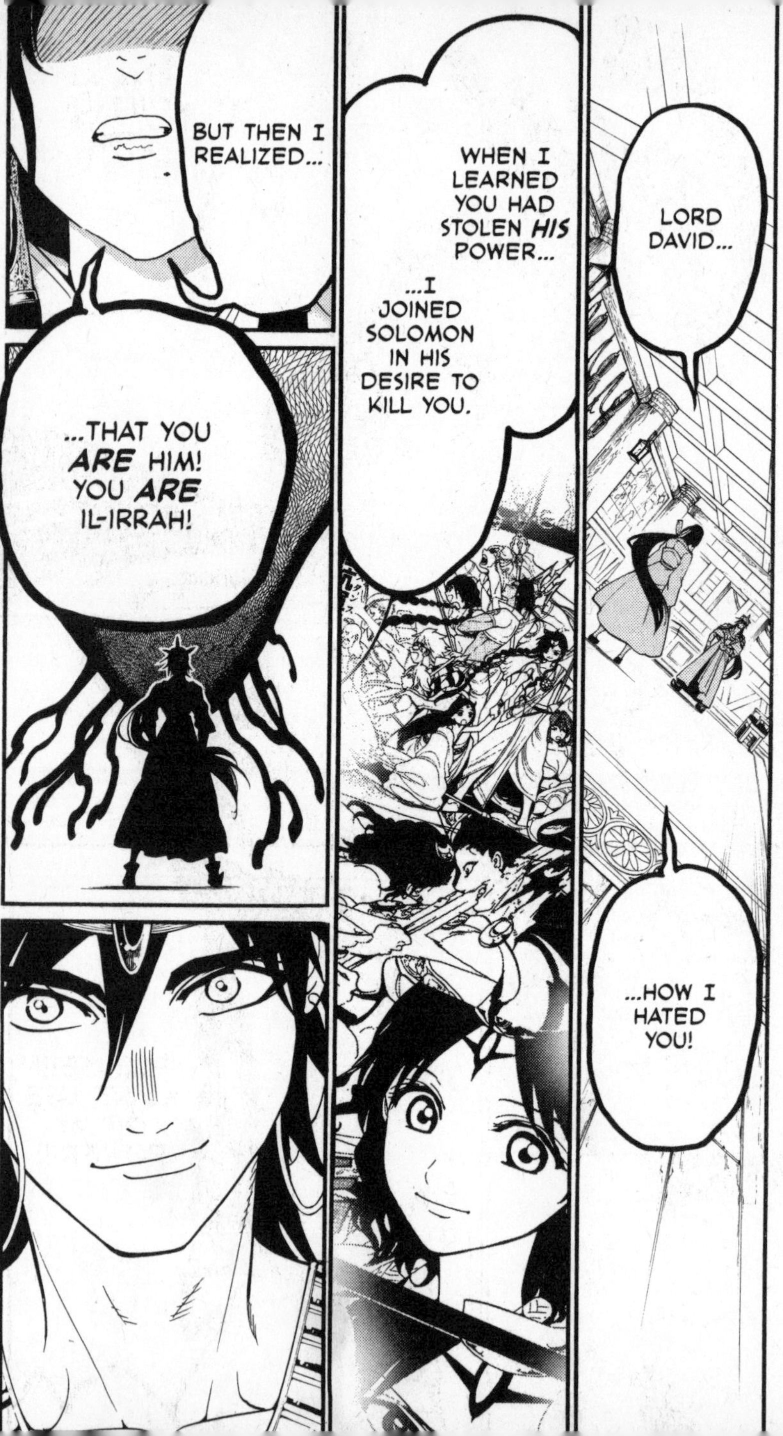
LORD DAVID...
...HOW I HATED YOU!
WHEN I LEARNED YOU HAD STOLEN *HIS* POWER...
...I JOINED SOLOMON IN HIS DESIRE TO KILL YOU.
BUT THEN I REALIZED...
...THAT YOU *ARE* HIM! YOU *ARE* IL-IRRAH!

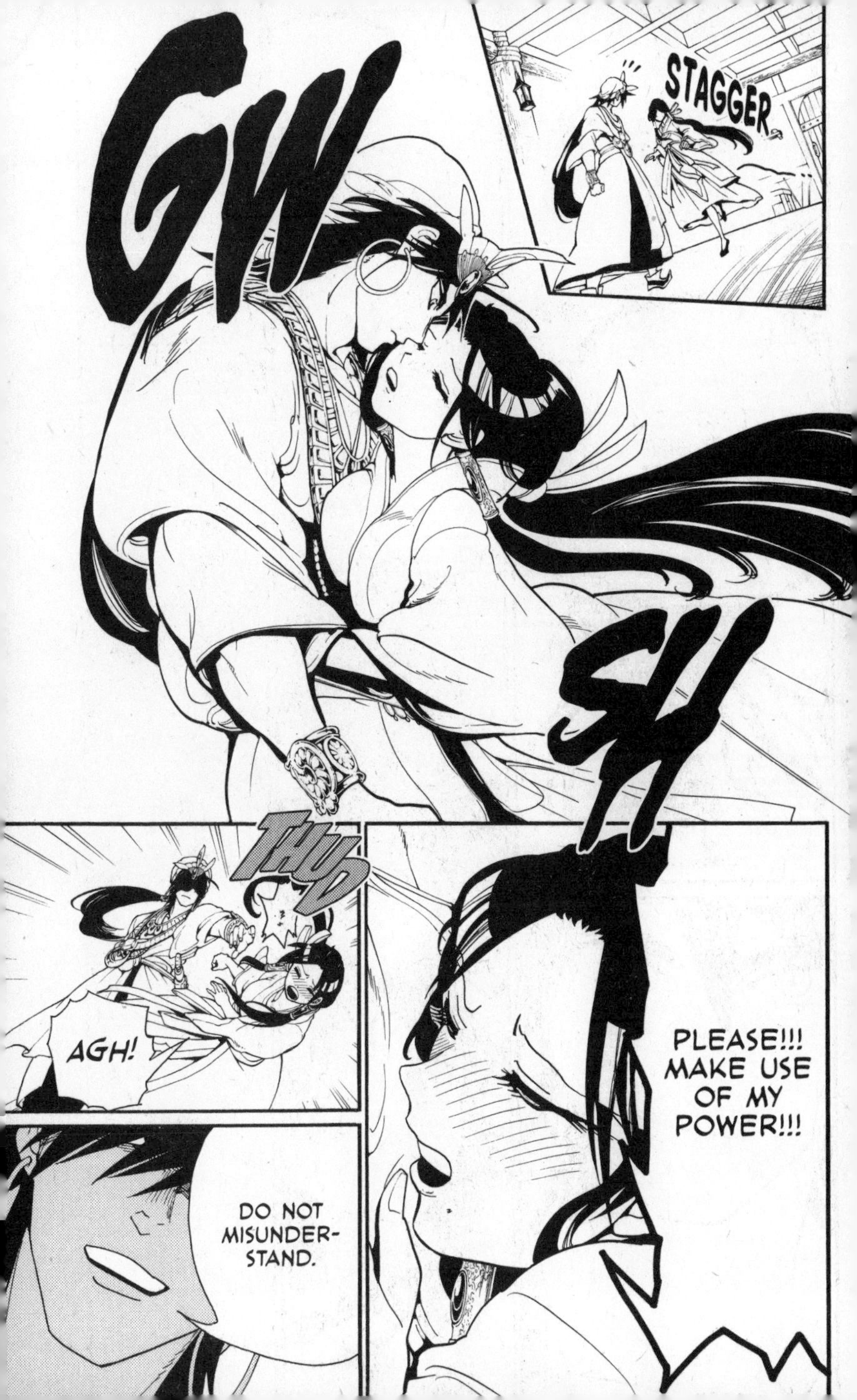
STAGGER
GW
SH
PLEASE!!! MAKE USE OF MY POWER!!!
THUD
AGH!
DO NOT MISUNDERSTAND.

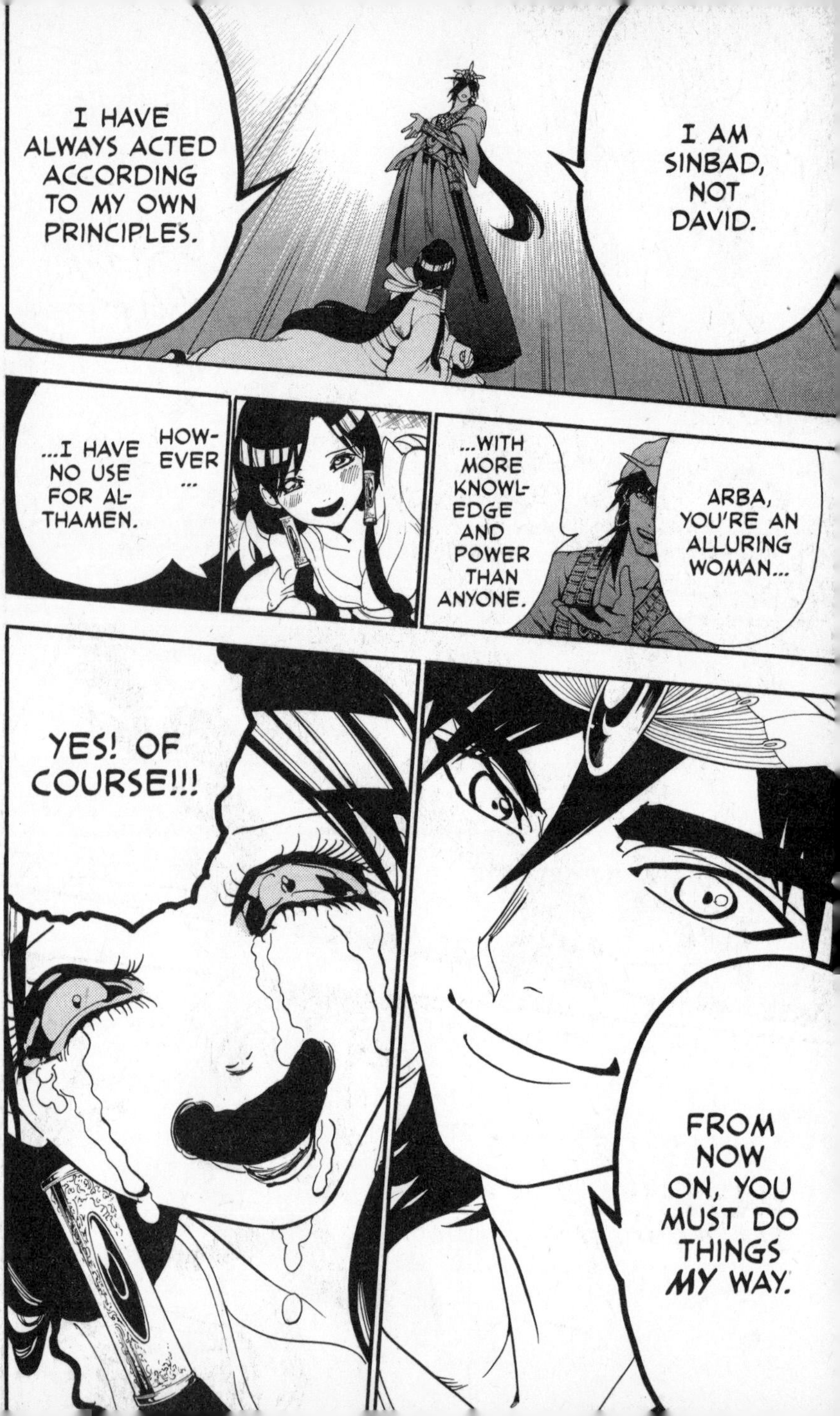
I AM SINBAD, NOT DAVID.
I HAVE ALWAYS ACTED ACCORDING TO MY OWN PRINCIPLES.
ARBA, YOU'RE AN ALLURING WOMAN...
...WITH MORE KNOWLEDGE AND POWER THAN ANYONE.
HOWEVER...
...I HAVE NO USE FOR AL-THAMEN.
FROM NOW ON, YOU MUST DO THINGS *MY* WAY.
YES! OF COURSE!!!

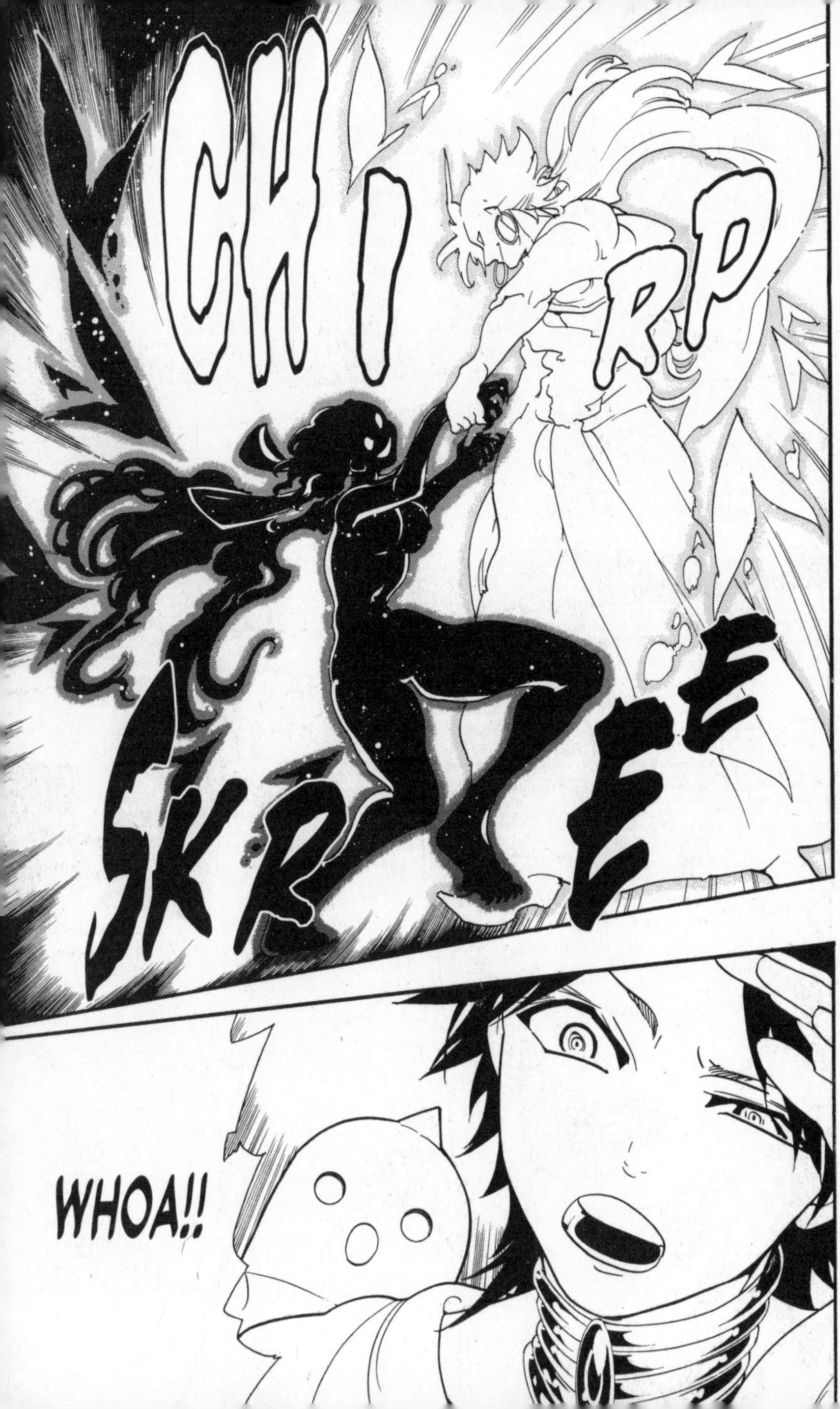
CHIRP
SKREEE
WHOA!!

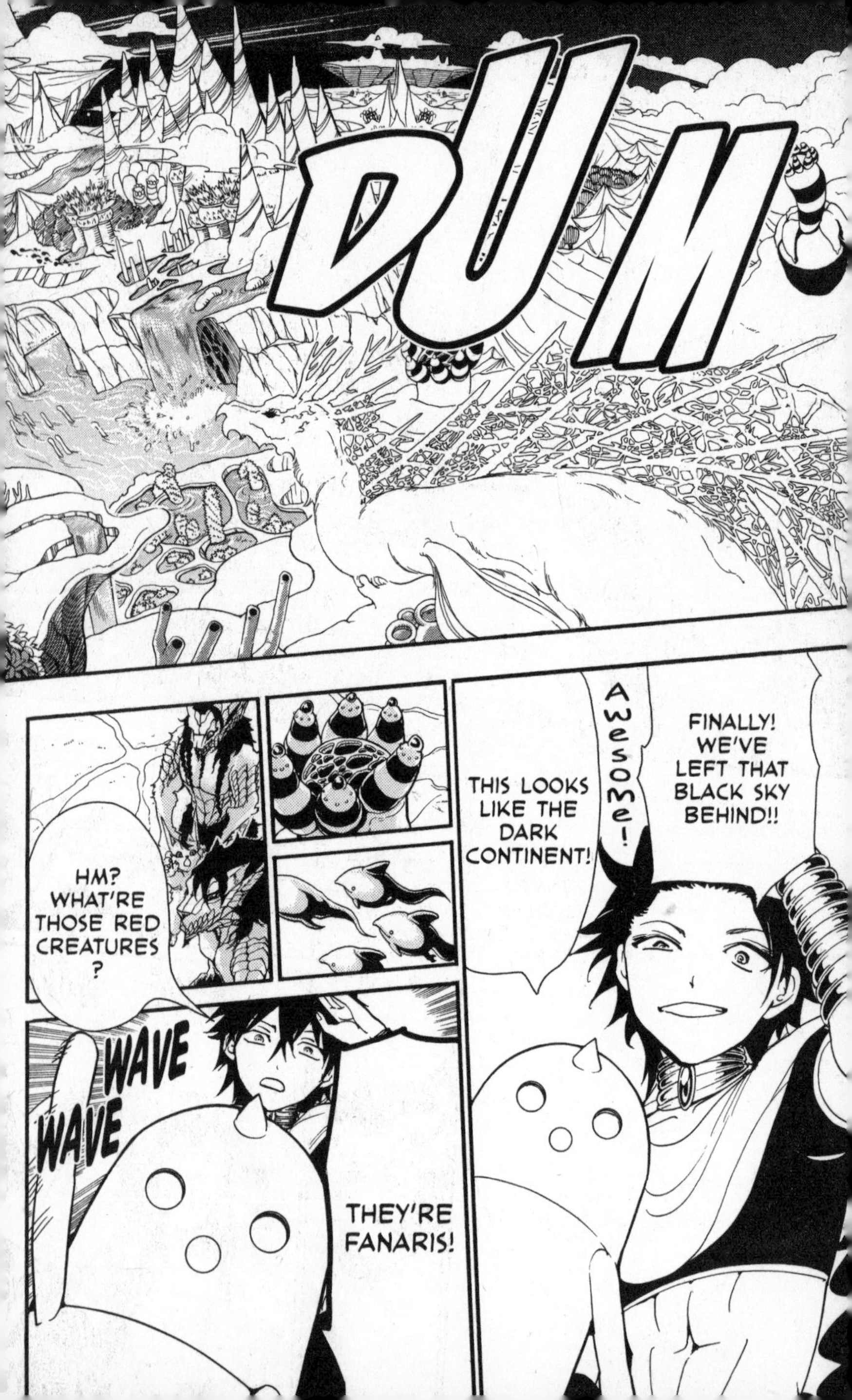
DUN
FINALLY! WE'VE LEFT THAT BLACK SKY BEHIND!!
Awesome!
THIS LOOKS LIKE THE DARK CONTINENT!
HM? WHAT'RE THOSE RED CREATURES?
THEY'RE FANARIS!
WAVE
WAVE

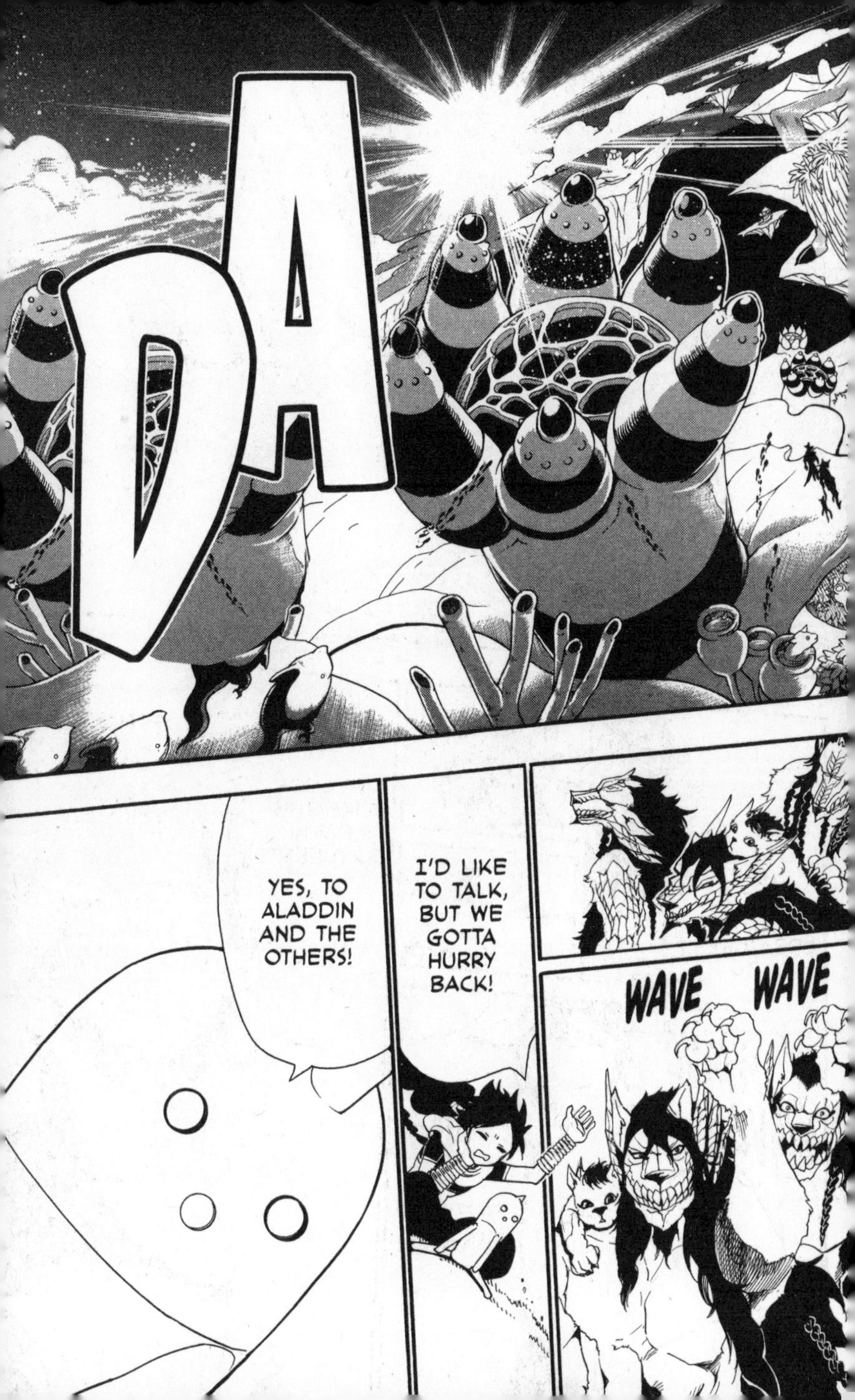
DA
WAVE WAVE
I'D LIKE TO TALK, BUT WE GOTTA HURRY BACK!
YES, TO ALADDIN AND THE OTHERS!

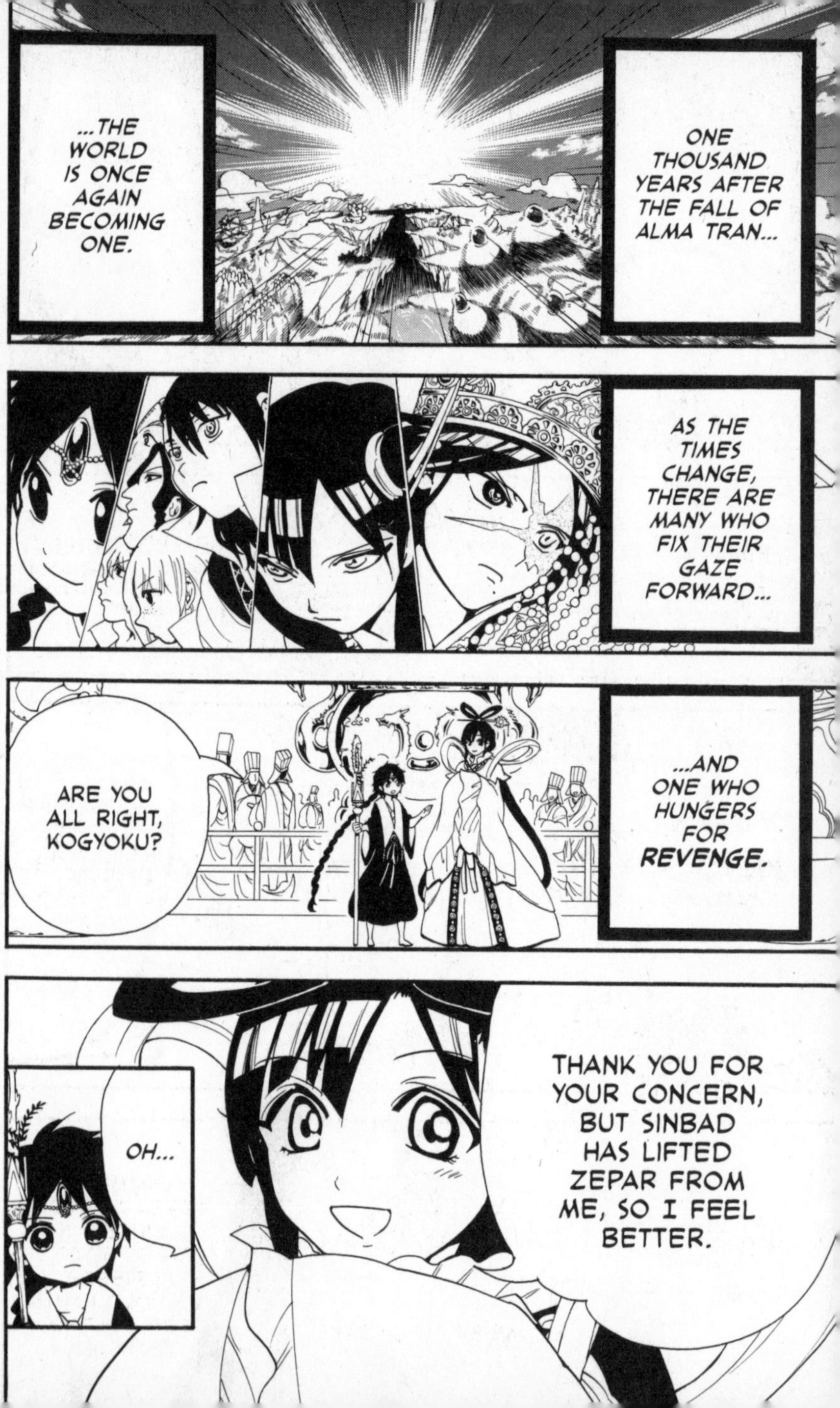
ONE THOUSAND YEARS AFTER THE FALL OF ALMA TRAN...
...THE WORLD IS ONCE AGAIN BECOMING ONE.
AS THE TIMES CHANGE, THERE ARE MANY WHO FIX THEIR GAZE FORWARD...
...AND ONE WHO HUNGERS FOR REVENGE.
ARE YOU ALL RIGHT, KOGYOKU?
THANK YOU FOR YOUR CONCERN, BUT SINBAD HAS LIFTED ZEPAR FROM ME, SO I FEEL BETTER.
OH...

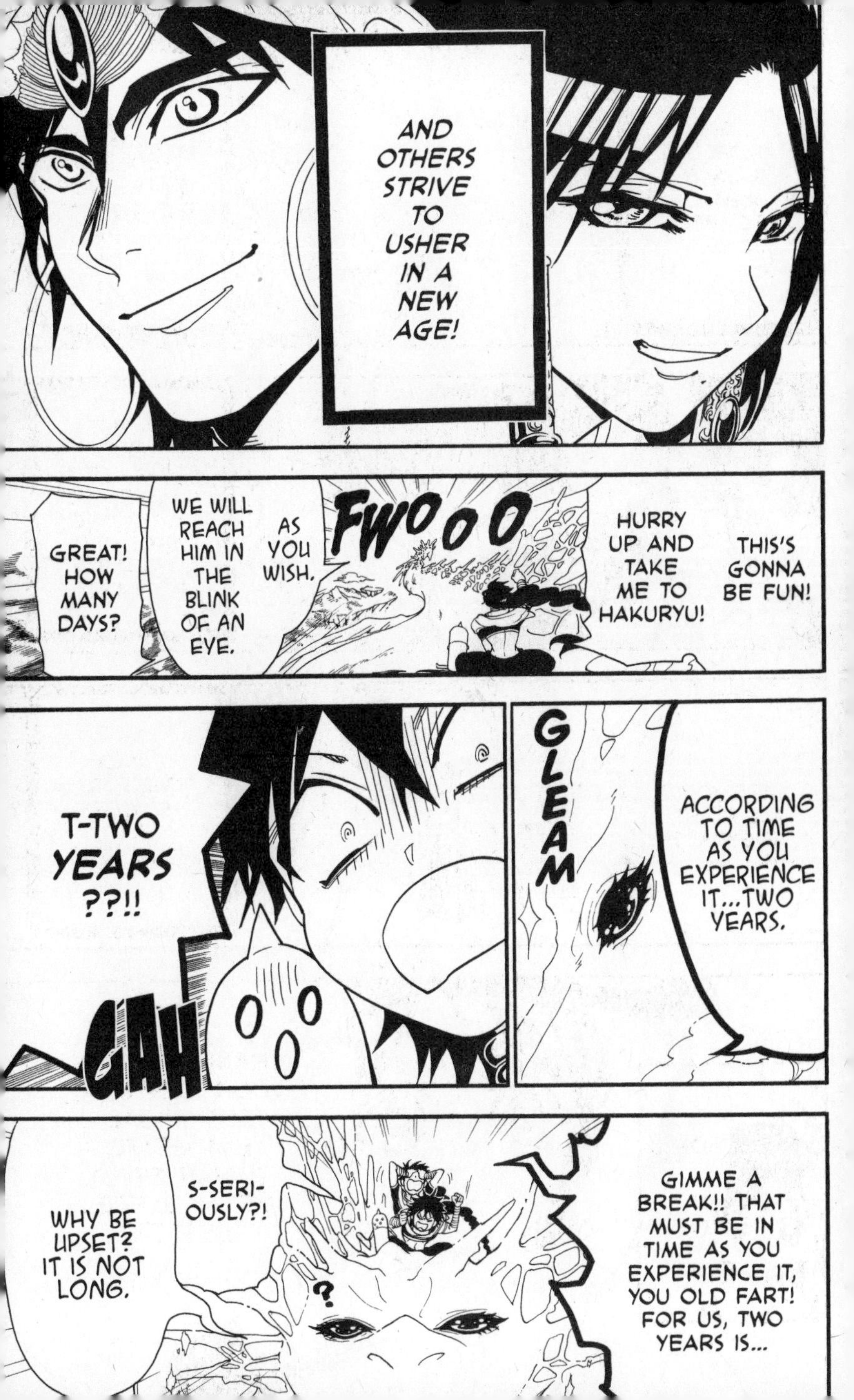
AND OTHERS STRIVE TO USHER IN A NEW AGE!
THIS'S GONNA BE FUN!
HURRY UP AND TAKE ME TO HAKURYU!
FWOOO
AS YOU WISH.
WE WILL REACH HIM IN THE BLINK OF AN EYE.
GREAT! HOW MANY DAYS?
GLEAM
ACCORDING TO TIME AS YOU EXPERIENCE IT...TWO YEARS.
T-TWO YEARS ??!!
GAH
GIMME A BREAK!! THAT MUST BE IN TIME AS YOU EXPERIENCE IT, YOU OLD FART! FOR US, TWO YEARS IS...
S-SERI-OUSLY?!
?
WHY BE UPSET? IT IS NOT LONG.

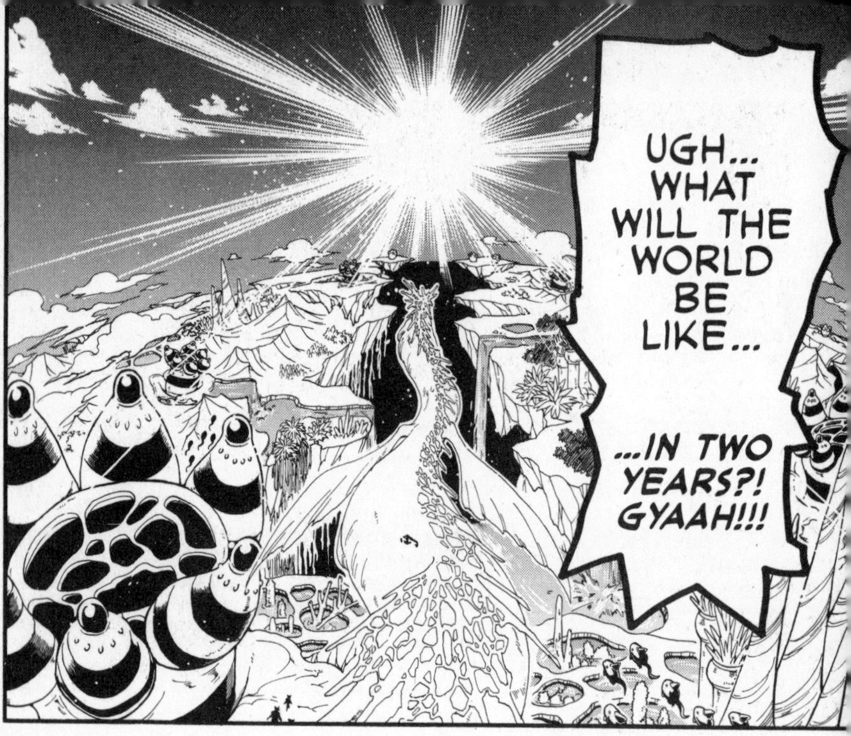
UGH... WHAT WILL THE WORLD BE LIKE...
...IN TWO YEARS?! GYAAH!!!

Magi
–Kou Empire Arc–
The End

Night 283: Alibaba's Return

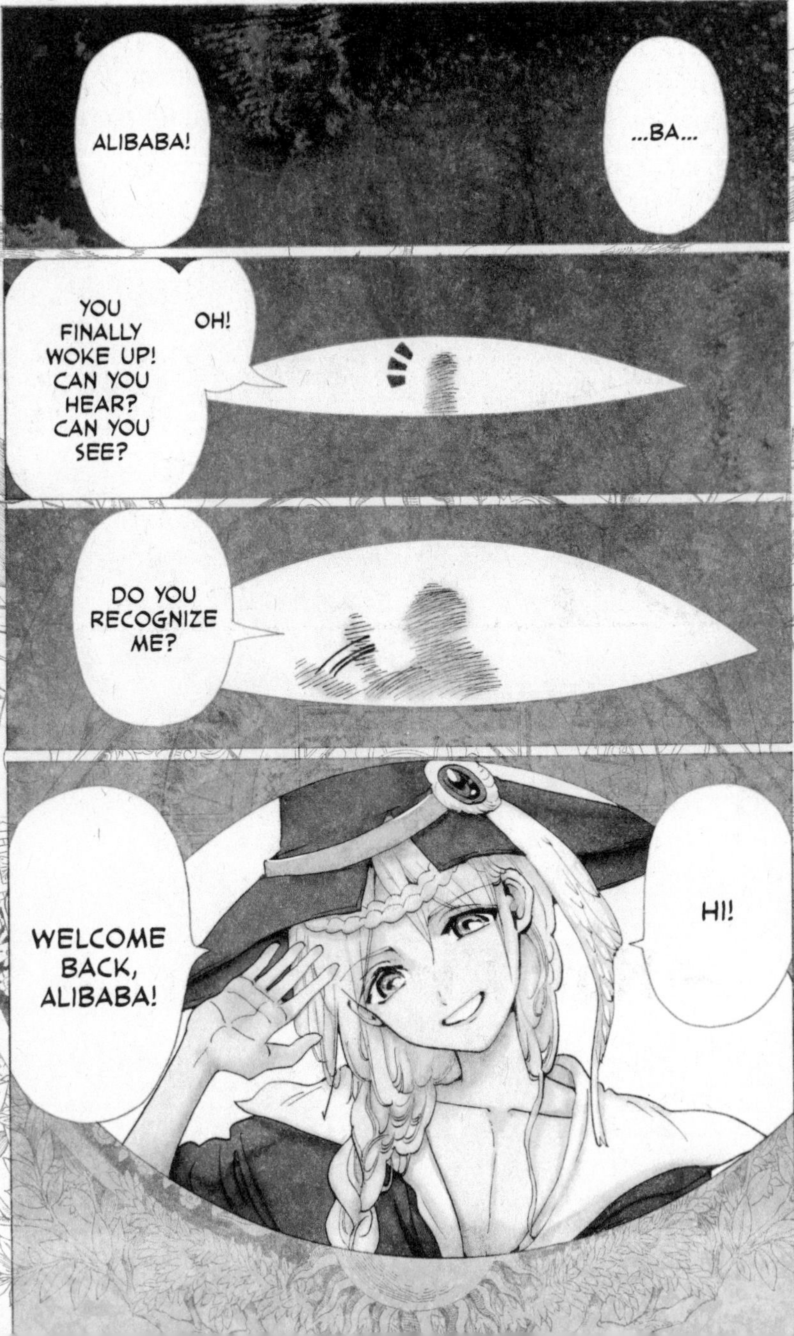
...BA...
ALIBABA!
OH!
YOU FINALLY WOKE UP! CAN YOU HEAR? CAN YOU SEE?
DO YOU RECOGNIZE ME?
HI!
WELCOME BACK, ALIBABA!

Night 283: Alibaba's Return

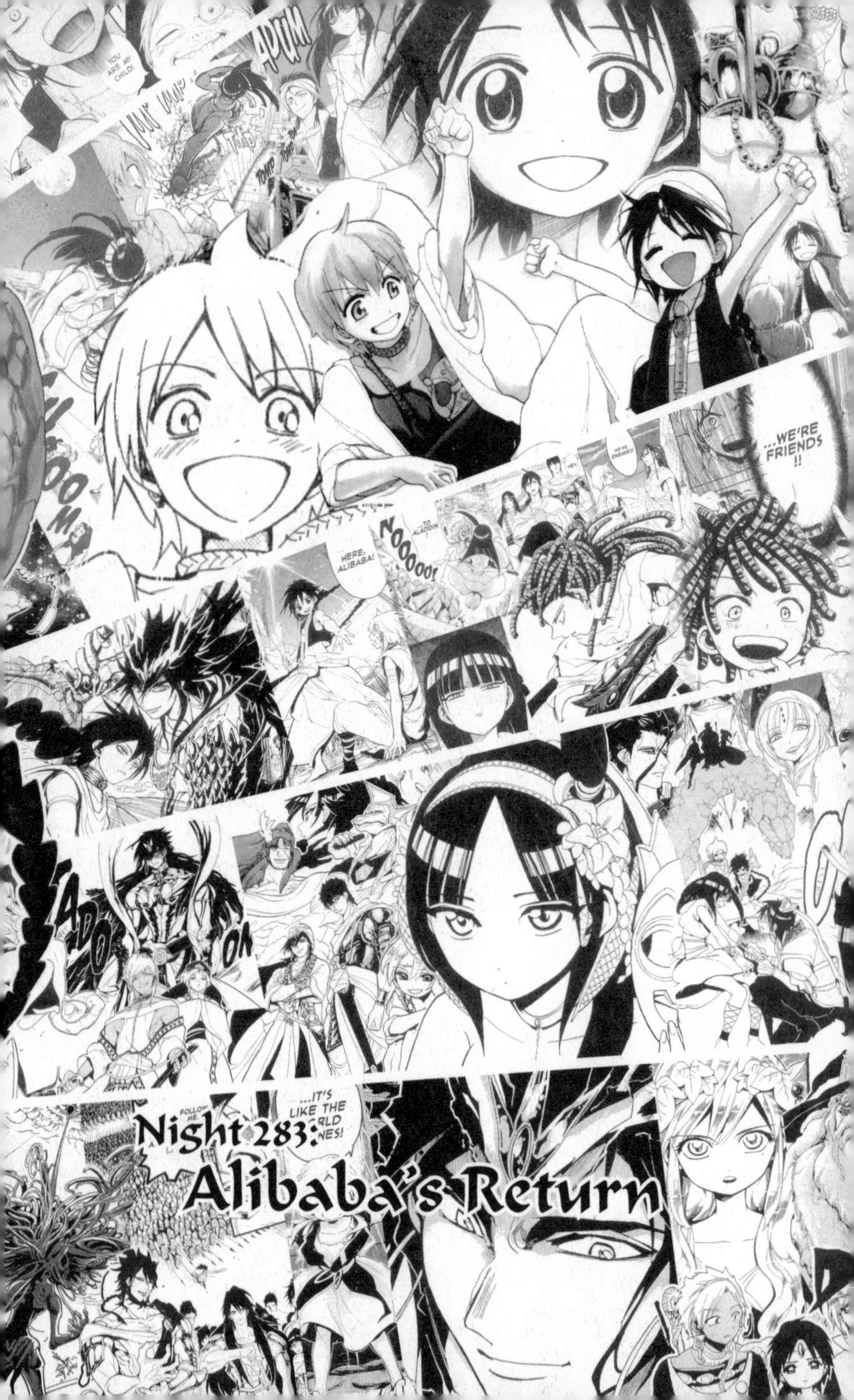
YOU ARE MY CHILD!
...WE'RE FRIENDS !!
WE'RE ENEMIES!
HEY.
TO ALADDIN!
NOOOOO!
HERE, ALIBABA!
FOLLOW ME.

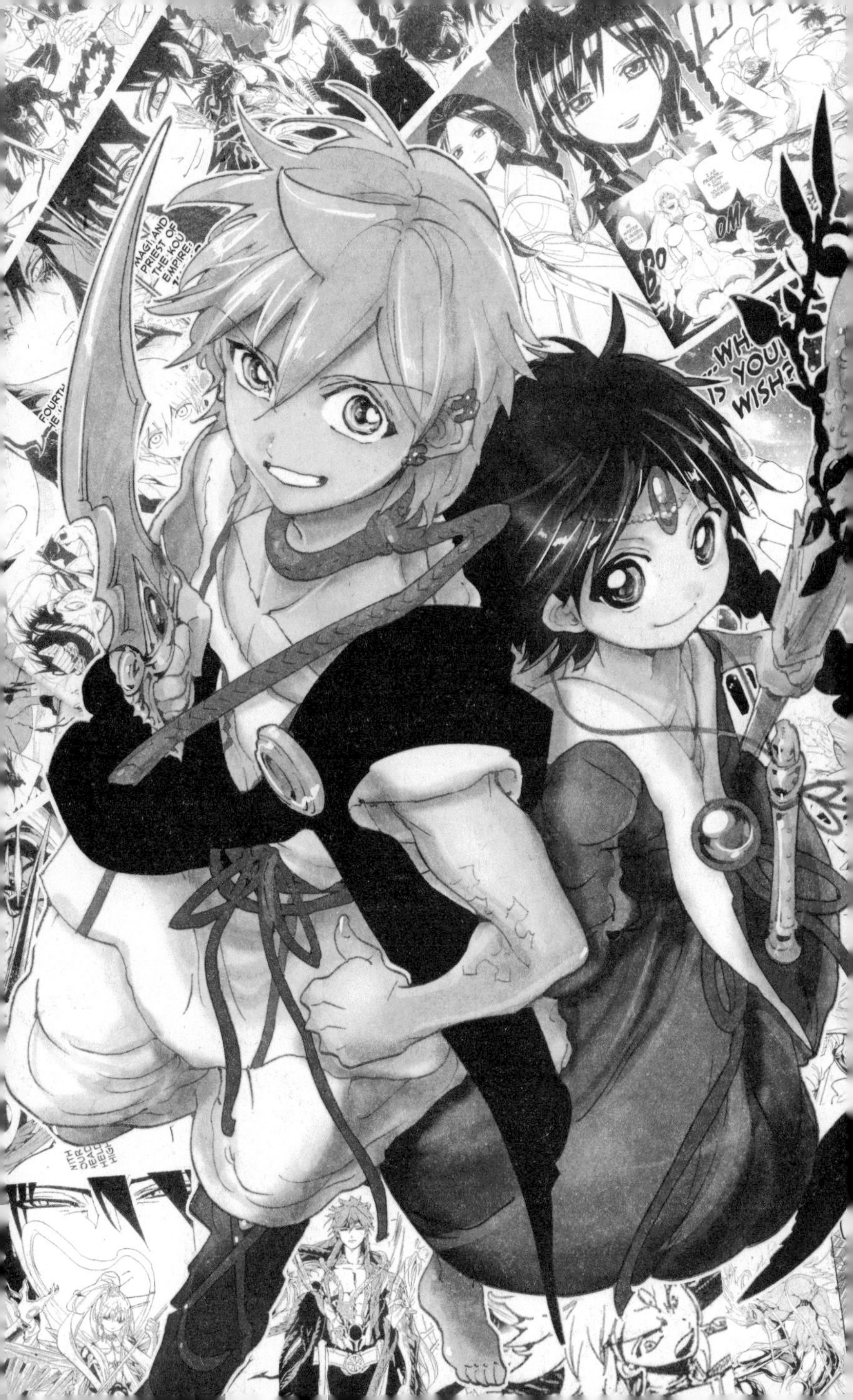
MAGI AND PRIEST OF THE KOU EMPIRE!
...WHA IS YOU WISH?
BO
OM
FOURTH

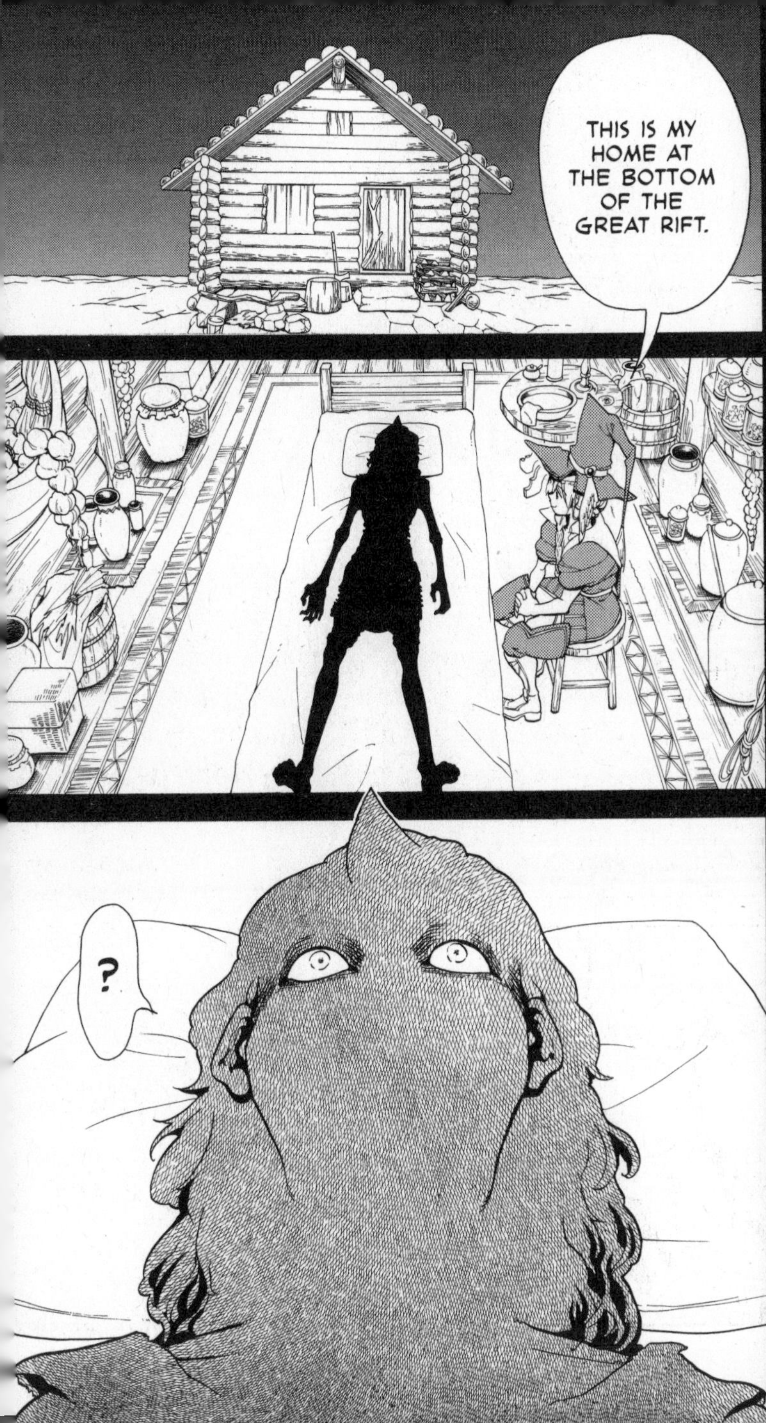
THIS IS MY HOME AT THE BOTTOM OF THE GREAT RIFT.
?

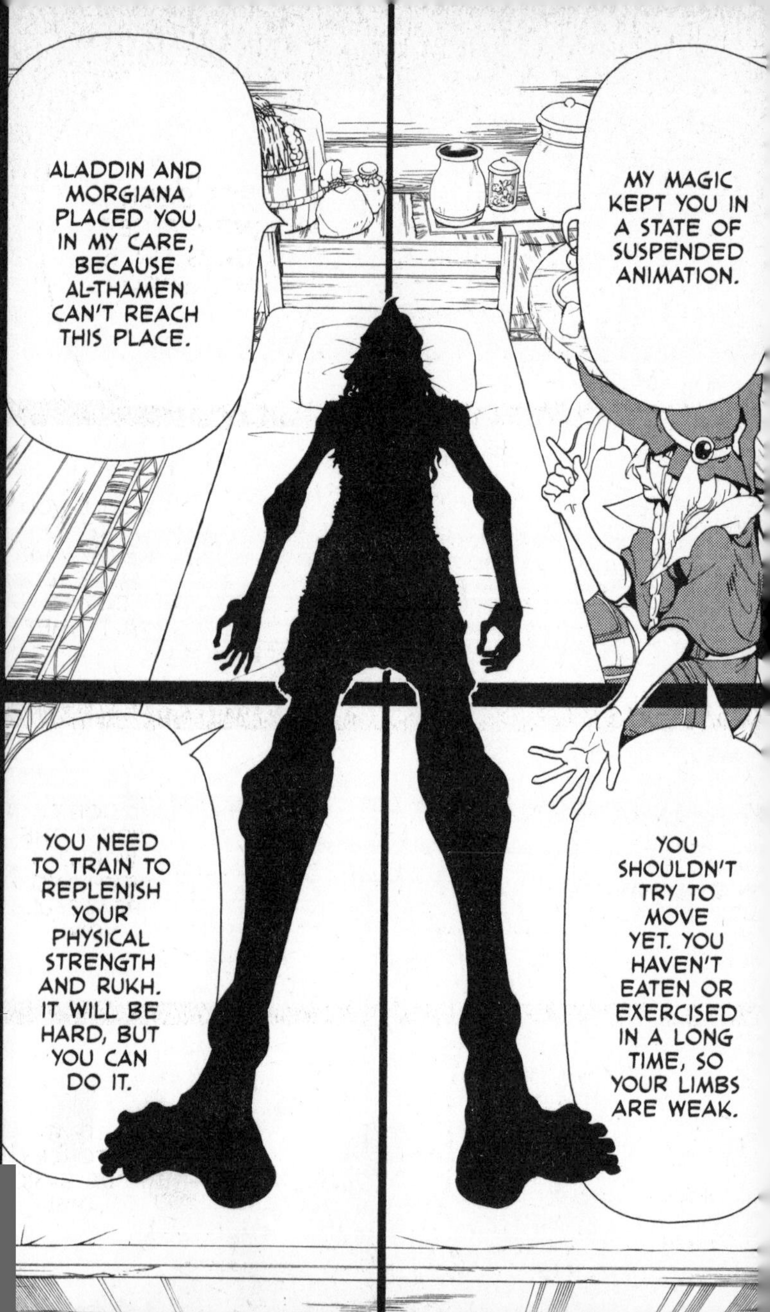
MY MAGIC KEPT YOU IN A STATE OF SUSPENDED ANIMATION.
ALADDIN AND MORGIANA PLACED YOU IN MY CARE, BECAUSE AL-THAMEN CAN'T REACH THIS PLACE.
YOU SHOULDN'T TRY TO MOVE YET. YOU HAVEN'T EATEN OR EXERCISED IN A LONG TIME, SO YOUR LIMBS ARE WEAK.
YOU NEED TO TRAIN TO REPLENISH YOUR PHYSICAL STRENGTH AND RUKH. IT WILL BE HARD, BUT YOU CAN DO IT.

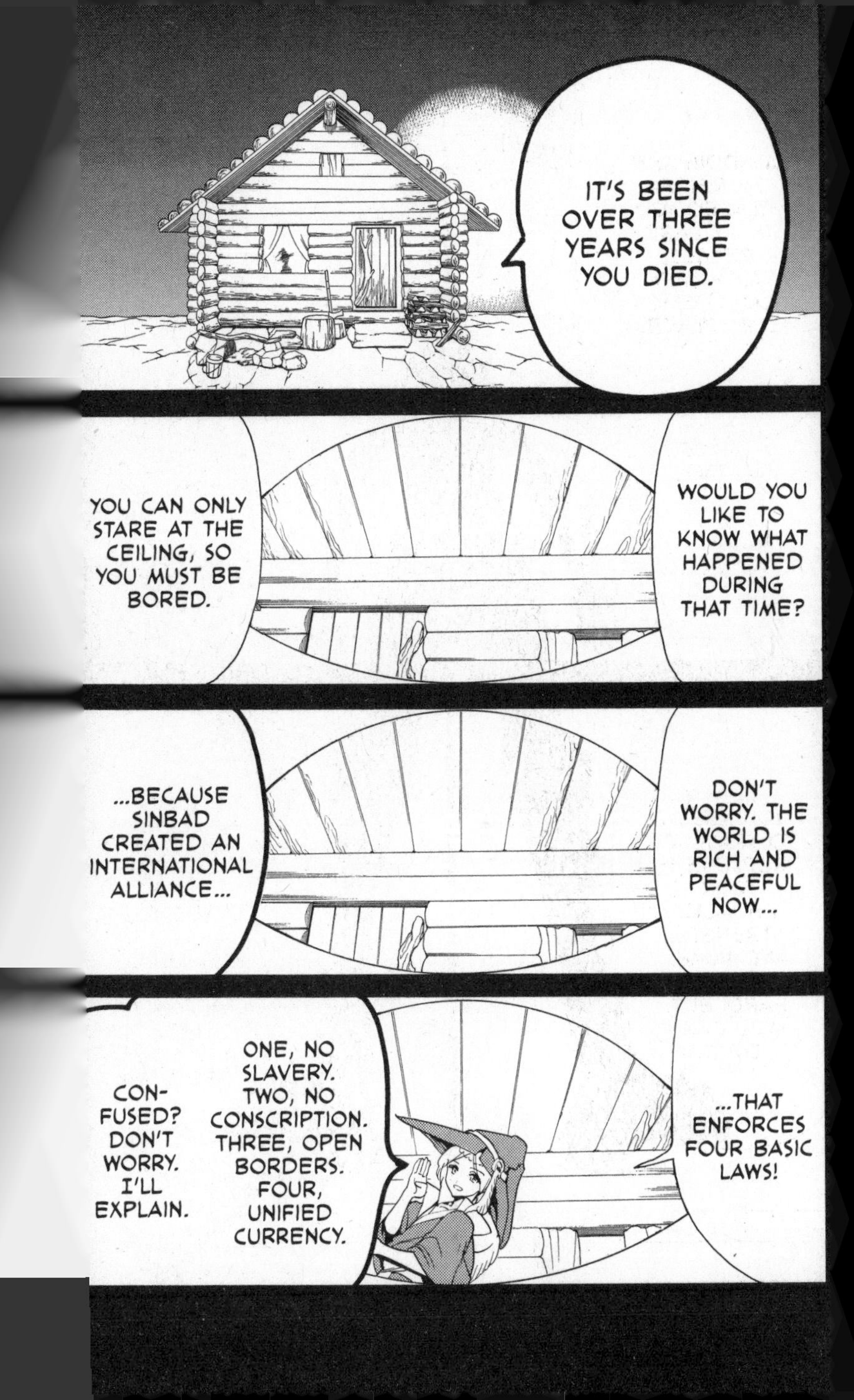
IT'S BEEN OVER THREE YEARS SINCE YOU DIED.
WOULD YOU LIKE TO KNOW WHAT HAPPENED DURING THAT TIME?
YOU CAN ONLY STARE AT THE CEILING, SO YOU MUST BE BORED.
DON'T WORRY. THE WORLD IS RICH AND PEACEFUL NOW...
...BECAUSE SINBAD CREATED AN INTERNATIONAL ALLIANCE...
...THAT ENFORCES FOUR BASIC LAWS!
ONE, NO SLAVERY. TWO, NO CONSCRIPTION. THREE, OPEN BORDERS. FOUR, UNIFIED CURRENCY.
CON-FUSED? DON'T WORRY. I'LL EXPLAIN.

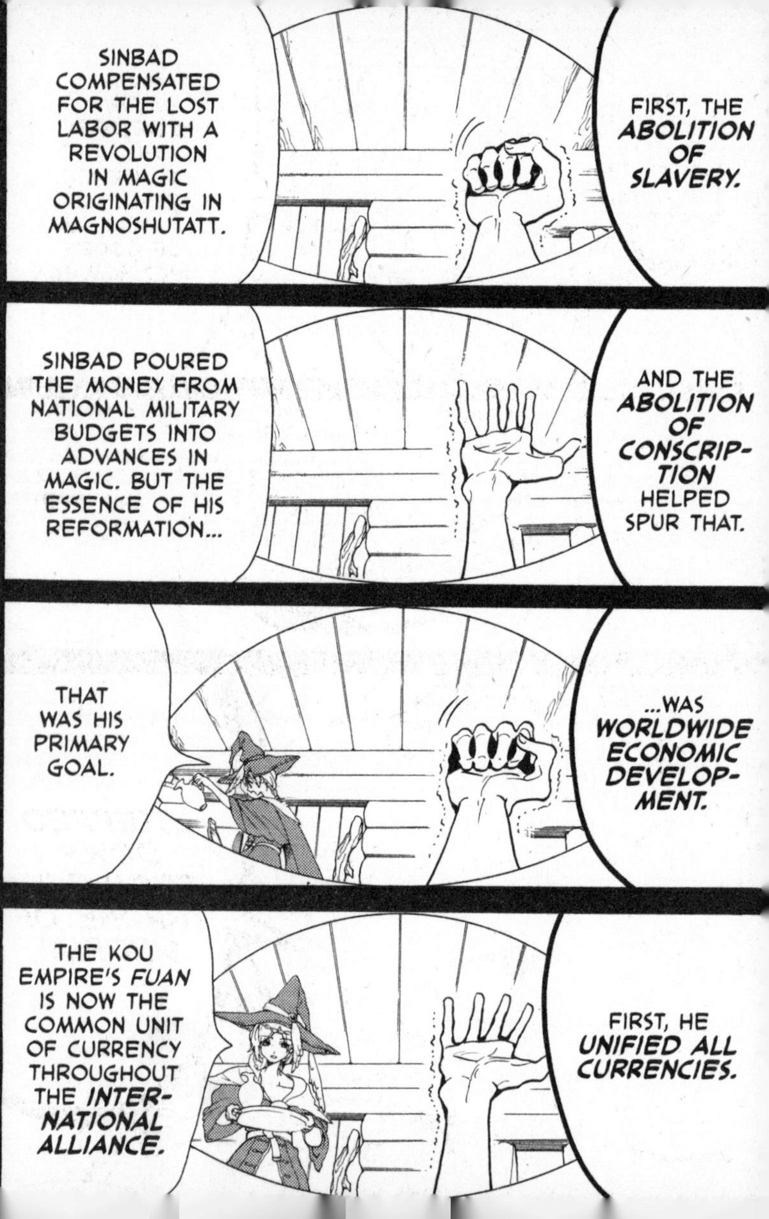

FIRST, THE *ABOLITION OF SLAVERY.*
SINBAD COMPENSATED FOR THE LOST LABOR WITH A REVOLUTION IN MAGIC ORIGINATING IN MAGNOSHUTATT.
AND THE *ABOLITION OF CONSCRIP-TION* HELPED SPUR THAT.
SINBAD POURED THE MONEY FROM NATIONAL MILITARY BUDGETS INTO ADVANCES IN MAGIC. BUT THE ESSENCE OF HIS REFORMATION...
...WAS *WORLDWIDE ECONOMIC DEVELOP-MENT.*
THAT WAS HIS PRIMARY GOAL.
FIRST, HE *UNIFIED ALL CURRENCIES.*
THE KOU EMPIRE'S *FUAN* IS NOW THE COMMON UNIT OF CURRENCY THROUGHOUT THE *INTER-NATIONAL ALLIANCE.*

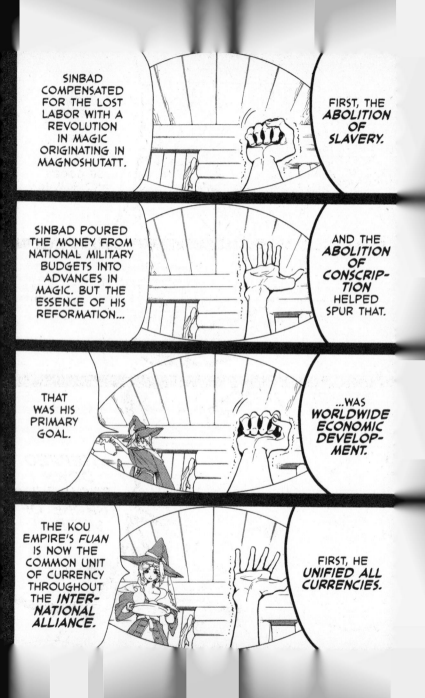

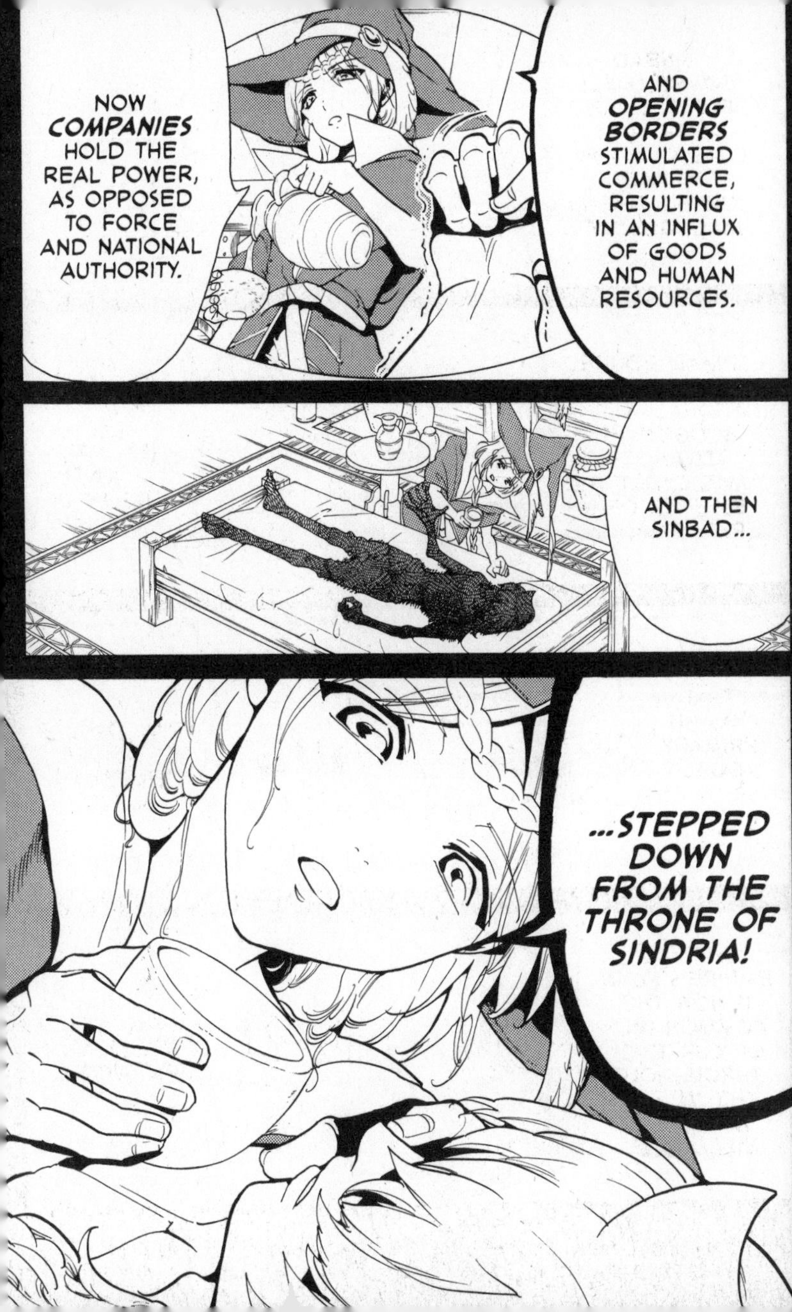
AND OPENING BORDERS STIMULATED COMMERCE, RESULTING IN AN INFLUX OF GOODS AND HUMAN RESOURCES.
NOW COMPANIES HOLD THE REAL POWER, AS OPPOSED TO FORCE AND NATIONAL AUTHORITY.
AND THEN SINBAD...
...STEPPED DOWN FROM THE THRONE OF SINDRIA!

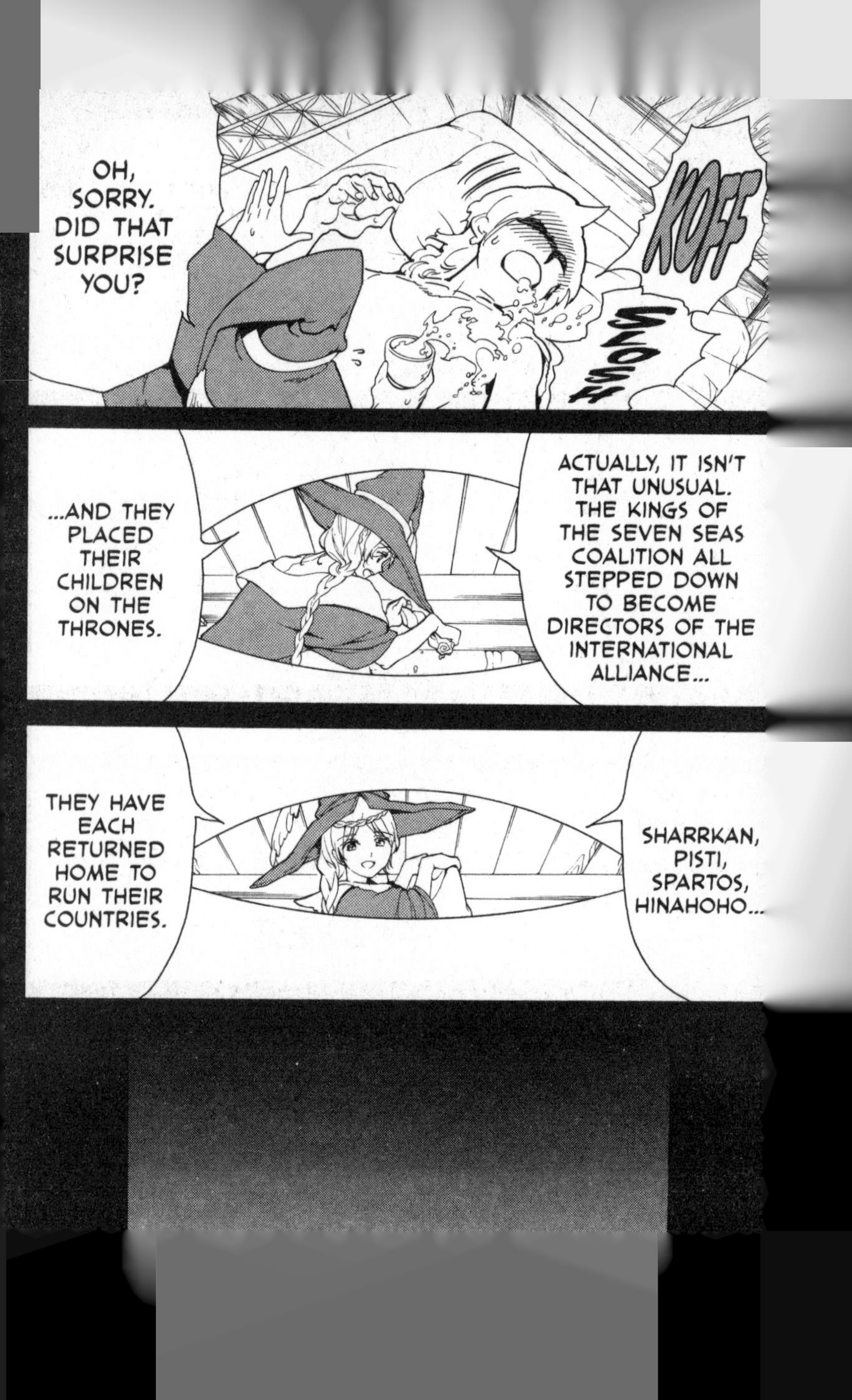
KOFF
SLOSH
OH, SORRY. DID THAT SURPRISE YOU?
ACTUALLY, IT ISN'T THAT UNUSUAL. THE KINGS OF THE SEVEN SEAS COALITION ALL STEPPED DOWN TO BECOME DIRECTORS OF THE INTERNATIONAL ALLIANCE...
...AND THEY PLACED THEIR CHILDREN ON THE THRONES.
SHARRKAN, PISTI, SPARTOS, HINAHOHO...
THEY HAVE EACH RETURNED HOME TO RUN THEIR COUNTRIES.

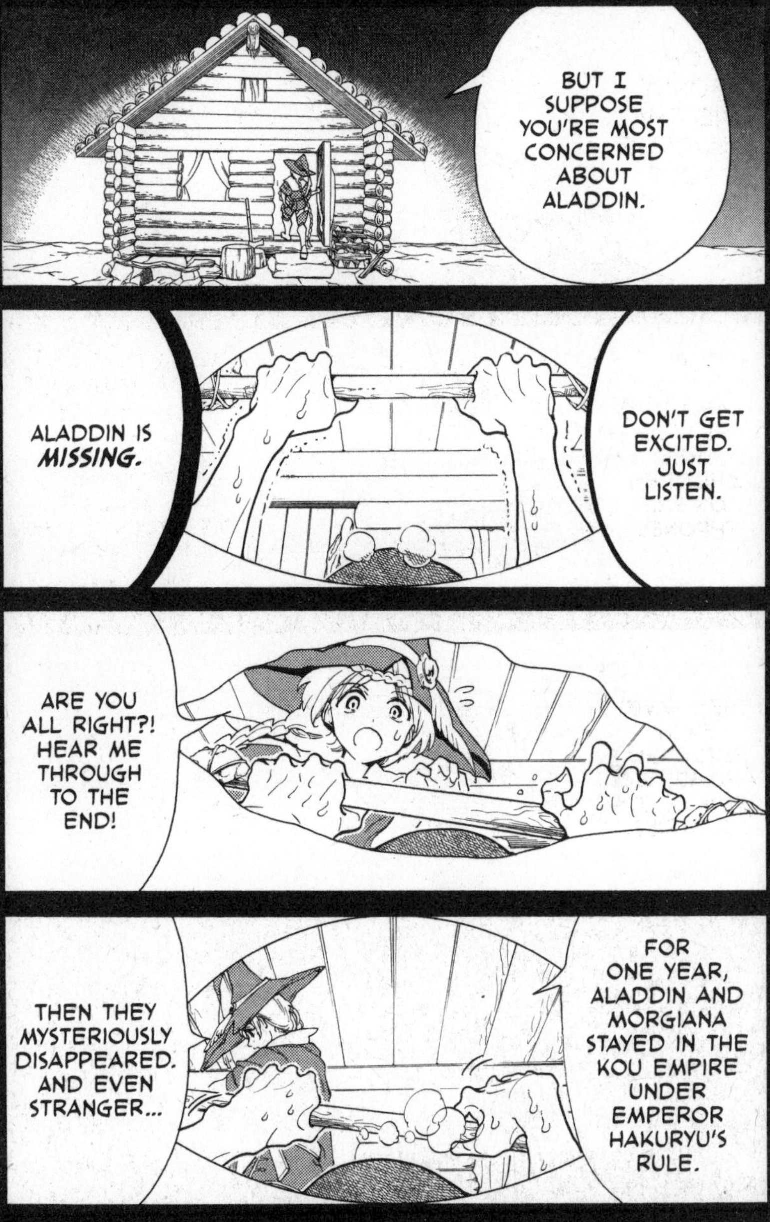
BUT I SUPPOSE YOU'RE MOST CONCERNED ABOUT ALADDIN.
DON'T GET EXCITED. JUST LISTEN.
ALADDIN IS *MISSING.*
ARE YOU ALL RIGHT?! HEAR ME THROUGH TO THE END!
FOR ONE YEAR, ALADDIN AND MORGIANA STAYED IN THE KOU EMPIRE UNDER EMPEROR HAKURYU'S RULE.
THEN THEY MYSTERIOUSLY DISAPPEARED. AND EVEN STRANGER...

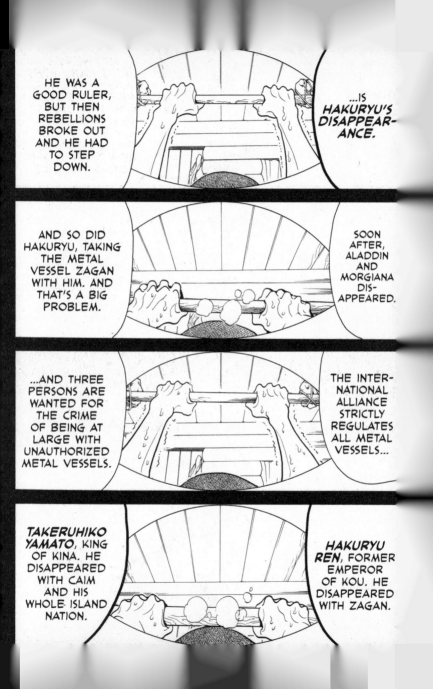

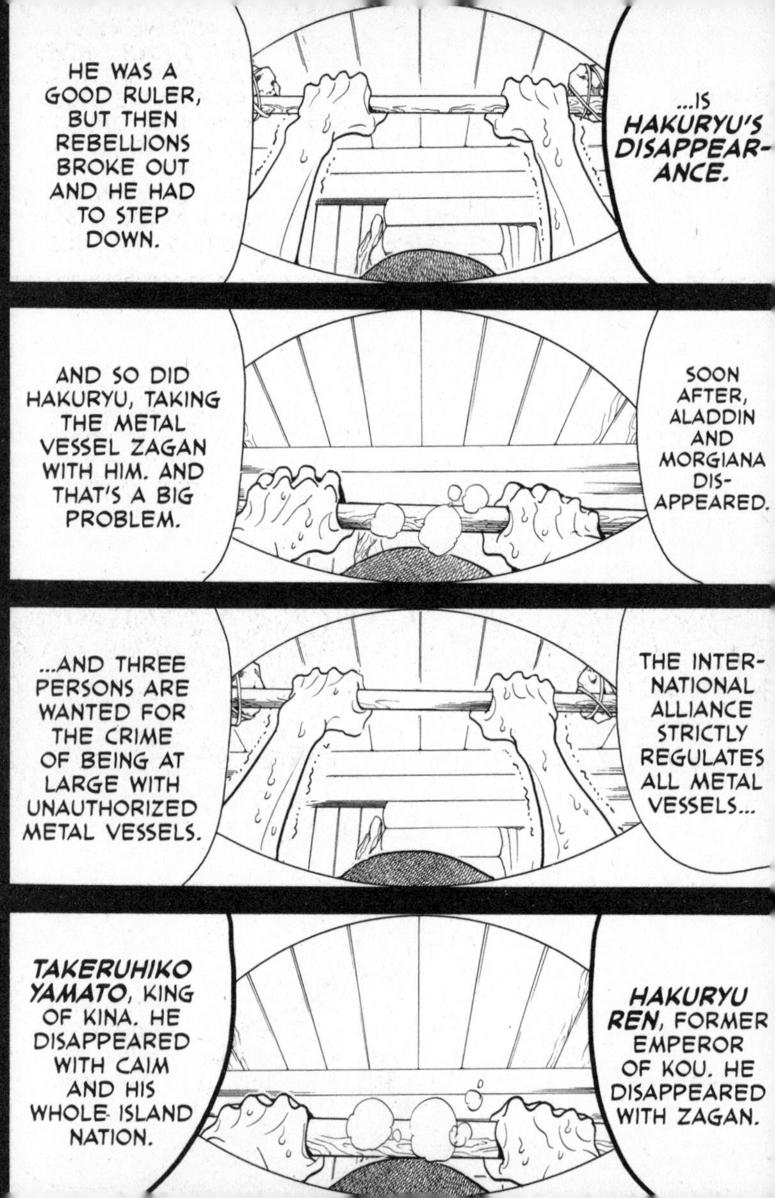
...IS ***HAKURYU'S DISAPPEARANCE.***
HE WAS A GOOD RULER, BUT THEN REBELLIONS BROKE OUT AND HE HAD TO STEP DOWN.
SOON AFTER, ALADDIN AND MORGIANA DISAPPEARED.
AND SO DID HAKURYU, TAKING THE METAL VESSEL ZAGAN WITH HIM. AND THAT'S A BIG PROBLEM.
THE INTERNATIONAL ALLIANCE STRICTLY REGULATES ALL METAL VESSELS...
...AND THREE PERSONS ARE WANTED FOR THE CRIME OF BEING AT LARGE WITH UNAUTHORIZED METAL VESSELS.
HAKURYU REN, FORMER EMPEROR OF KOU. HE DISAPPEARED WITH ZAGAN.
TAKERUHIKO YAMATO, KING OF KINA. HE DISAPPEARED WITH CAIM AND HIS WHOLE ISLAND NATION.

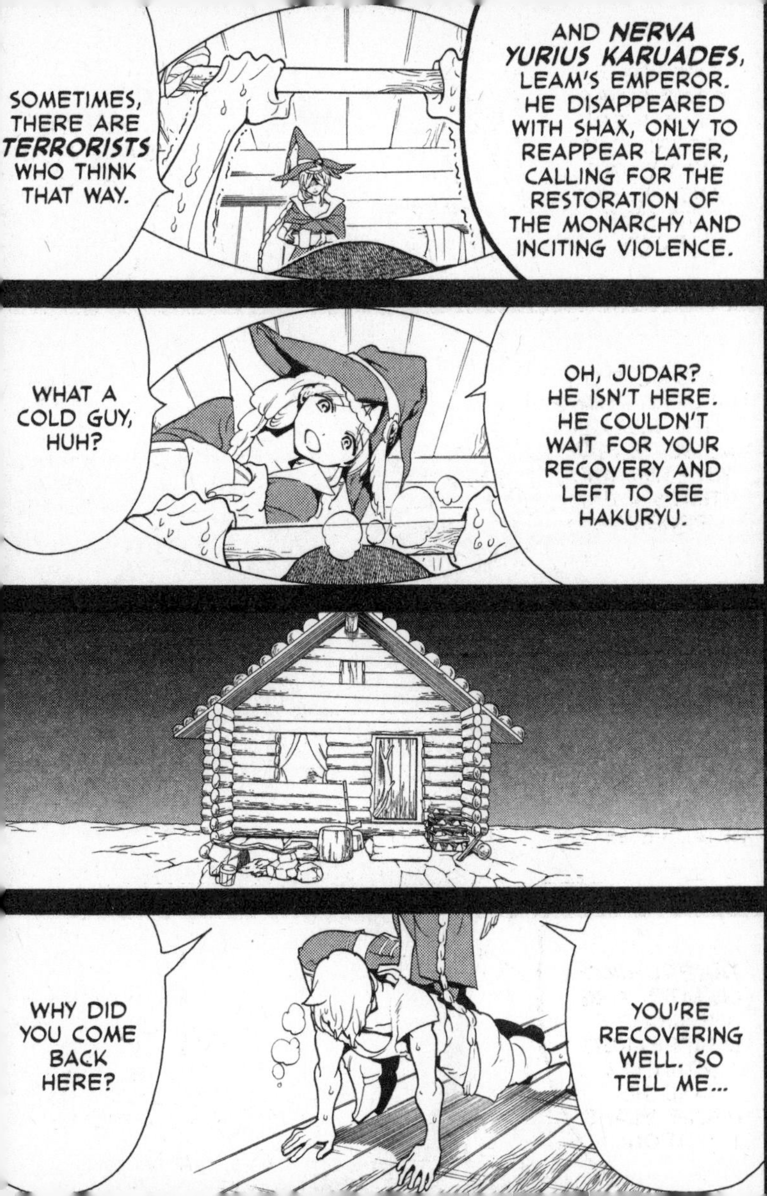
AND NERVA YURIUS KARUADES, LEAM'S EMPEROR. HE DISAPPEARED WITH SHAX, ONLY TO REAPPEAR LATER, CALLING FOR THE RESTORATION OF THE MONARCHY AND INCITING VIOLENCE.
SOMETIMES, THERE ARE TERRORISTS WHO THINK THAT WAY.
OH, JUDAR? HE ISN'T HERE. HE COULDN'T WAIT FOR YOUR RECOVERY AND LEFT TO SEE HAKURYU.
WHAT A COLD GUY, HUH?
YOU'RE RECOVERING WELL. SO TELL ME...
WHY DID YOU COME BACK HERE?

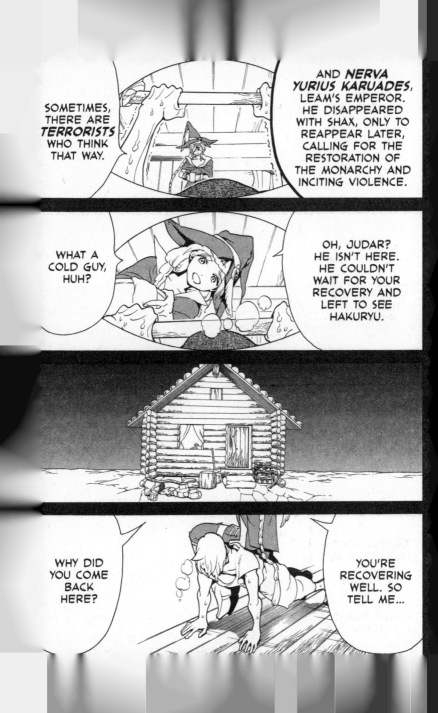

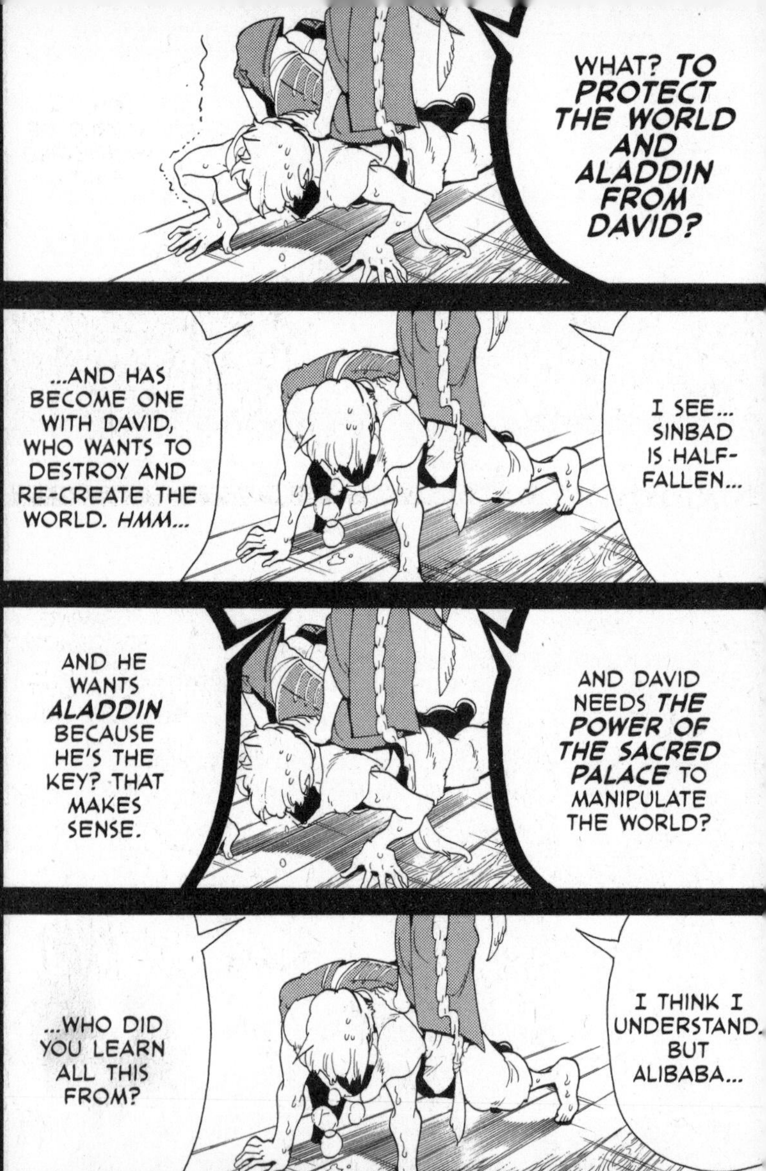
WHAT? TO PROTECT THE WORLD AND ALADDIN FROM DAVID?
I SEE... SINBAD IS HALF-FALLEN...
...AND HAS BECOME ONE WITH DAVID, WHO WANTS TO DESTROY AND RE-CREATE THE WORLD. HMM...
AND DAVID NEEDS THE POWER OF THE SACRED PALACE TO MANIPULATE THE WORLD?
AND HE WANTS ALADDIN BECAUSE HE'S THE KEY? THAT MAKES SENSE.
I THINK I UNDERSTAND. BUT ALIBABA...
...WHO DID YOU LEARN ALL THIS FROM?

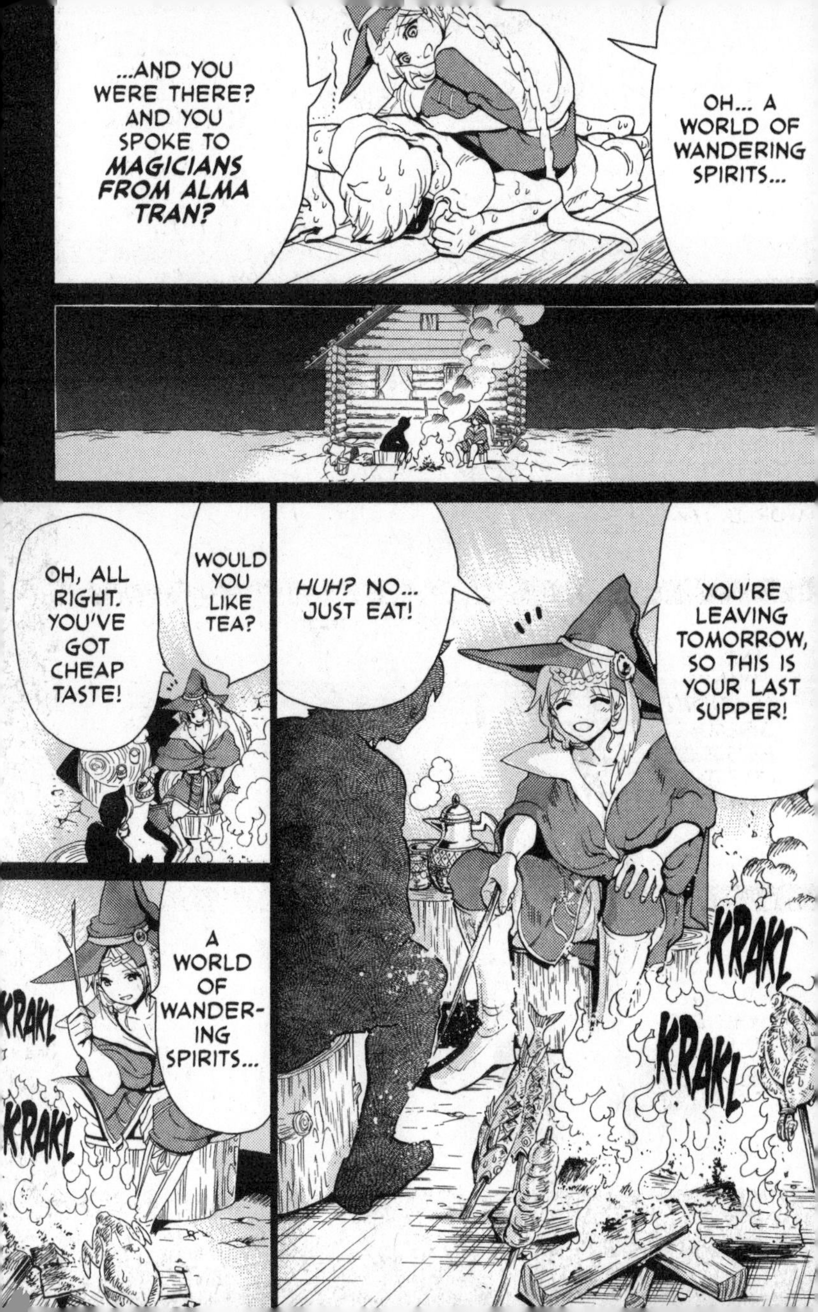

OH... A WORLD OF WANDERING SPIRITS...
...AND YOU WERE THERE? AND YOU SPOKE TO *MAGICIANS FROM ALMA TRAN?*
YOU'RE LEAVING TOMORROW, SO THIS IS YOUR LAST SUPPER!
HUH? NO... JUST EAT!
KRAKL
KRAKL
WOULD YOU LIKE TEA?
OH, ALL RIGHT. YOU'VE GOT CHEAP TASTE!
A WORLD OF WANDER-ING SPIRITS...
KRAKL
KRAKL

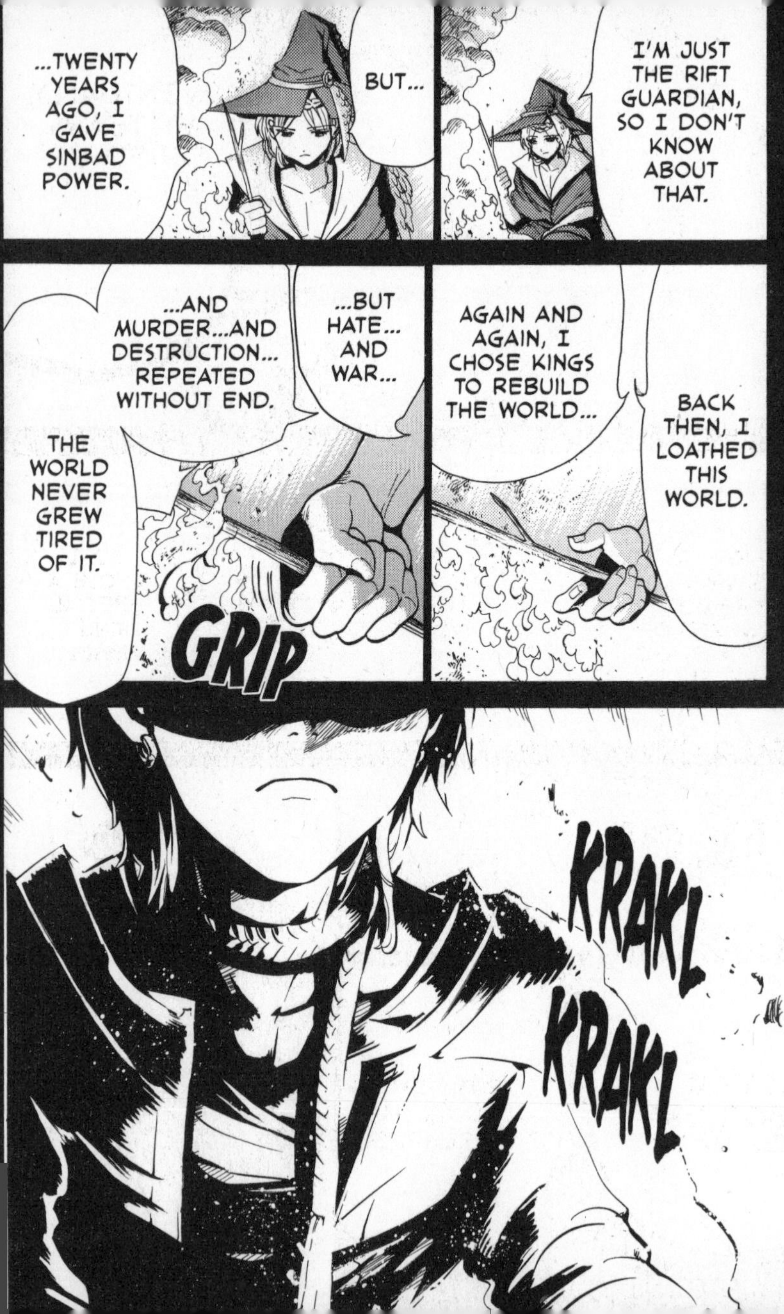
I'M JUST THE RIFT GUARDIAN, SO I DON'T KNOW ABOUT THAT.
BUT...
...TWENTY YEARS AGO, I GAVE SINBAD POWER.
BACK THEN, I LOATHED THIS WORLD.
AGAIN AND AGAIN, I CHOSE KINGS TO REBUILD THE WORLD...
...BUT HATE... AND WAR...
...AND MURDER...AND DESTRUCTION... REPEATED WITHOUT END.
THE WORLD NEVER GREW TIRED OF IT.
GRIP
KRAKL
KRAKL

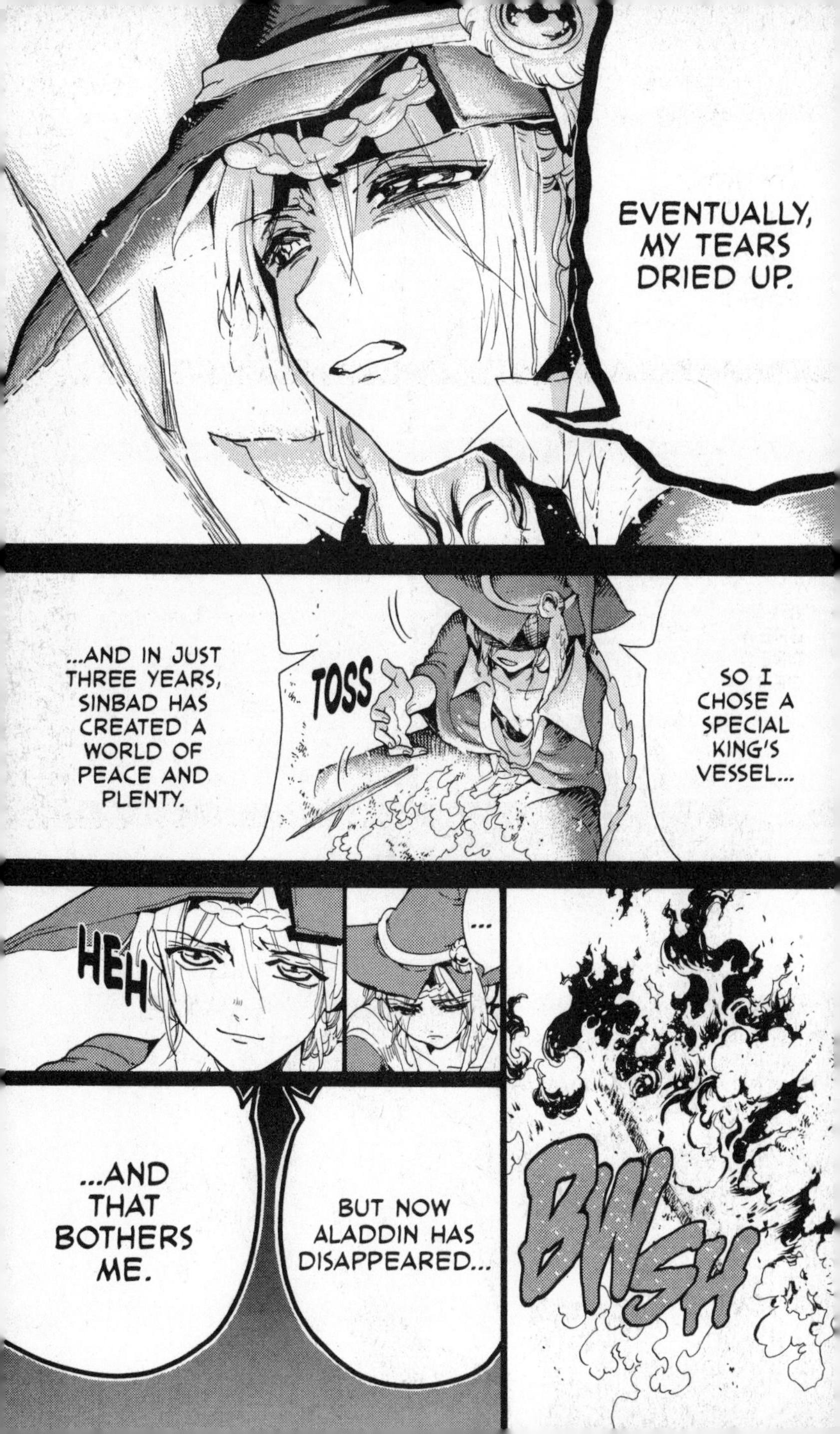
EVENTUALLY, MY TEARS DRIED UP.
SO I CHOSE A SPECIAL KING'S VESSEL...
TOSS
...AND IN JUST THREE YEARS, SINBAD HAS CREATED A WORLD OF PEACE AND PLENTY.
BWSH
...
HEH
BUT NOW ALADDIN HAS DISAPPEARED...
...AND THAT BOTHERS ME.

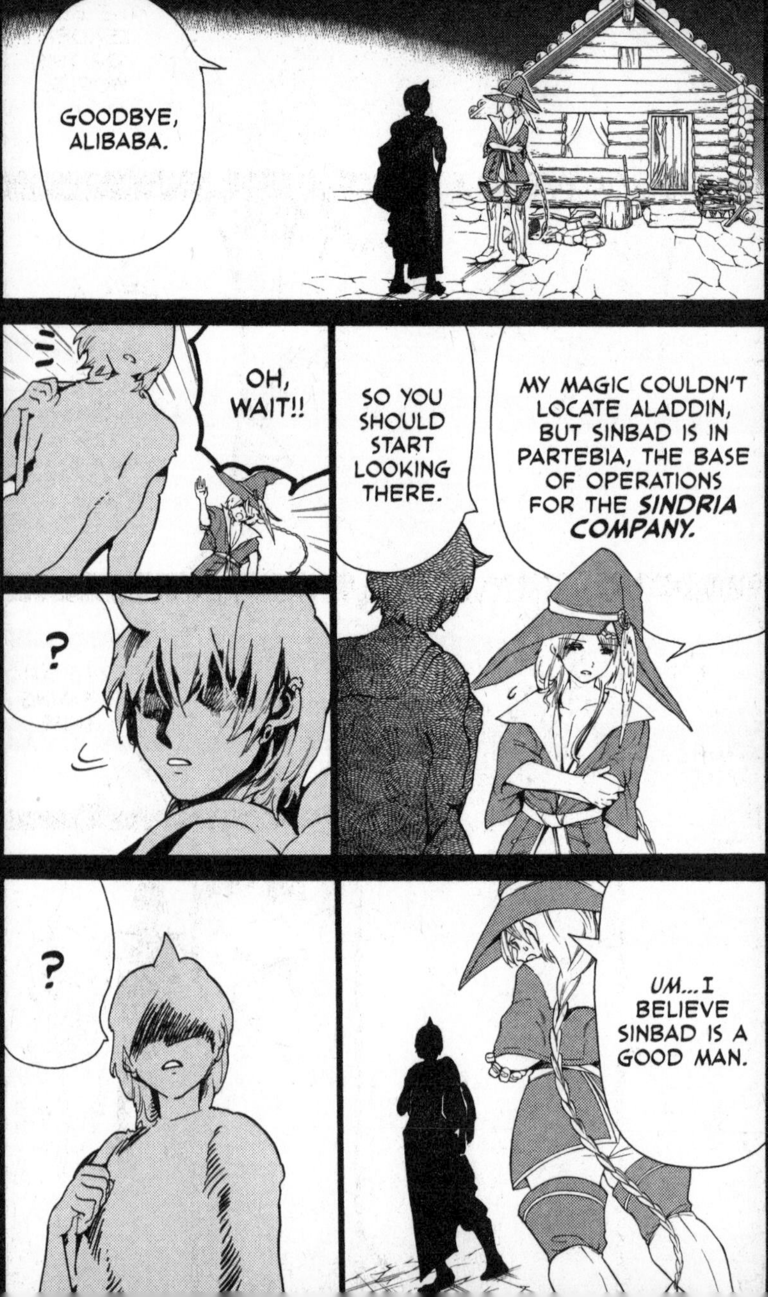
GOODBYE, ALIBABA.
MY MAGIC COULDN'T LOCATE ALADDIN, BUT SINBAD IS IN PARTEBIA, THE BASE OF OPERATIONS FOR THE *SINDRIA COMPANY.*
SO YOU SHOULD START LOOKING THERE.
OH, WAIT!!
?
UM...I BELIEVE SINBAD IS A GOOD MAN.
?

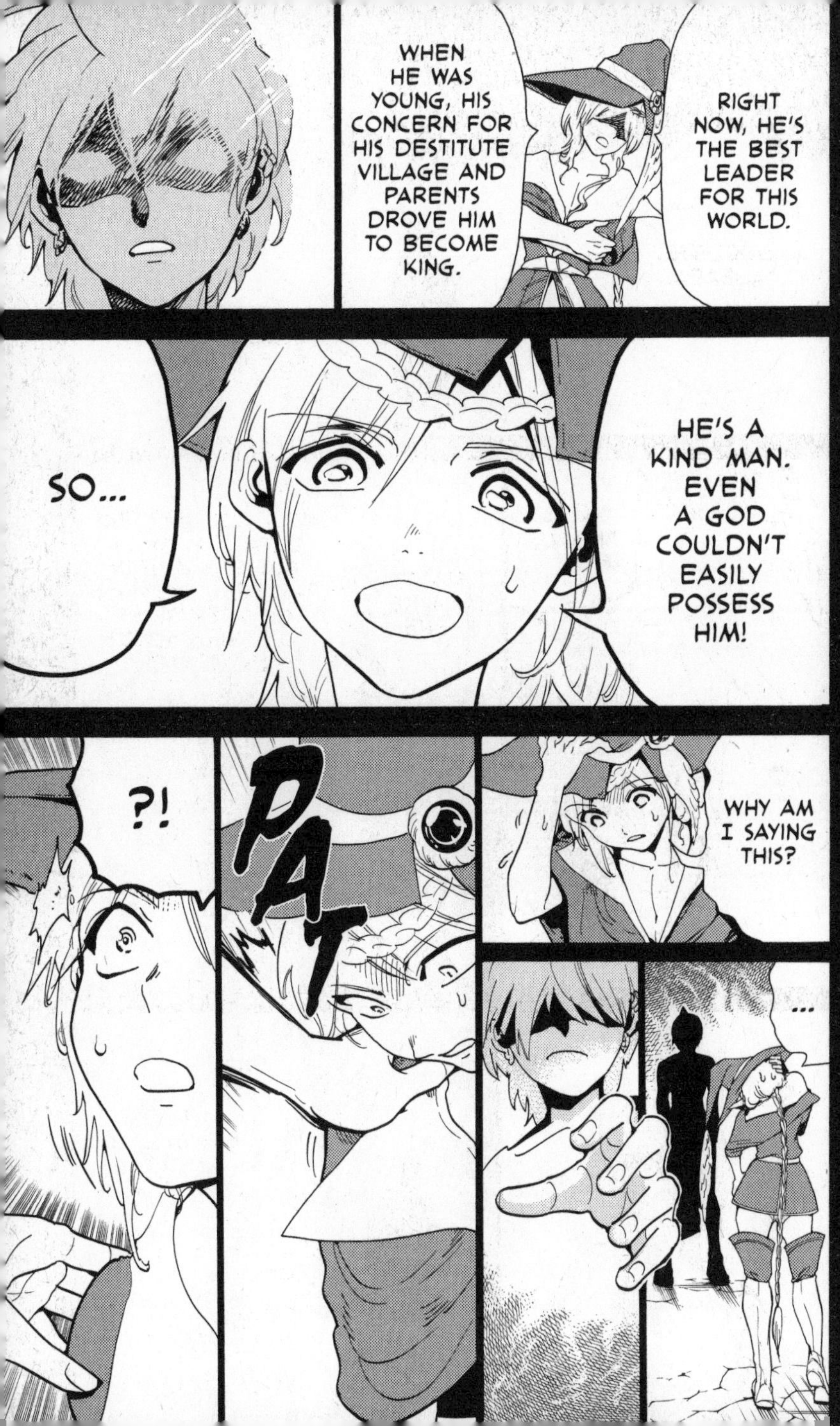
RIGHT NOW, HE'S THE BEST LEADER FOR THIS WORLD.
WHEN HE WAS YOUNG, HIS CONCERN FOR HIS DESTITUTE VILLAGE AND PARENTS DROVE HIM TO BECOME KING.
HE'S A KIND MAN. EVEN A GOD COULDN'T EASILY POSSESS HIM!
SO...
WHY AM I SAYING THIS?
...
PAT
?!

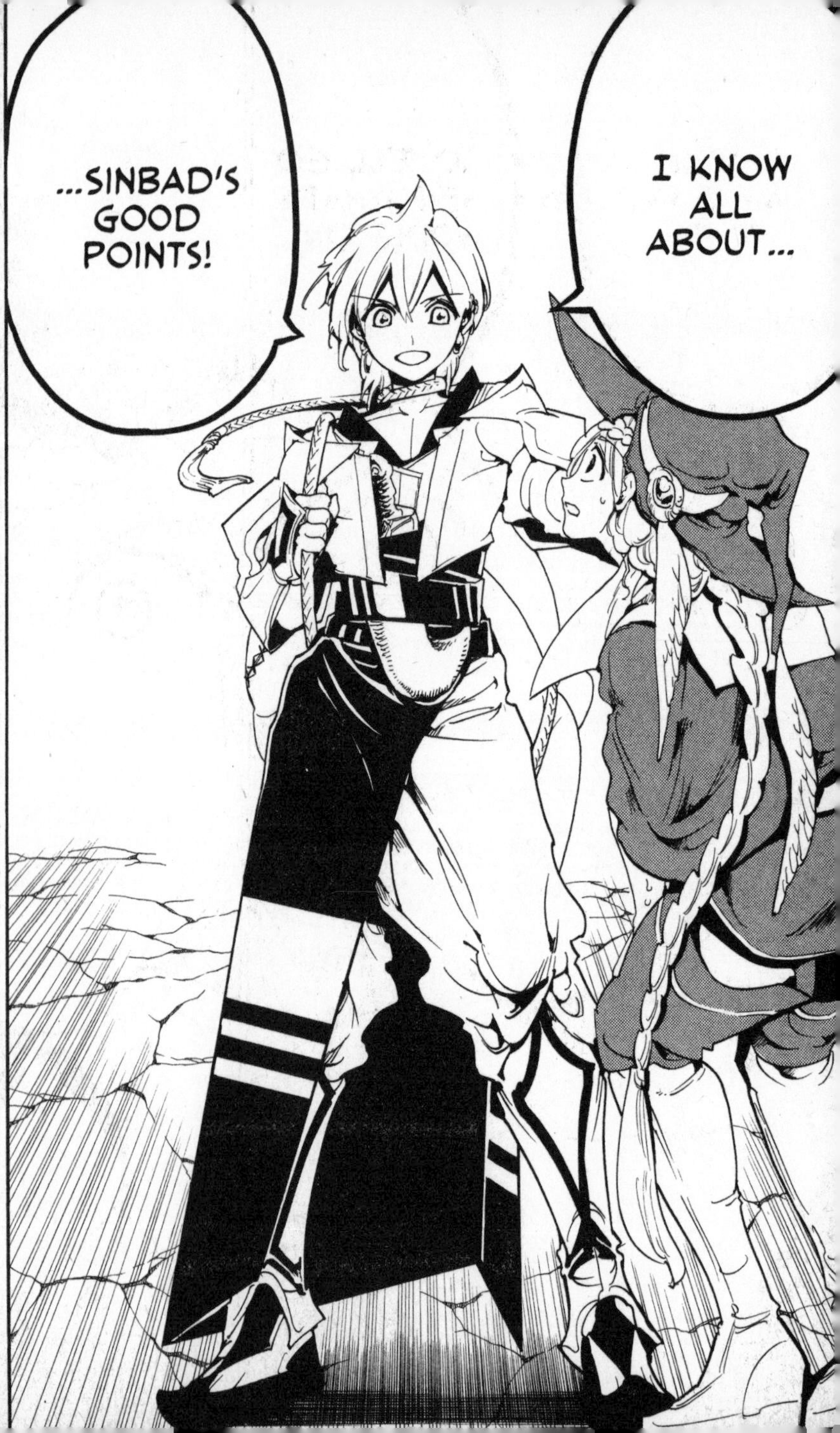
I KNOW ALL ABOUT...
...SINBAD'S GOOD POINTS!

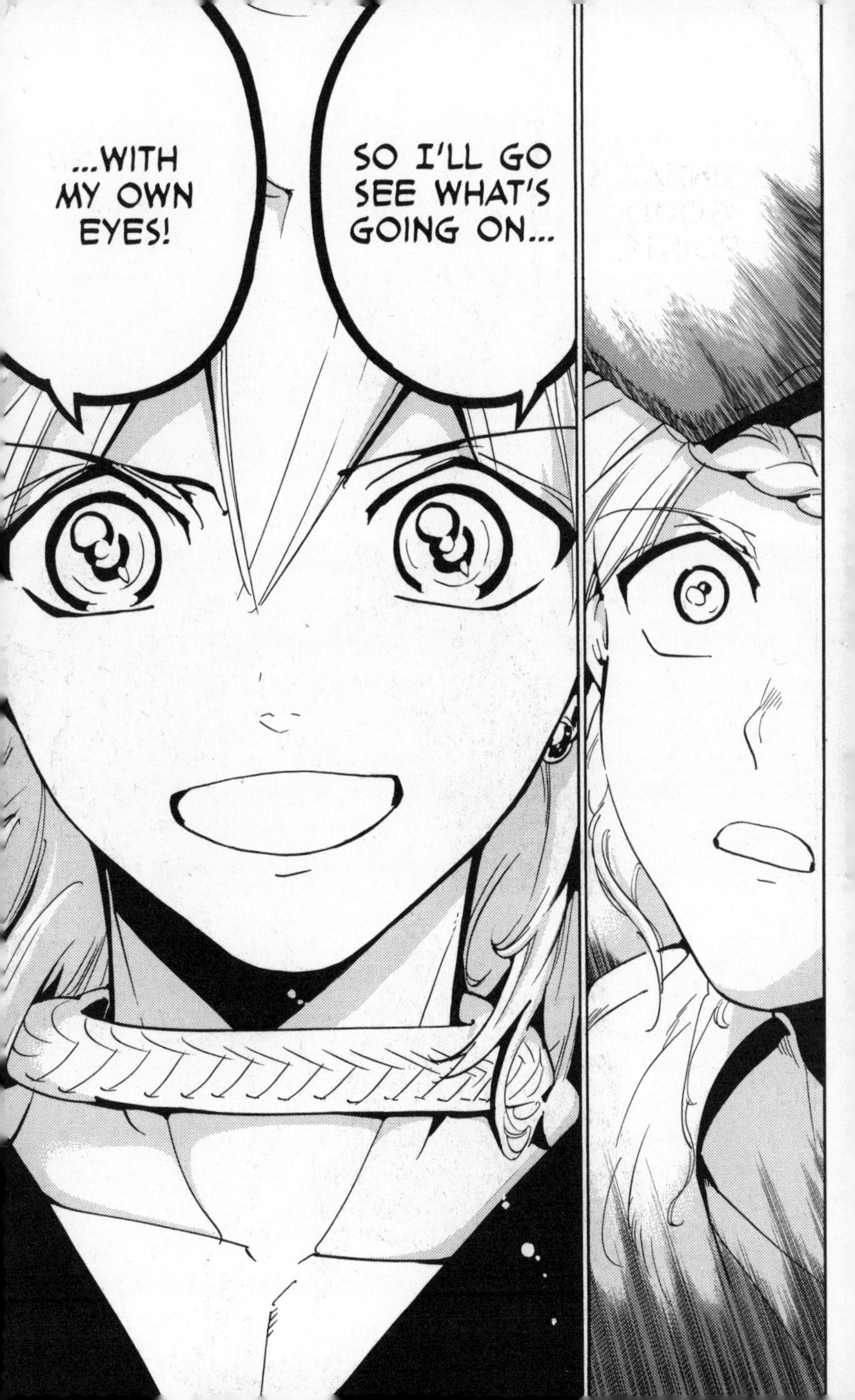
SO I'LL GO SEE WHAT'S GOING ON...
...WITH MY OWN EYES!

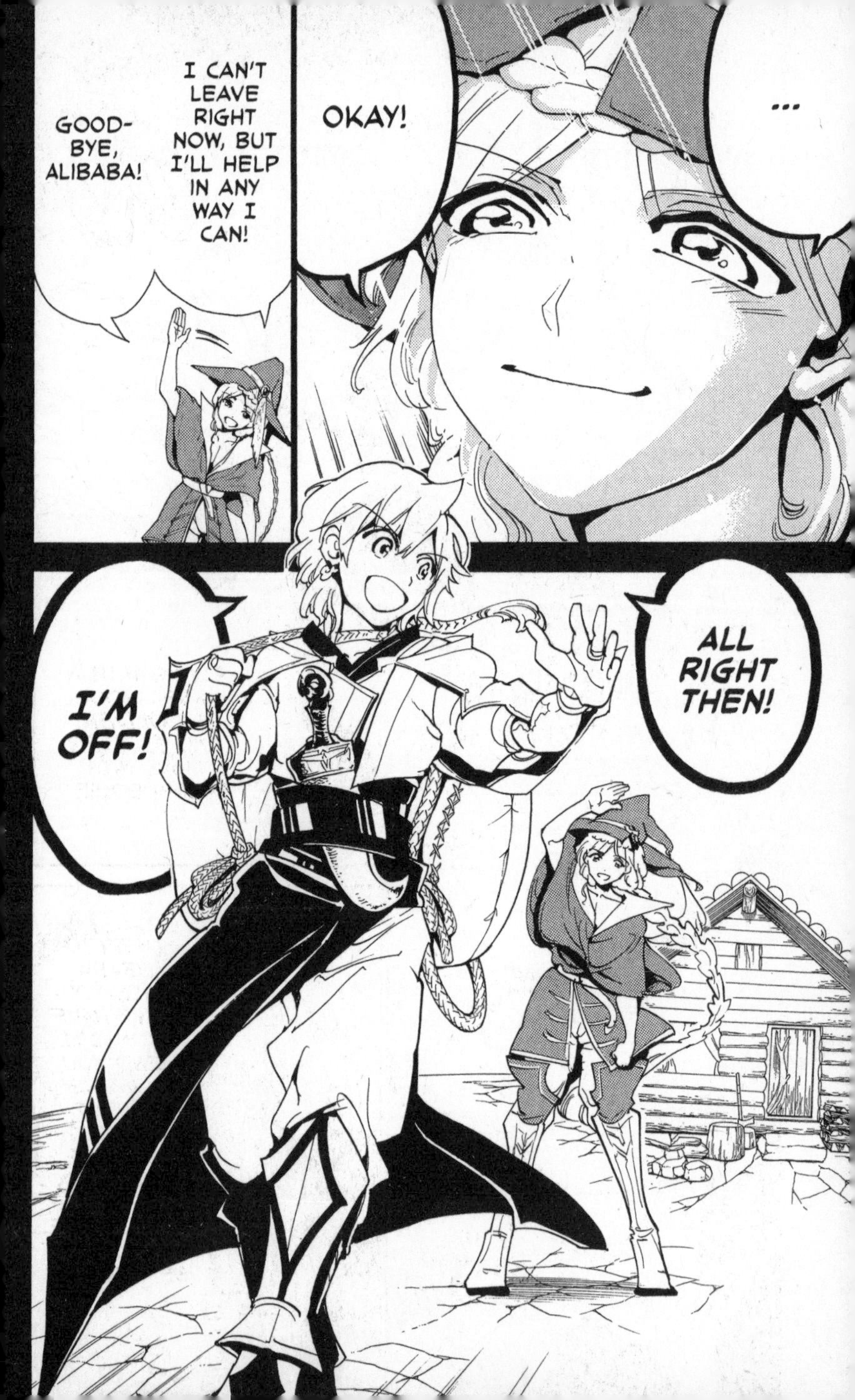
...
OKAY!
I CAN'T LEAVE RIGHT NOW, BUT I'LL HELP IN ANY WAY I CAN!
GOOD-BYE, ALIBABA!
ALL RIGHT THEN!
I'M OFF!

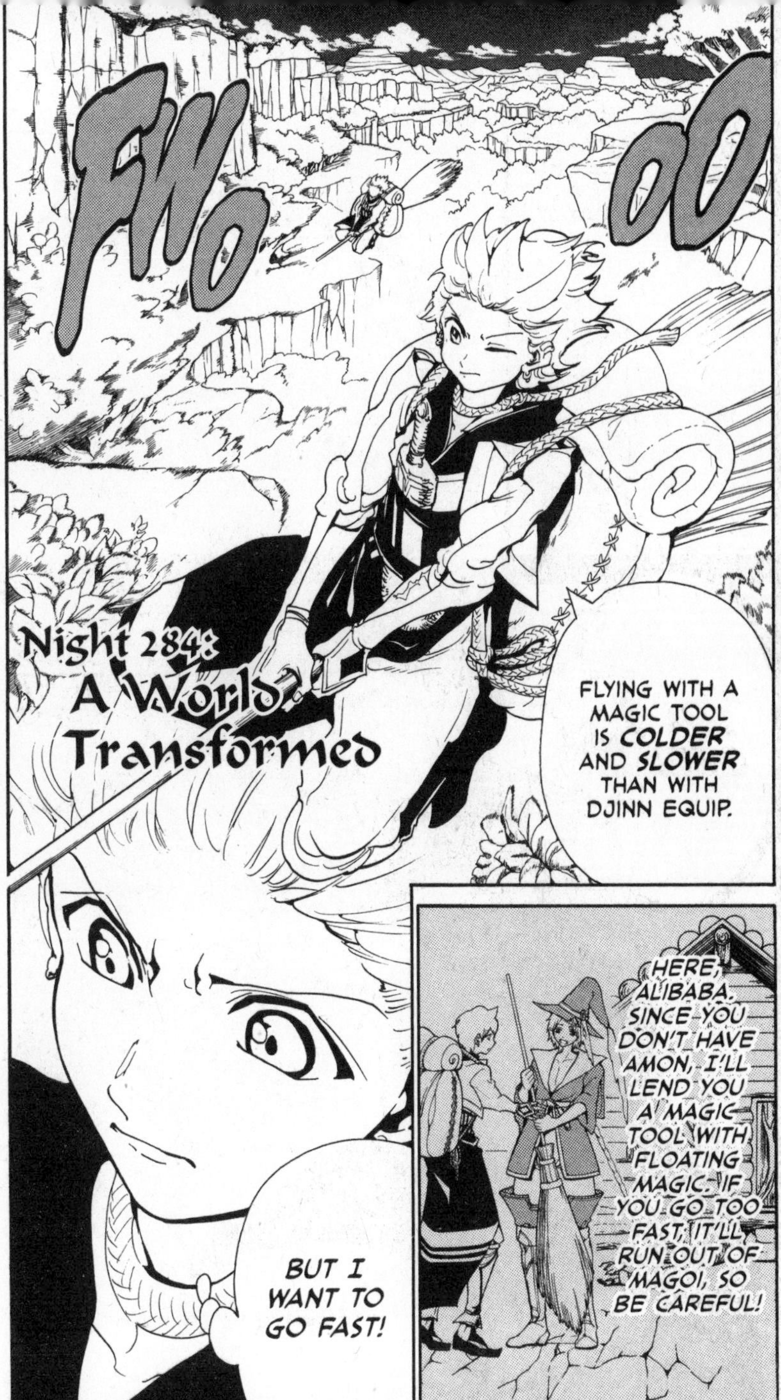
FWOOOO
Night 284: A World Transformed
FLYING WITH A MAGIC TOOL IS COLDER AND SLOWER THAN WITH DJINN EQUIP.
HERE, ALIBABA. SINCE YOU DON'T HAVE AMON, I'LL LEND YOU A MAGIC TOOL WITH FLOATING MAGIC. IF YOU GO TOO FAST, IT'LL RUN OUT OF MAGOI, SO BE CAREFUL!
BUT I WANT TO GO FAST!

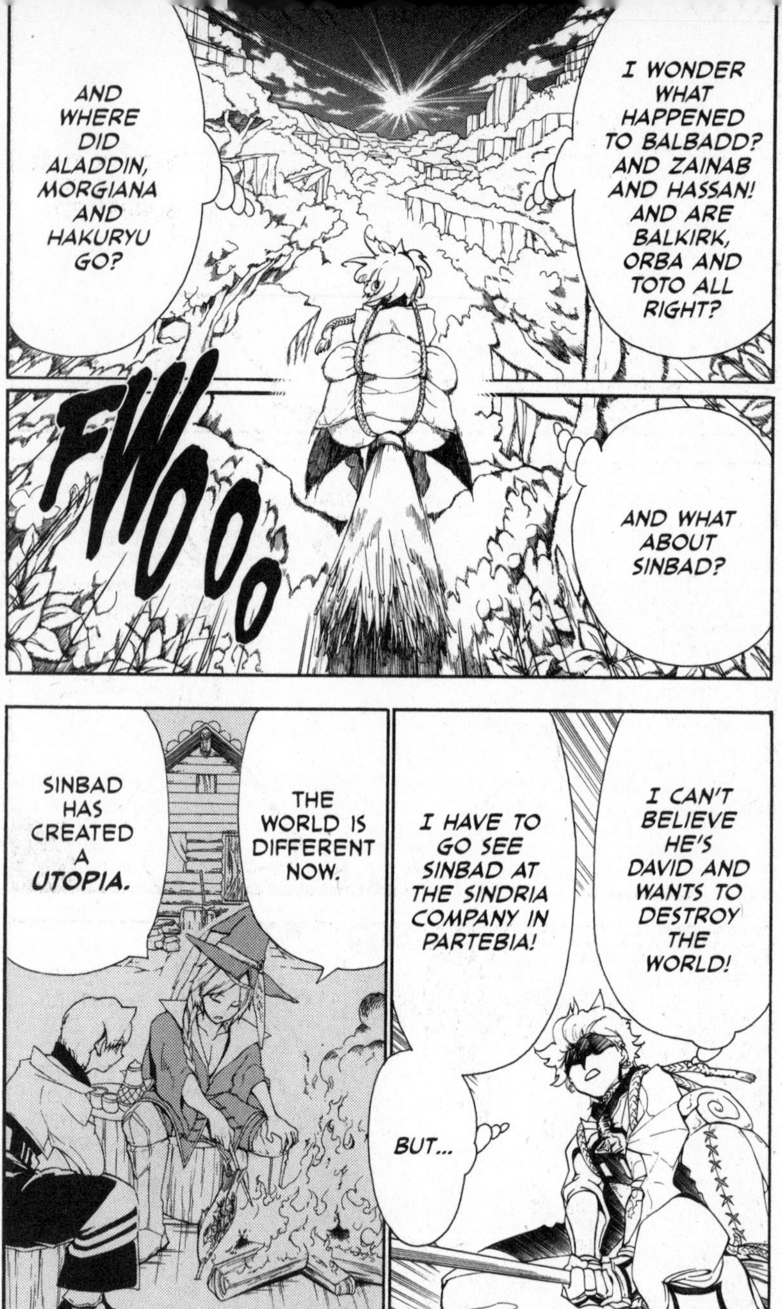
I WONDER WHAT HAPPENED TO BALBADD? AND ZAINAB AND HASSAN! AND ARE BALKIRK, ORBA AND TOTO ALL RIGHT?
AND WHERE DID ALADDIN, MORGIANA AND HAKURYU GO?
AND WHAT ABOUT SINBAD?
FWOOOO
I CAN'T BELIEVE HE'S DAVID AND WANTS TO DESTROY THE WORLD!
I HAVE TO GO SEE SINBAD AT THE SINDRIA COMPANY IN PARTEBIA!
BUT...
THE WORLD IS DIFFERENT NOW.
SINBAD HAS CREATED A UTOPIA.

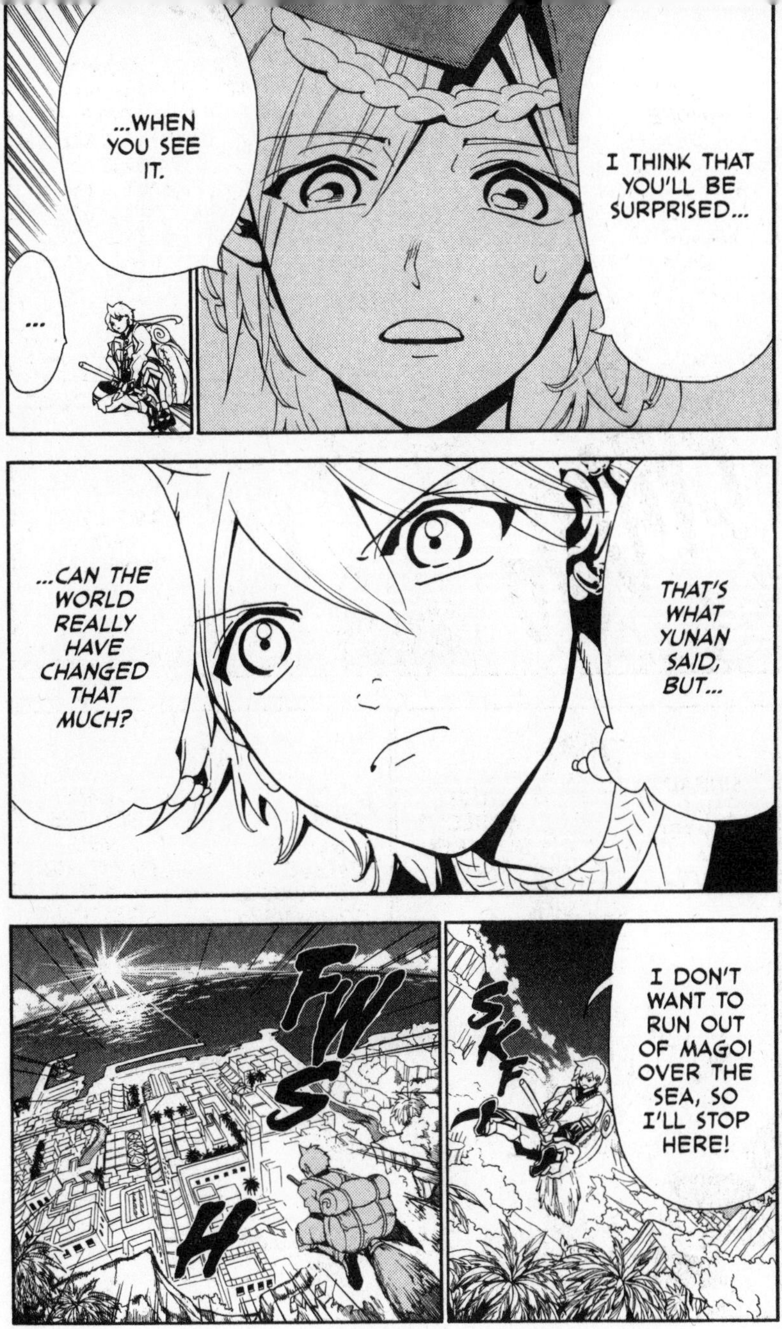
I THINK THAT YOU'LL BE SURPRISED...
...WHEN YOU SEE IT.
...
THAT'S WHAT YUNAN SAID, BUT...
...CAN THE WORLD REALLY HAVE CHANGED THAT MUCH?
I DON'T WANT TO RUN OUT OF MAGOI OVER THE SEA, SO I'LL STOP HERE!
SKF
FWSH

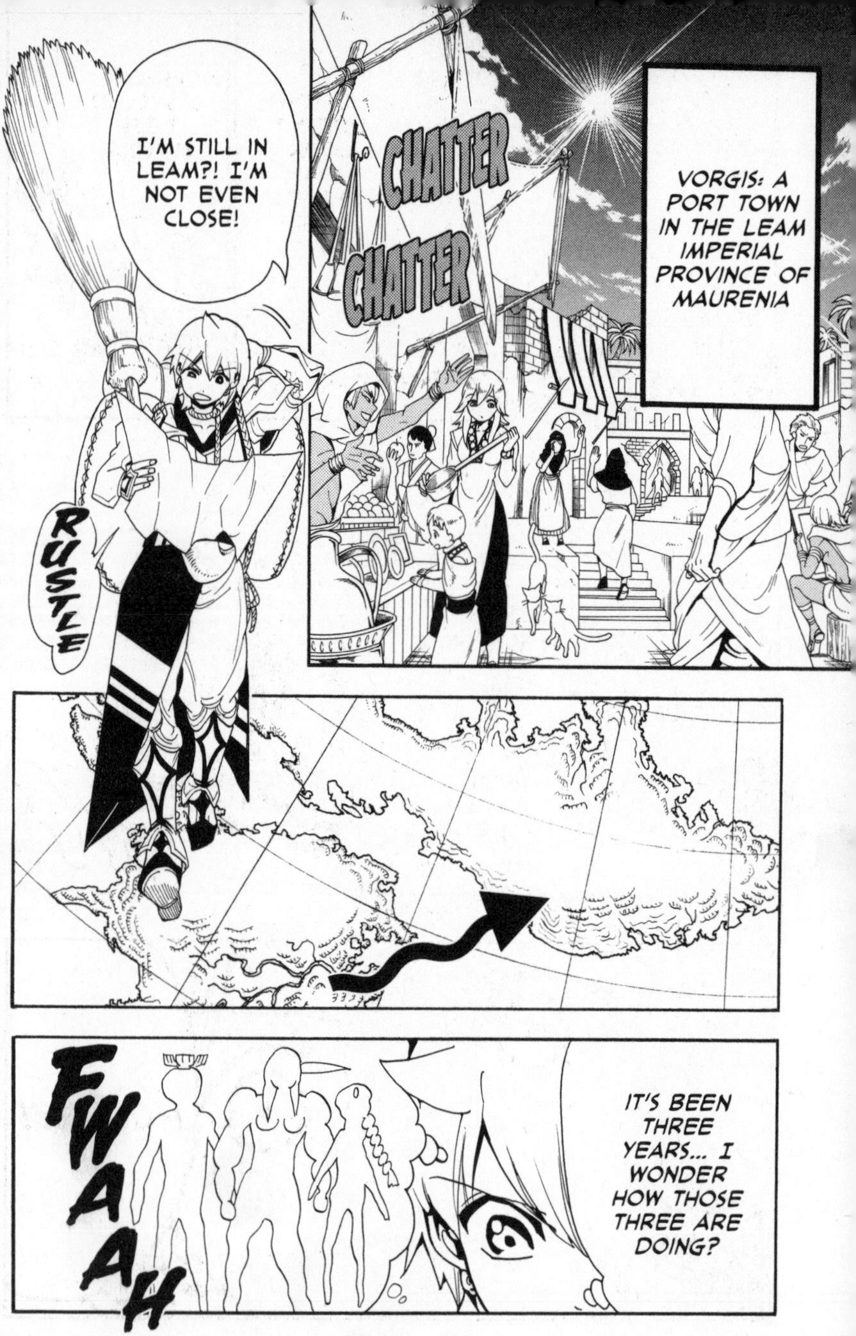
VORGIS: A PORT TOWN IN THE LEAM IMPERIAL PROVINCE OF MAURENIA
CHATTER
CHATTER
I'M STILL IN LEAM?! I'M NOT EVEN CLOSE!
RUSTLE
IT'S BEEN THREE YEARS... I WONDER HOW THOSE THREE ARE DOING?
FWAAH

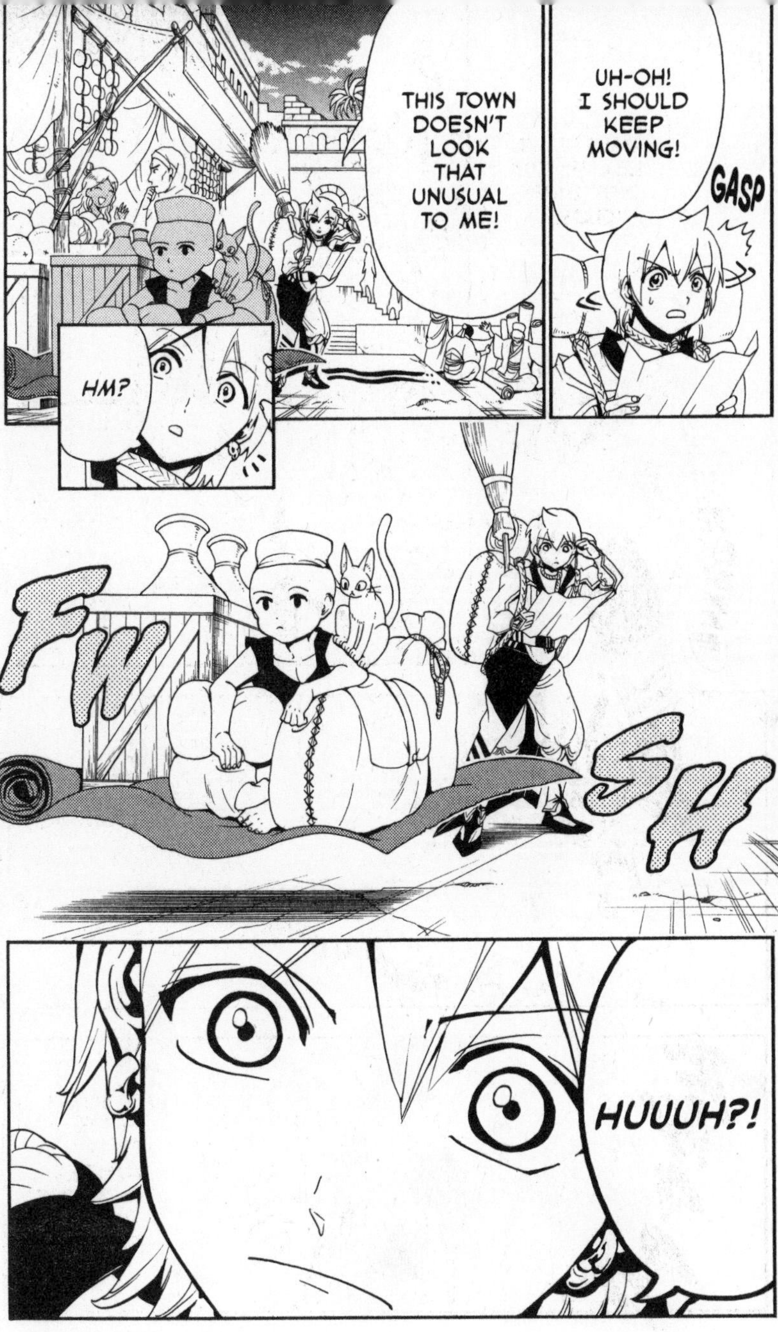
UH-OH! I SHOULD KEEP MOVING!
GASP
THIS TOWN DOESN'T LOOK THAT UNUSUAL TO ME!
HM?
FWSH
HUUUH?!

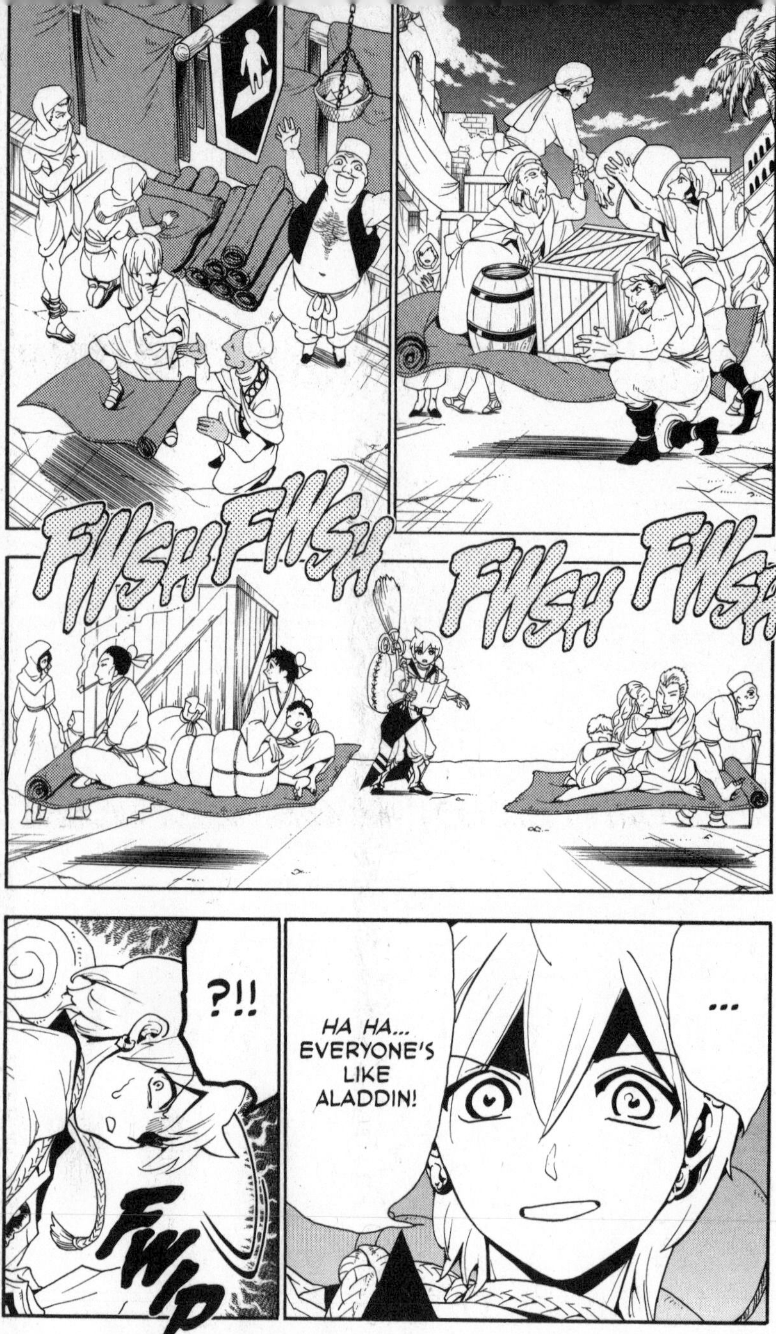
FWSH FWSH
FWSH FWSH
...
HA HA... EVERYONE'S LIKE ALADDIN!
?!!
FWIP

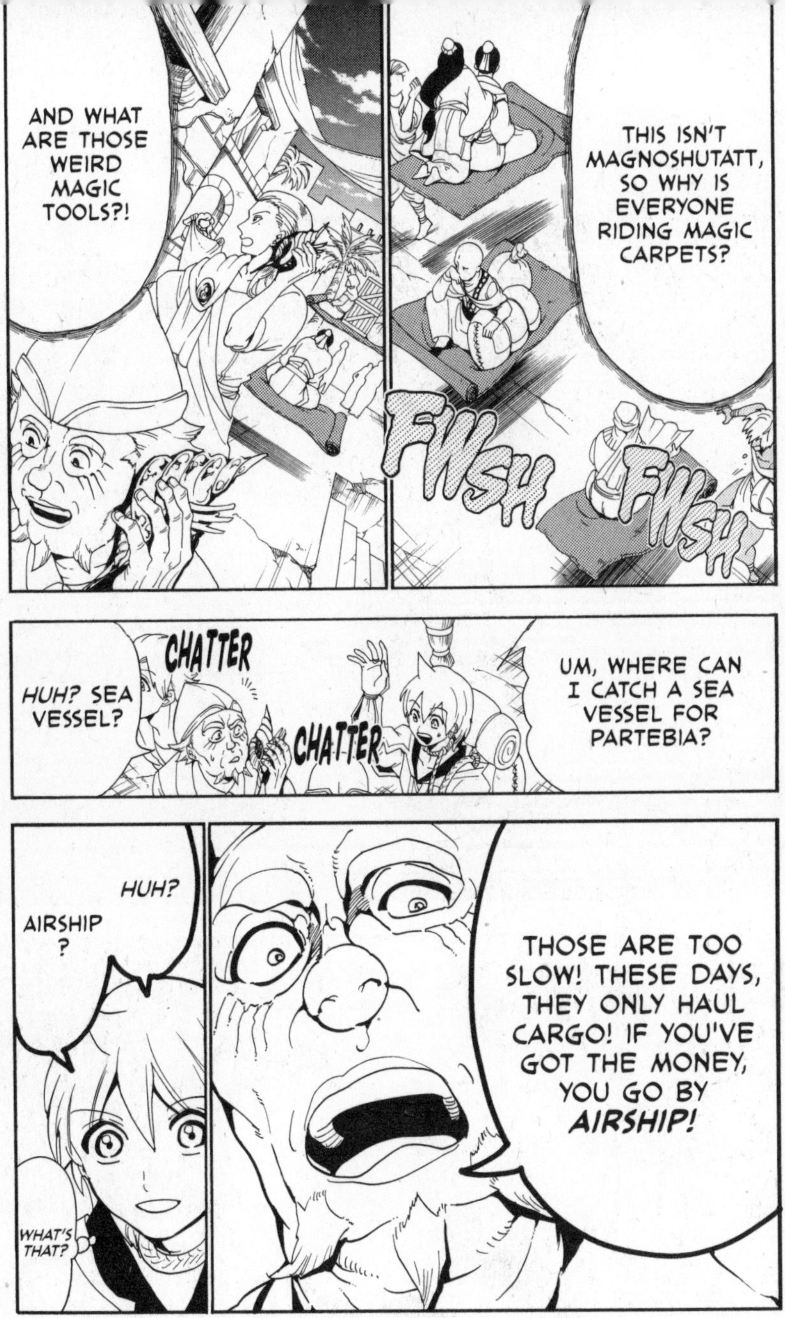
THIS ISN'T MAGNOSHUTATT, SO WHY IS EVERYONE RIDING MAGIC CARPETS?
FWSH
FWSH
AND WHAT ARE THOSE WEIRD MAGIC TOOLS?!
UM, WHERE CAN I CATCH A SEA VESSEL FOR PARTEBIA?
CHATTER
CHATTER
HUH? SEA VESSEL?
THOSE ARE TOO SLOW! THESE DAYS, THEY ONLY HAUL CARGO! IF YOU'VE GOT THE MONEY, YOU GO BY AIRSHIP!
HUH?
AIRSHIP?
WHAT'S THAT?

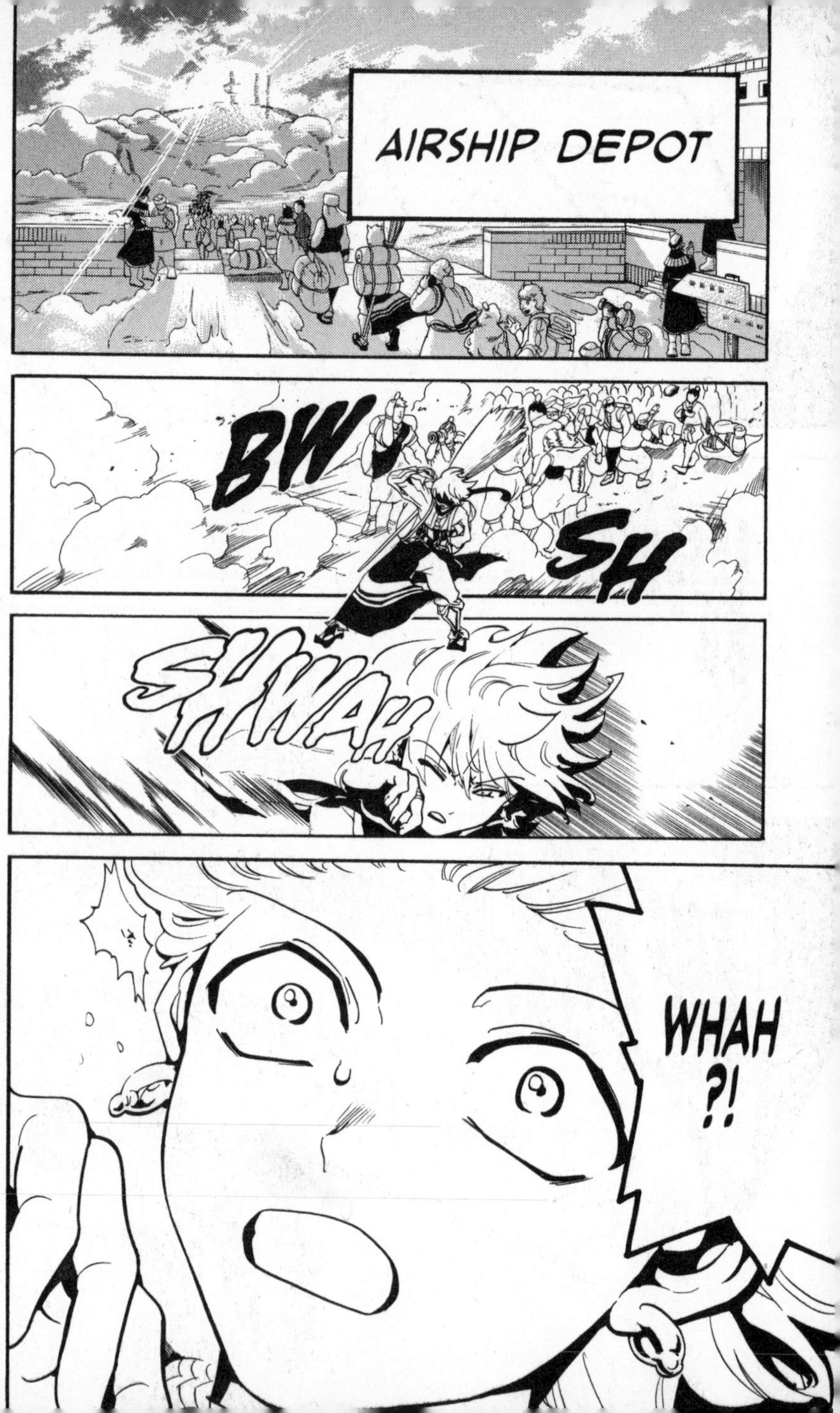
AIRSHIP DEPOT
BW
SH
SHWAH
WHAH ?!

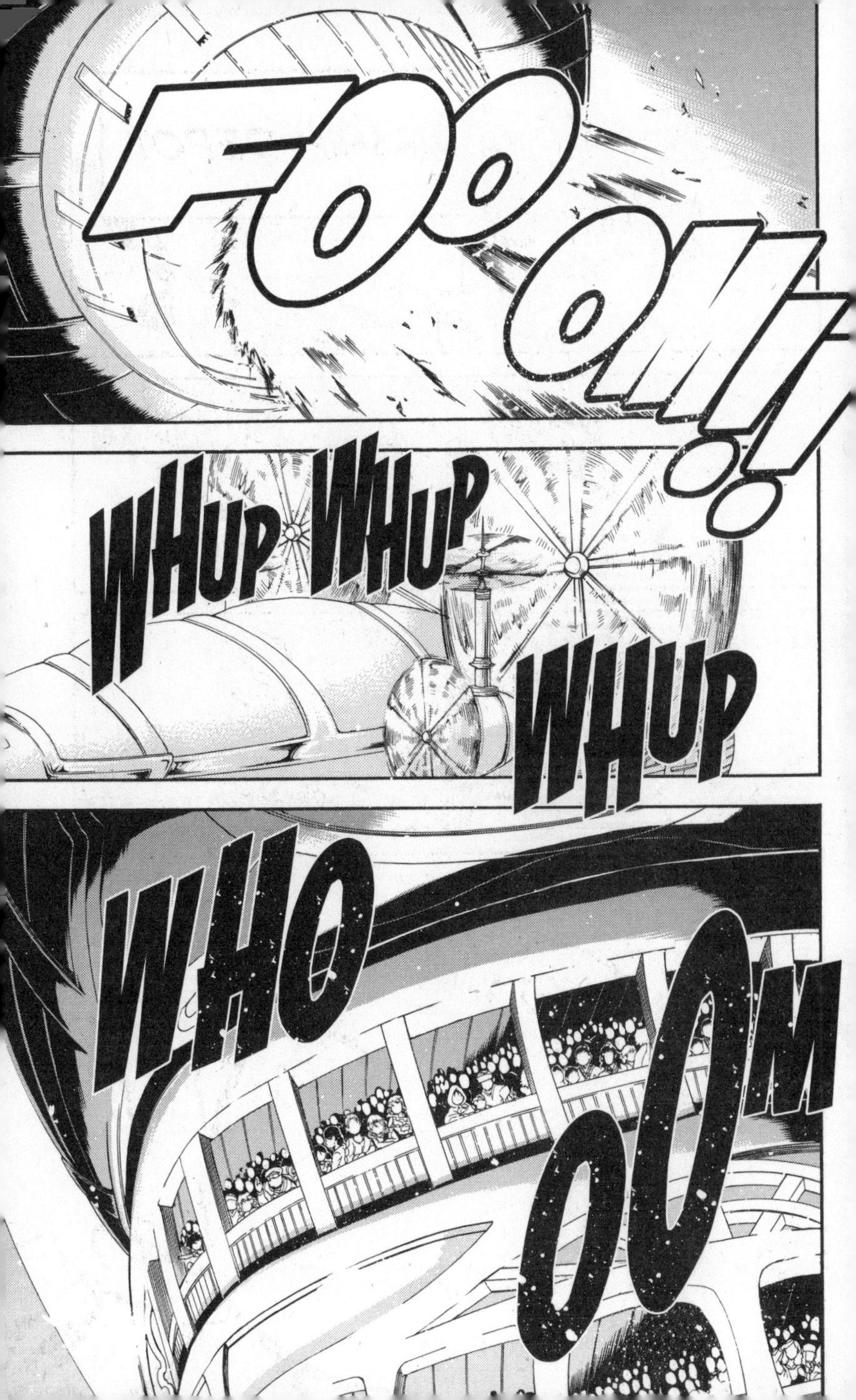
FOOOM!!
WHUP WHUP
WHUP
WHOOOM

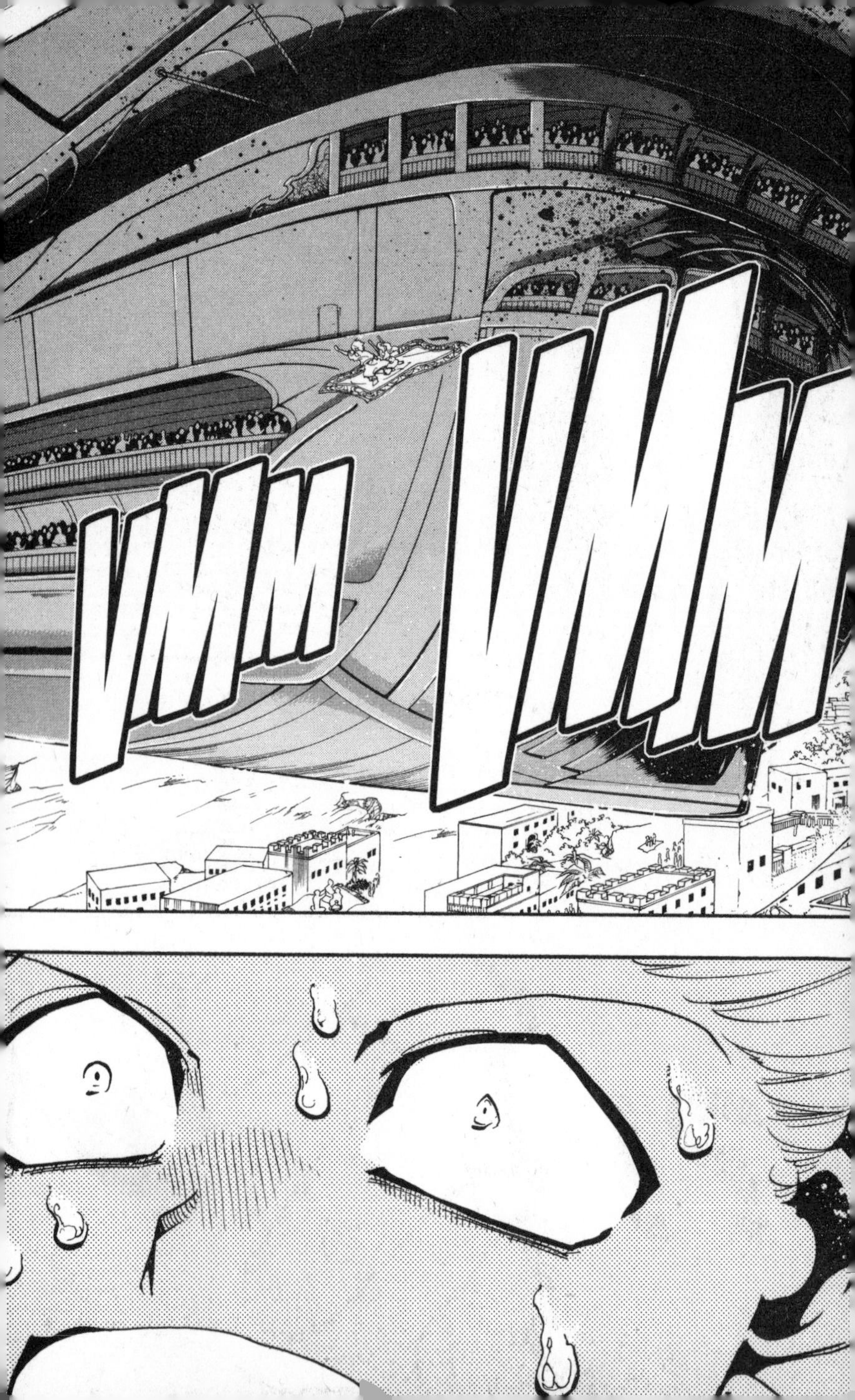
VMM VMM

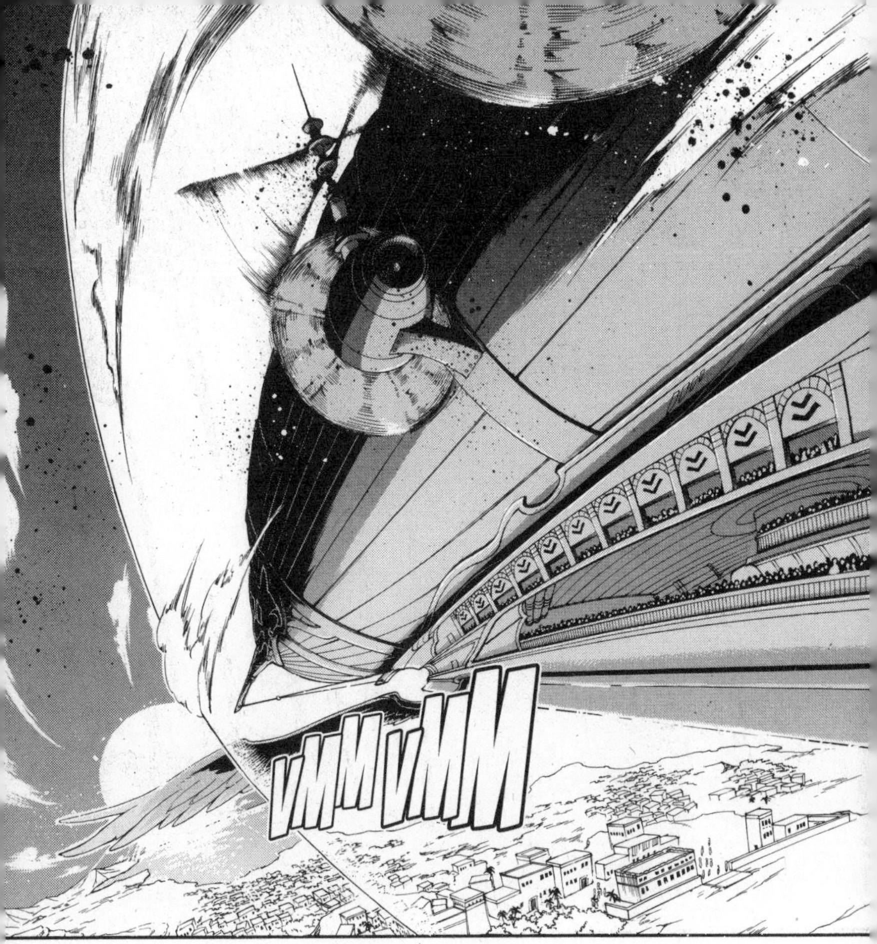
VMM VMM
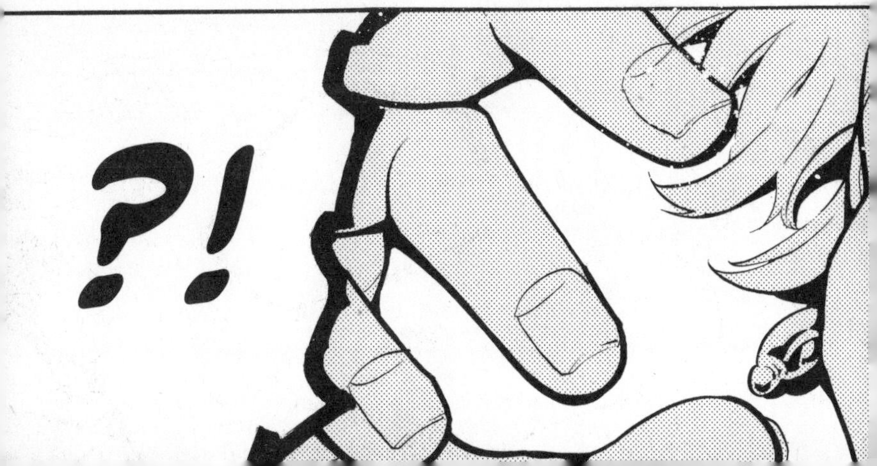
?!

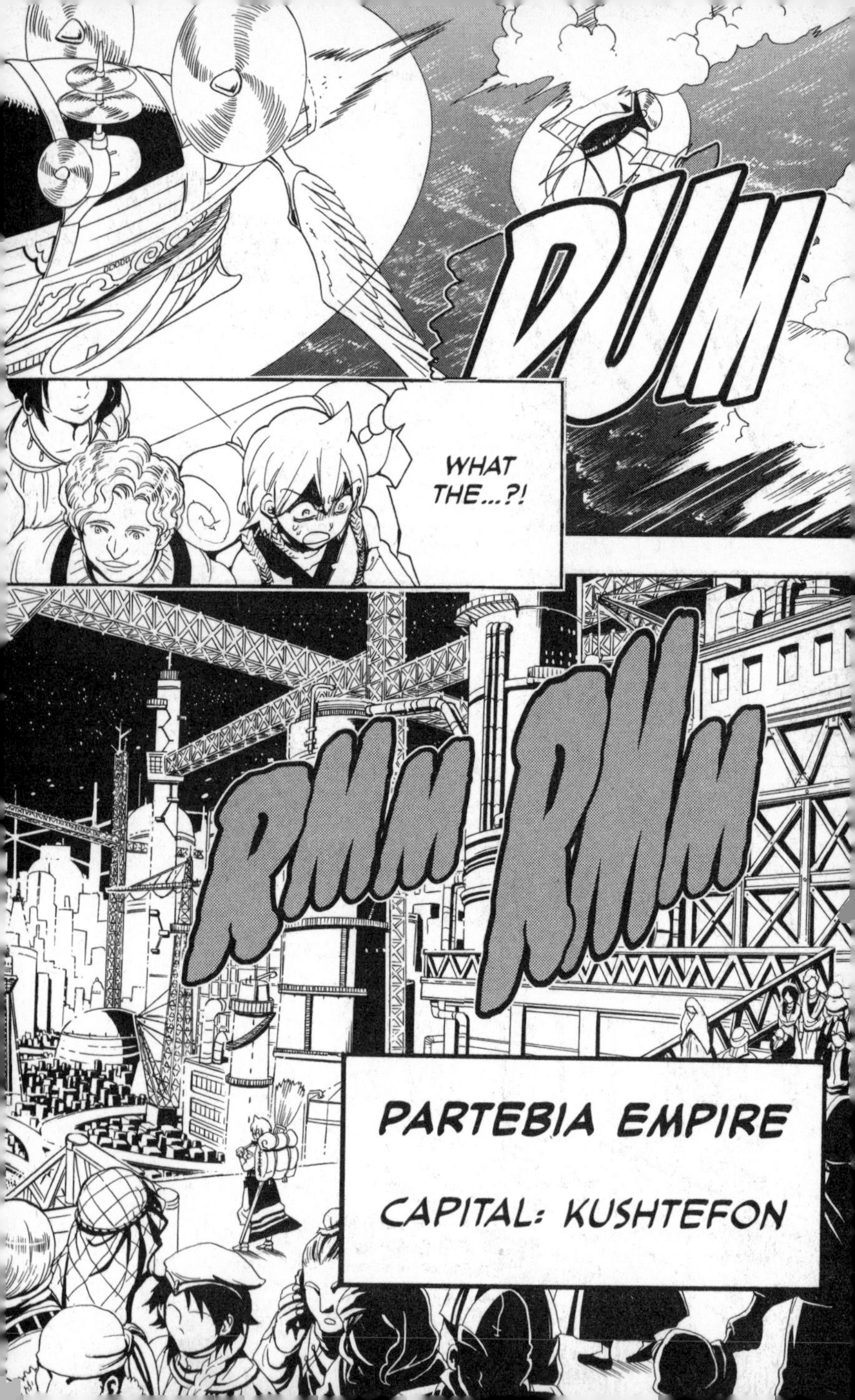
DUM
WHAT THE...?!
RMMM RMMM
PARTEBIA EMPIRE
CAPITAL: KUSHTEFON

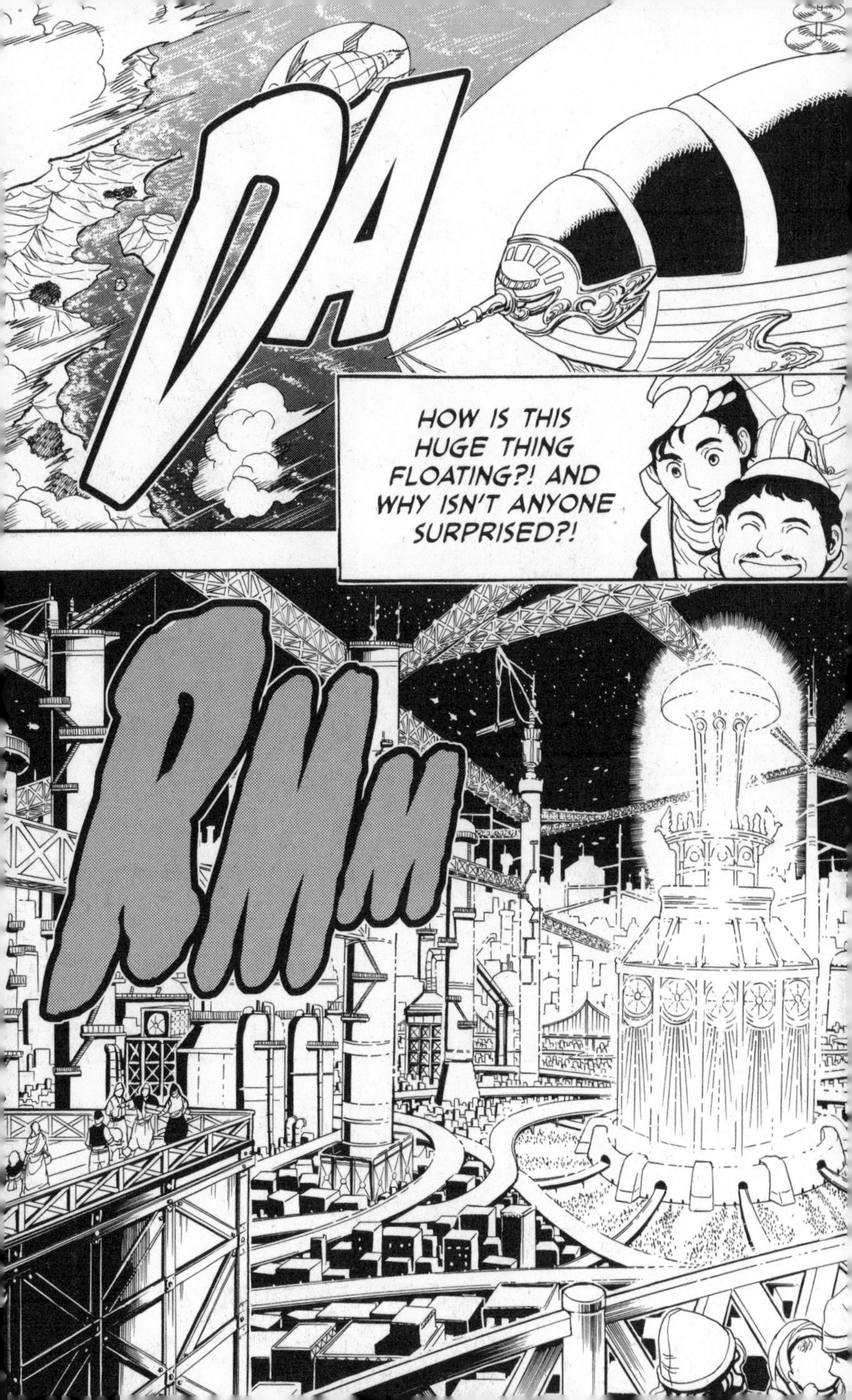
HOW IS THIS HUGE THING FLOATING?! AND WHY ISN'T ANYONE SURPRISED?!

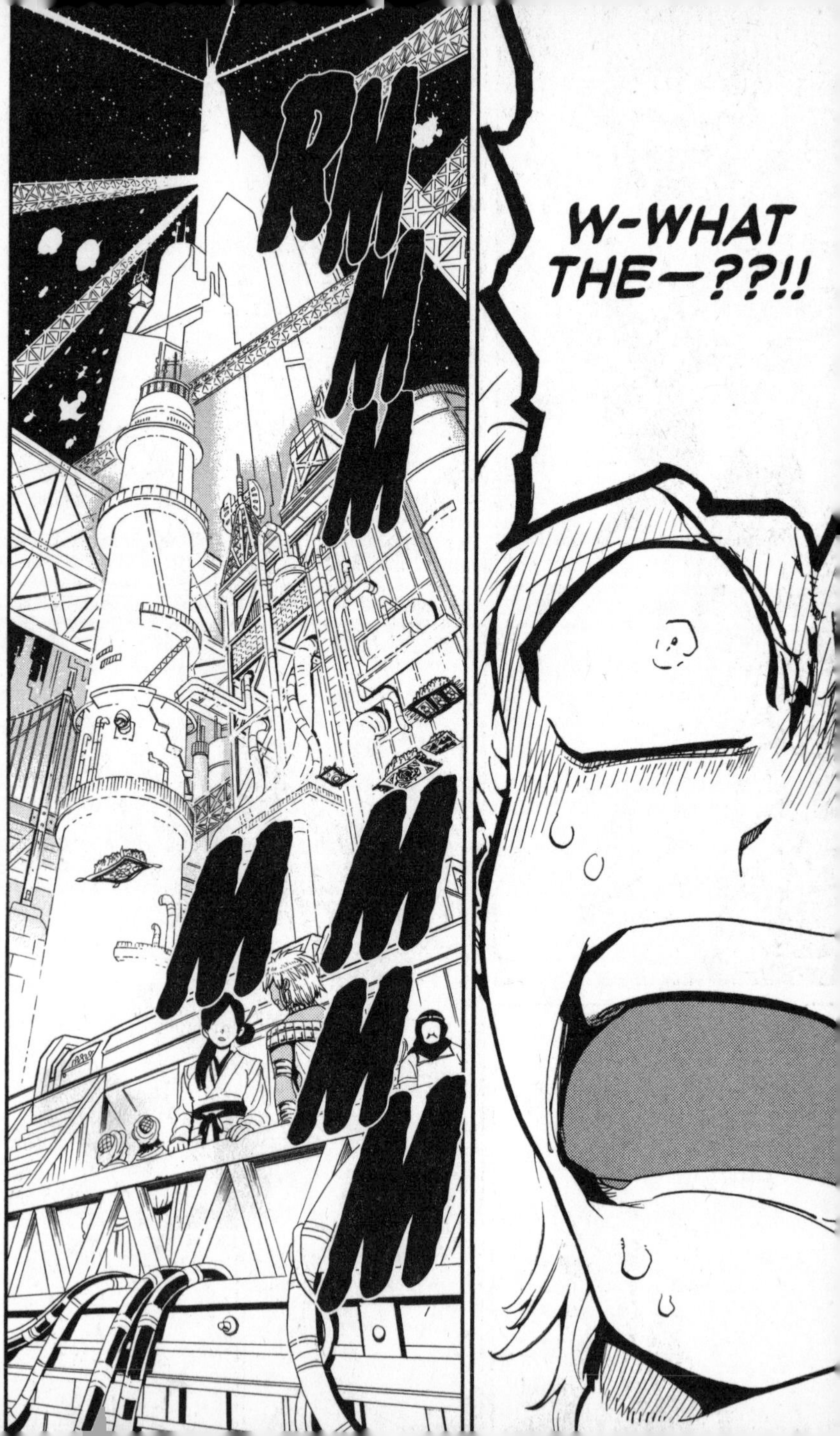
W-WHAT THE—??!!

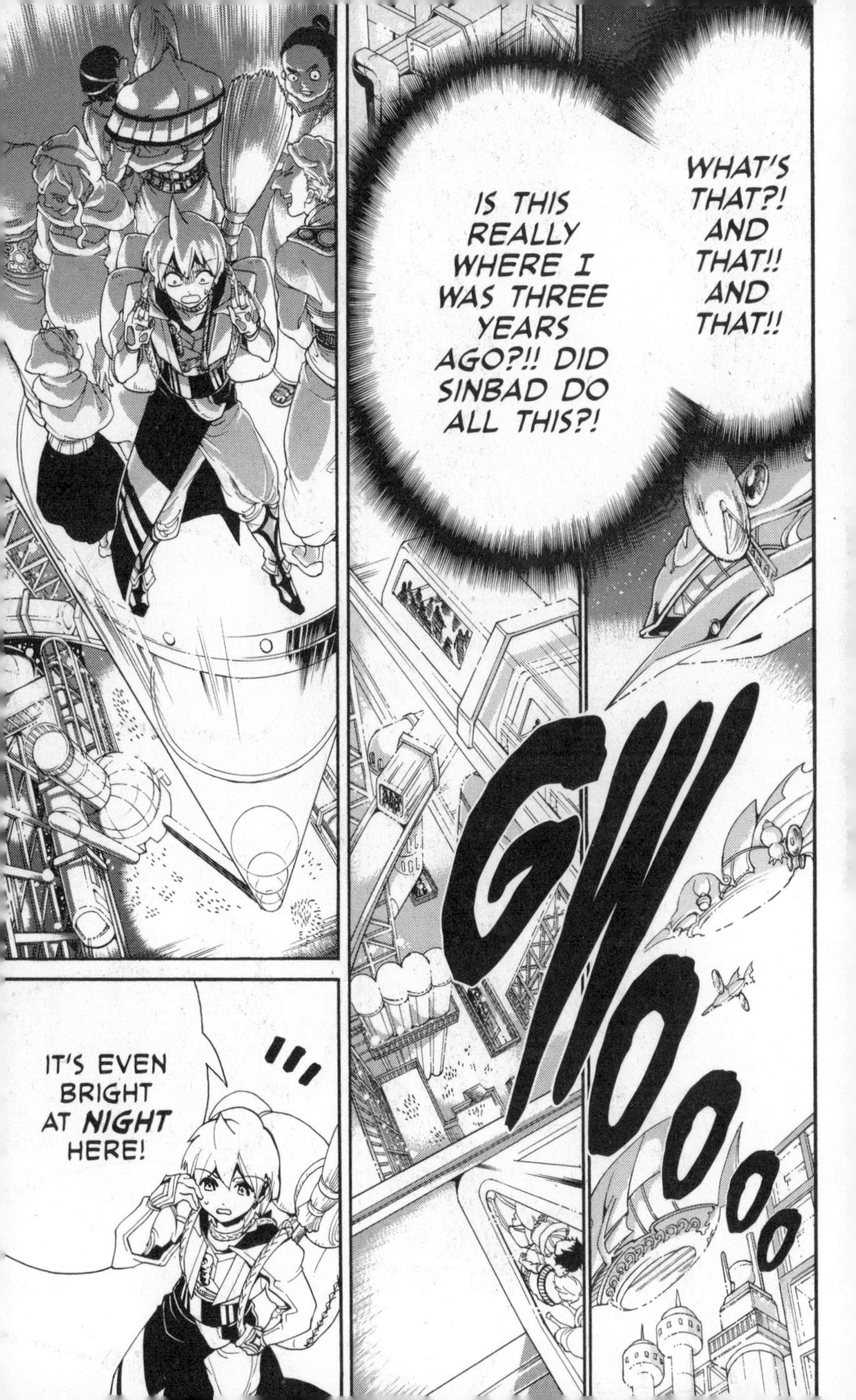
WHAT'S THAT?! AND THAT!! AND THAT!!
IS THIS REALLY WHERE I WAS THREE YEARS AGO?!! DID SINBAD DO ALL THIS?!
GWOOoo
...
IT'S EVEN BRIGHT AT NIGHT HERE!

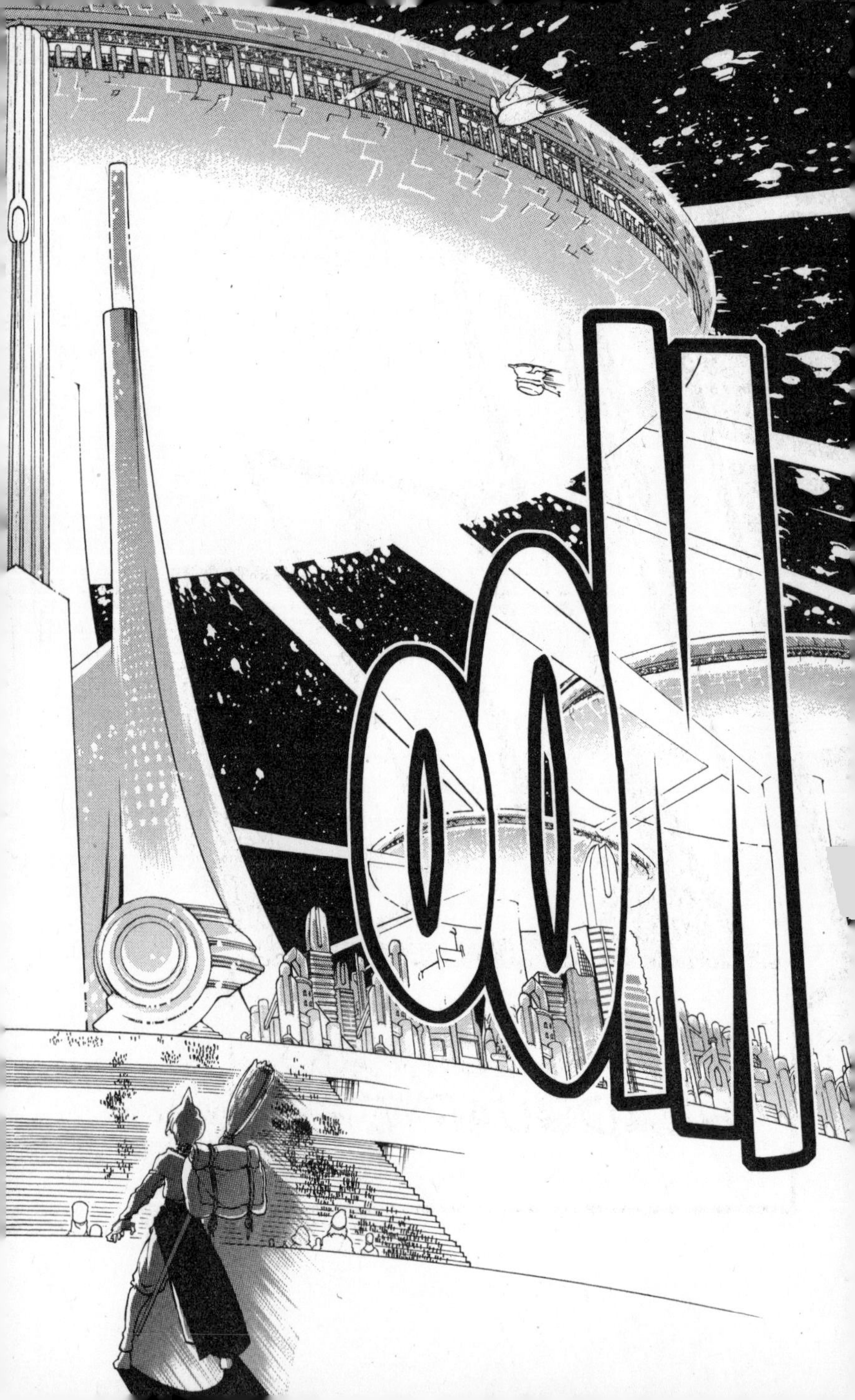

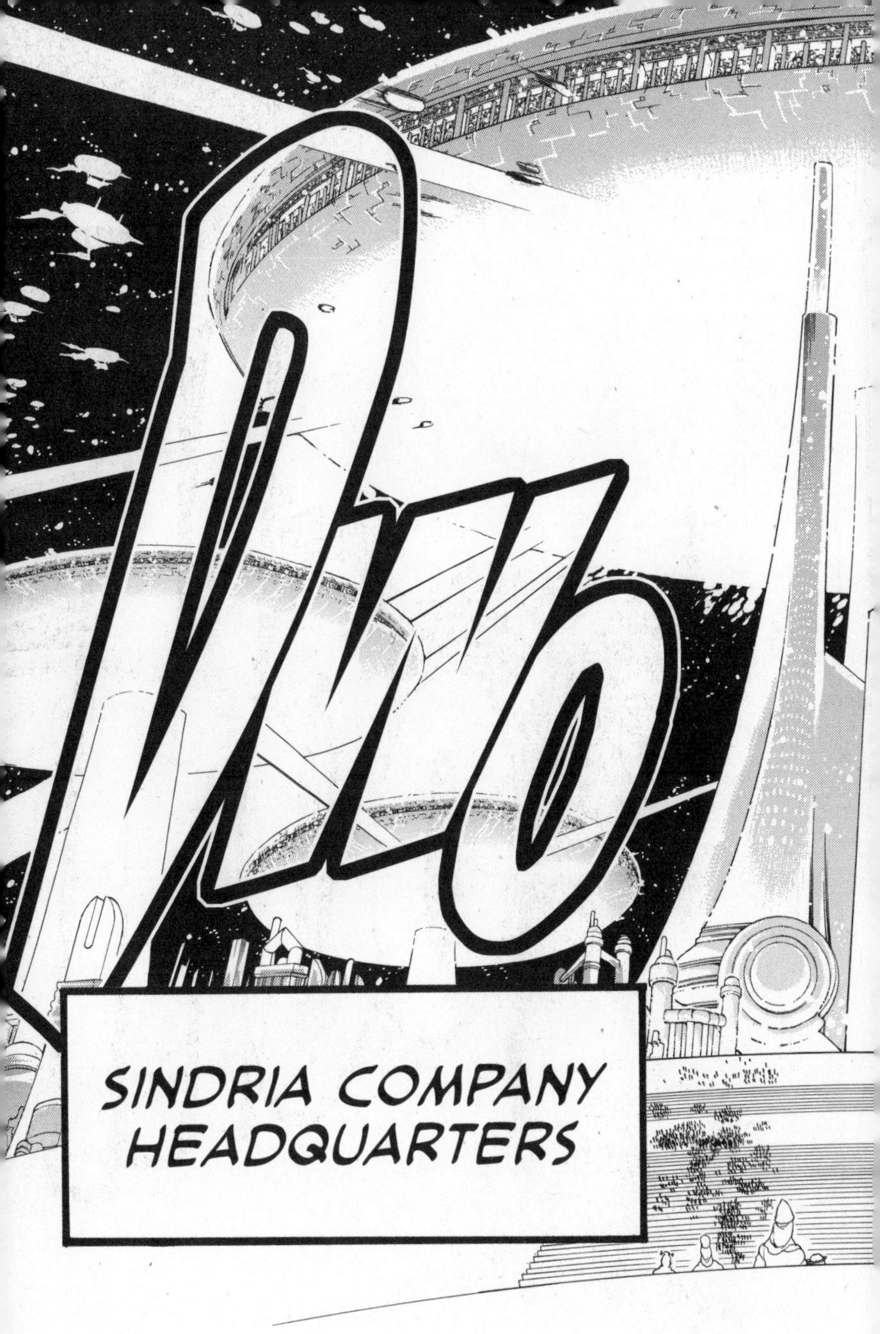
SINDRIA COMPANY HEADQUARTERS

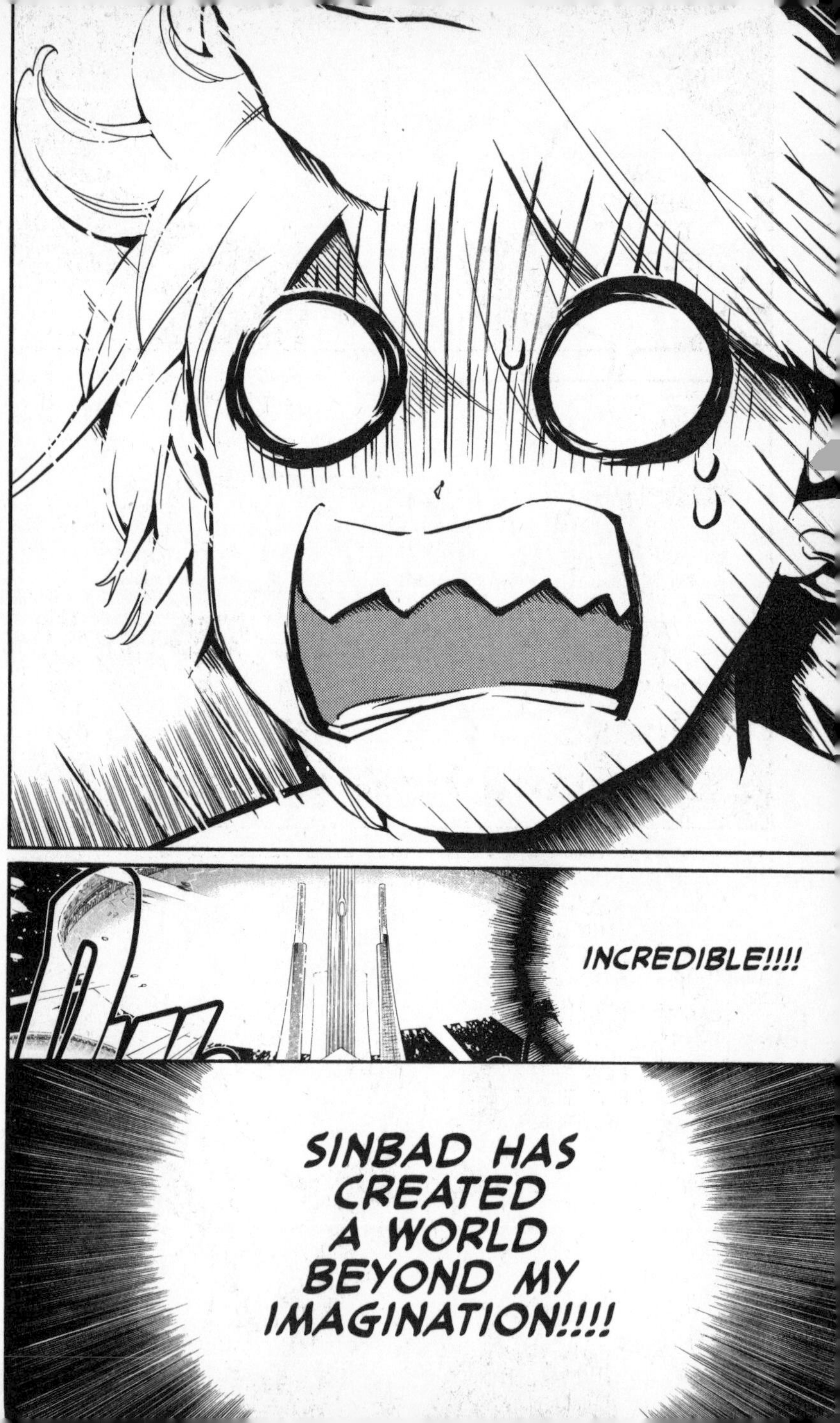
INCREDIBLE!!!!
SINBAD HAS CREATED A WORLD BEYOND MY IMAGINATION!!!!

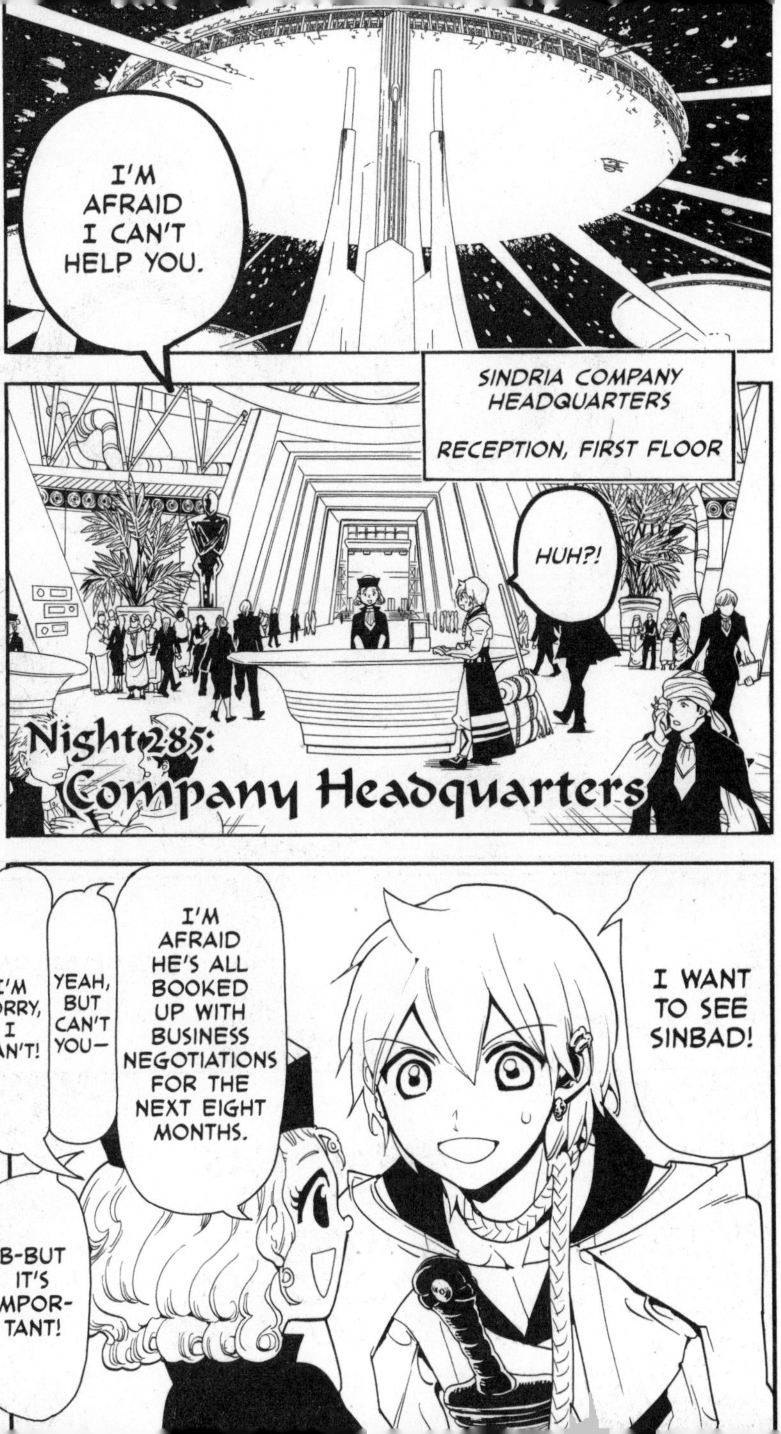
I'M AFRAID I CAN'T HELP YOU.
SINDRIA COMPANY HEADQUARTERS
RECEPTION, FIRST FLOOR
HUH?!
Night 285: Company Headquarters
I WANT TO SEE SINBAD!
I'M AFRAID HE'S ALL BOOKED UP WITH BUSINESS NEGOTIATIONS FOR THE NEXT EIGHT MONTHS.
YEAH, BUT CAN'T YOU—
I'M SORRY, I CAN'T!
B-BUT IT'S IMPORTANT!

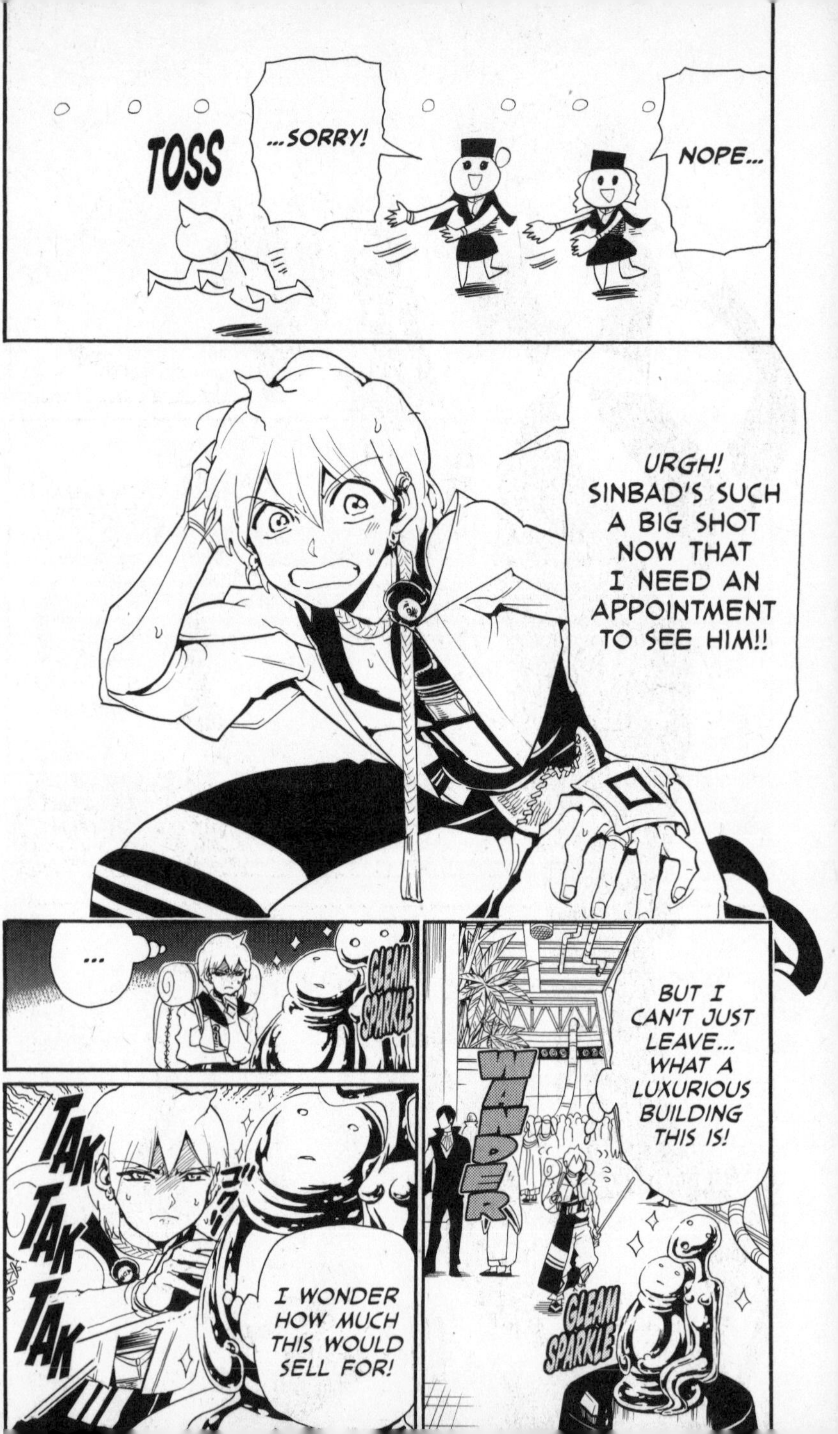
NOPE...
...SORRY!
TOSS
URGH! SINBAD'S SUCH A BIG SHOT NOW THAT I NEED AN APPOINTMENT TO SEE HIM!!
BUT I CAN'T JUST LEAVE... WHAT A LUXURIOUS BUILDING THIS IS!
WANDER
GLEAM SPARKLE
...
GLEAM SPARKLE
TAK TAK TAK
I WONDER HOW MUCH THIS WOULD SELL FOR!

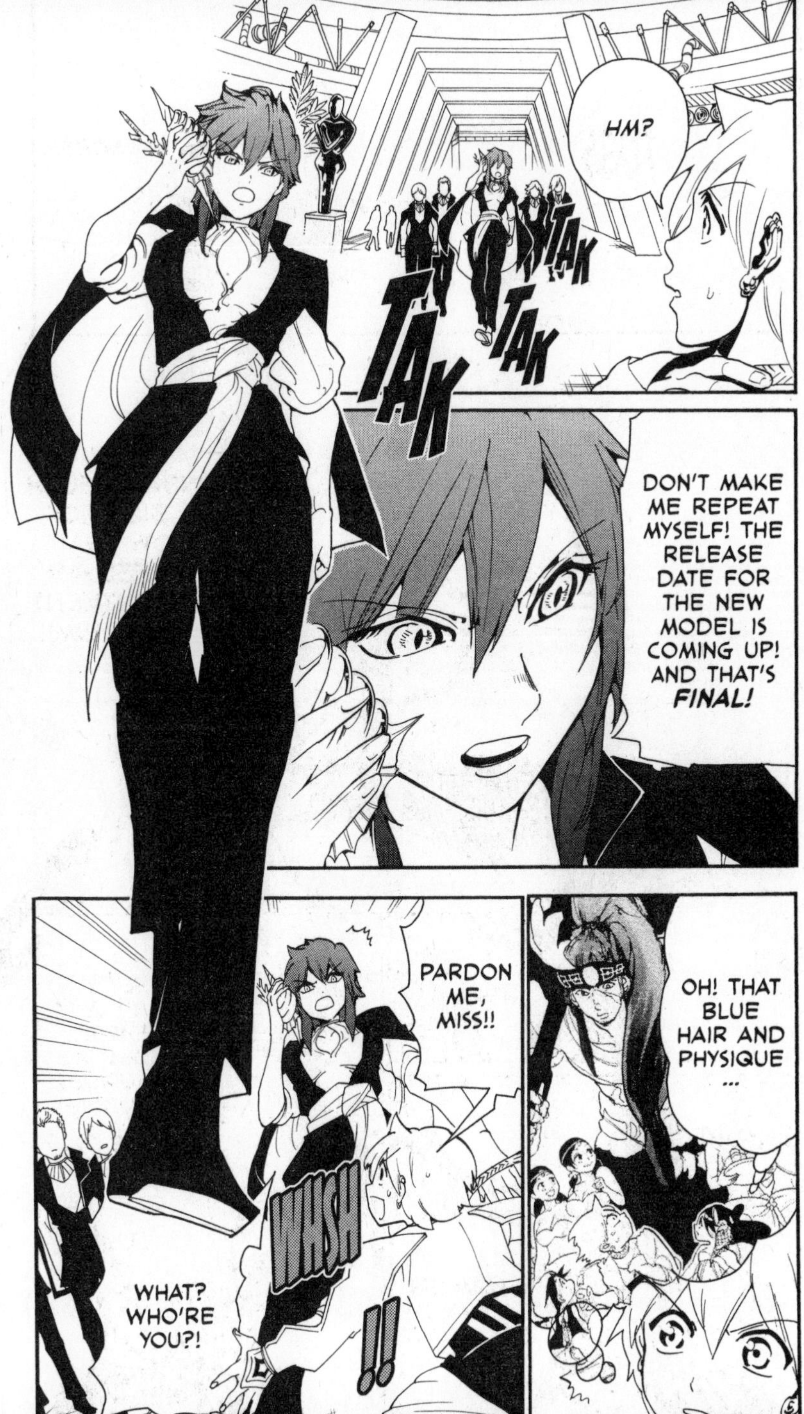
HM?
TAK
TAK
TAK
TAK
DON'T MAKE ME REPEAT MYSELF! THE RELEASE DATE FOR THE NEW MODEL IS COMING UP! AND THAT'S *FINAL!*
OH! THAT BLUE HAIR AND PHYSIQUE ...
PARDON ME, MISS!!
WHSH
!!
WHAT? WHO'RE YOU?!

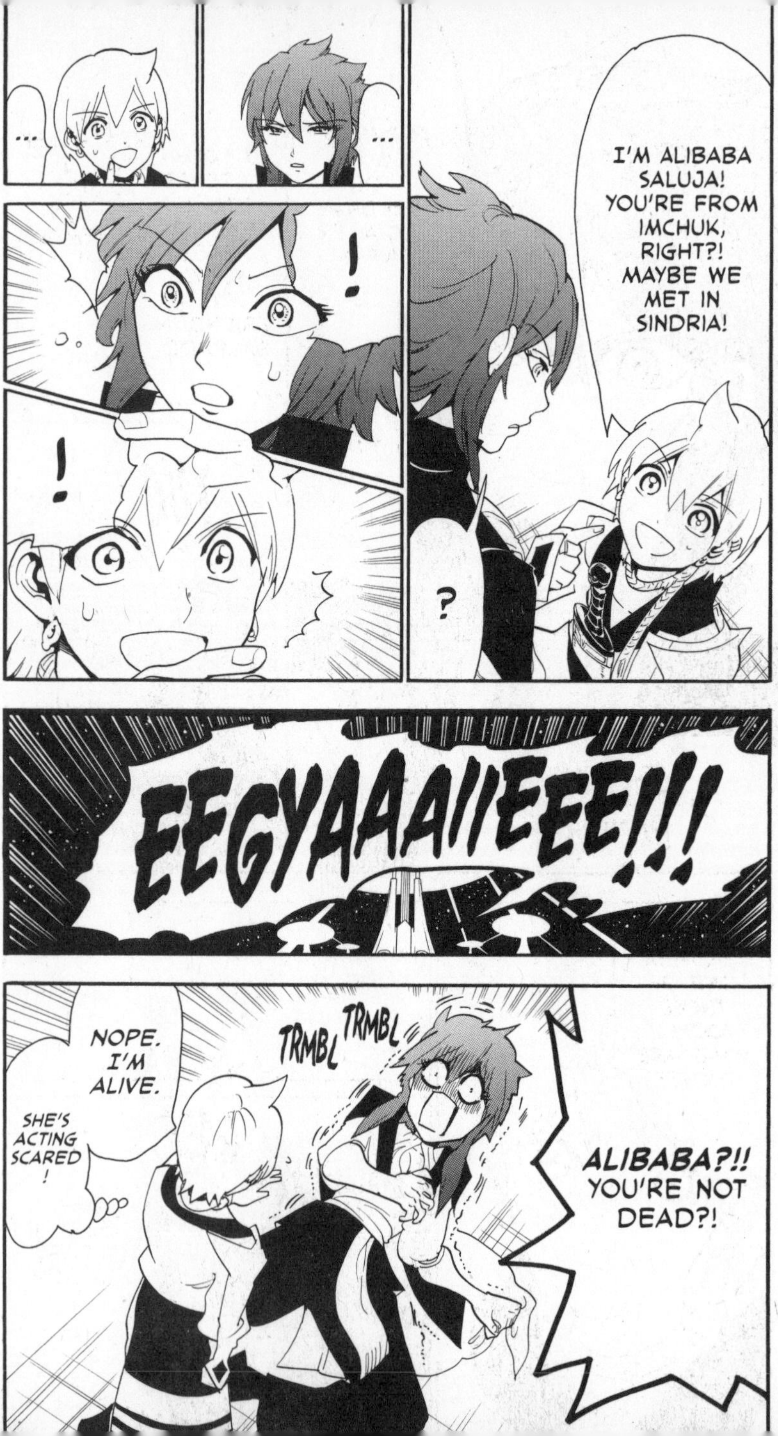
I'M ALIBABA SALUJA! YOU'RE FROM IMCHUK, RIGHT?! MAYBE WE MET IN SINDRIA!
?
...
...
!
!
EEGYAAAIIEEE!!!
ALIBABA?!! YOU'RE NOT DEAD?!
TRMBL
TRMBL
NOPE. I'M ALIVE.
SHE'S ACTING SCARED!

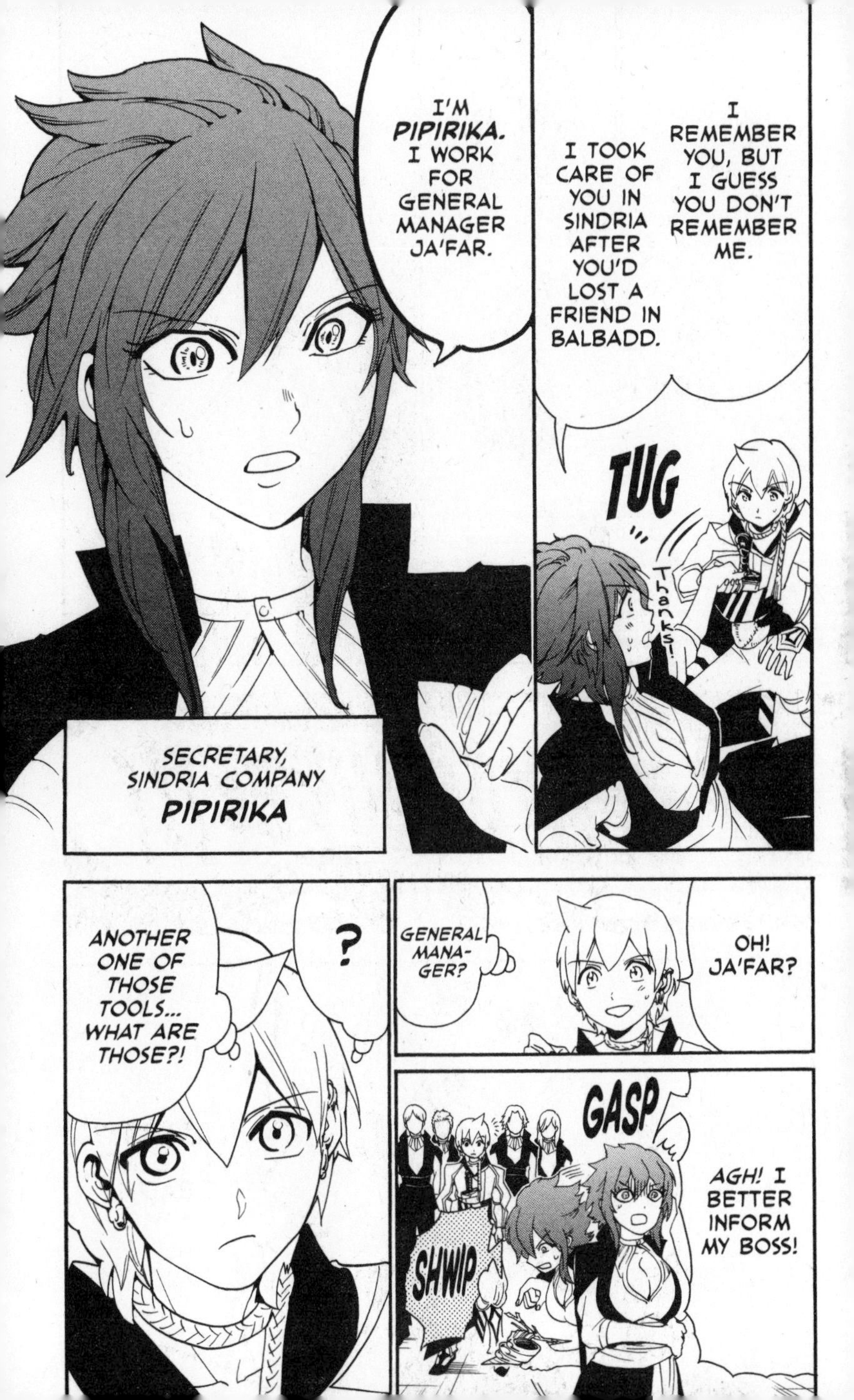

I REMEMBER YOU, BUT I GUESS YOU DON'T REMEMBER ME.
I TOOK CARE OF YOU IN SINDRIA AFTER YOU'D LOST A FRIEND IN BALBADD.
TUG
Thanks!
I'M PIPIRIKA. I WORK FOR GENERAL MANAGER JA'FAR.
SECRETARY, SINDRIA COMPANY PIPIRIKA
OH! JA'FAR?
GENERAL MANA-GER?
GASP
AGH! I BETTER INFORM MY BOSS!
SHWIP
?
ANOTHER ONE OF THOSE TOOLS... WHAT ARE THOSE?!

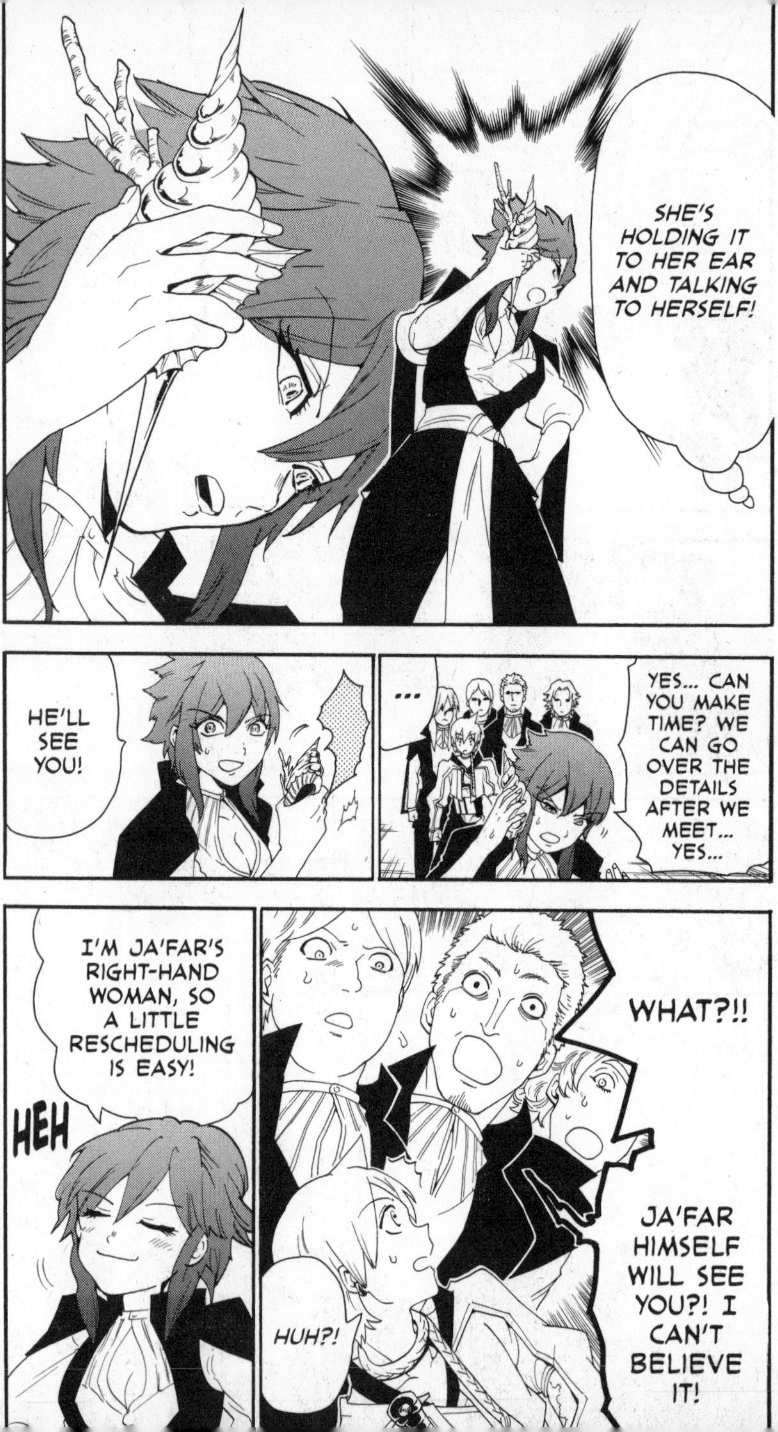
SHE'S HOLDING IT TO HER EAR AND TALKING TO HERSELF!
YES... CAN YOU MAKE TIME? WE CAN GO OVER THE DETAILS AFTER WE MEET... YES...
...
HE'LL SEE YOU!
WHAT?!!
JA'FAR HIMSELF WILL SEE YOU?! I CAN'T BELIEVE IT!
HUH?!
I'M JA'FAR'S RIGHT-HAND WOMAN, SO A LITTLE RESCHEDULING IS EASY!
HEH

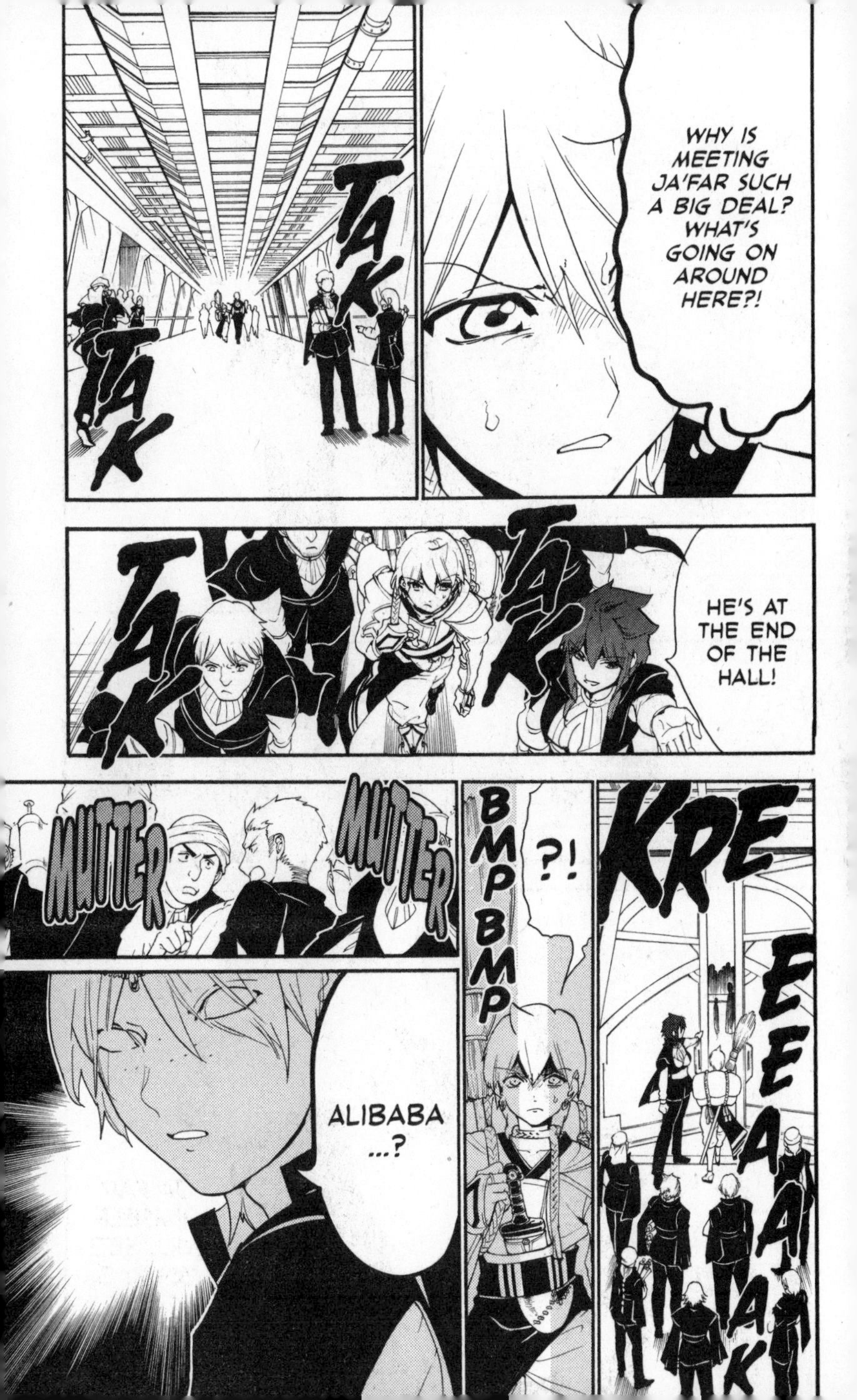
WHY IS MEETING JA'FAR SUCH A BIG DEAL? WHAT'S GOING ON AROUND HERE?!
TAK
TAK
HE'S AT THE END OF THE HALL!
TAK
TAK
KREEEAAK
?!
BMP BMP
MUTTER
MUTTER
ALIBABA ...?

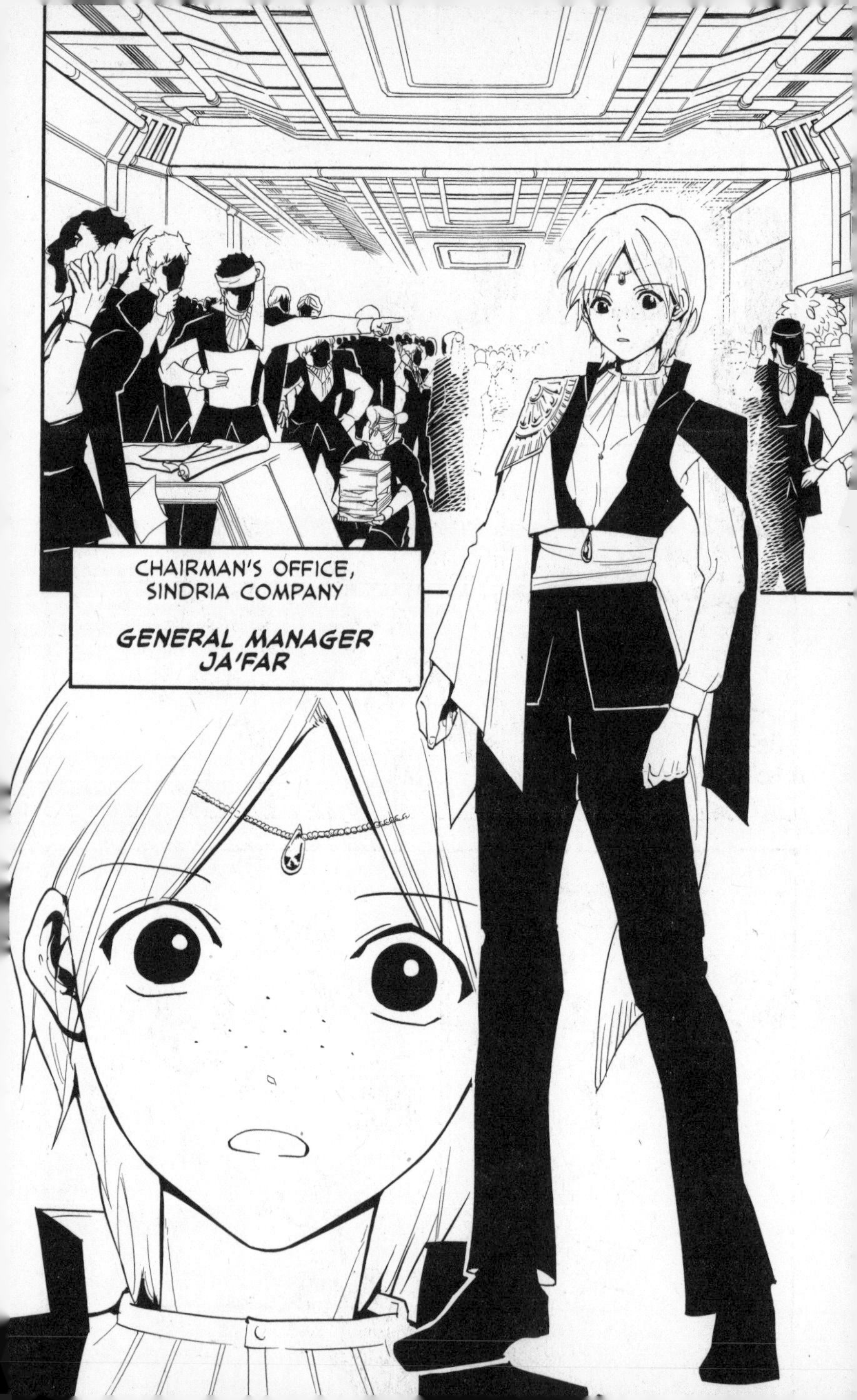
CHAIRMAN'S OFFICE, SINDRIA COMPANY
GENERAL MANAGER JA'FAR

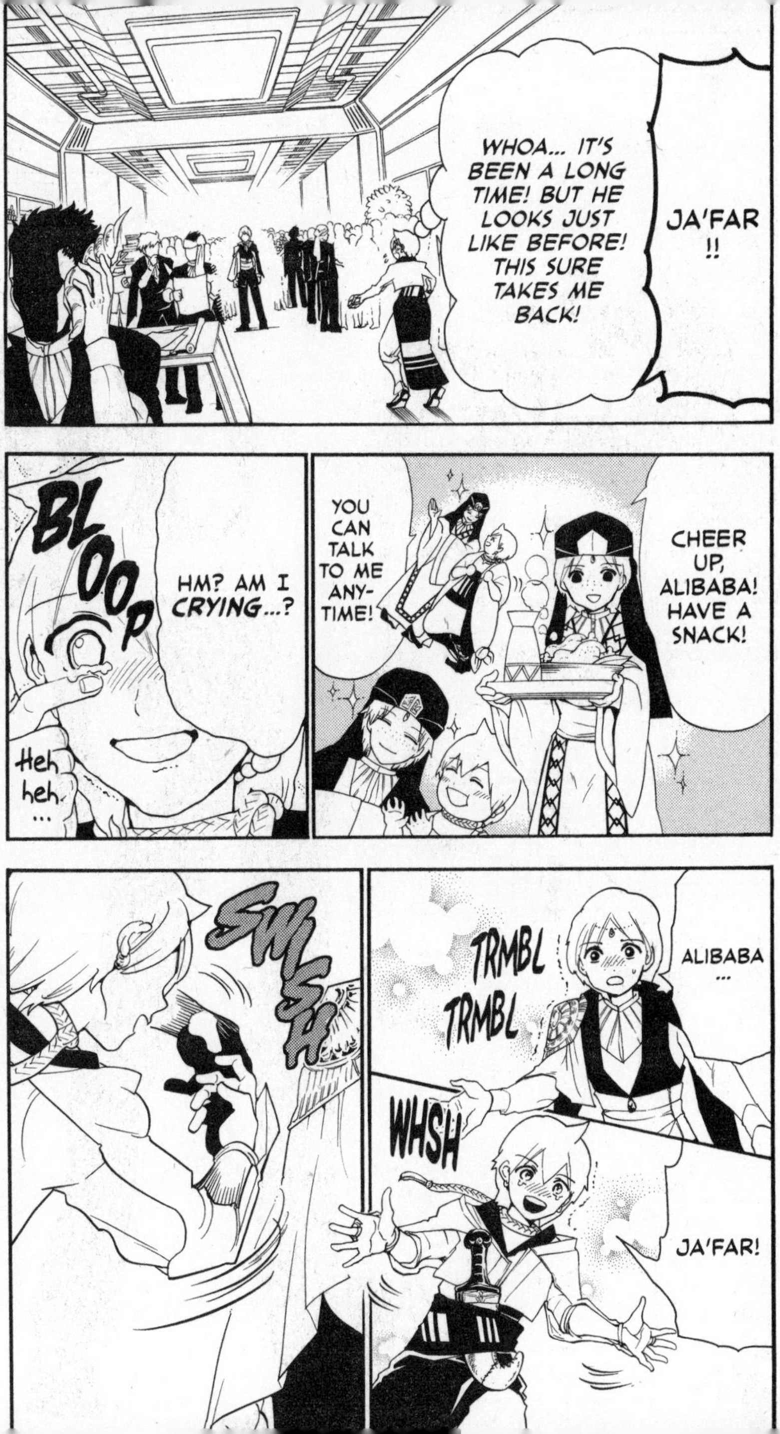
JA'FAR !!
WHOA... IT'S BEEN A LONG TIME! BUT HE LOOKS JUST LIKE BEFORE! THIS SURE TAKES ME BACK!
CHEER UP, ALIBABA! HAVE A SNACK!
YOU CAN TALK TO ME ANY-TIME!
HM? AM I CRYING...?
BLOOP
Heh heh...
ALIBABA...
TRMBL TRMBL
WHSH
JA'FAR!
SWISH

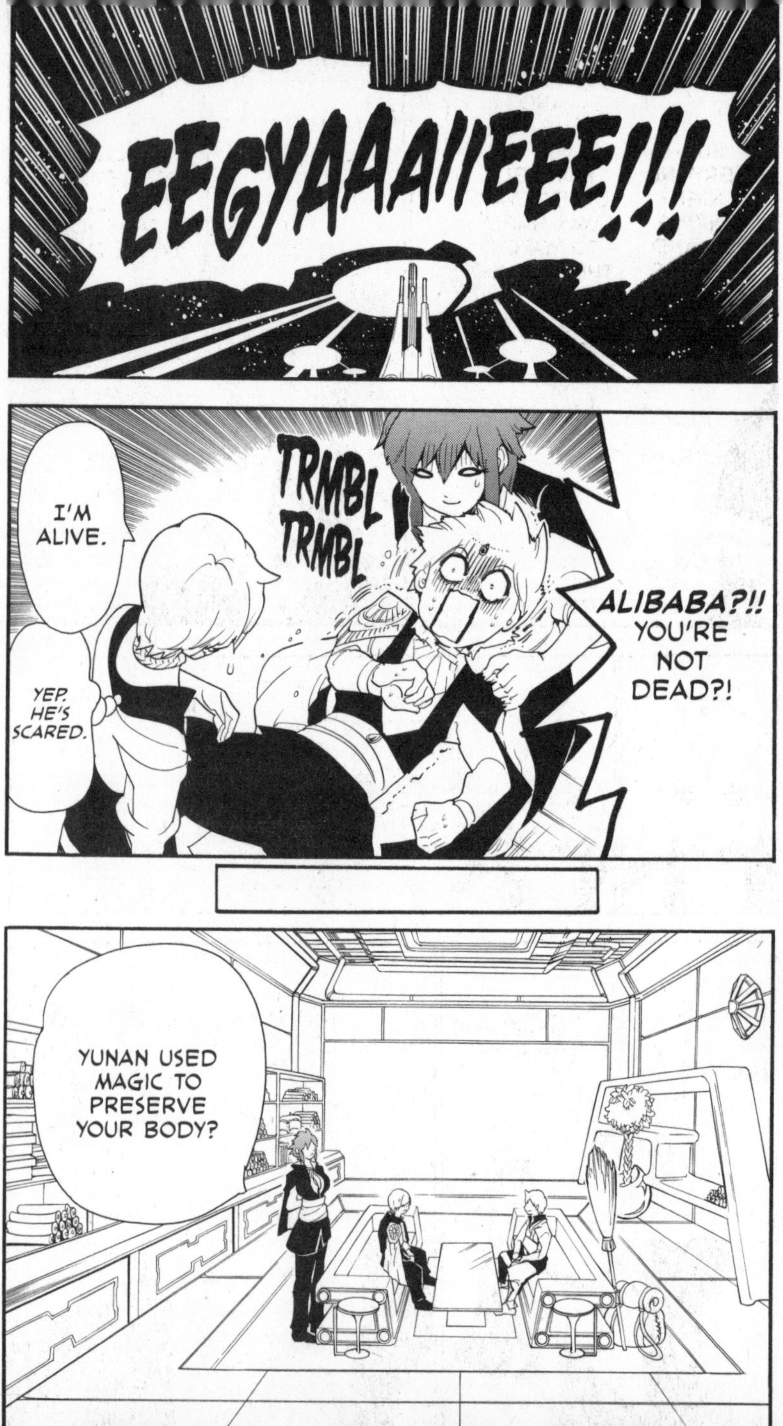
EEGYAAAIIEEE!!!
ALIBABA?!! YOU'RE NOT DEAD?!
TRMBL TRMBL
I'M ALIVE.
YEP. HE'S SCARED.
YUNAN USED MAGIC TO PRESERVE YOUR BODY?

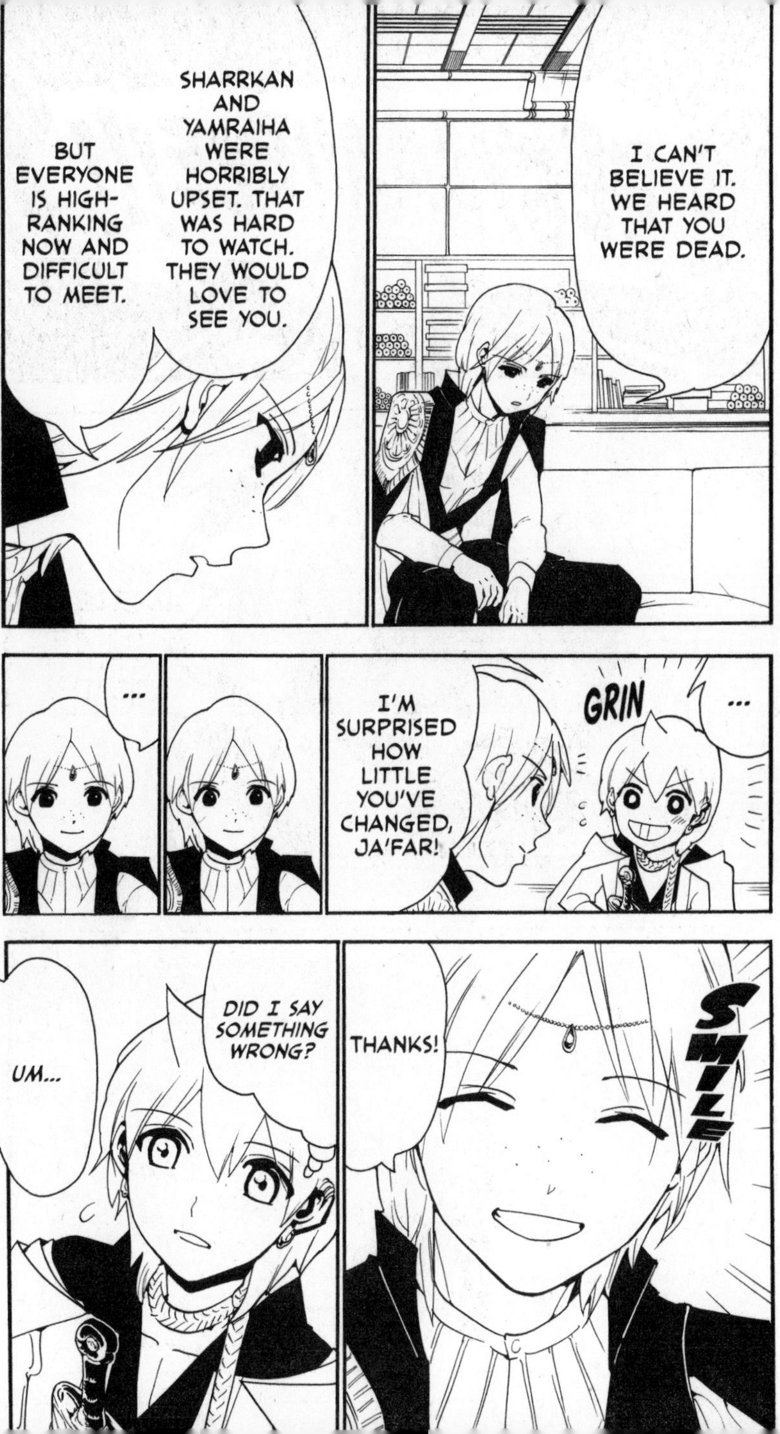
I CAN'T BELIEVE IT. WE HEARD THAT YOU WERE DEAD.
SHARRKAN AND YAMRAIHA WERE HORRIBLY UPSET. THAT WAS HARD TO WATCH. THEY WOULD LOVE TO SEE YOU.
BUT EVERYONE IS HIGH-RANKING NOW AND DIFFICULT TO MEET.
...
GRIN
I'M SURPRISED HOW LITTLE YOU'VE CHANGED, JA'FAR!
...
SMILE
THANKS!
DID I SAY SOMETHING WRONG?
UM...

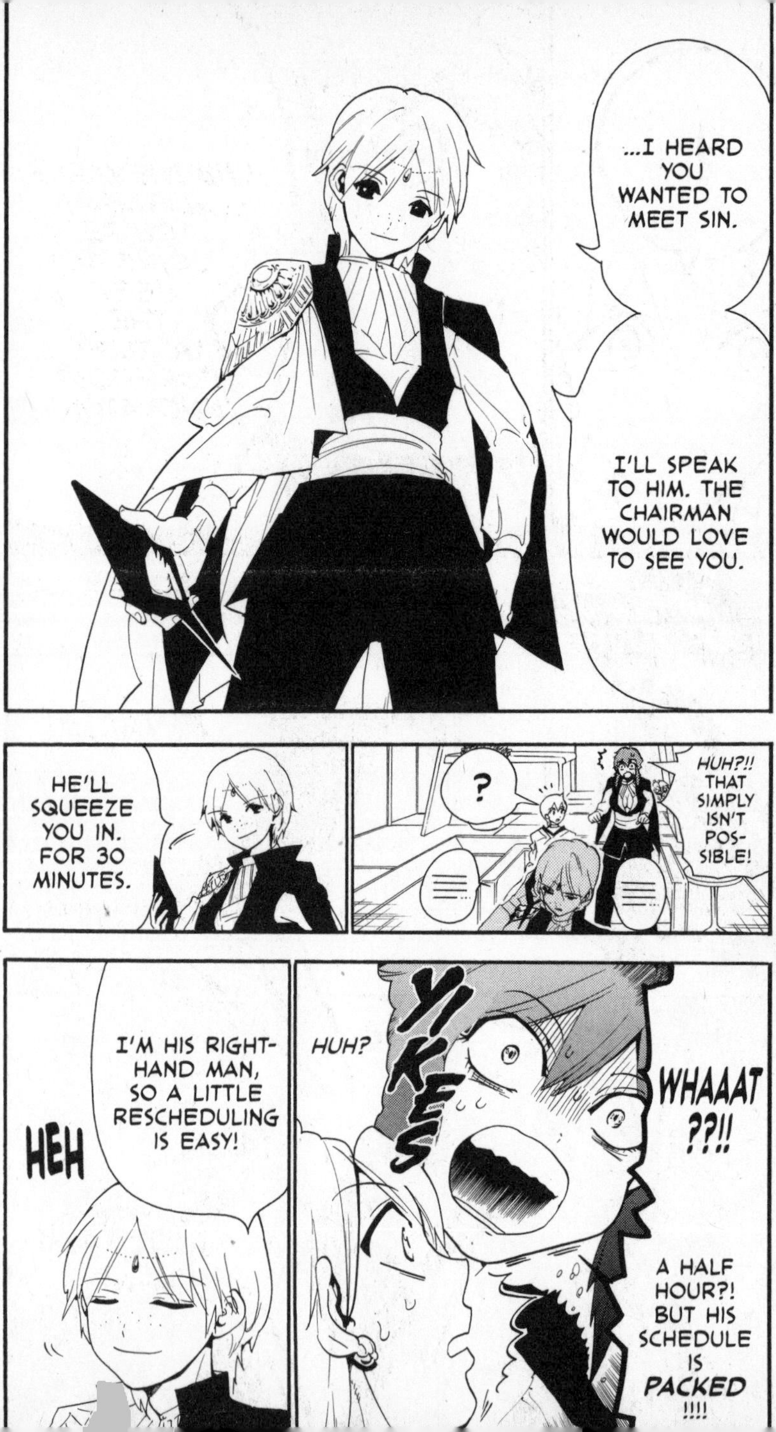
...I HEARD YOU WANTED TO MEET SIN.
I'LL SPEAK TO HIM. THE CHAIRMAN WOULD LOVE TO SEE YOU.
HUH?!! THAT SIMPLY ISN'T POS-SIBLE!
?
HE'LL SQUEEZE YOU IN. FOR 30 MINUTES.
WHAAAT ??!!
YIKES
HUH?
A HALF HOUR?! BUT HIS SCHEDULE IS PACKED !!!!
I'M HIS RIGHT-HAND MAN, SO A LITTLE RESCHEDULING IS EASY!
HEH

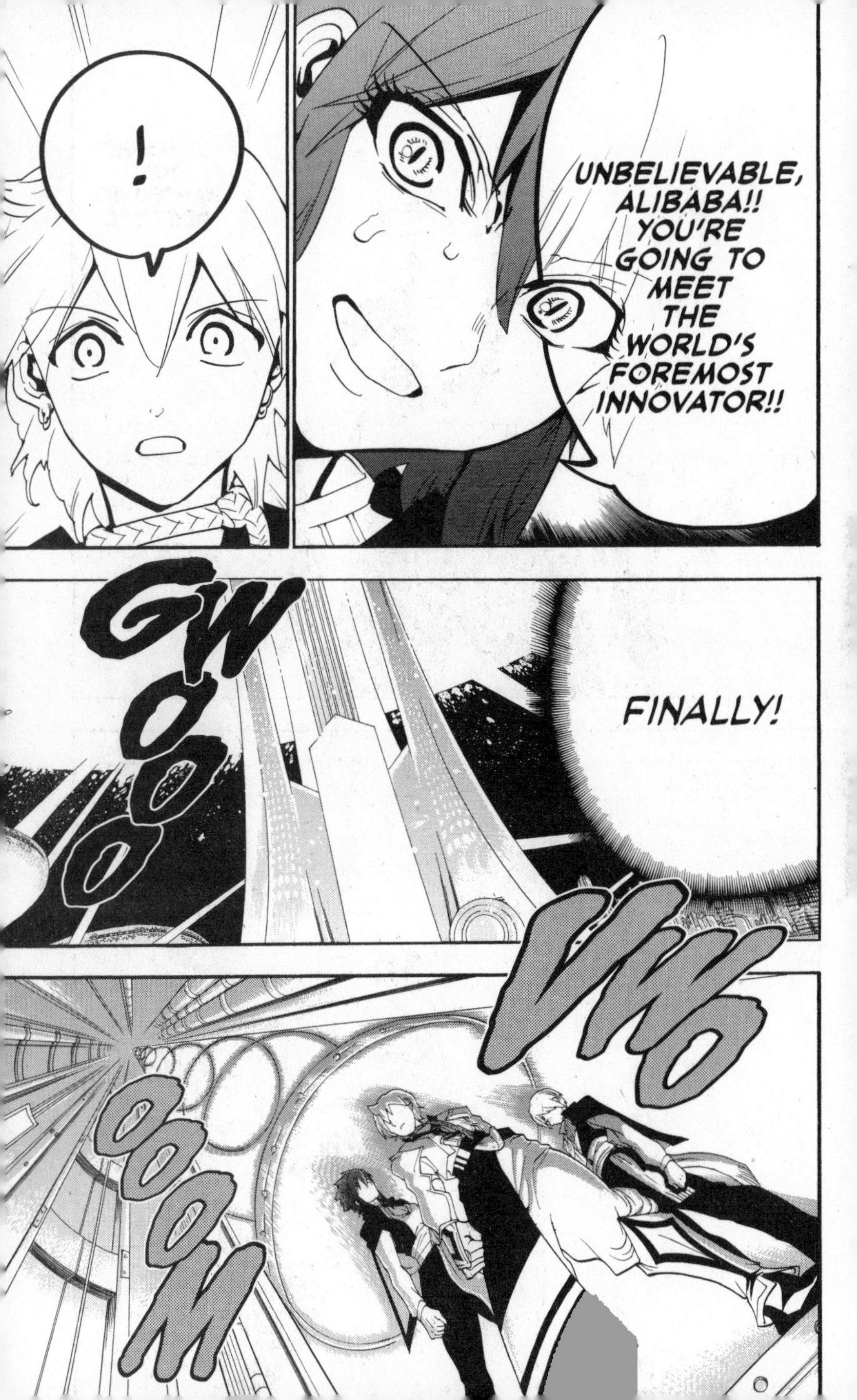
UNBELIEVABLE, ALIBABA!! YOU'RE GOING TO MEET THE WORLD'S FOREMOST INNOVATOR!!
!
FINALLY!
GWOOO
VWOOOOOM

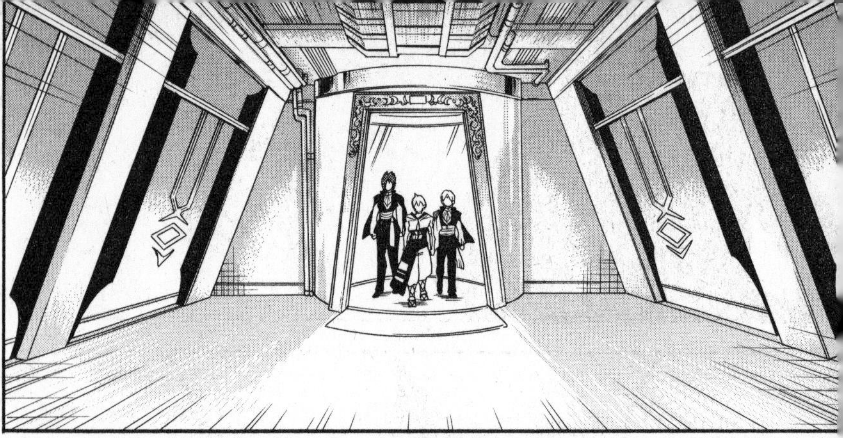

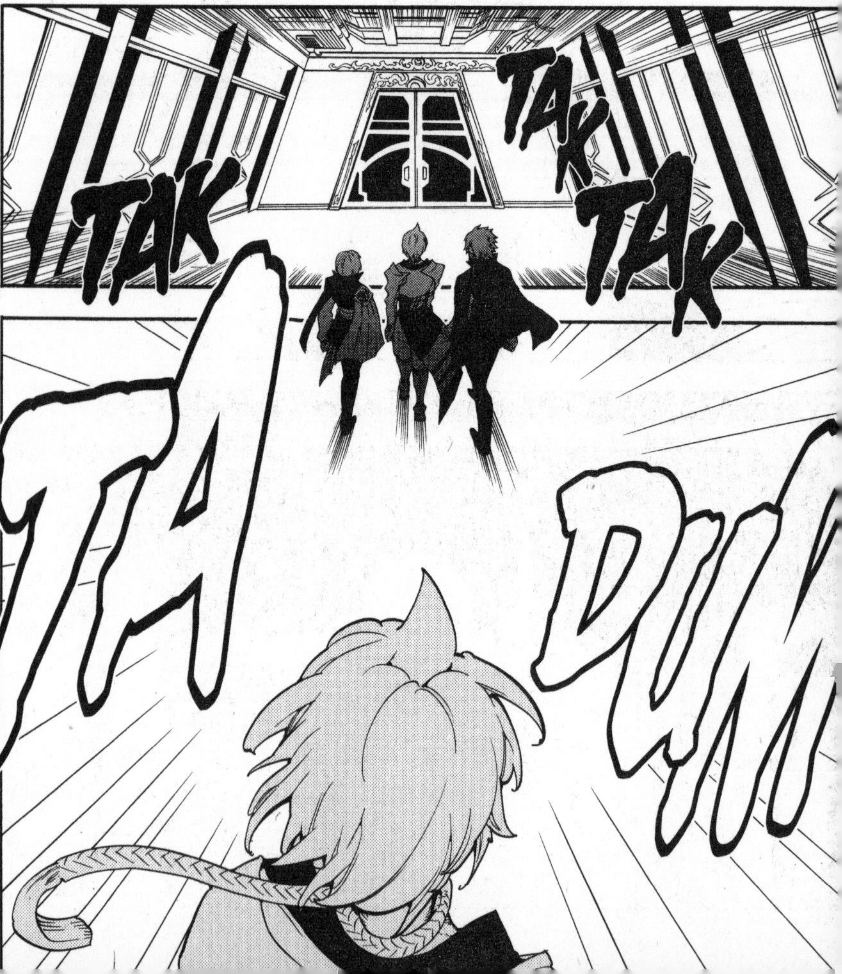
TAK
TAK
TAK
TA DUM

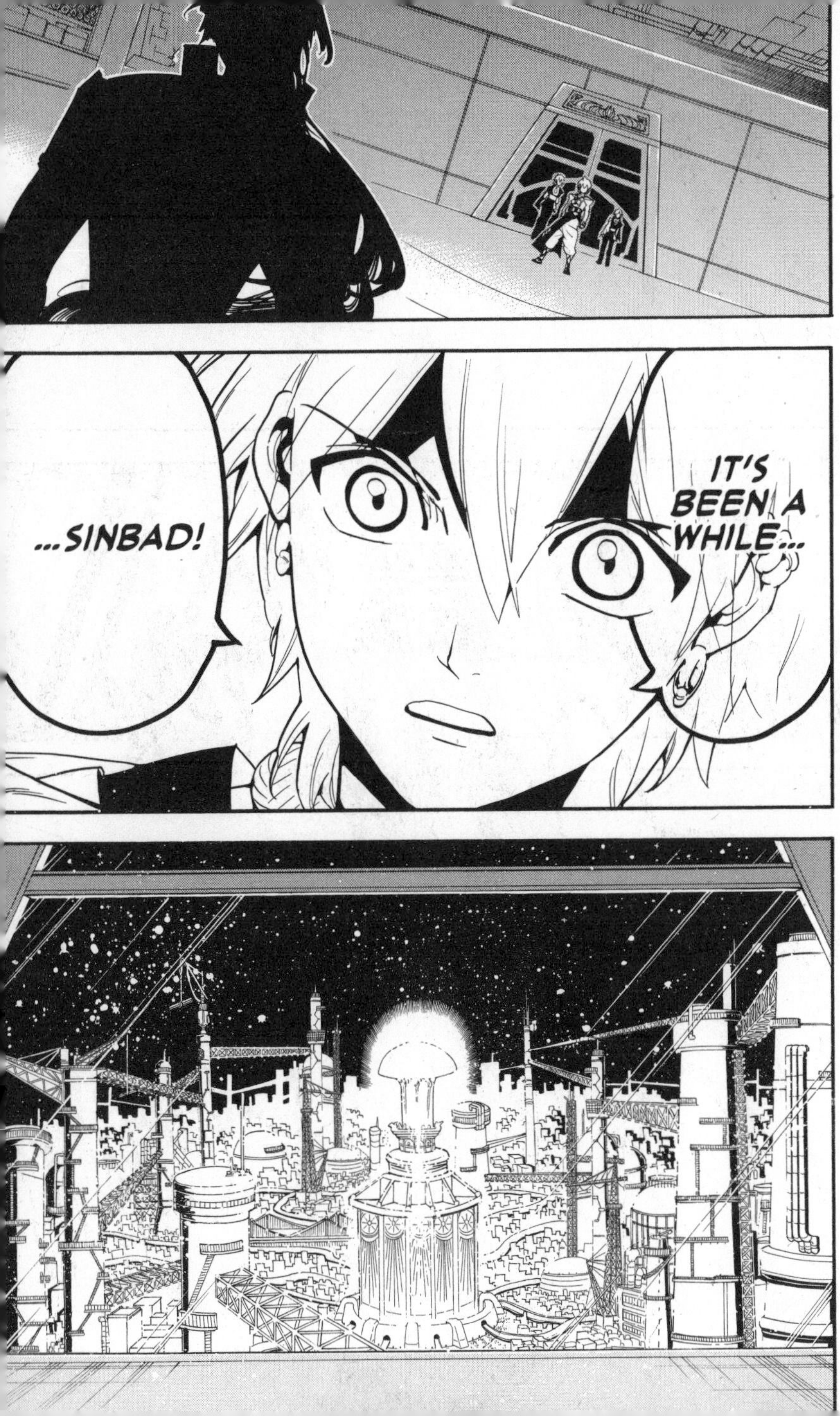
IT'S BEEN A WHILE...
...SINBAD!

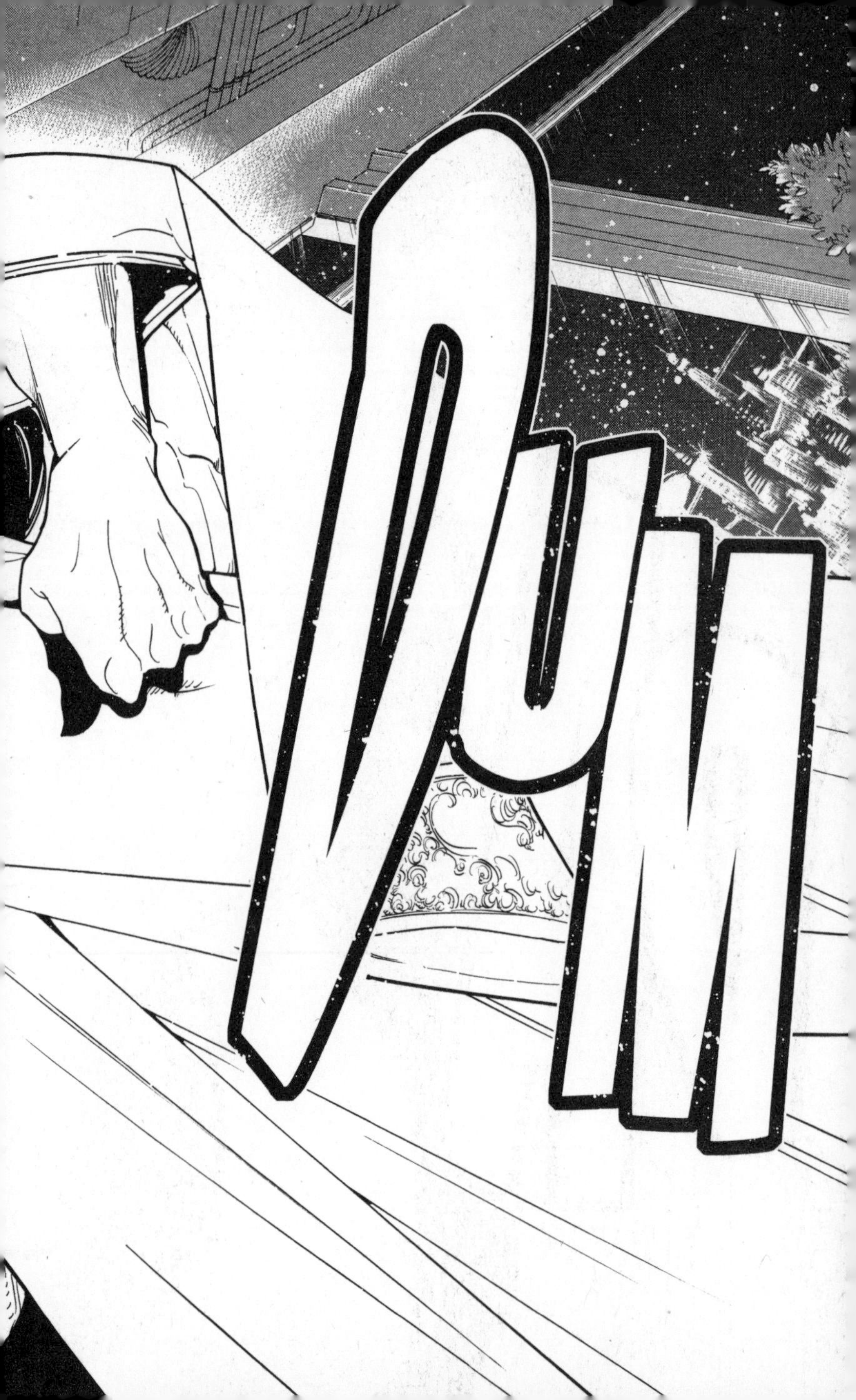
VUM

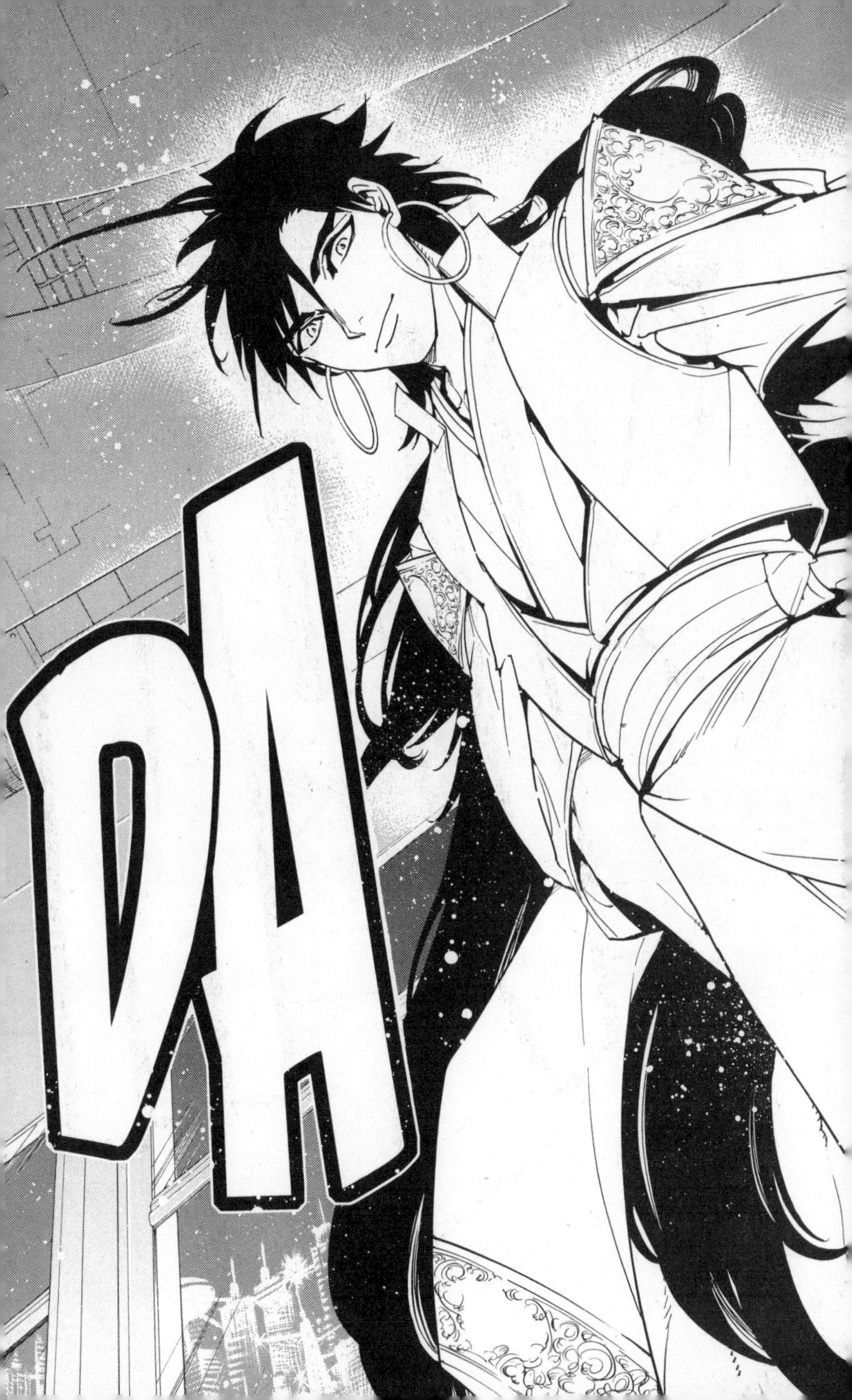
DA

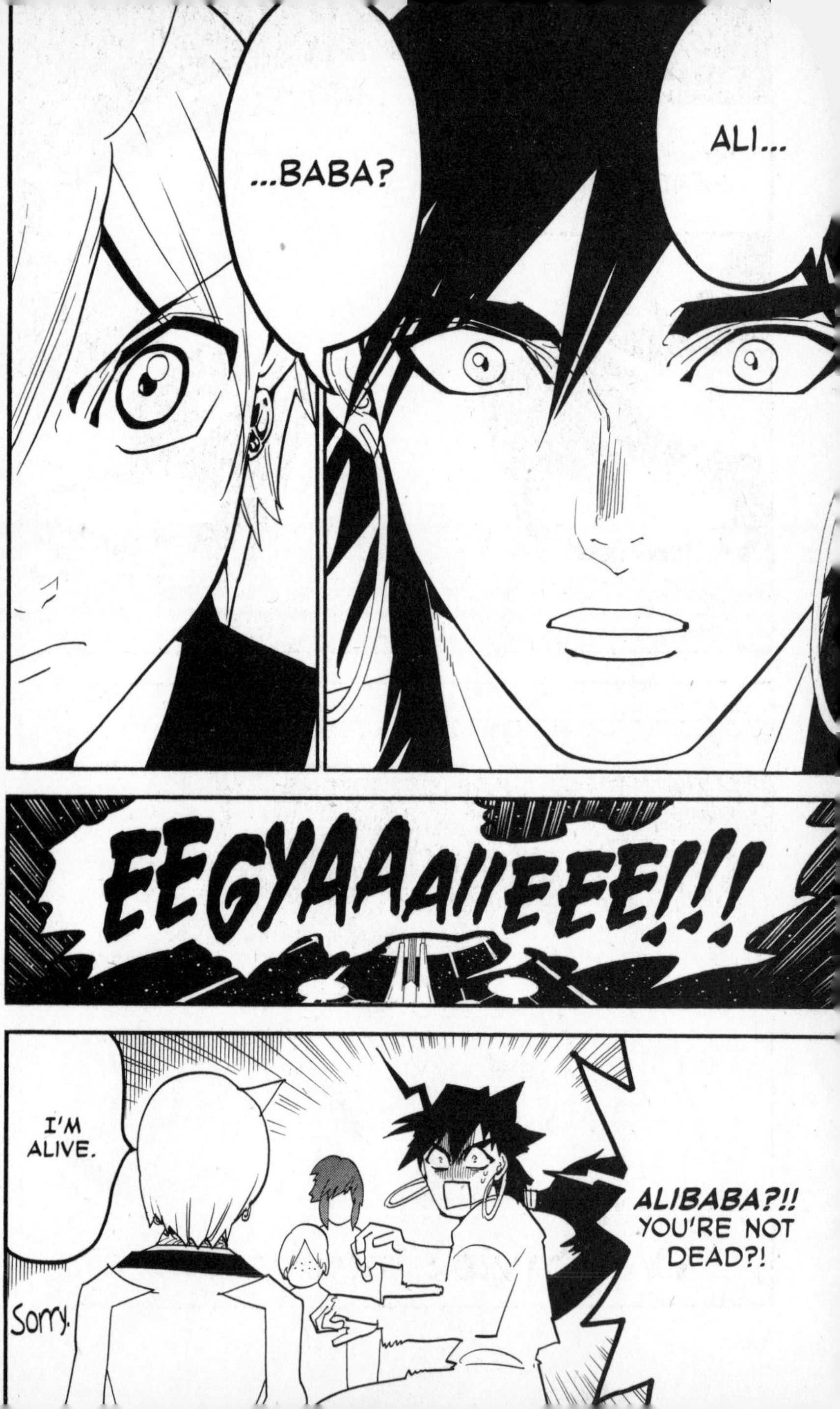
ALI...
...BABA?
EEGYAAAIIEEE!!!
ALIBABA?!! YOU'RE NOT DEAD?!
I'M ALIVE.
Sorry.

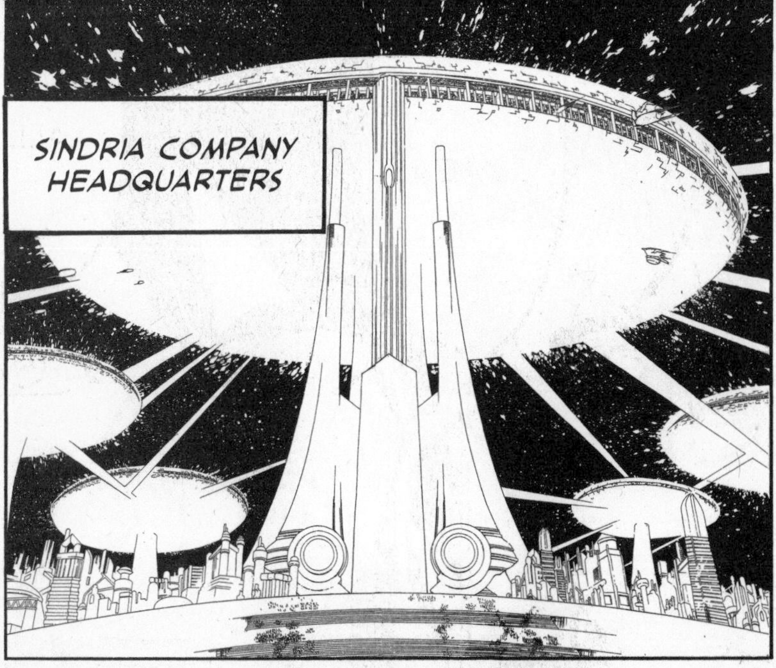
SINDRIA COMPANY HEADQUARTERS
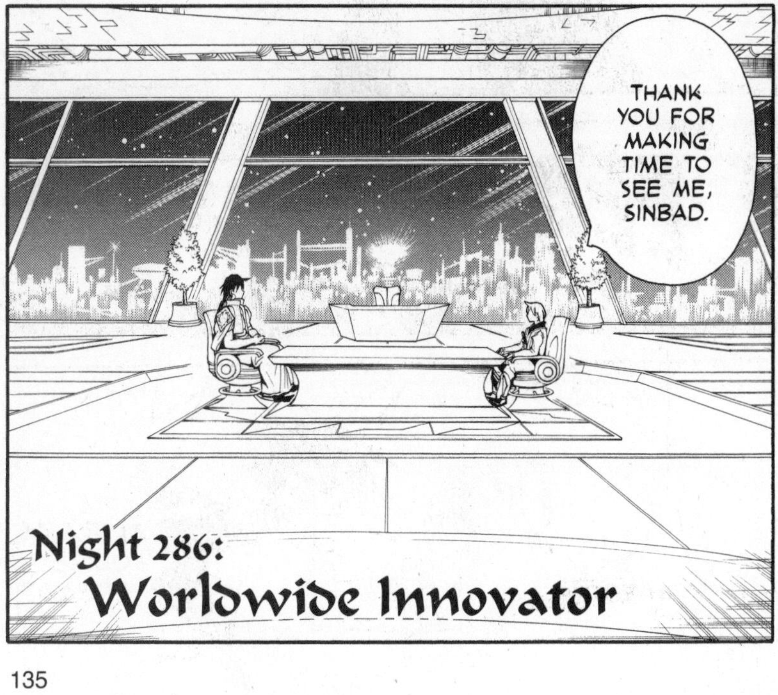
THANK YOU FOR MAKING TIME TO SEE ME, SINBAD.
Night 286:
Worldwide Innovator

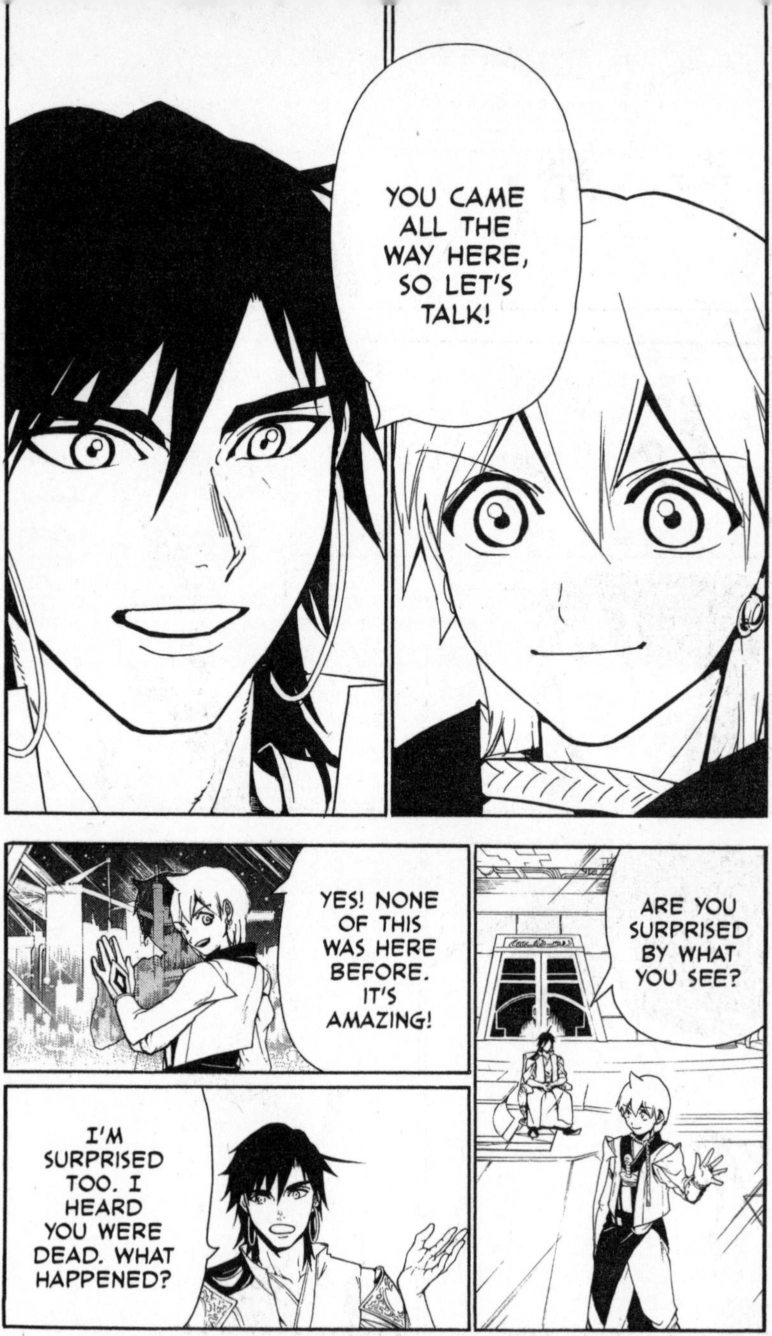
YOU CAME ALL THE WAY HERE, SO LET'S TALK!
ARE YOU SURPRISED BY WHAT YOU SEE?
YES! NONE OF THIS WAS HERE BEFORE. IT'S AMAZING!
I'M SURPRISED TOO. I HEARD YOU WERE DEAD. WHAT HAPPENED?

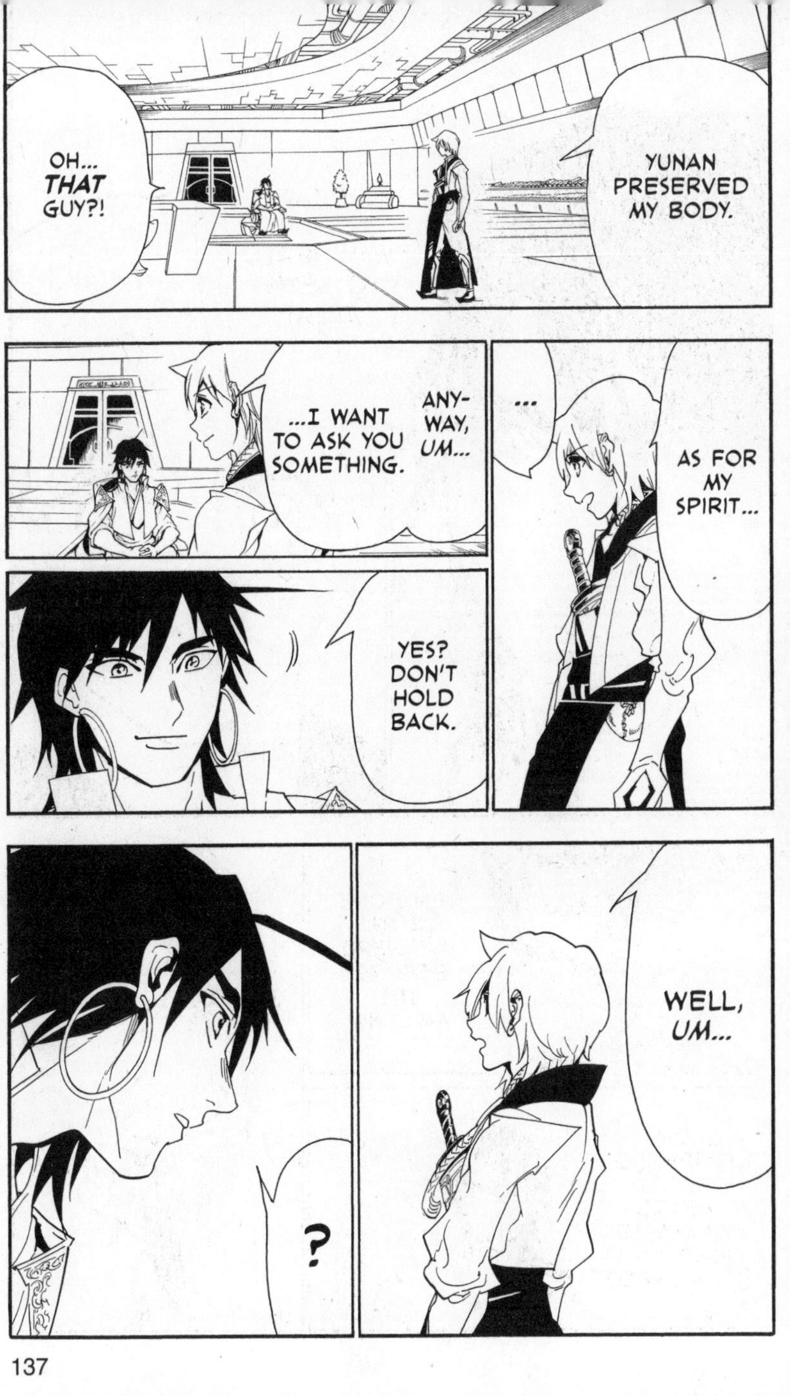
YUNAN PRESERVED MY BODY.
OH... *THAT* GUY?!
AS FOR MY SPIRIT...
...
ANY-WAY, *UM*...
...I WANT TO ASK YOU SOMETHING.
YES? DON'T HOLD BACK.
WELL, *UM*...
?

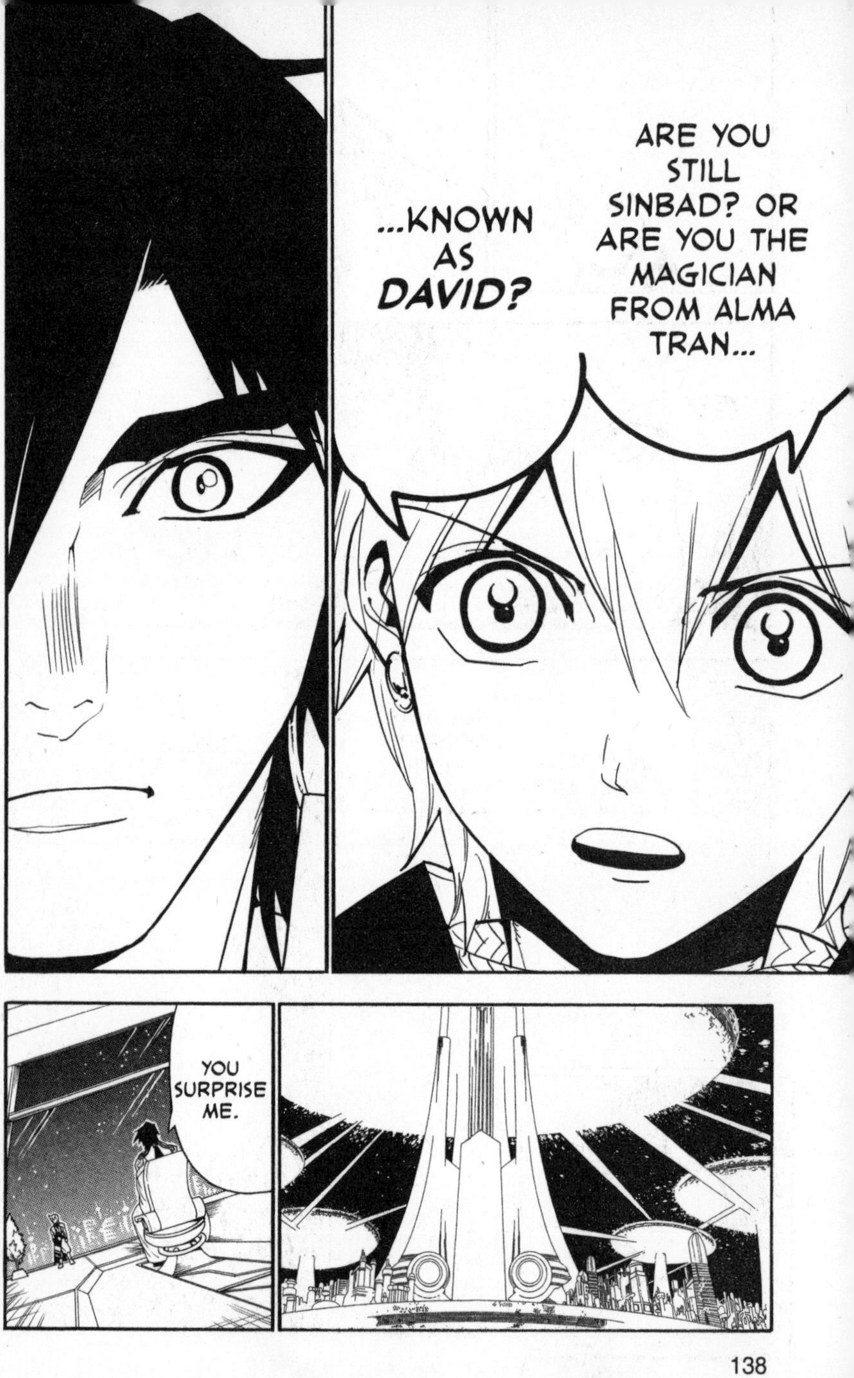
ARE YOU STILL SINBAD? OR ARE YOU THE MAGICIAN FROM ALMA TRAN...
...KNOWN AS *DAVID?*
YOU SURPRISE ME.

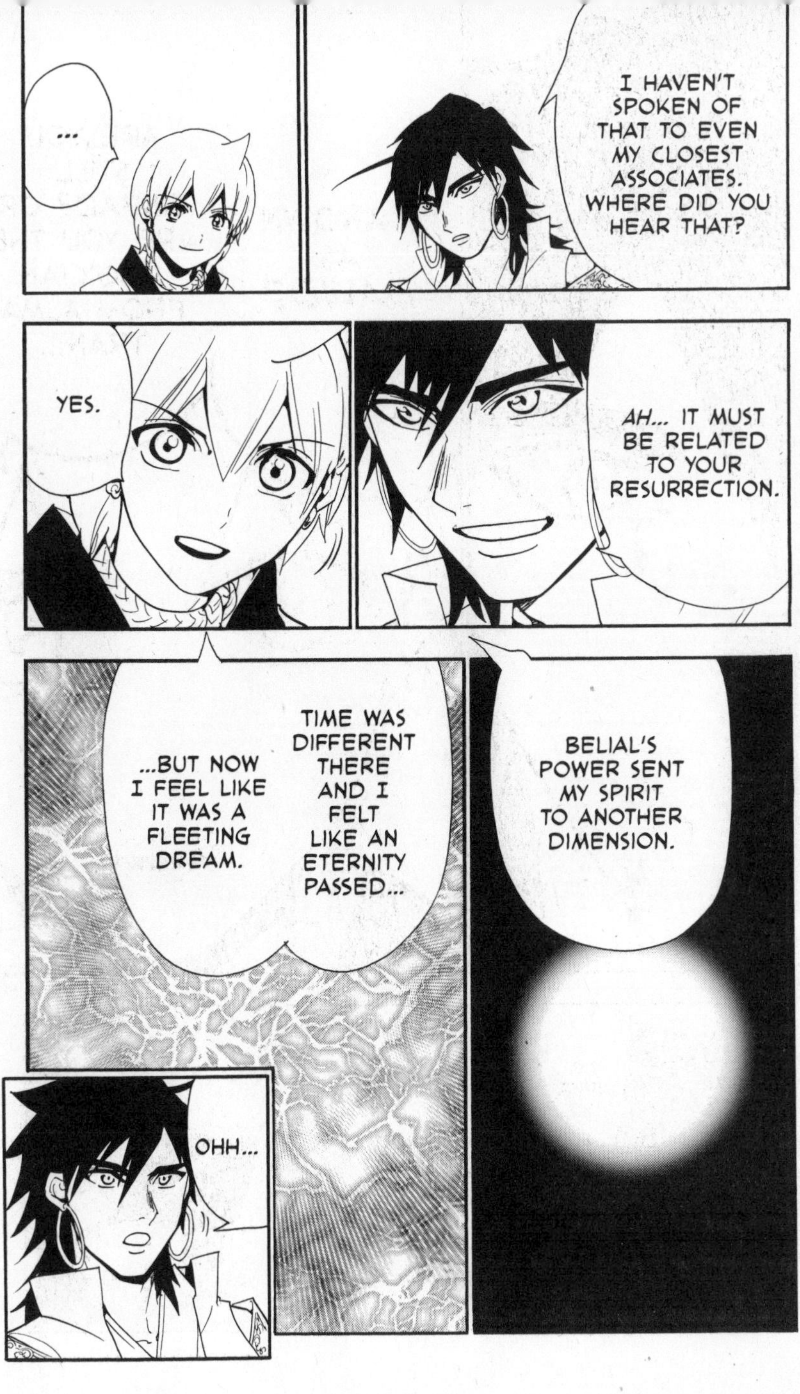
I HAVEN'T SPOKEN OF THAT TO EVEN MY CLOSEST ASSOCIATES. WHERE DID YOU HEAR THAT?
...
AH... IT MUST BE RELATED TO YOUR RESURRECTION.
YES.
BELIAL'S POWER SENT MY SPIRIT TO ANOTHER DIMENSION.
TIME WAS DIFFERENT THERE AND I FELT LIKE AN ETERNITY PASSED...
...BUT NOW I FEEL LIKE IT WAS A FLEETING DREAM.
OHH...

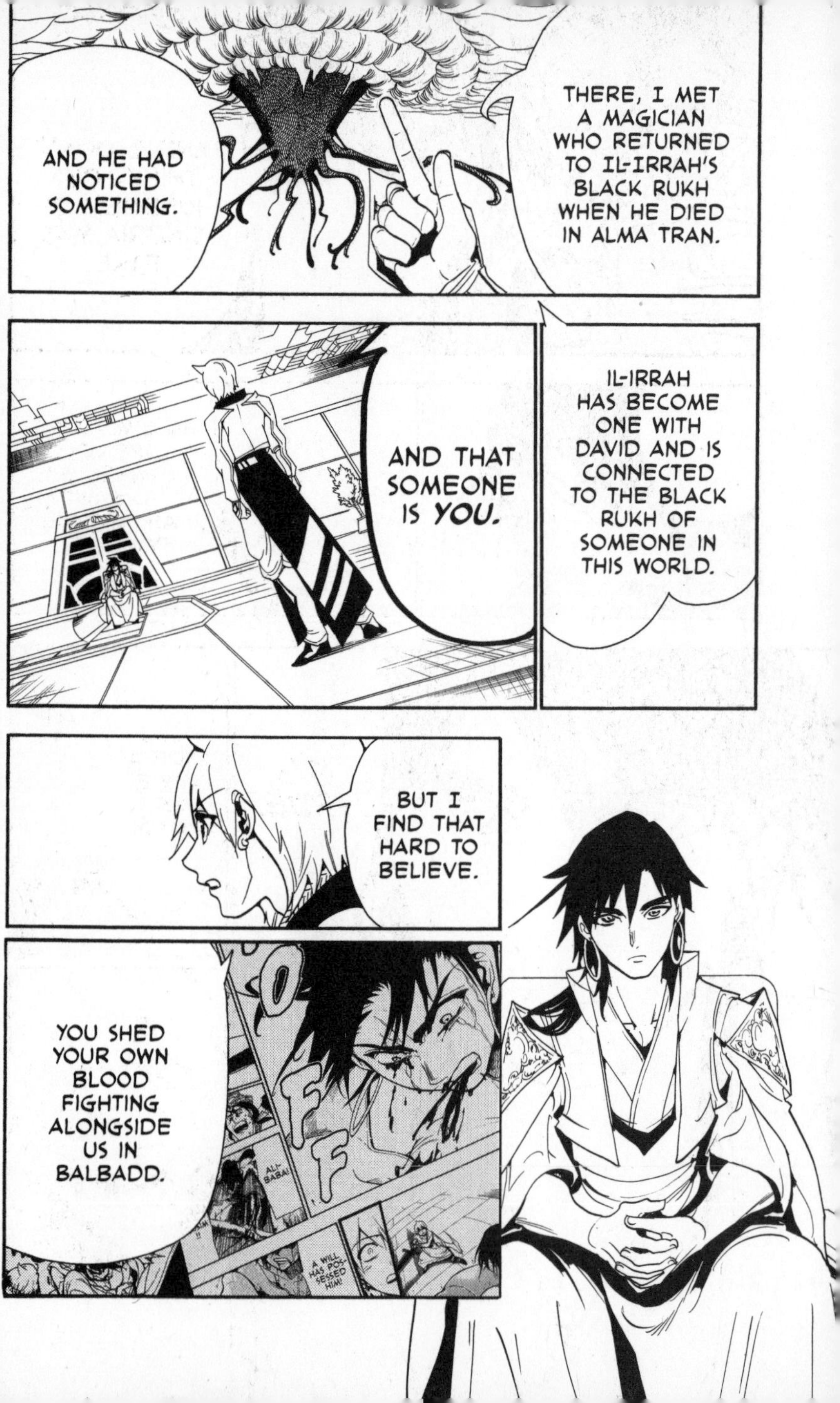
THERE, I MET A MAGICIAN WHO RETURNED TO IL-IRRAH'S BLACK RUKH WHEN HE DIED IN ALMA TRAN.
AND HE HAD NOTICED SOMETHING.
IL-IRRAH HAS BECOME ONE WITH DAVID AND IS CONNECTED TO THE BLACK RUKH OF SOMEONE IN THIS WORLD.
AND THAT SOMEONE IS *YOU.*
BUT I FIND THAT HARD TO BELIEVE.
YOU SHED YOUR OWN BLOOD FIGHTING ALONGSIDE US IN BALBADD.
AL-BABA!
A WILL HAS POS-SESSED HIM!

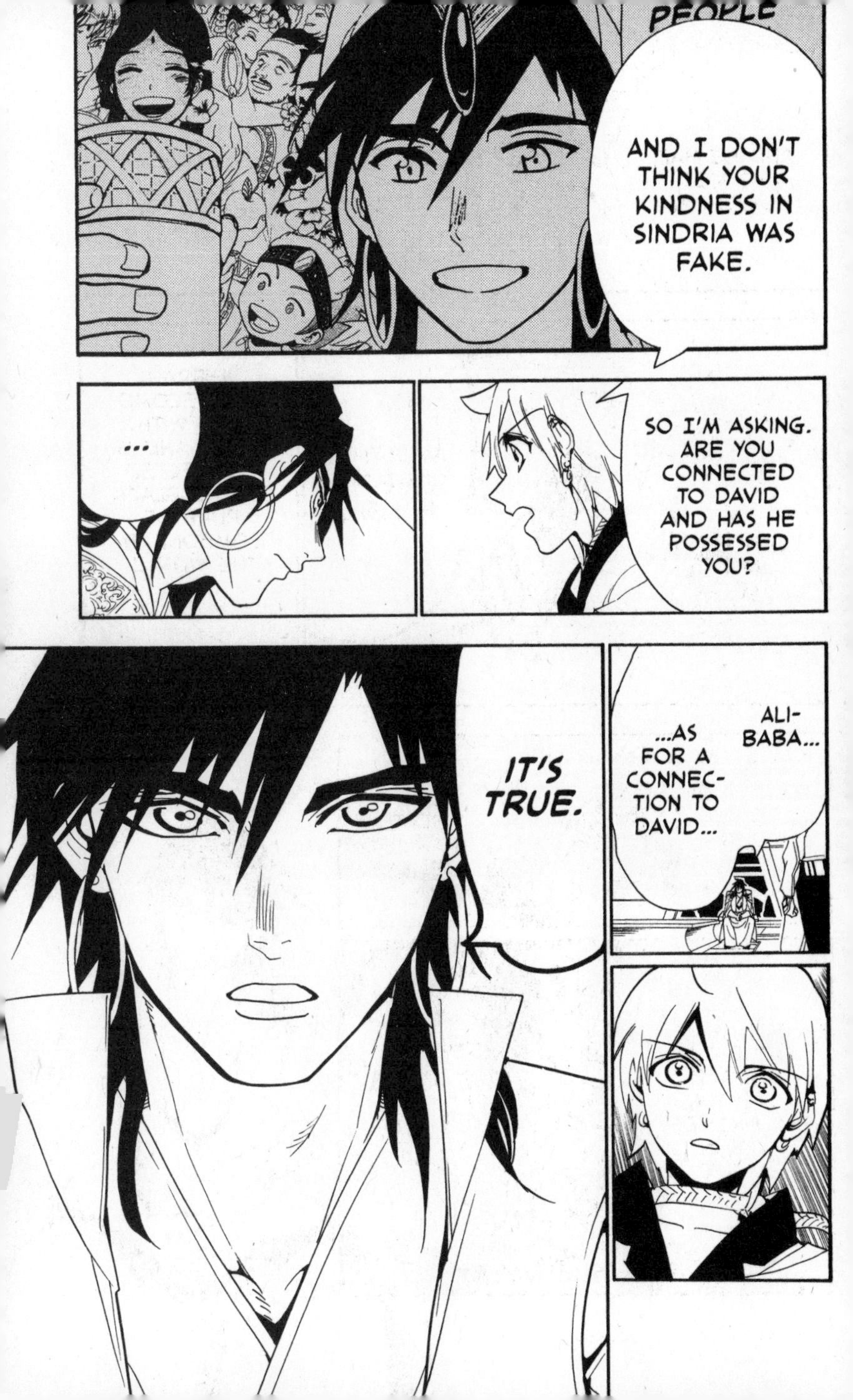
PEOPLE
AND I DON'T THINK YOUR KINDNESS IN SINDRIA WAS FAKE.
SO I'M ASKING. ARE YOU CONNECTED TO DAVID AND HAS HE POSSESSED YOU?
...
ALI-BABA...
...AS FOR A CONNECTION TO DAVID...
IT'S TRUE.

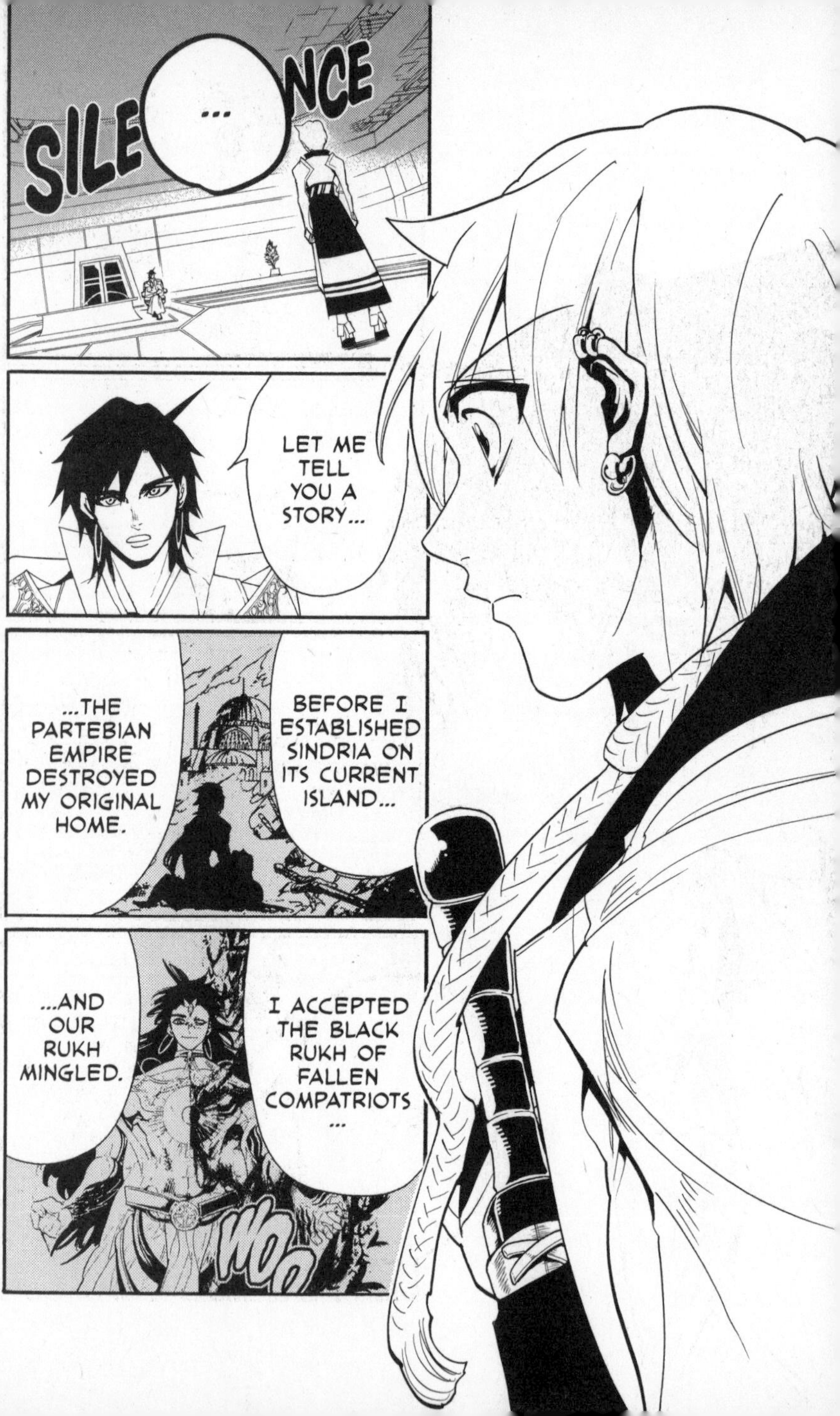
SILENCE
...
LET ME TELL YOU A STORY...
BEFORE I ESTABLISHED SINDRIA ON ITS CURRENT ISLAND...
...THE PARTEBIAN EMPIRE DESTROYED MY ORIGINAL HOME.
I ACCEPTED THE BLACK RUKH OF FALLEN COMPATRIOTS ...
...AND OUR RUKH MINGLED.
WOO

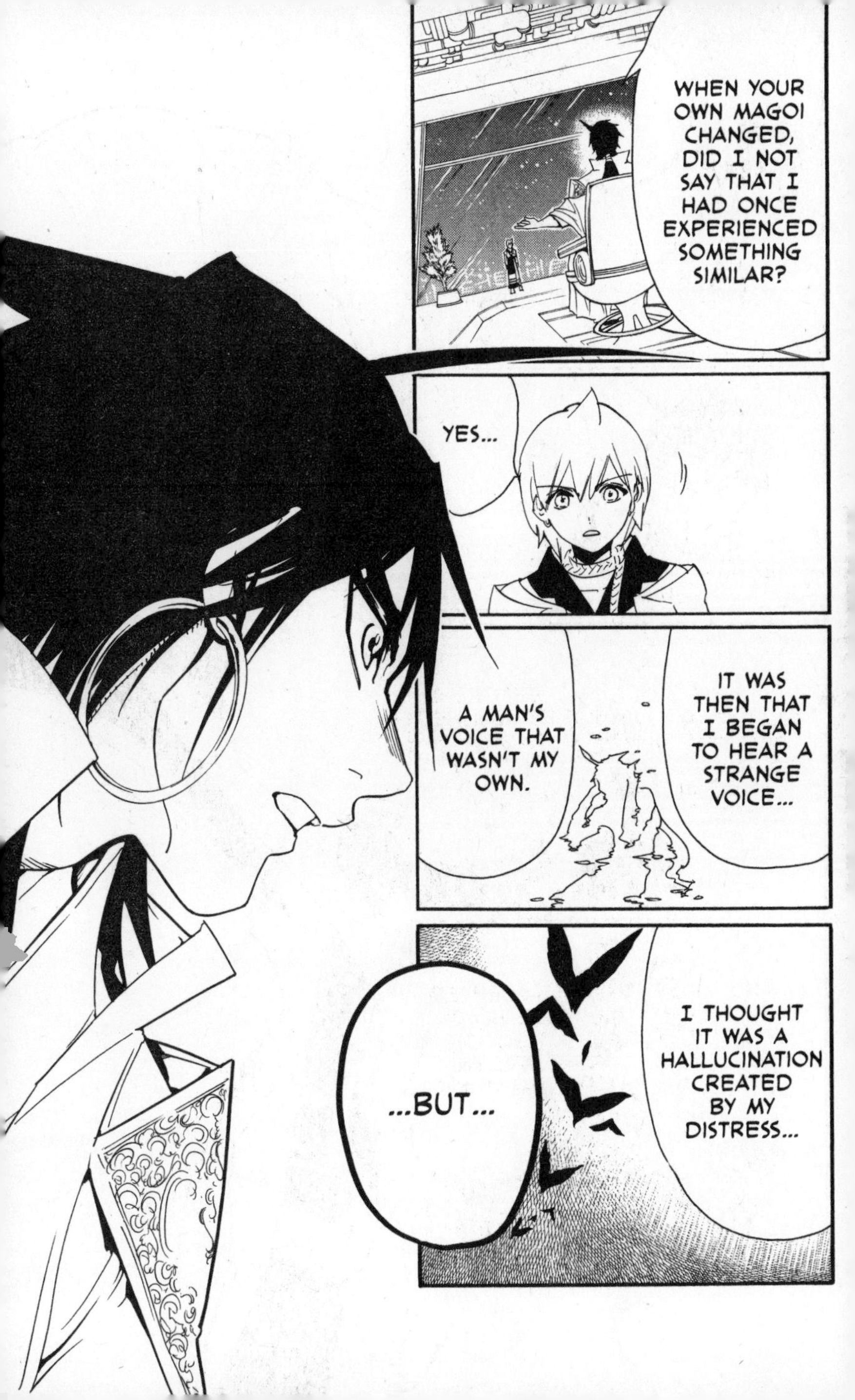
WHEN YOUR OWN MAGOI CHANGED, DID I NOT SAY THAT I HAD ONCE EXPERIENCED SOMETHING SIMILAR?
YES...
IT WAS THEN THAT I BEGAN TO HEAR A STRANGE VOICE...
A MAN'S VOICE THAT WASN'T MY OWN.
I THOUGHT IT WAS A HALLUCINATION CREATED BY MY DISTRESS...
...BUT...

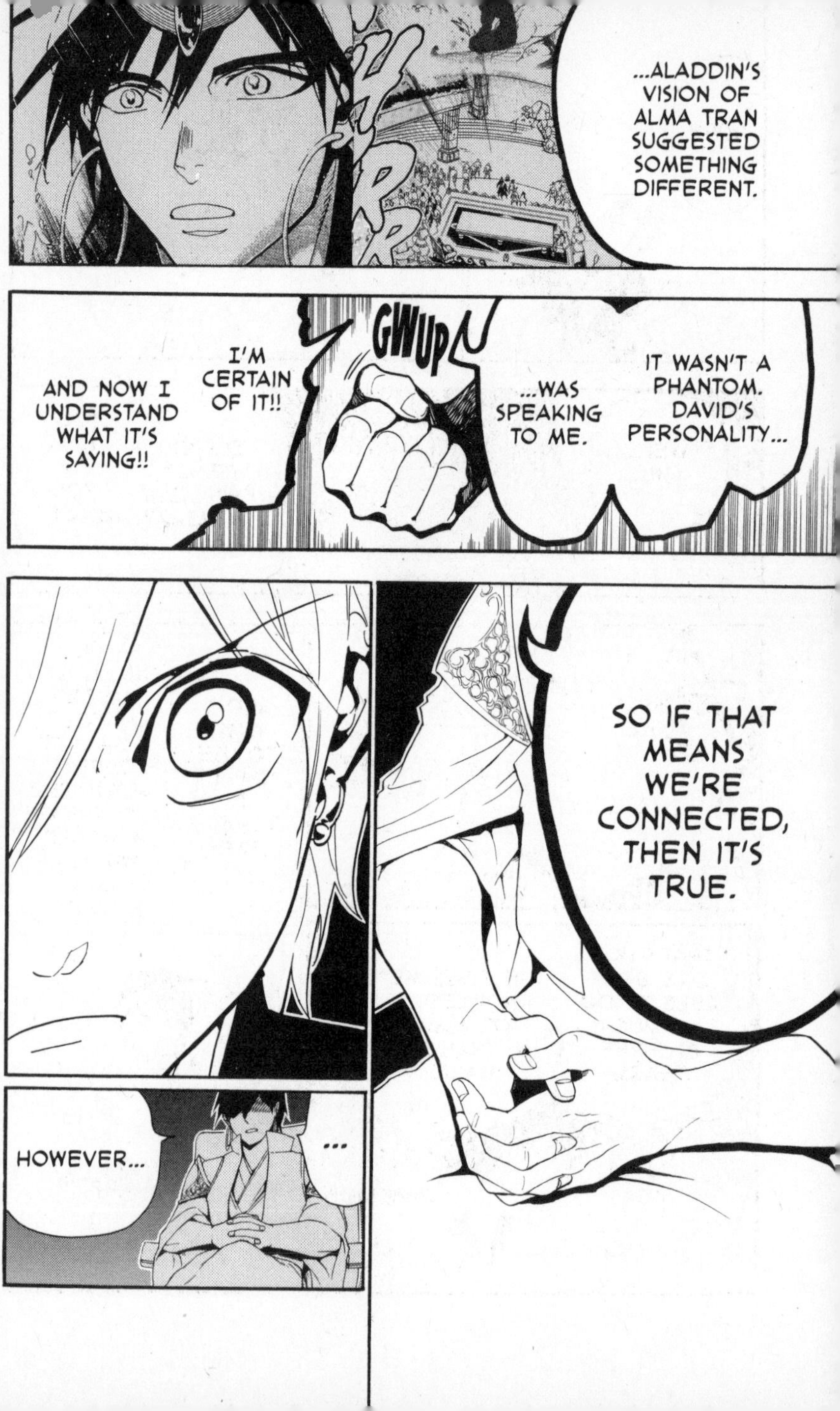
...ALADDIN'S VISION OF ALMA TRAN SUGGESTED SOMETHING DIFFERENT.
IT WASN'T A PHANTOM. DAVID'S PERSONALITY...
...WAS SPEAKING TO ME.
GWUP
I'M CERTAIN OF IT!!
AND NOW I UNDERSTAND WHAT IT'S SAYING!!
SO IF THAT MEANS WE'RE CONNECTED, THEN IT'S TRUE.
...
HOWEVER...

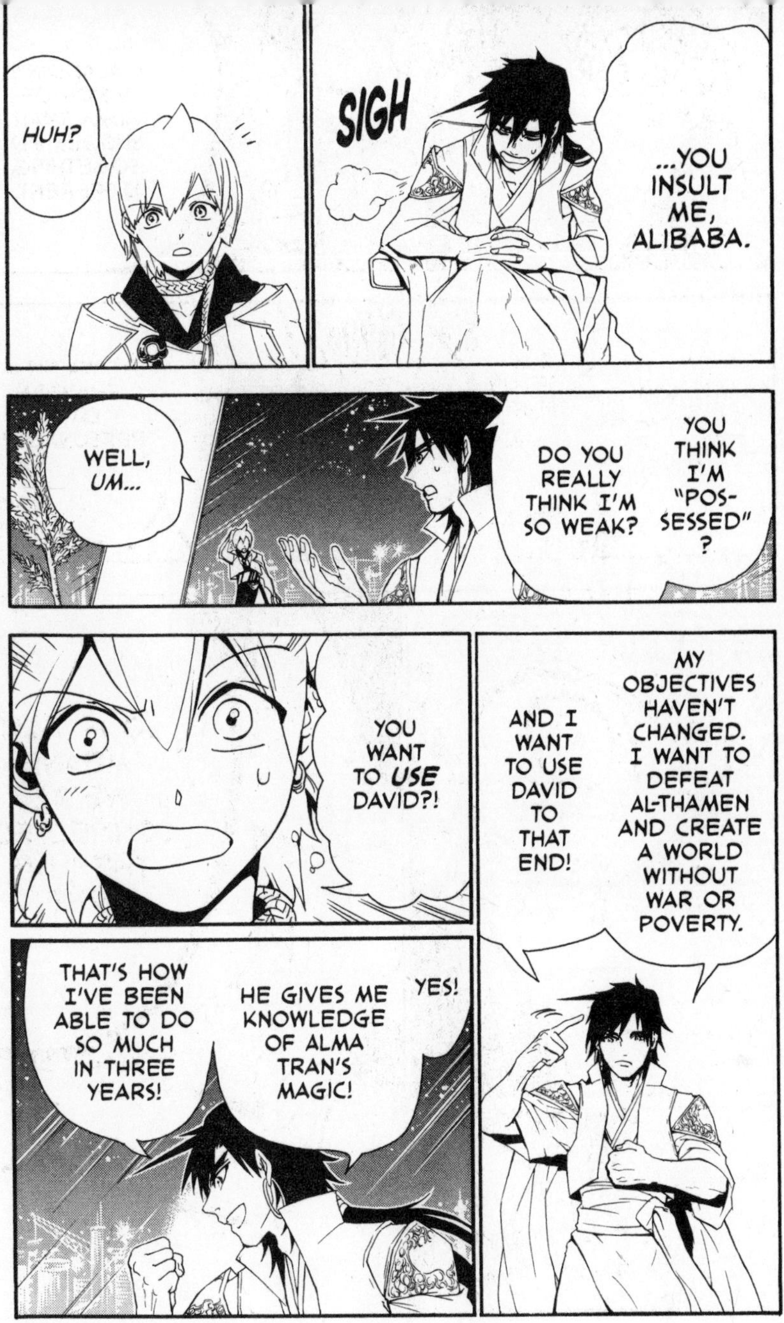
...YOU INSULT ME, ALIBABA.
SIGH
HUH?
YOU THINK I'M "POS-SESSED"?
DO YOU REALLY THINK I'M SO WEAK?
WELL, UM...
MY OBJECTIVES HAVEN'T CHANGED. I WANT TO DEFEAT AL-THAMEN AND CREATE A WORLD WITHOUT WAR OR POVERTY.
AND I WANT TO USE DAVID TO THAT END!
YOU WANT TO *USE* DAVID?!
YES!
HE GIVES ME KNOWLEDGE OF ALMA TRAN'S MAGIC!
THAT'S HOW I'VE BEEN ABLE TO DO SO MUCH IN THREE YEARS!

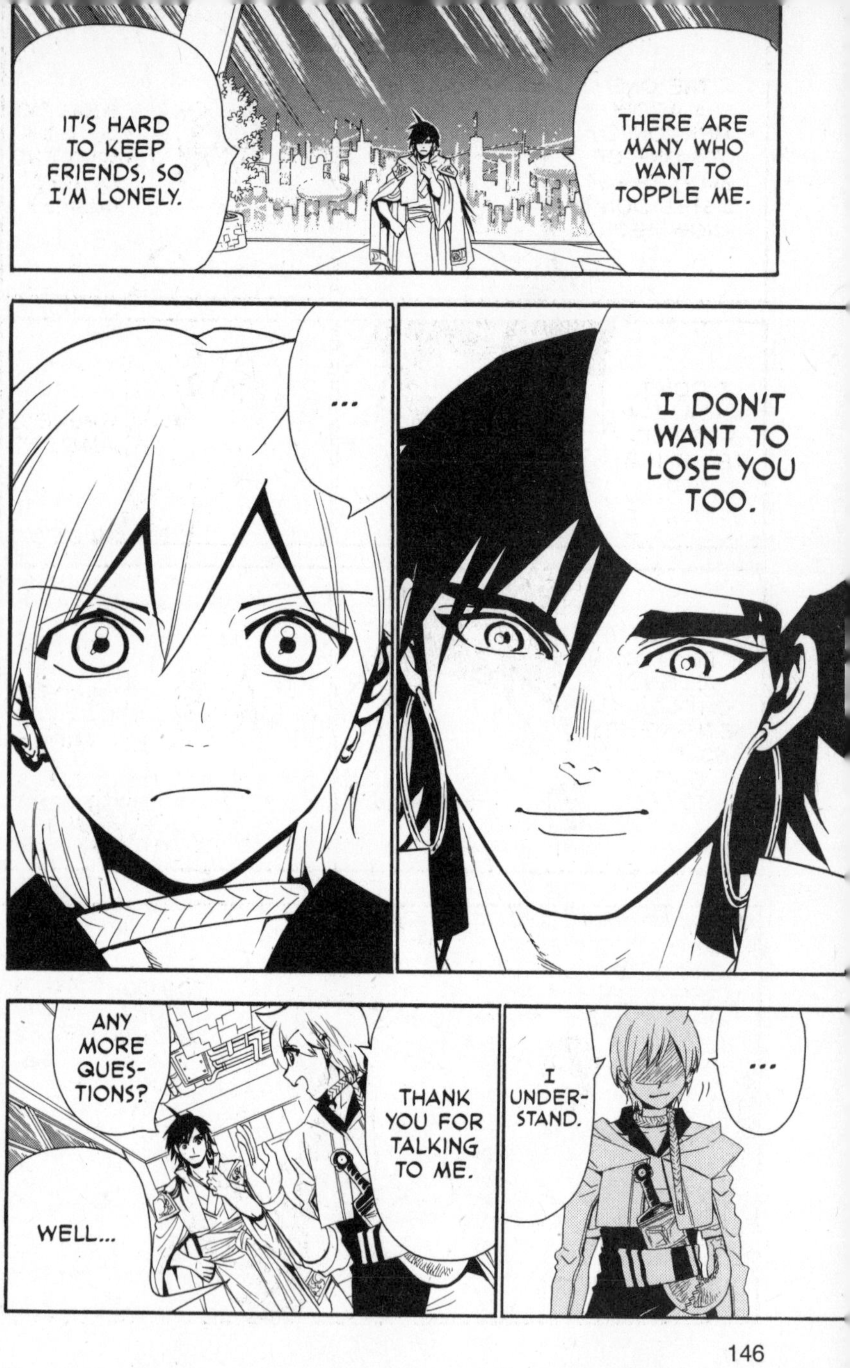
THERE ARE MANY WHO WANT TO TOPPLE ME.
IT'S HARD TO KEEP FRIENDS, SO I'M LONELY.
I DON'T WANT TO LOSE YOU TOO.
...
...
I UNDERSTAND.
THANK YOU FOR TALKING TO ME.
ANY MORE QUES-TIONS?
WELL...

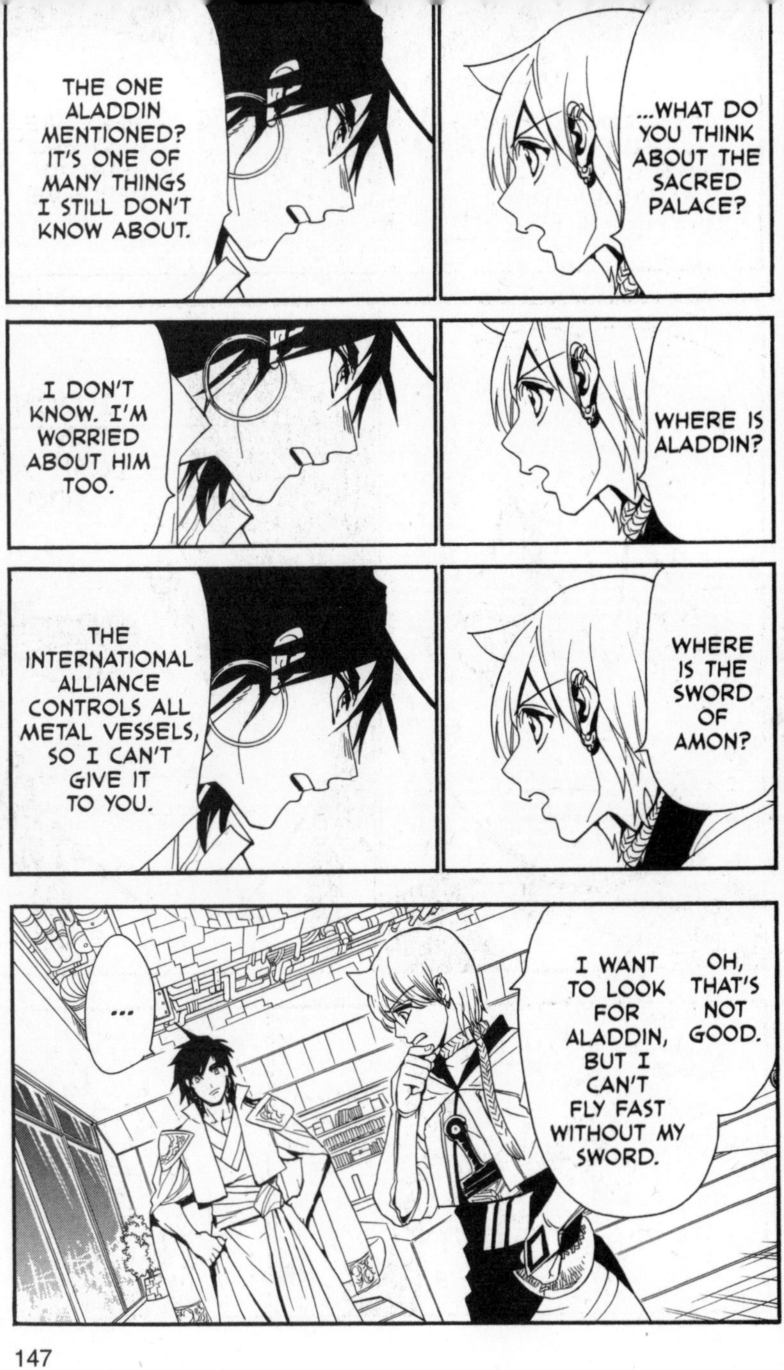
...WHAT DO YOU THINK ABOUT THE SACRED PALACE?
THE ONE ALADDIN MENTIONED? IT'S ONE OF MANY THINGS I STILL DON'T KNOW ABOUT.
WHERE IS ALADDIN?
I DON'T KNOW. I'M WORRIED ABOUT HIM TOO.
WHERE IS THE SWORD OF AMON?
THE INTERNATIONAL ALLIANCE CONTROLS ALL METAL VESSELS, SO I CAN'T GIVE IT TO YOU.
OH, THAT'S NOT GOOD.
I WANT TO LOOK FOR ALADDIN, BUT I CAN'T FLY FAST WITHOUT MY SWORD.
...

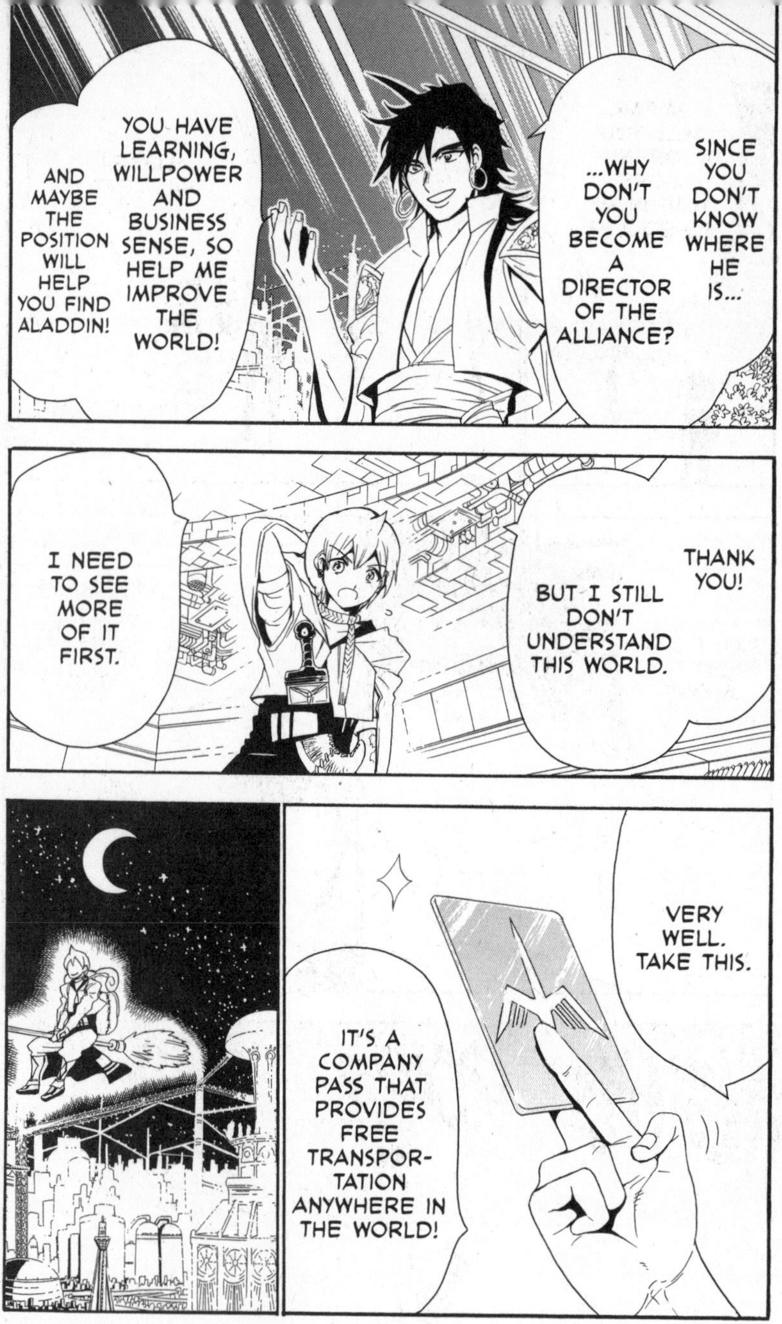
SINCE YOU DON'T KNOW WHERE HE IS...
...WHY DON'T YOU BECOME A DIRECTOR OF THE ALLIANCE?
YOU HAVE LEARNING, WILLPOWER AND BUSINESS SENSE, SO HELP ME IMPROVE THE WORLD!
AND MAYBE THE POSITION WILL HELP YOU FIND ALADDIN!
THANK YOU!
BUT I STILL DON'T UNDERSTAND THIS WORLD.
I NEED TO SEE MORE OF IT FIRST.
VERY WELL. TAKE THIS.
IT'S A COMPANY PASS THAT PROVIDES FREE TRANSPOR-TATION ANYWHERE IN THE WORLD!

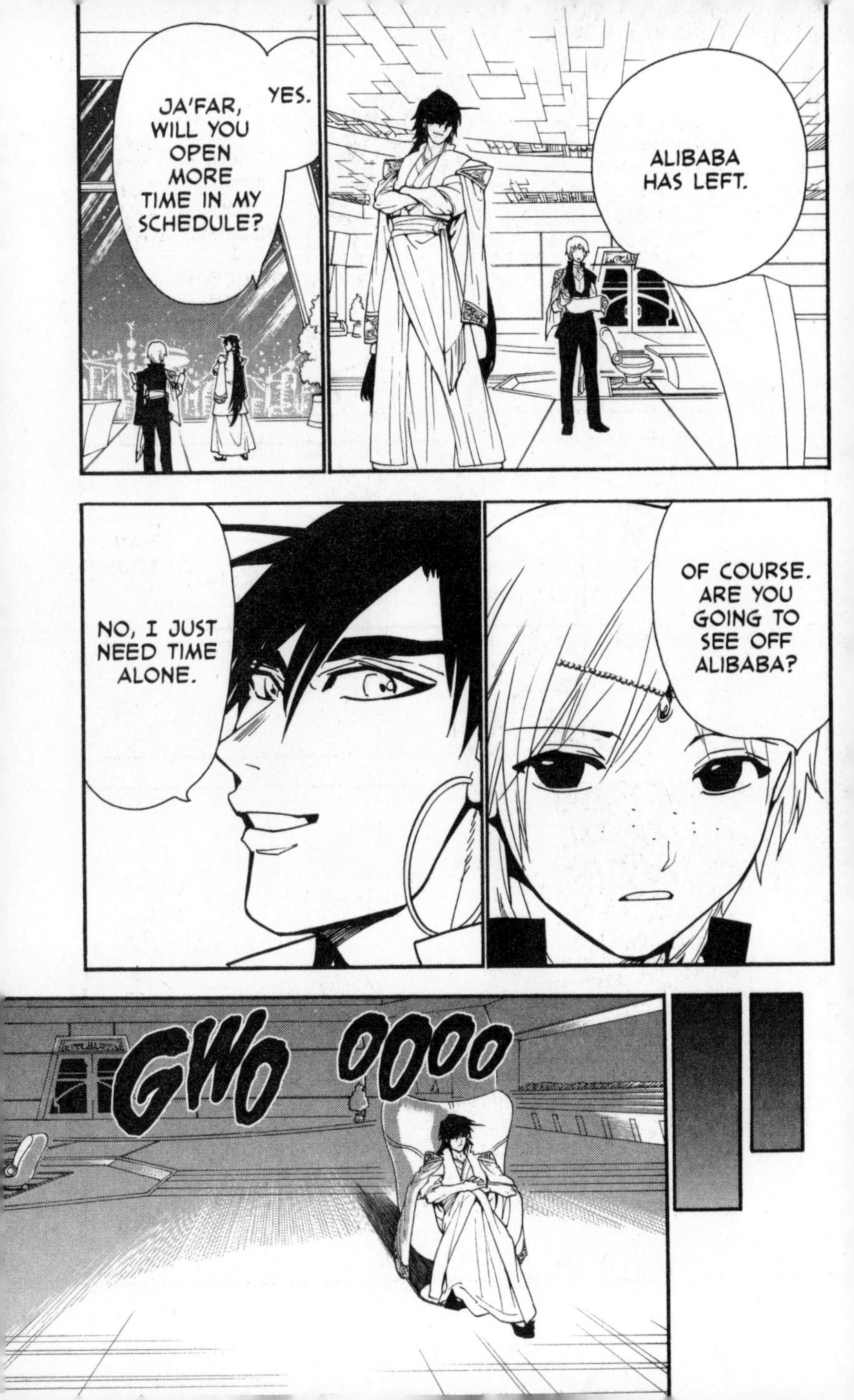
ALIBABA HAS LEFT.
YES.
JA'FAR, WILL YOU OPEN MORE TIME IN MY SCHEDULE?
OF COURSE. ARE YOU GOING TO SEE OFF ALIBABA?
NO, I JUST NEED TIME ALONE.
GWOOOOO

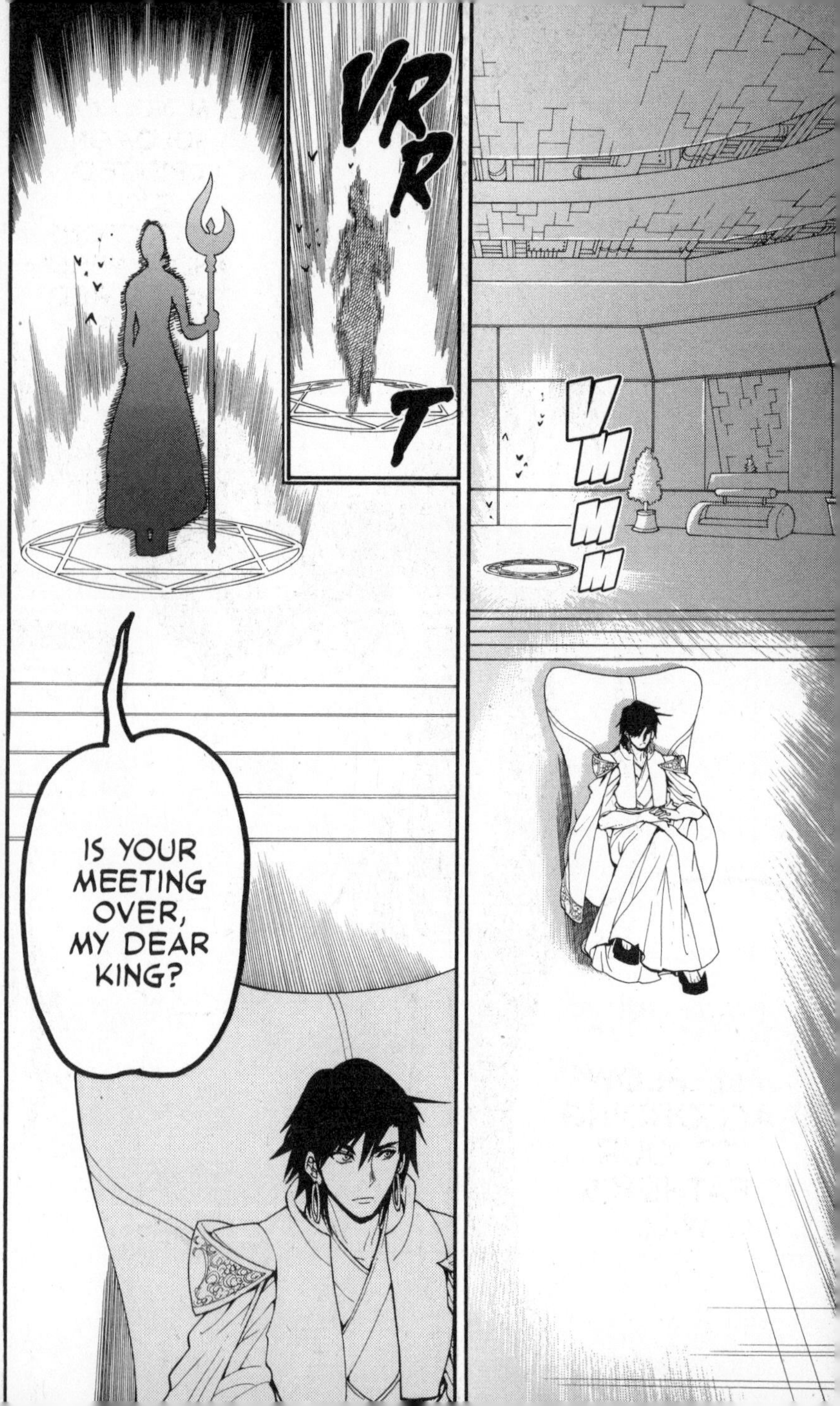
VMMM
VRR
T
IS YOUR MEETING OVER, MY DEAR KING?

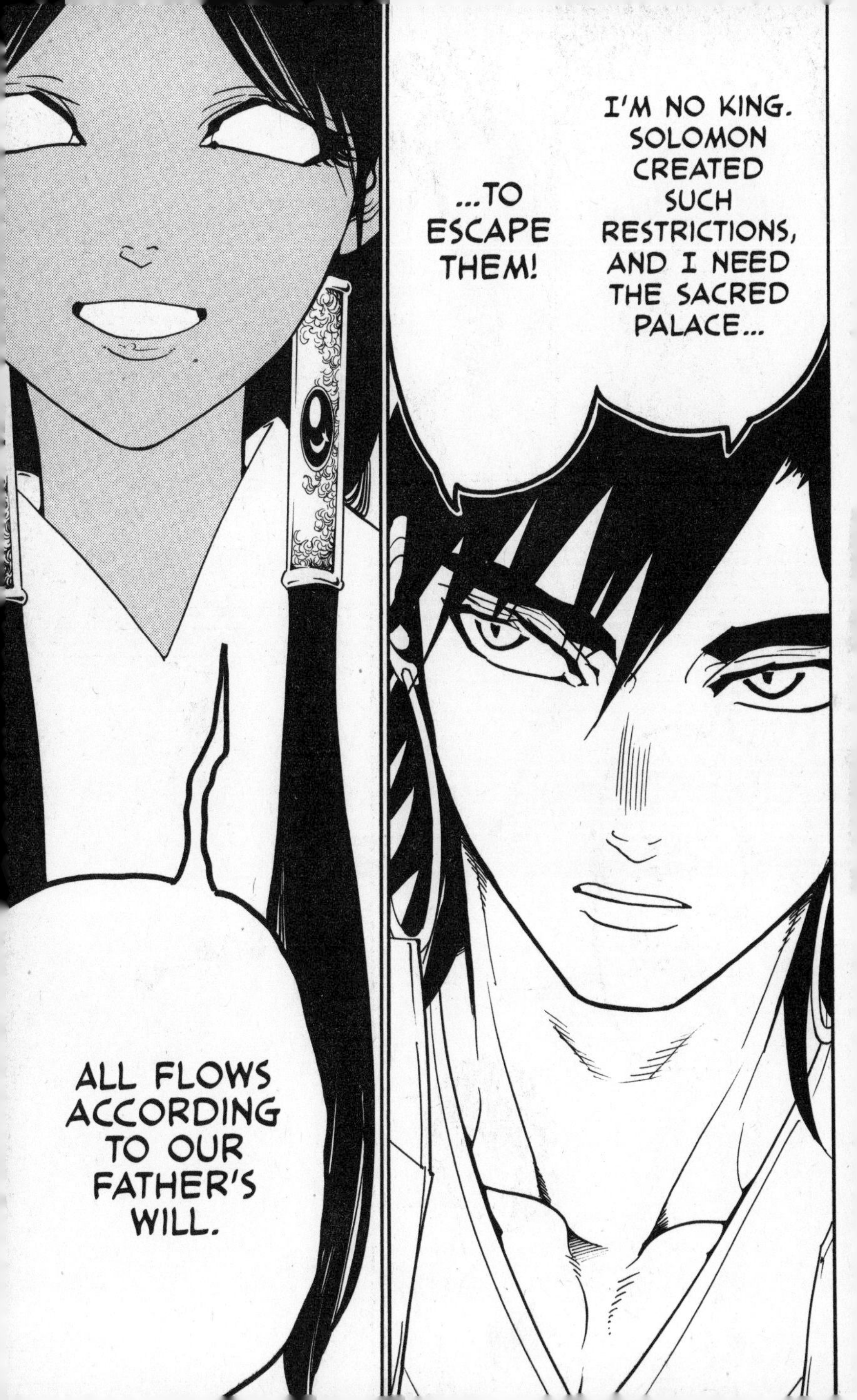
I'M NO KING. SOLOMON CREATED SUCH RESTRICTIONS, AND I NEED THE SACRED PALACE...
...TO ESCAPE THEM!
ALL FLOWS ACCORDING TO OUR FATHER'S WILL.

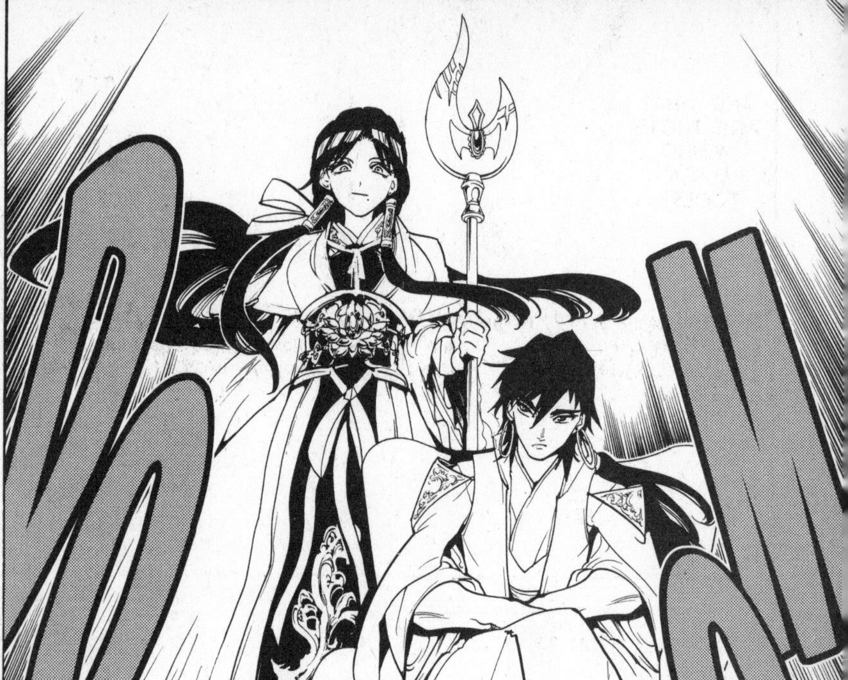

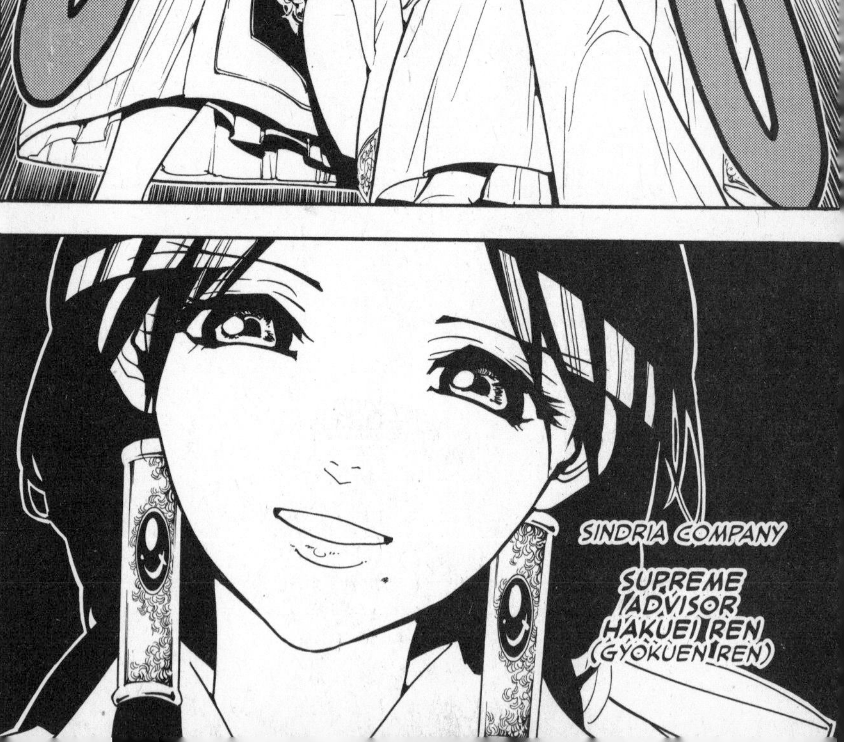
SINDRIA COMPANY
SUPREME ADVISOR HAKUEI REN (GYOKUEN REN)

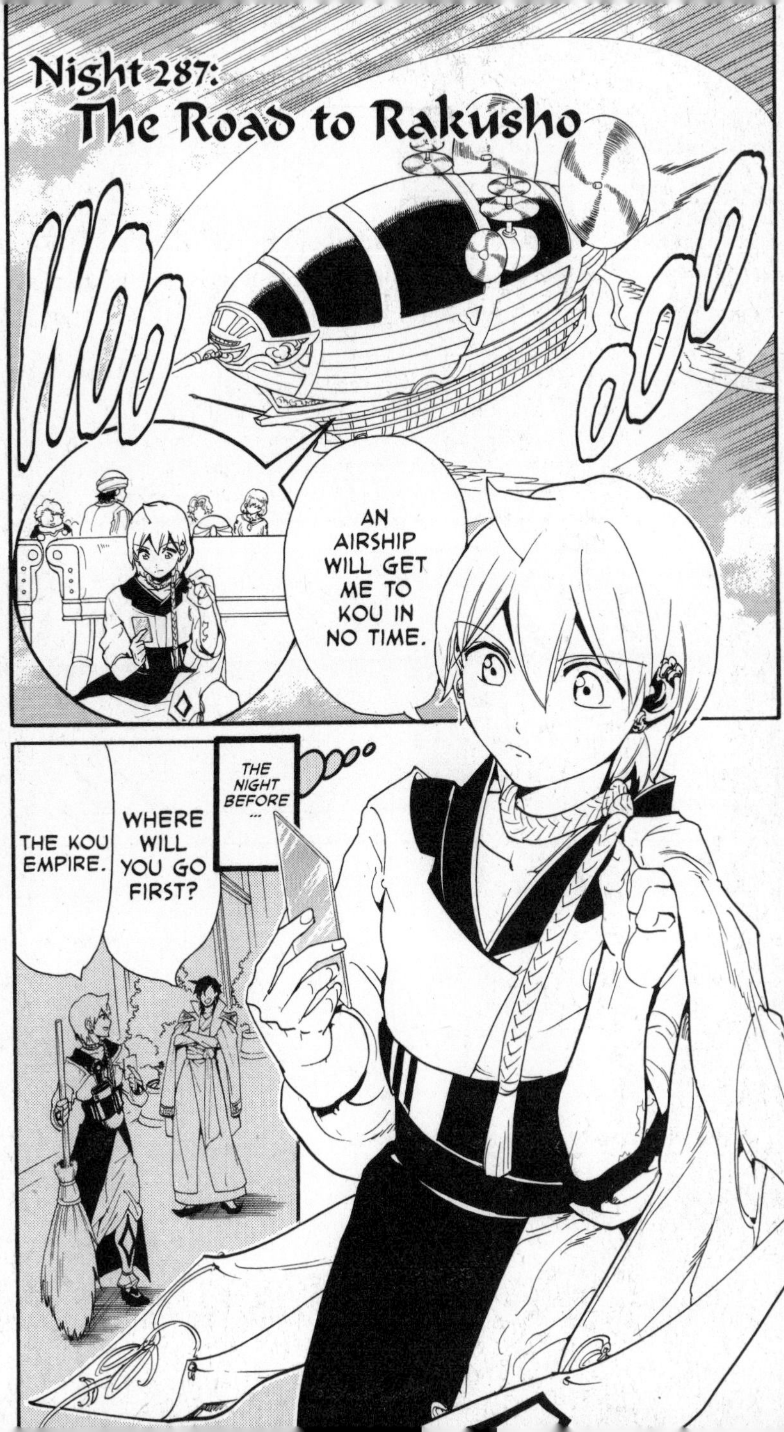
Night 287:
The Road to Rakusho
WOOOOOOO
AN AIRSHIP WILL GET ME TO KOU IN NO TIME.
THE NIGHT BEFORE...
WHERE WILL YOU GO FIRST?
THE KOU EMPIRE.

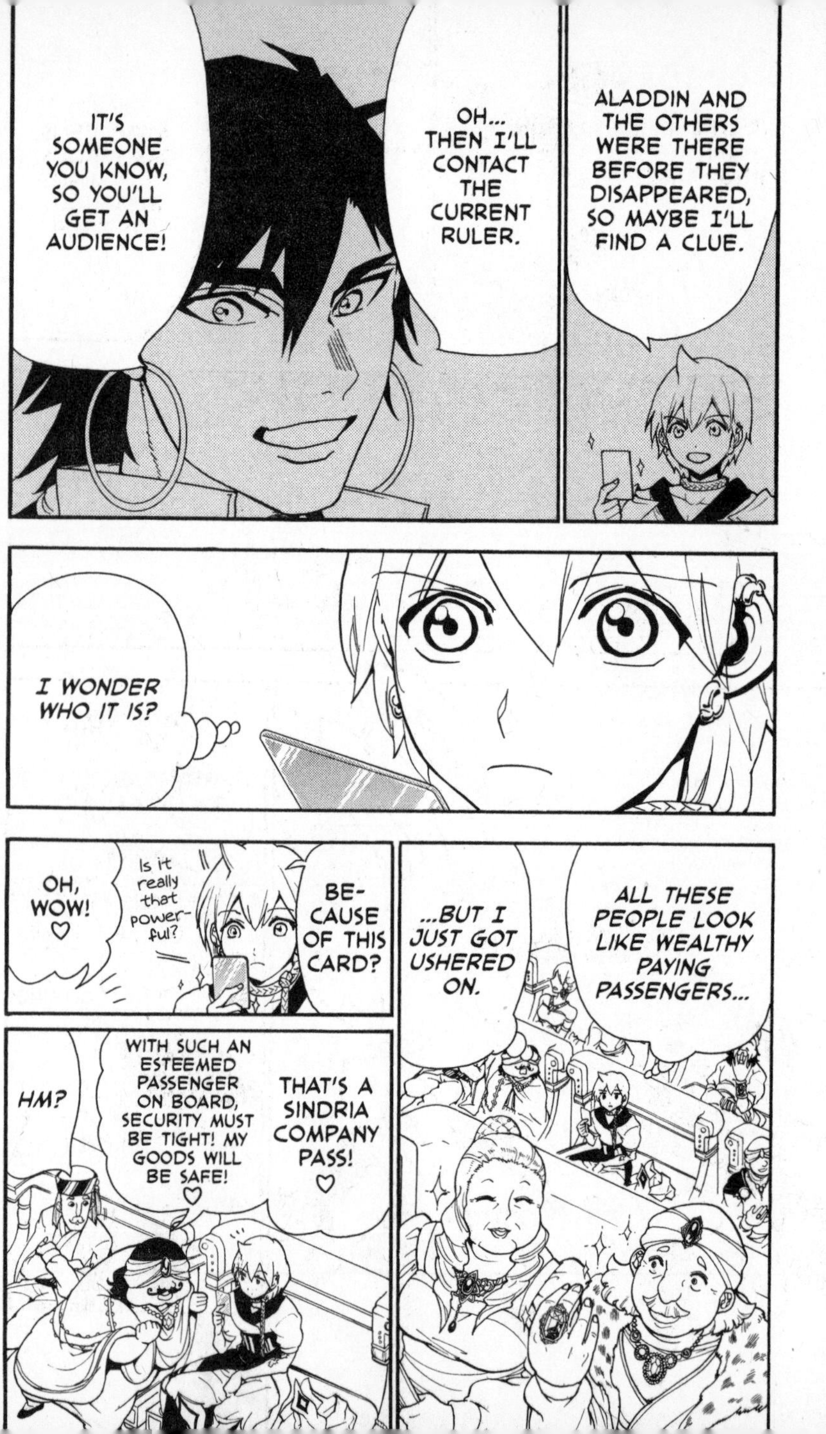
ALADDIN AND THE OTHERS WERE THERE BEFORE THEY DISAPPEARED, SO MAYBE I'LL FIND A CLUE.
OH... THEN I'LL CONTACT THE CURRENT RULER.
IT'S SOMEONE YOU KNOW, SO YOU'LL GET AN AUDIENCE!
I WONDER WHO IT IS?
ALL THESE PEOPLE LOOK LIKE WEALTHY PAYING PASSENGERS...
...BUT I JUST GOT USHERED ON.
BE-CAUSE OF THIS CARD?
Is it really that power-ful?
OH, WOW! ♡
THAT'S A SINDRIA COMPANY PASS! ♡
WITH SUCH AN ESTEEMED PASSENGER ON BOARD, SECURITY MUST BE TIGHT! MY GOODS WILL BE SAFE! ♡
HM?

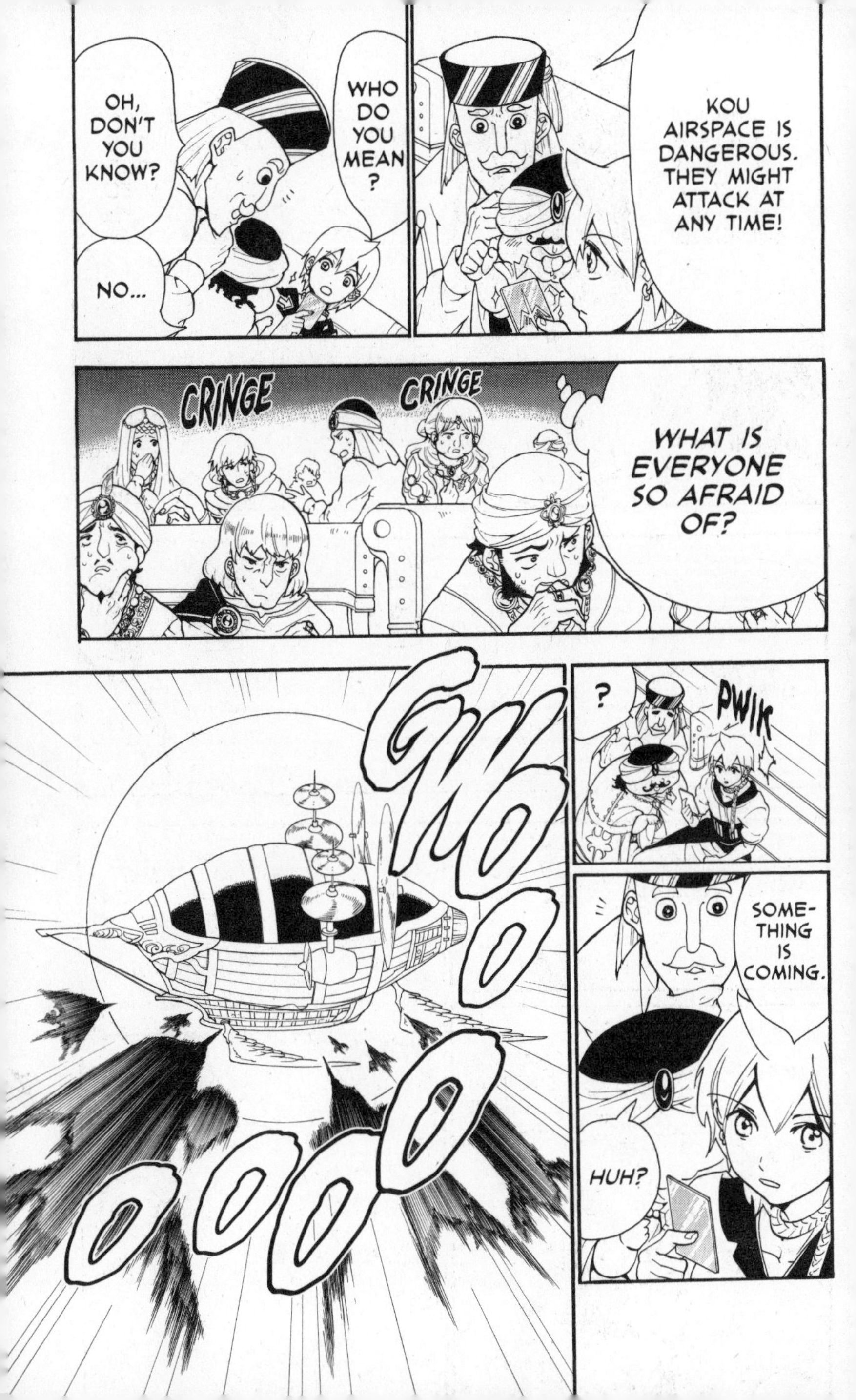

KOU AIRSPACE IS DANGEROUS. THEY MIGHT ATTACK AT ANY TIME!
WHO DO YOU MEAN?
OH, DON'T YOU KNOW?
NO...
CRINGE
WHAT IS EVERYONE SO AFRAID OF?
CRINGE
PWIK
?
SOME-THING IS COMING.
HUH?
GWOOOOOOOO

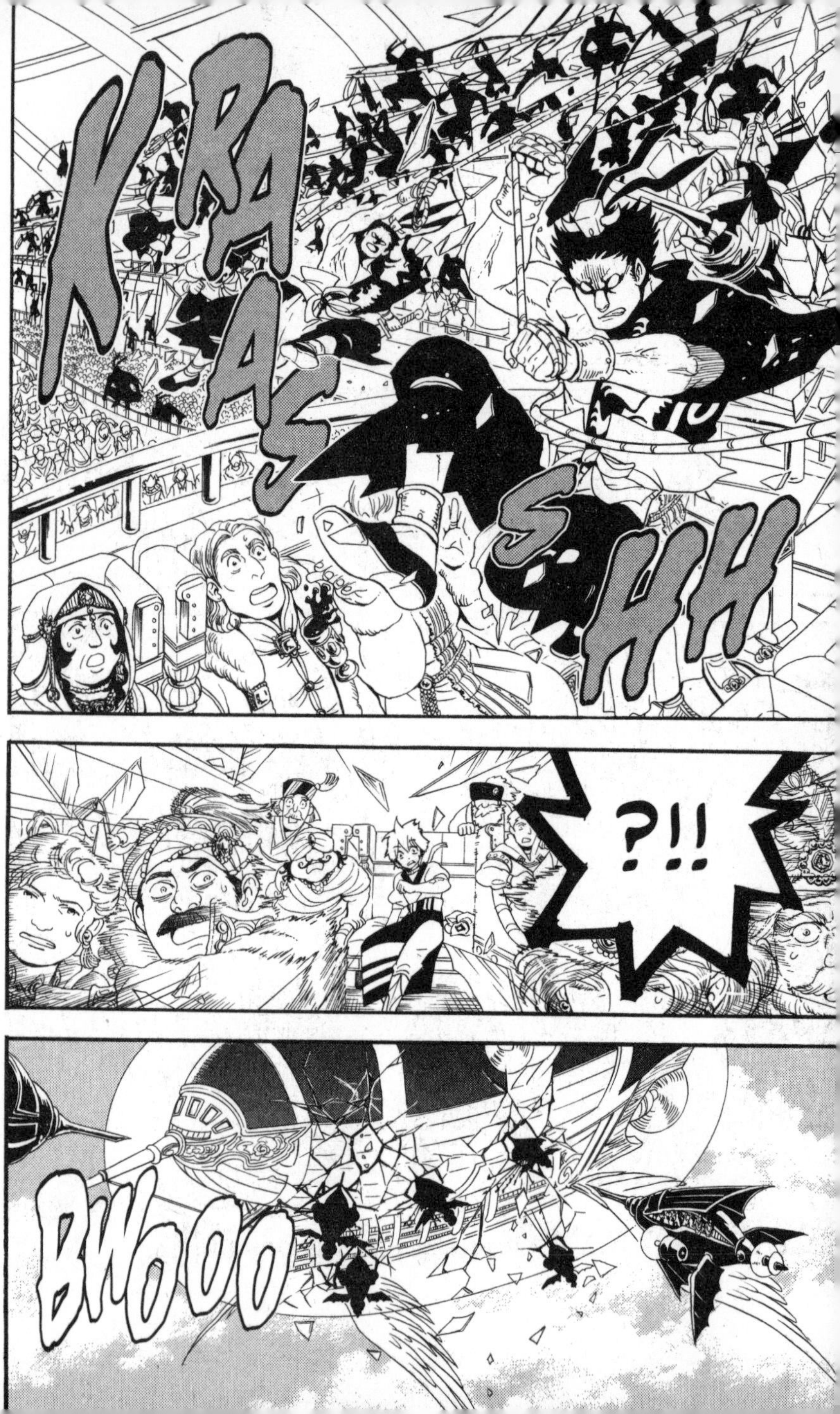
KRASSHH
?!!
BWOOO

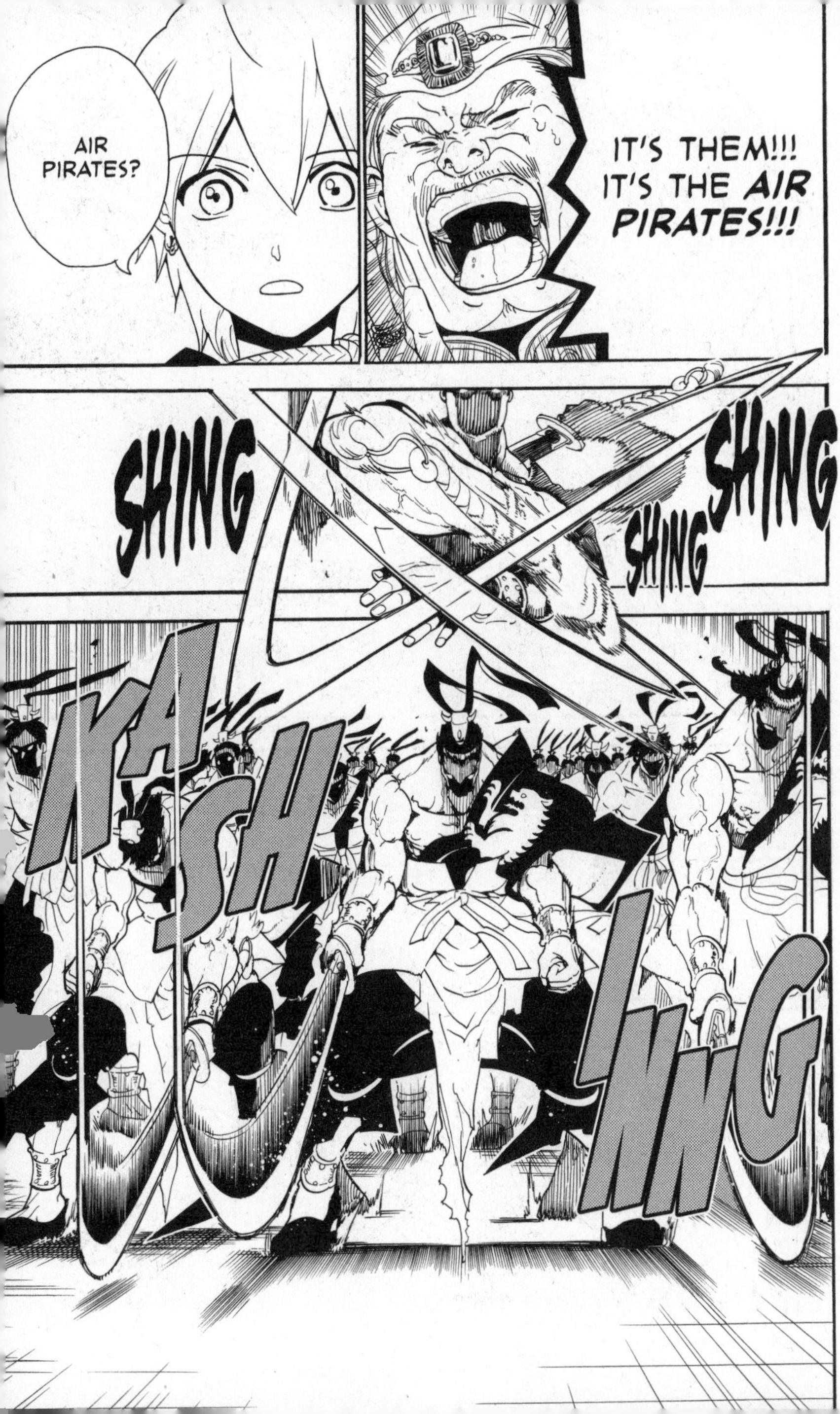
IT'S THEM!!! IT'S THE AIR PIRATES!!!
AIR PIRATES?
SHING
SHING
SHING
KASHING

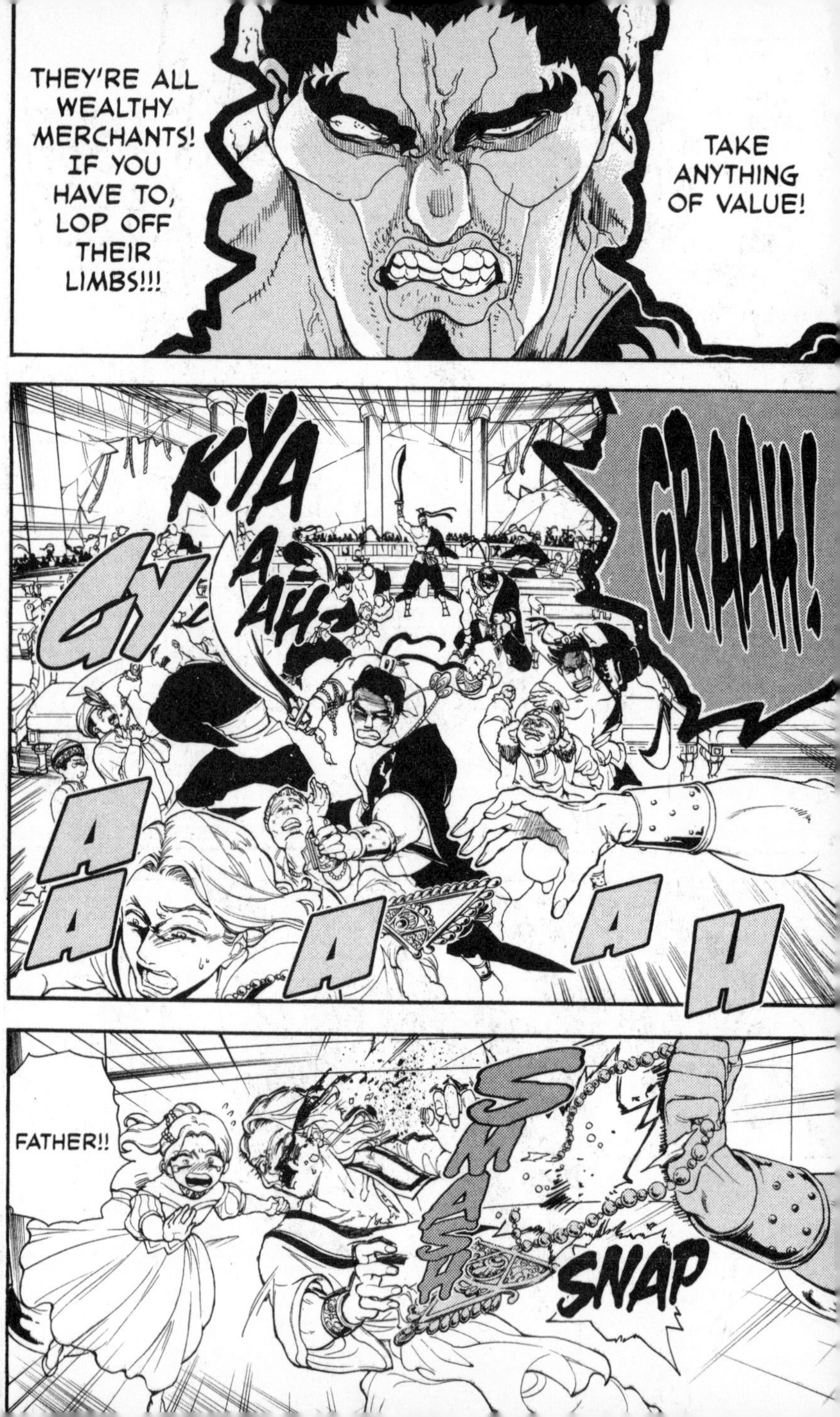
TAKE ANYTHING OF VALUE!
THEY'RE ALL WEALTHY MERCHANTS! IF YOU HAVE TO, LOP OFF THEIR LIMBS!!!
GRAAH!
KYAAAH
AAAAAH
SNAP
SMASH
FATHER!!

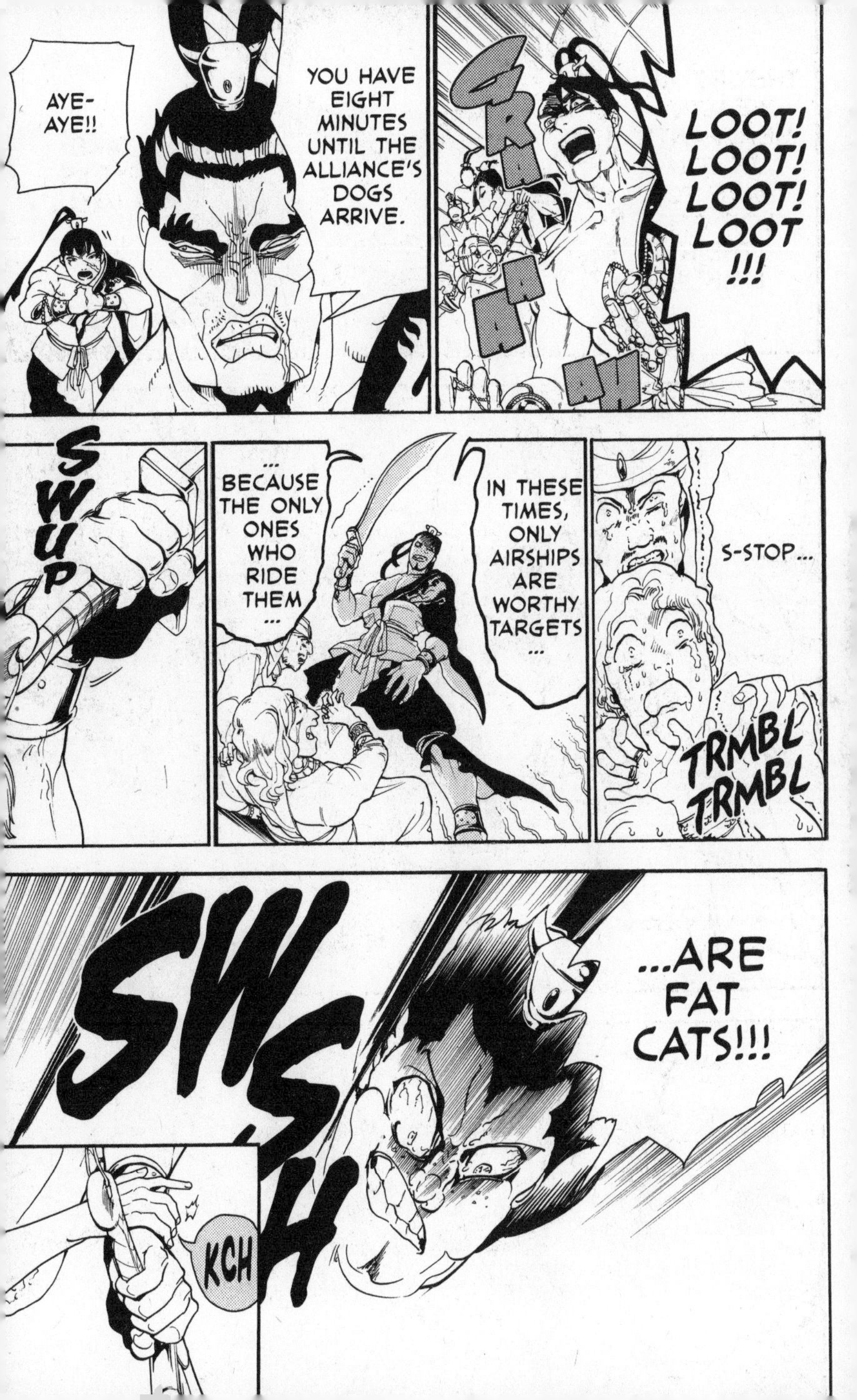
GRAAAAH
LOOT! LOOT! LOOT! LOOT!!!
YOU HAVE EIGHT MINUTES UNTIL THE ALLIANCE'S DOGS ARRIVE.
AYE-AYE!!
S-STOP...
TRMBL TRMBL
IN THESE TIMES, ONLY AIRSHIPS ARE WORTHY TARGETS...
...BECAUSE THE ONLY ONES WHO RIDE THEM...
SWUP
...ARE FAT CATS!!!
SWISH
KCH

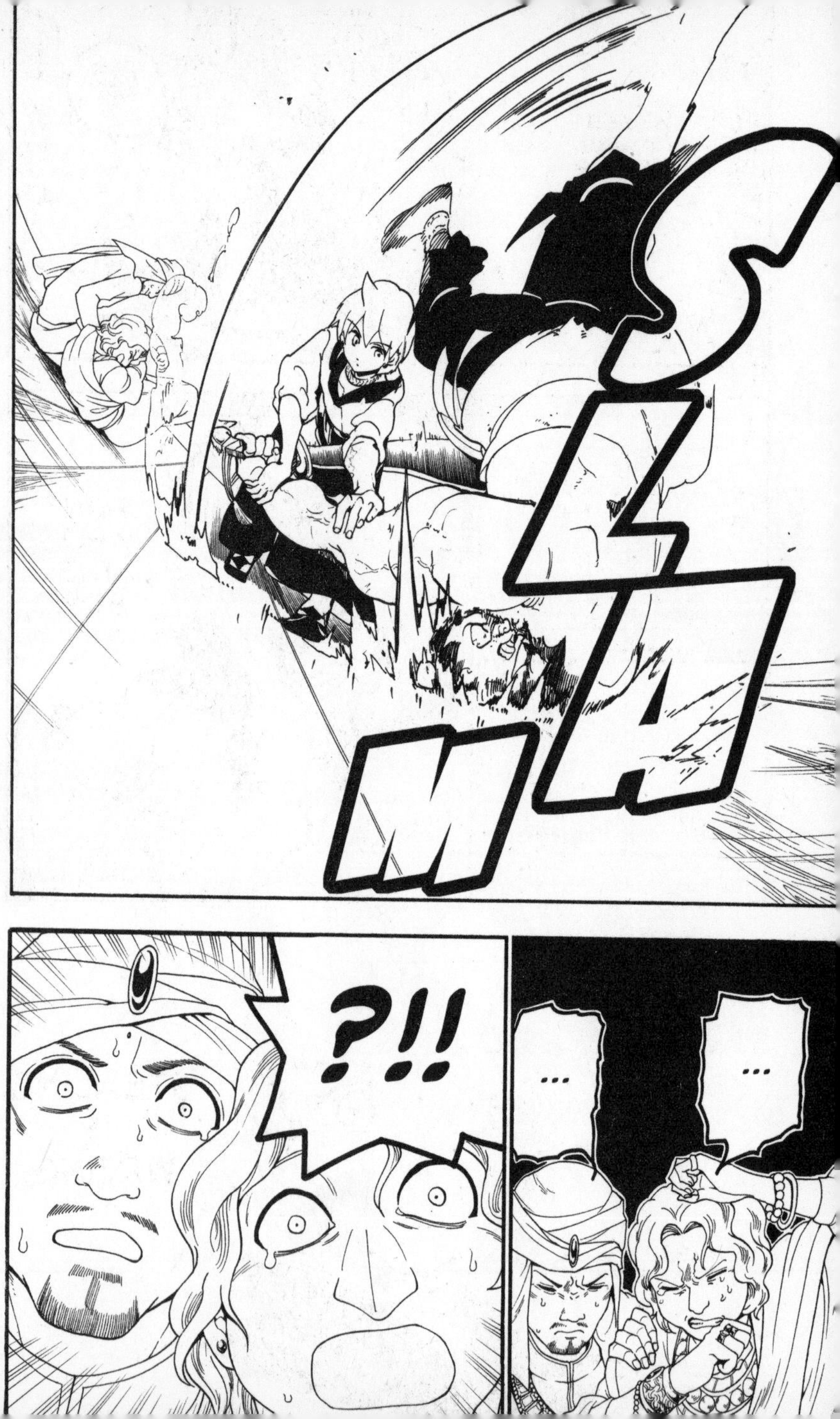
SLAM
?!!
...
...

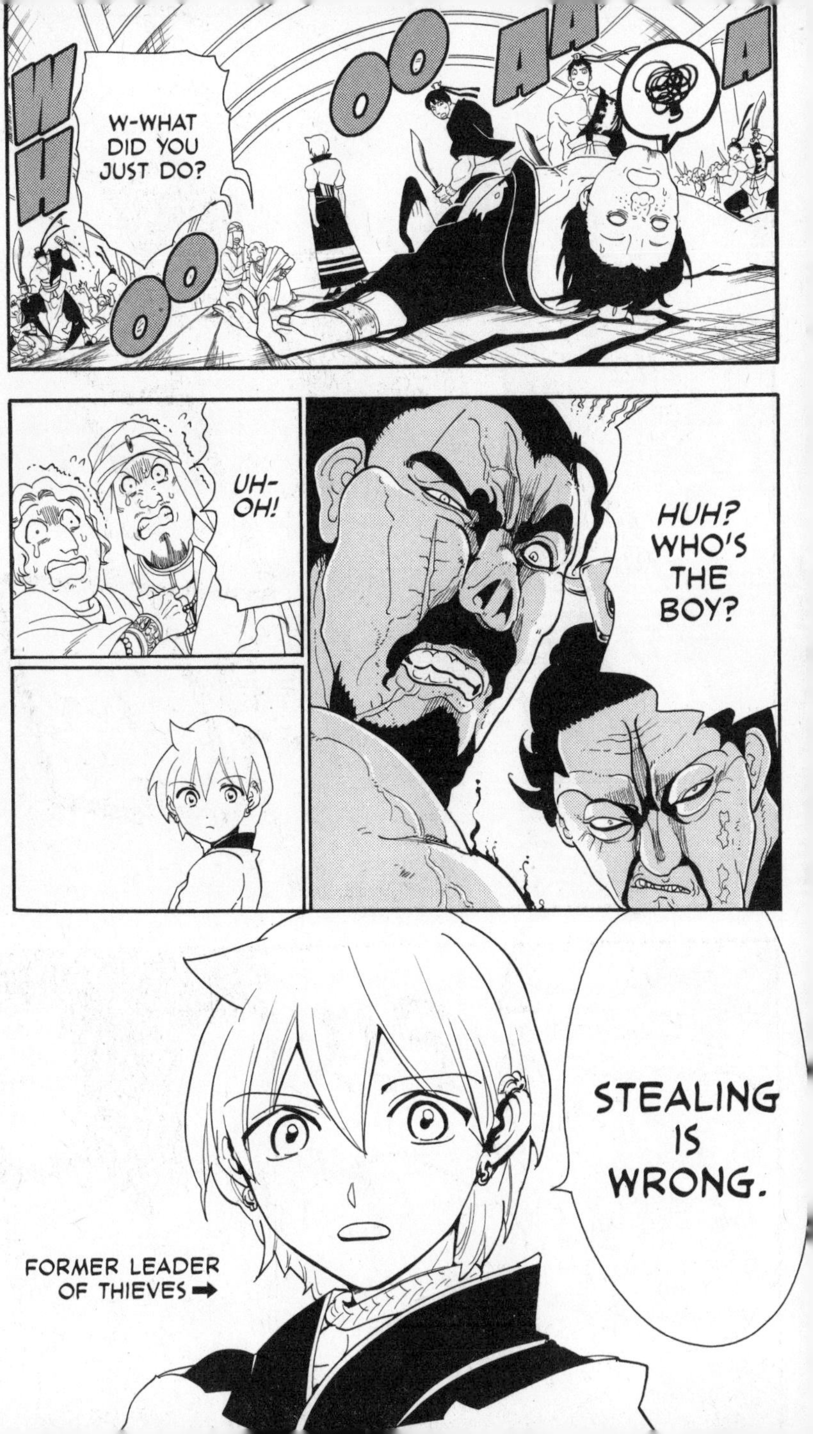
WHOOOOOAAA
W-WHAT DID YOU JUST DO?
HUH? WHO'S THE BOY?
UH-OH!
STEALING IS WRONG.
FORMER LEADER OF THIEVES ➡

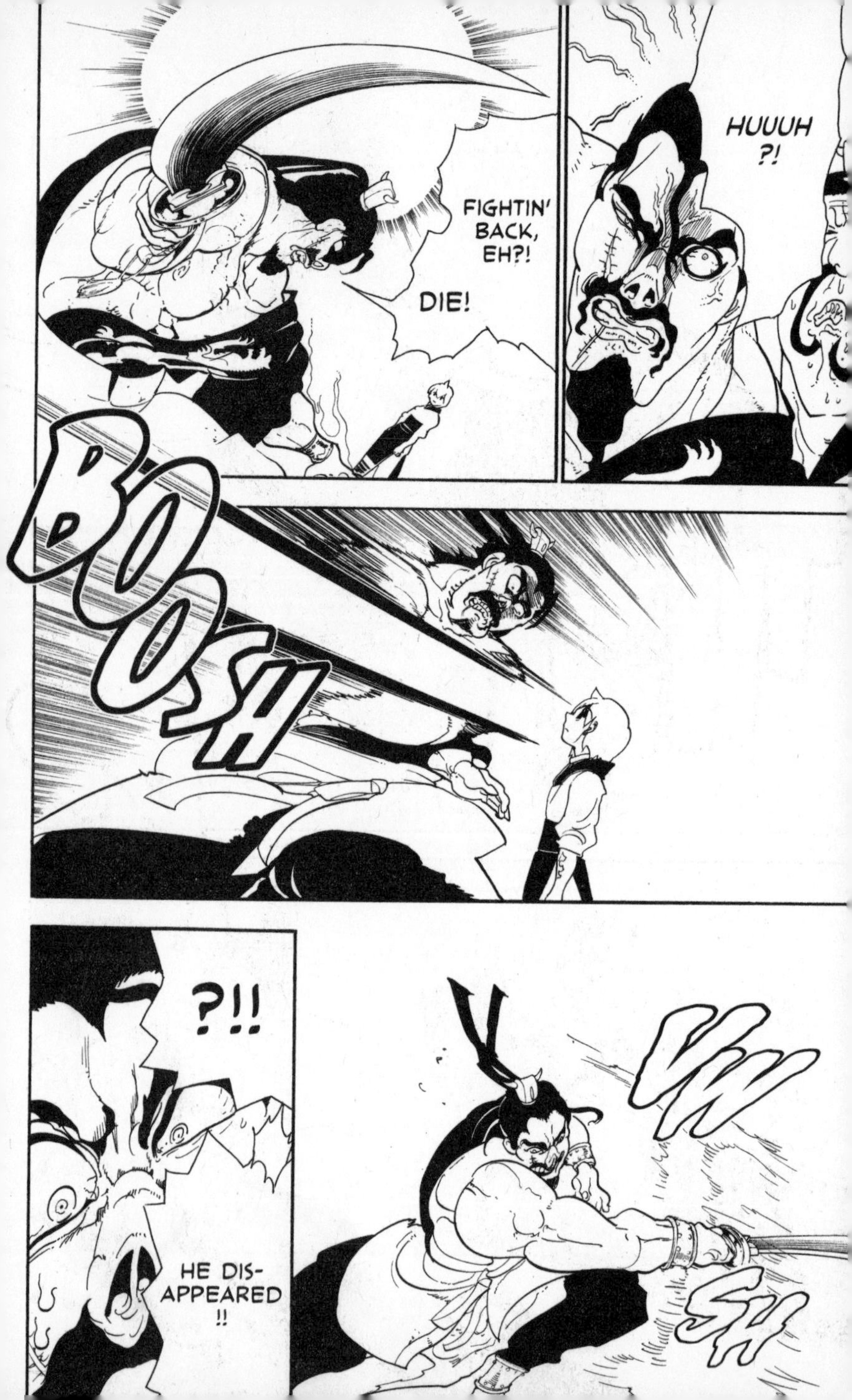
HUUUH ?!
FIGHTIN' BACK, EH?!
DIE!
BOOSH
VWSH
?!!
HE DIS-APPEARED !!

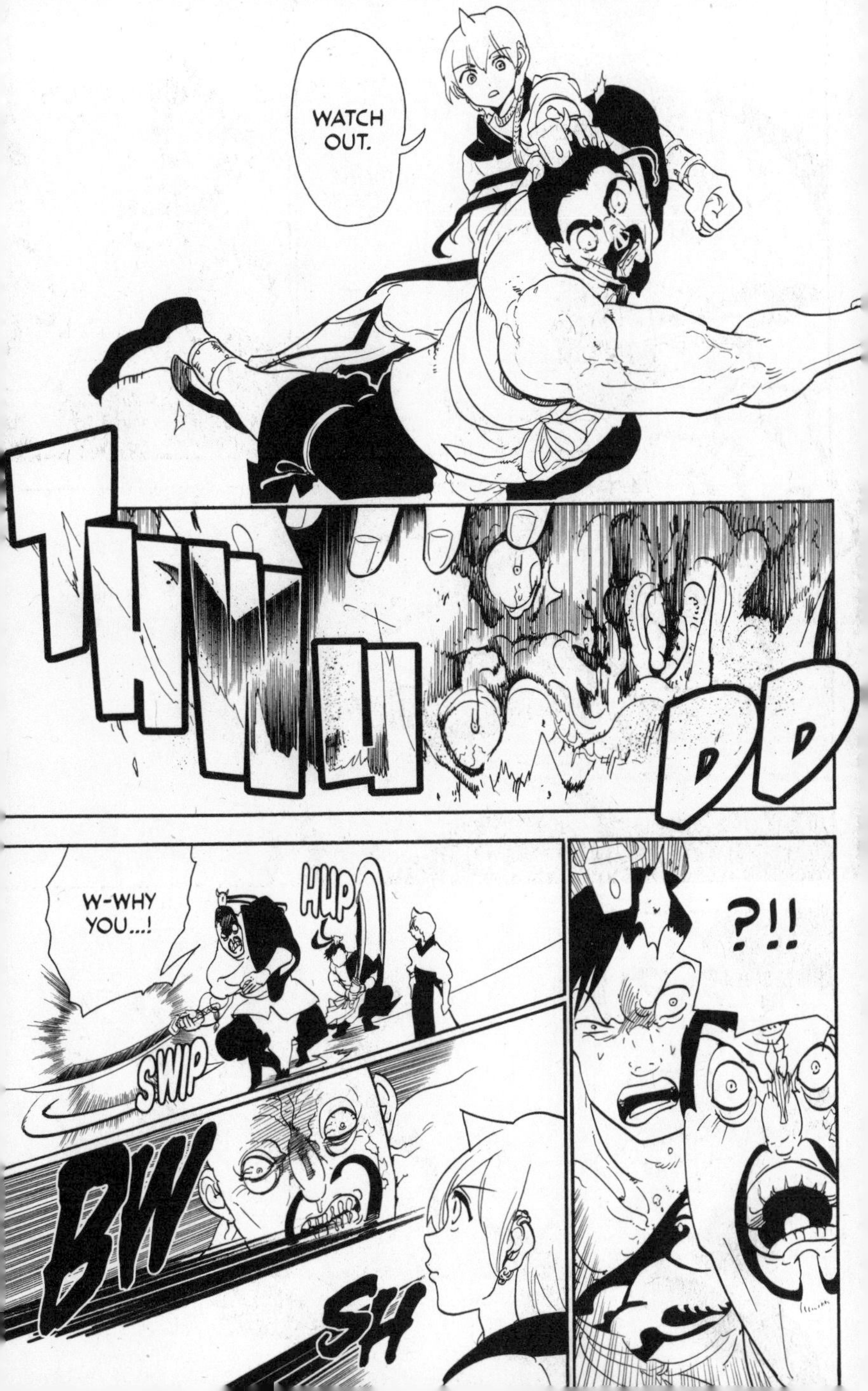
WATCH OUT.
THWUDD
?!!
HUP
W-WHY YOU...!
SWIP
BW
SH

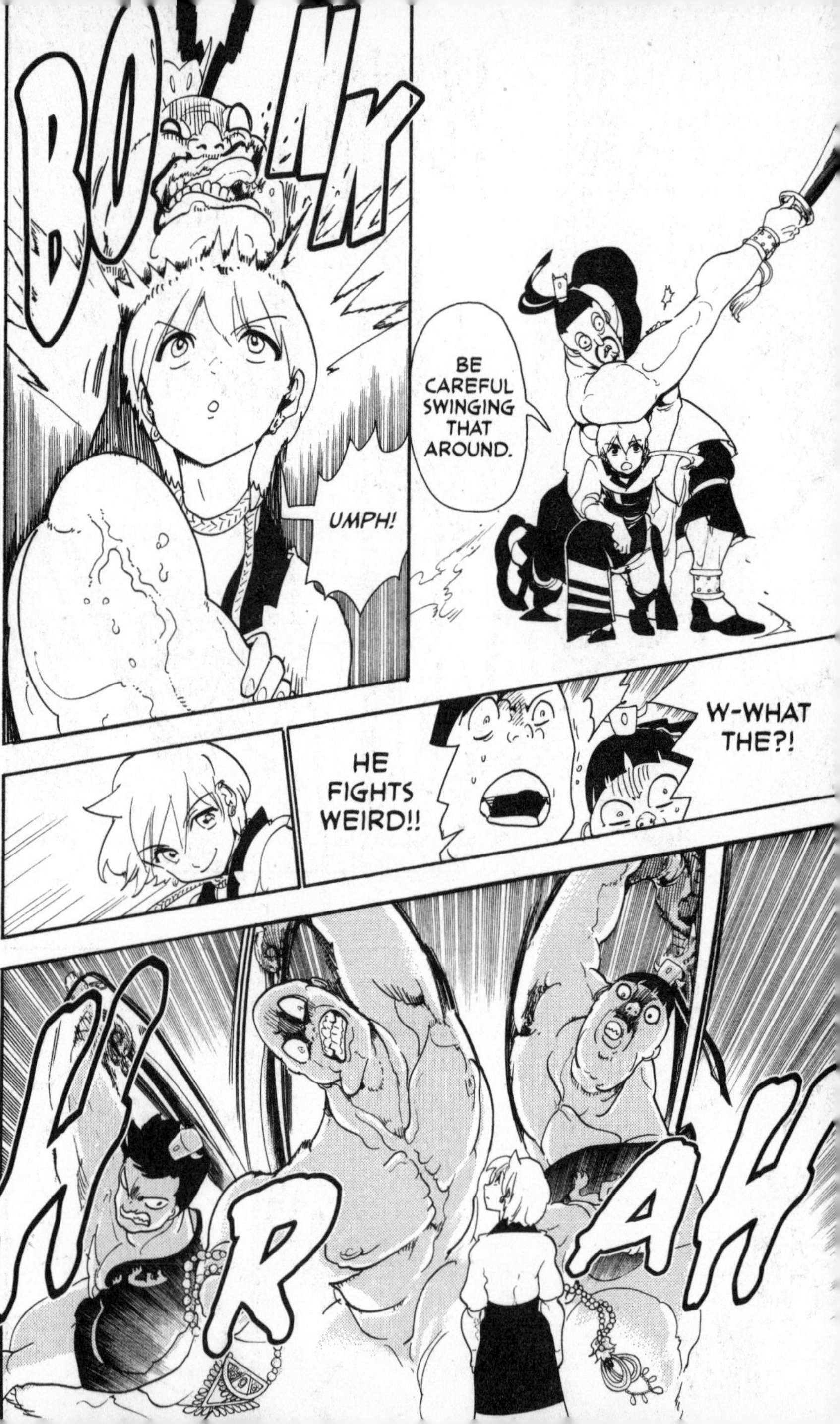
BE CAREFUL SWINGING THAT AROUND.
BONK
UMPH!
W-WHAT THE?!
HE FIGHTS WEIRD!!
HRAH

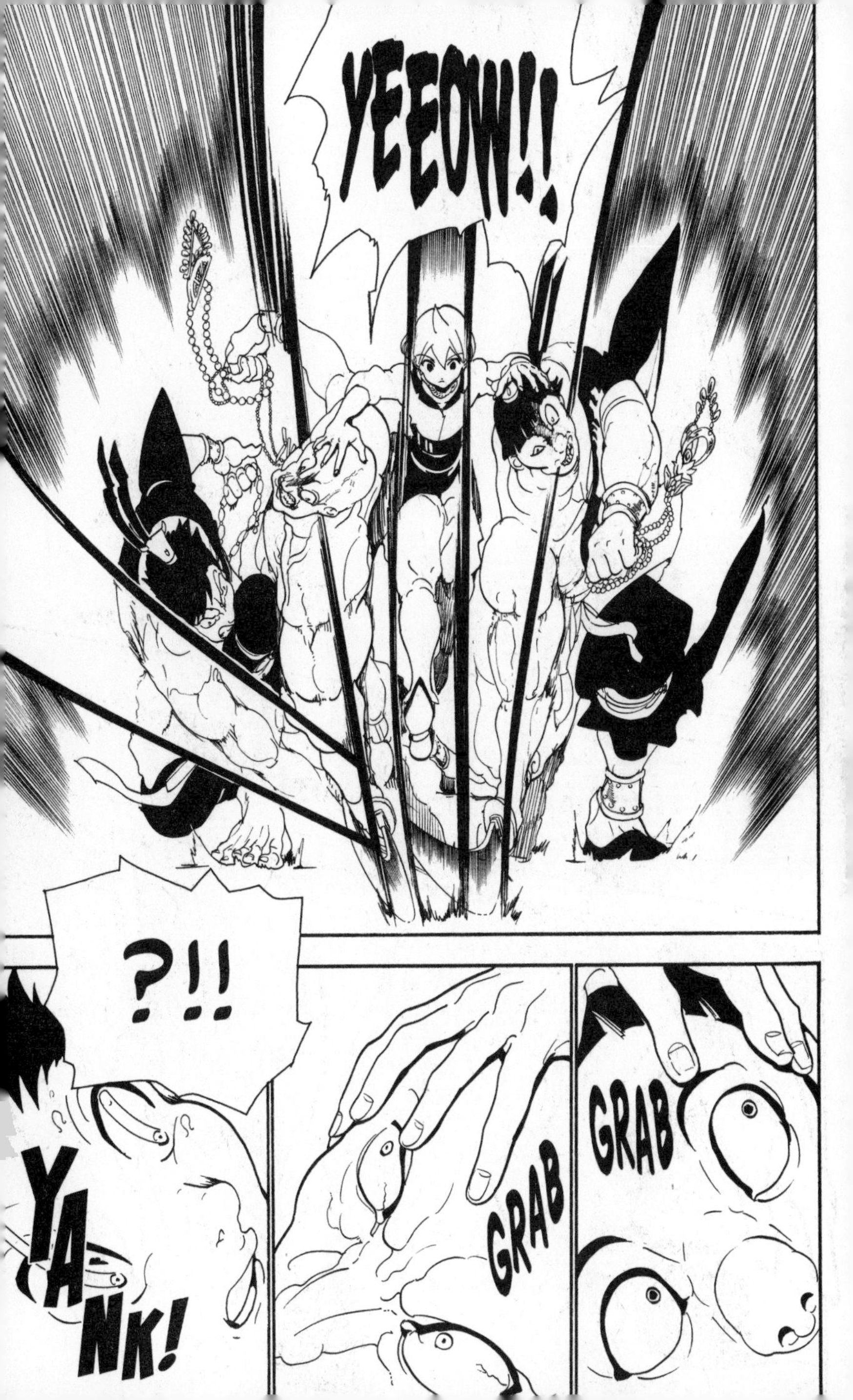
YEEOW!!
GRAB
GRAB
?!!
YANK!

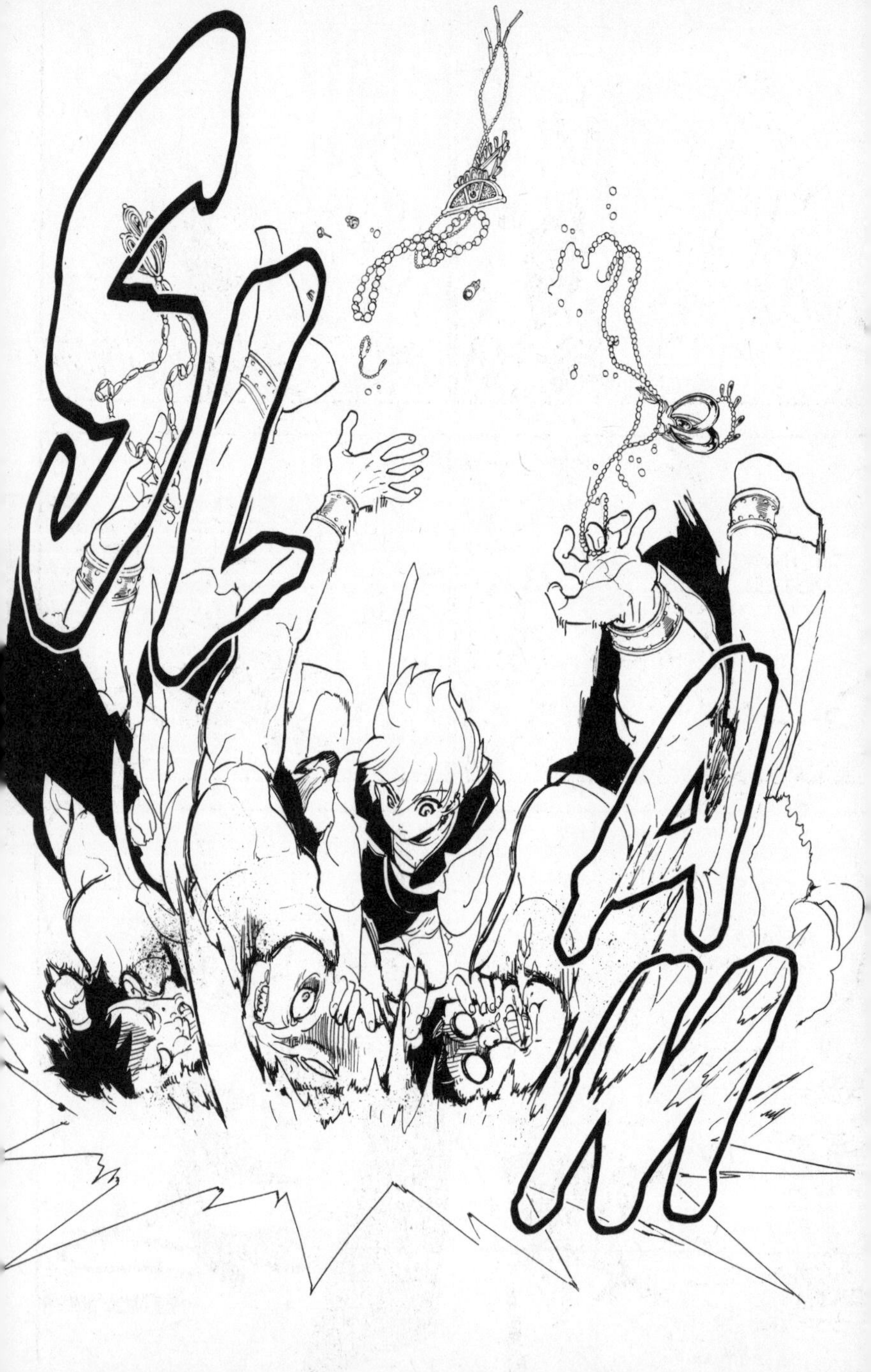
SLAM

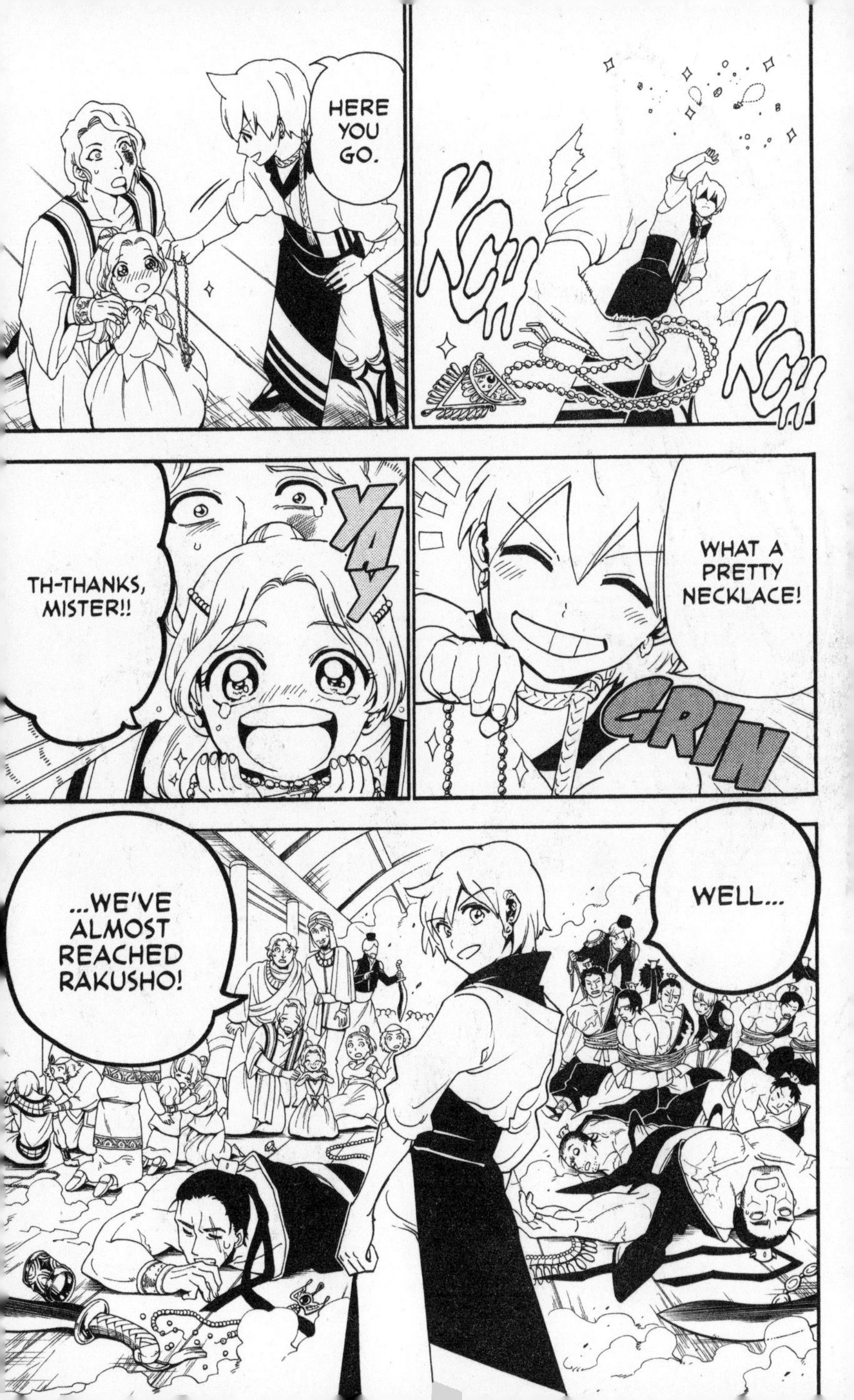
KCH
KCH
HERE YOU GO.
WHAT A PRETTY NECKLACE!
GRIN
YAY
TH-THANKS, MISTER!!
WELL...
...WE'VE ALMOST REACHED RAKUSHO!

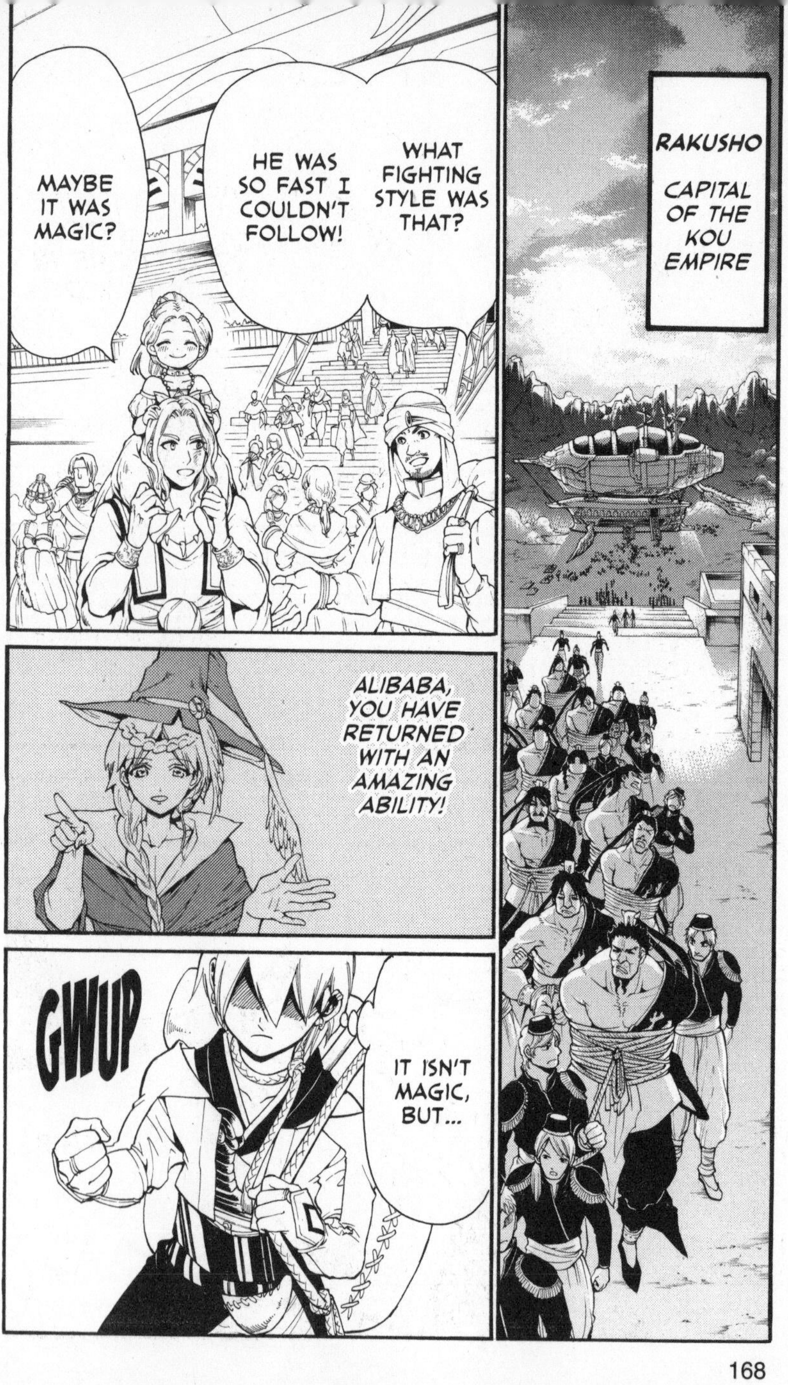
RAKUSHO
CAPITAL OF THE KOU EMPIRE
WHAT FIGHTING STYLE WAS THAT?
HE WAS SO FAST I COULDN'T FOLLOW!
MAYBE IT WAS MAGIC?
ALIBABA, YOU HAVE RETURNED WITH AN AMAZING ABILITY!
IT ISN'T MAGIC, BUT...
GWUP

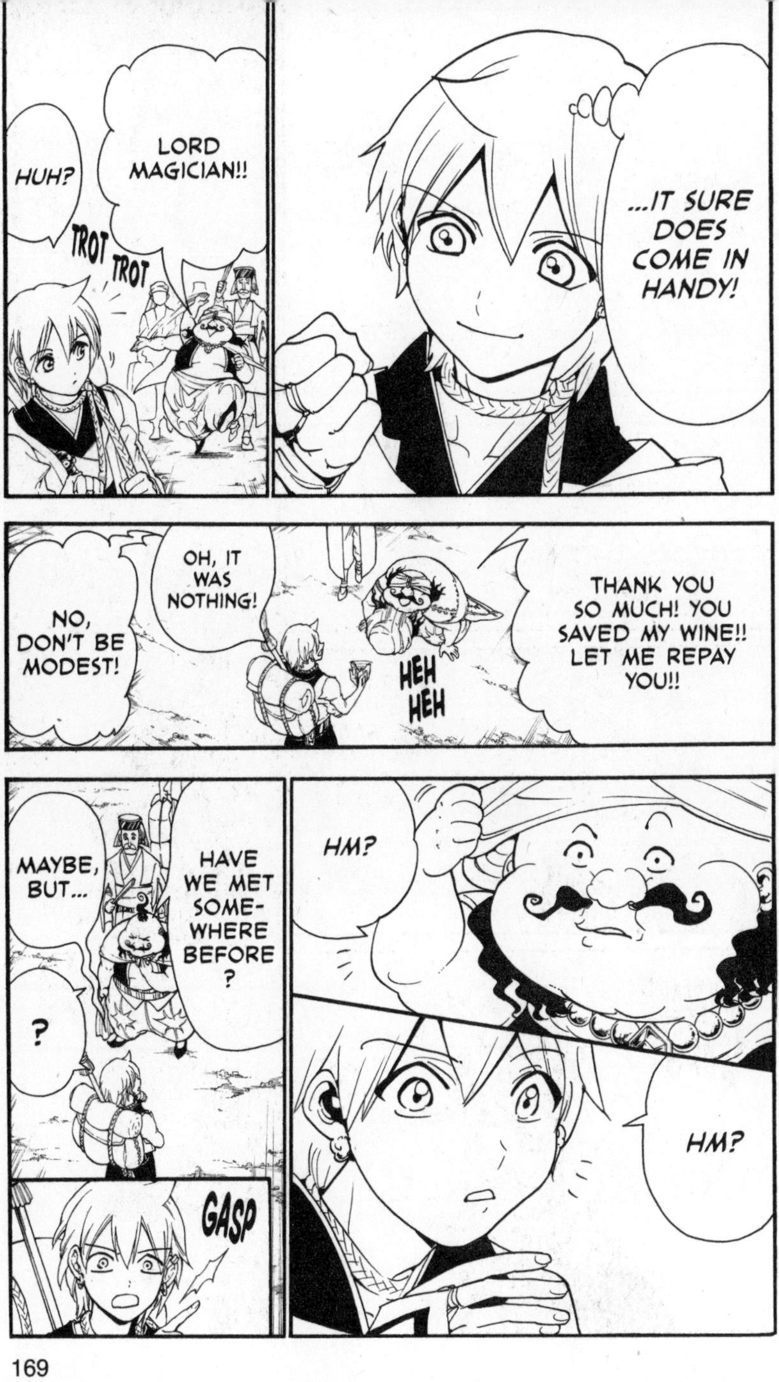
...IT SURE DOES COME IN HANDY!
LORD MAGICIAN!!
HUH?
TROT TROT
THANK YOU SO MUCH! YOU SAVED MY WINE!! LET ME REPAY YOU!!
HEH HEH
OH, IT WAS NOTHING!
NO, DON'T BE MODEST!
HM?
HM?
HAVE WE MET SOME-WHERE BEFORE?
MAYBE, BUT...
?
GASP

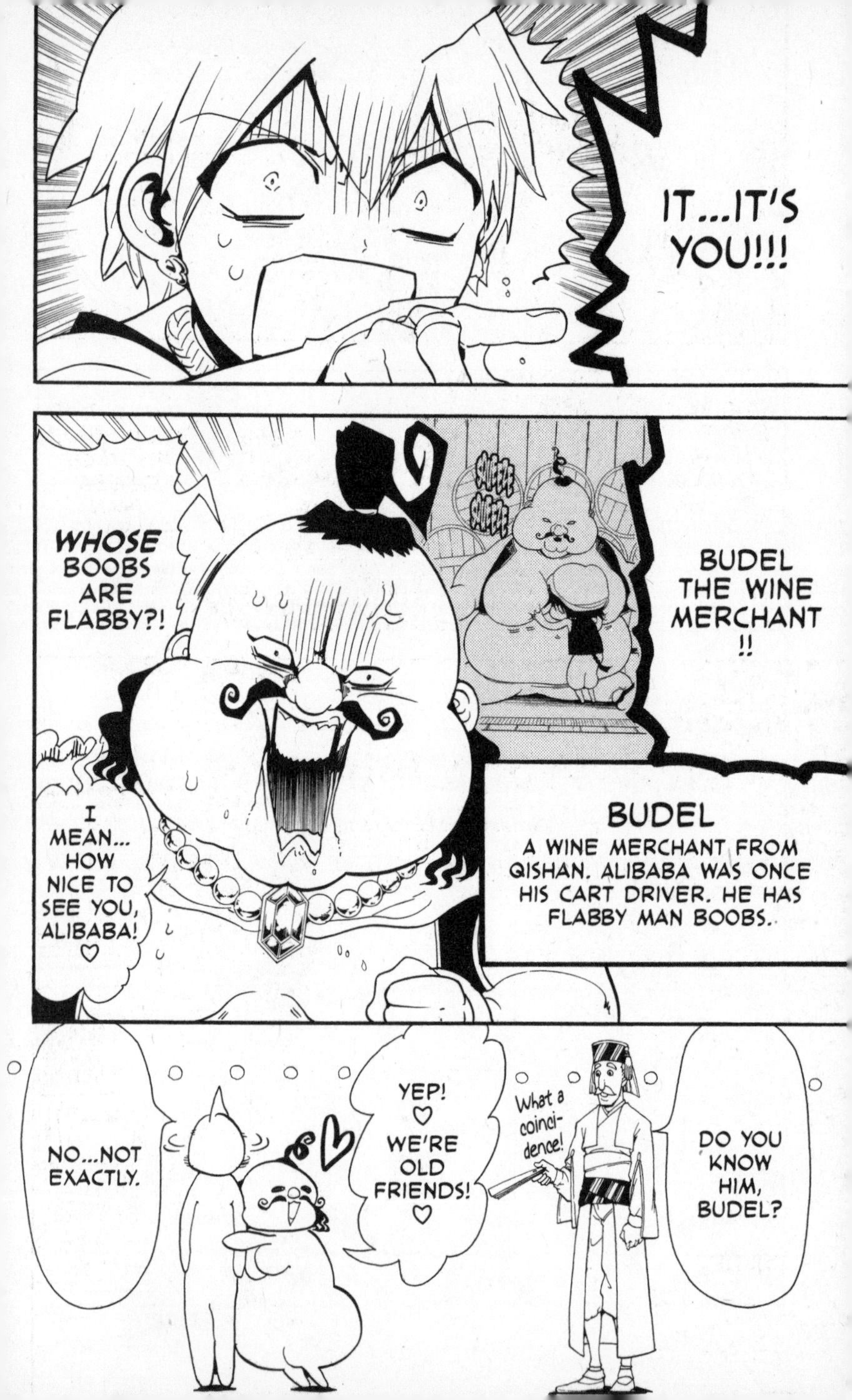
IT...IT'S YOU!!!
BUDEL THE WINE MERCHANT !!
BUDEL
A WINE MERCHANT FROM QISHAN. ALIBABA WAS ONCE HIS CART DRIVER. HE HAS FLABBY MAN BOOBS.
WHOSE BOOBS ARE FLABBY?!
I MEAN... HOW NICE TO SEE YOU, ALIBABA! ♡
DO YOU KNOW HIM, BUDEL?
What a coinci-dence!
YEP! ♡ WE'RE OLD FRIENDS! ♡
NO...NOT EXACTLY.

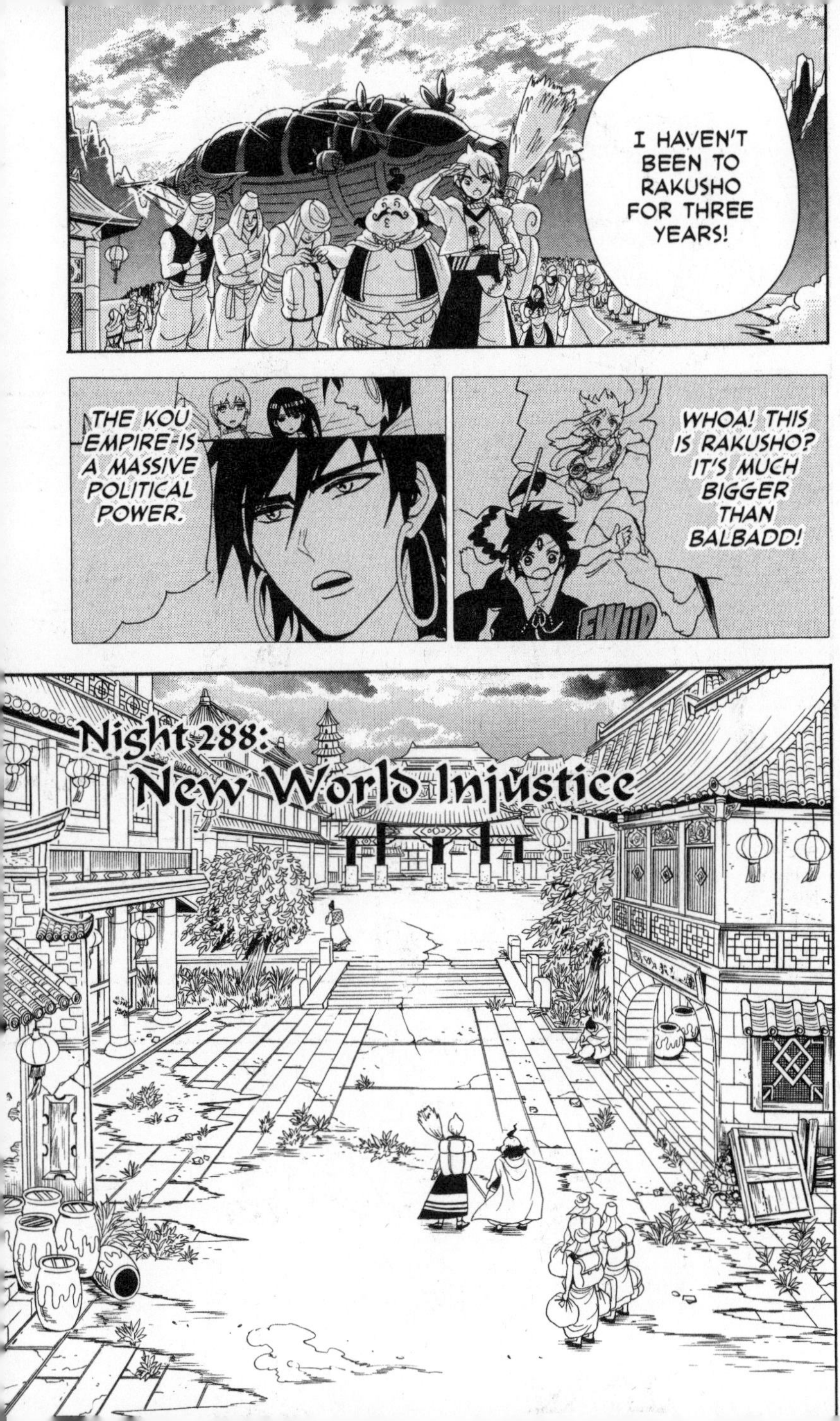
I HAVEN'T BEEN TO RAKUSHO FOR THREE YEARS!
WHOA! THIS IS RAKUSHO? IT'S MUCH BIGGER THAN BALBADD!
THE KOU EMPIRE IS A MASSIVE POLITICAL POWER.
Night 288:
New World Injustice

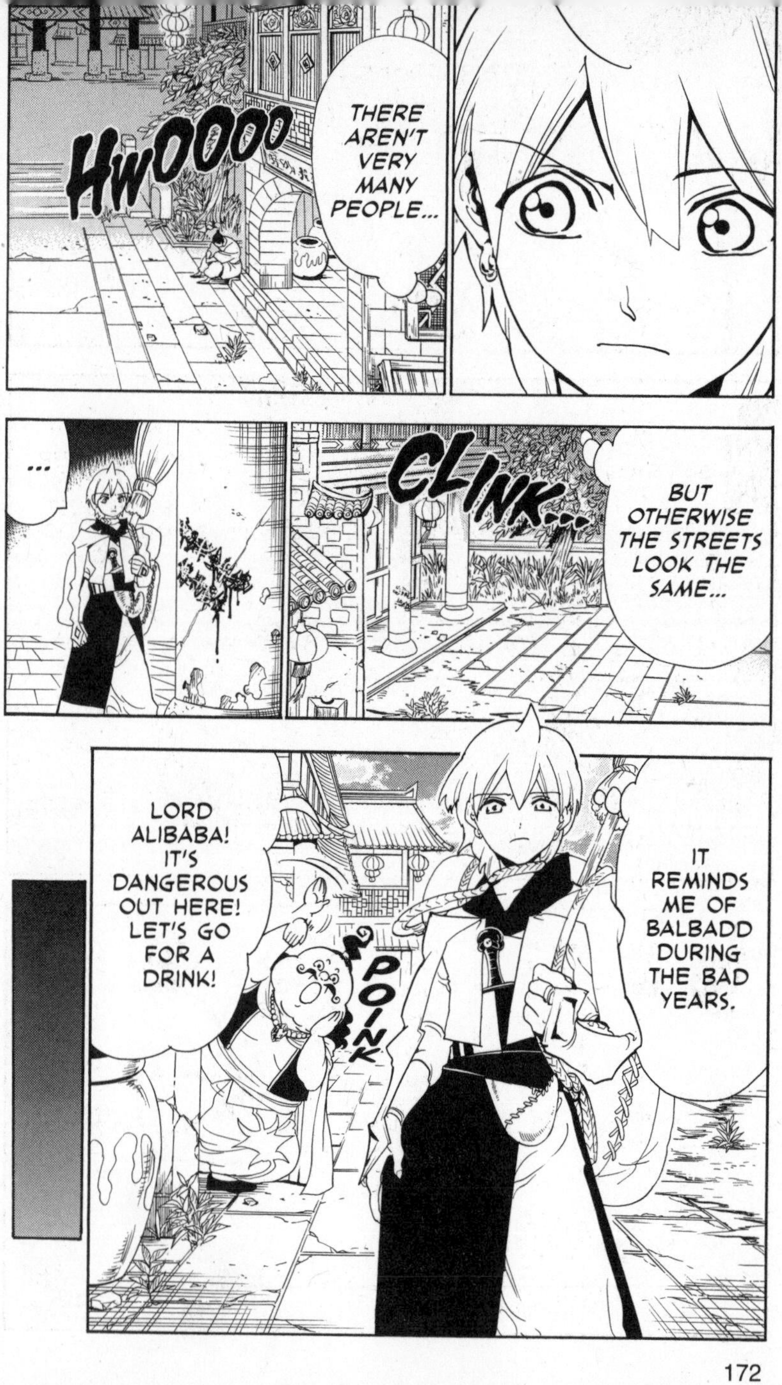
THERE AREN'T VERY MANY PEOPLE...
HWOOOO
BUT OTHERWISE THE STREETS LOOK THE SAME...
CLINK...
...
IT REMINDS ME OF BALBADD DURING THE BAD YEARS.
LORD ALIBABA! IT'S DANGEROUS OUT HERE! LET'S GO FOR A DRINK!
POINK

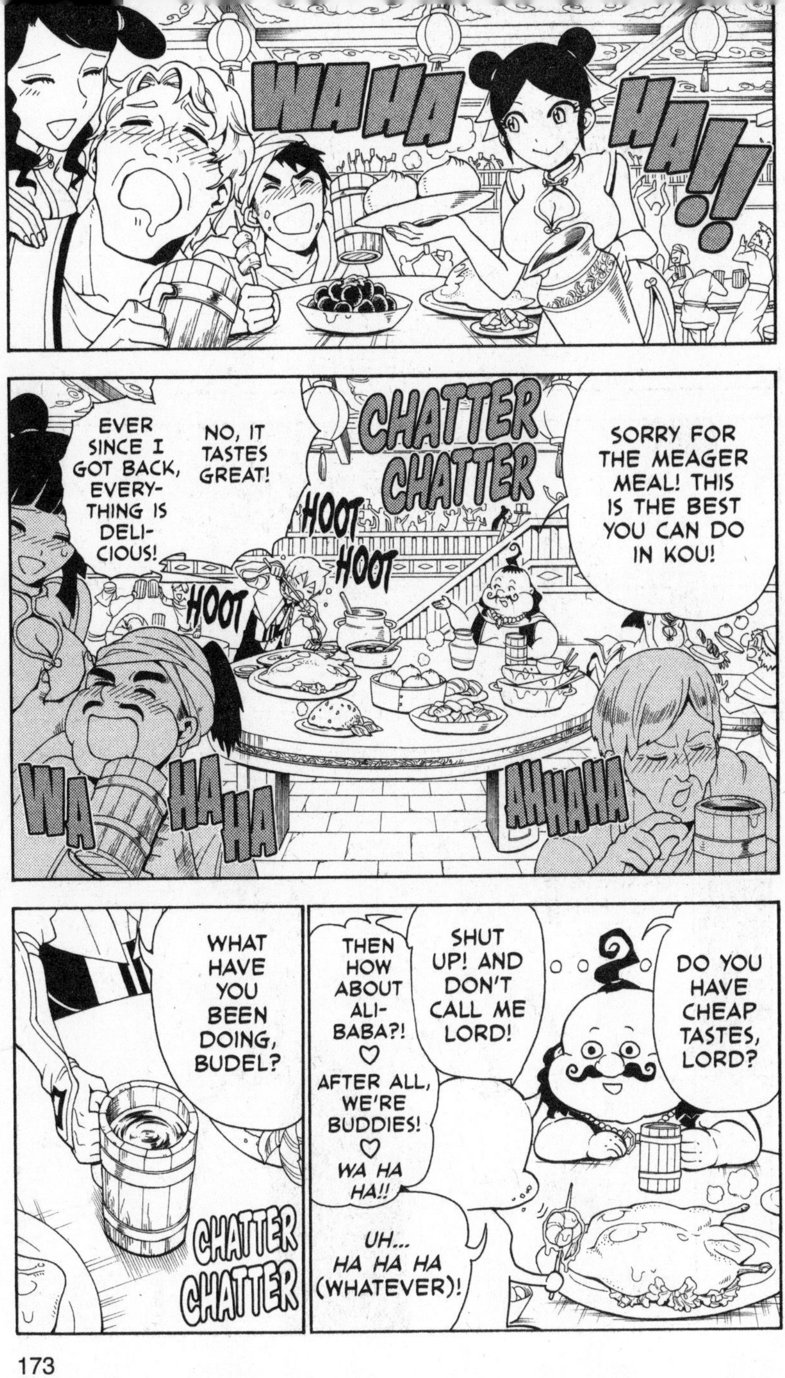
WAHA HA!!!
SORRY FOR THE MEAGER MEAL! THIS IS THE BEST YOU CAN DO IN KOU!
CHATTER CHATTER
NO, IT TASTES GREAT!
EVER SINCE I GOT BACK, EVERYTHING IS DELICIOUS!
HOOT HOOT
HOOT
AHHAHA
WA HA HA HA
DO YOU HAVE CHEAP TASTES, LORD?
SHUT UP! AND DON'T CALL ME LORD!
THEN HOW ABOUT ALI-BABA?! ♡ AFTER ALL, WE'RE BUDDIES! ♡ WA HA HA!!
UH... HA HA HA (WHATEVER)!
WHAT HAVE YOU BEEN DOING, BUDEL?
CHATTER CHATTER

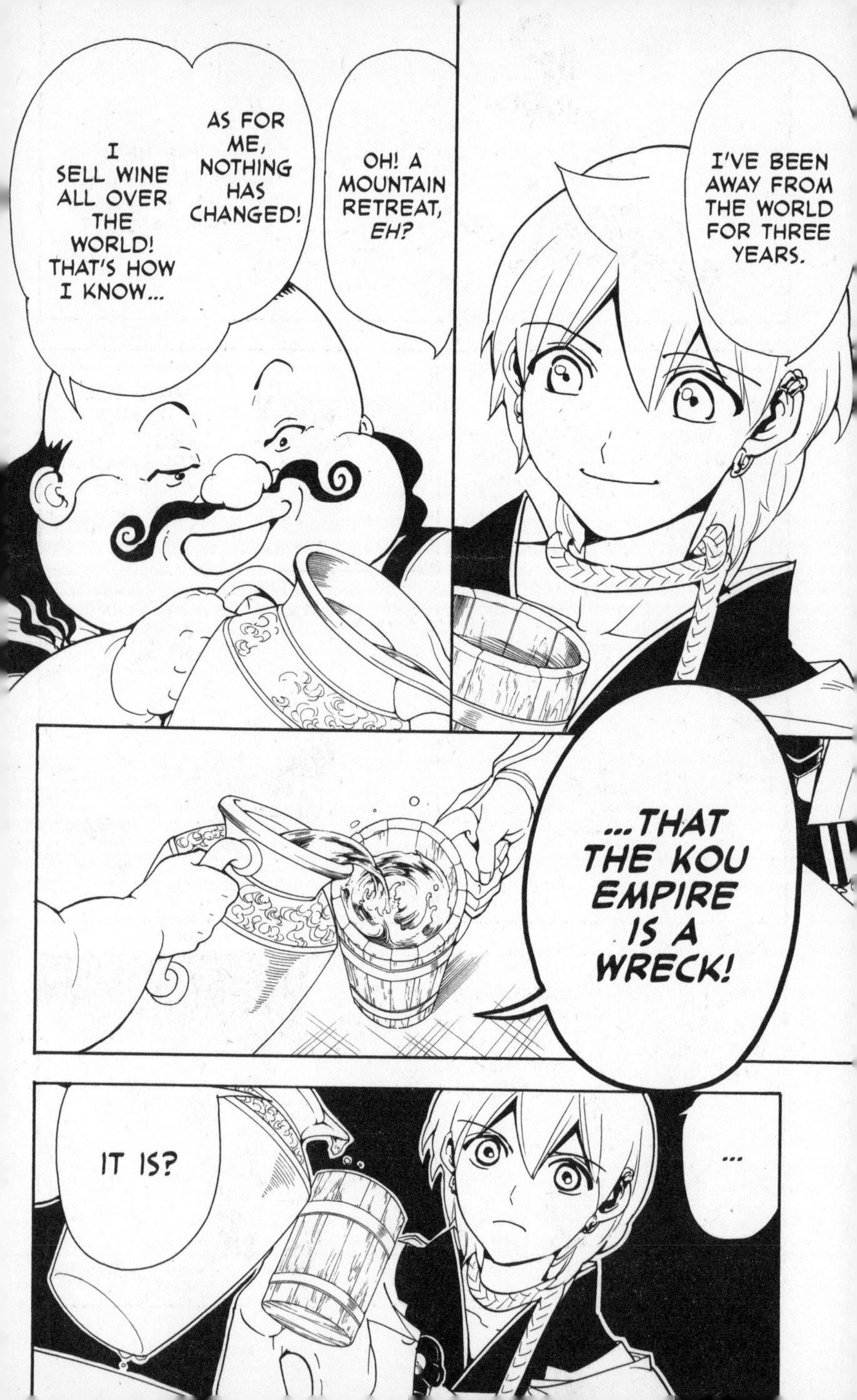
I'VE BEEN AWAY FROM THE WORLD FOR THREE YEARS.
OH! A MOUNTAIN RETREAT, *EH?*
AS FOR ME, NOTHING HAS CHANGED!
I SELL WINE ALL OVER THE WORLD! THAT'S HOW I KNOW...
...THAT THE KOU EMPIRE IS A WRECK!
...
IT IS?

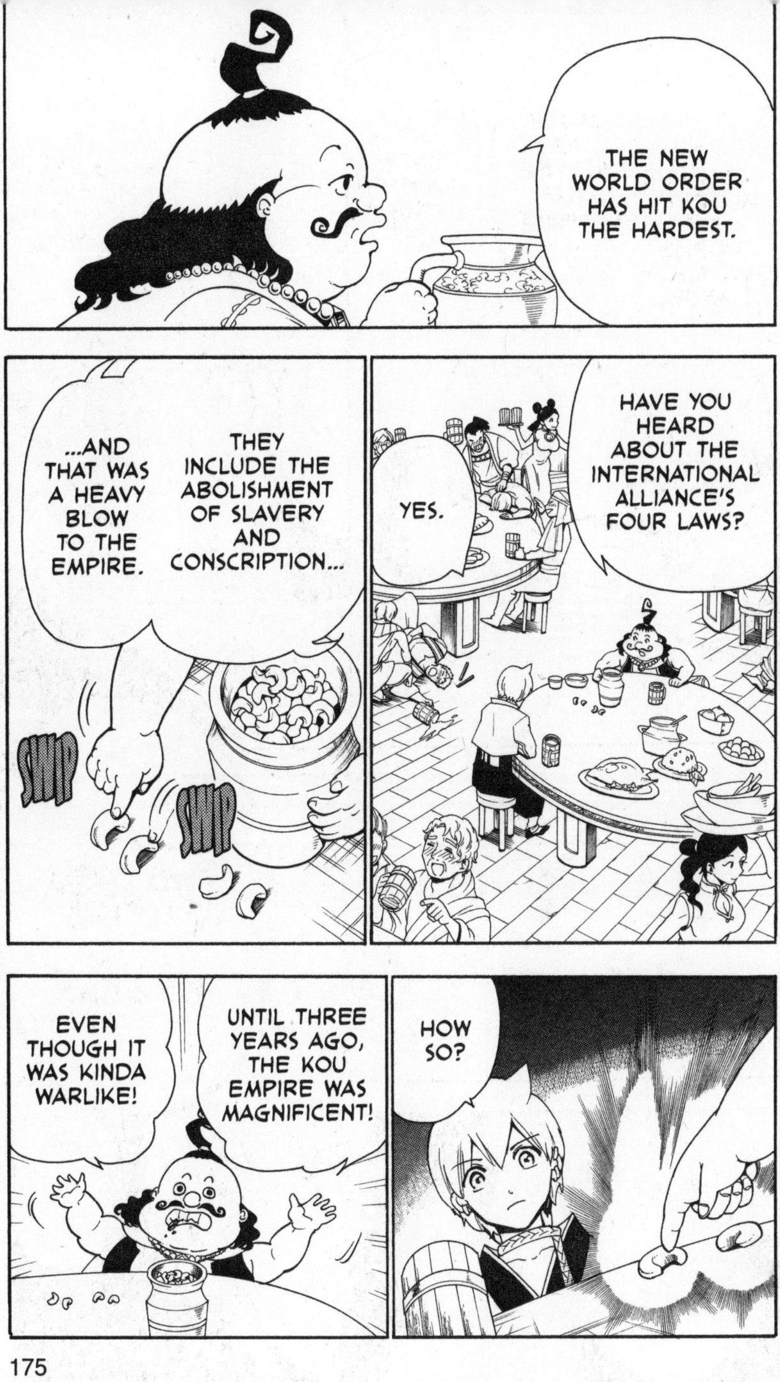
THE NEW WORLD ORDER HAS HIT KOU THE HARDEST.
HAVE YOU HEARD ABOUT THE INTERNATIONAL ALLIANCE'S FOUR LAWS?
YES.
THEY INCLUDE THE ABOLISHMENT OF SLAVERY AND CONSCRIPTION...
...AND THAT WAS A HEAVY BLOW TO THE EMPIRE.
SWIP
SWIP
HOW SO?
UNTIL THREE YEARS AGO, THE KOU EMPIRE WAS MAGNIFICENT!
EVEN THOUGH IT WAS KINDA WARLIKE!

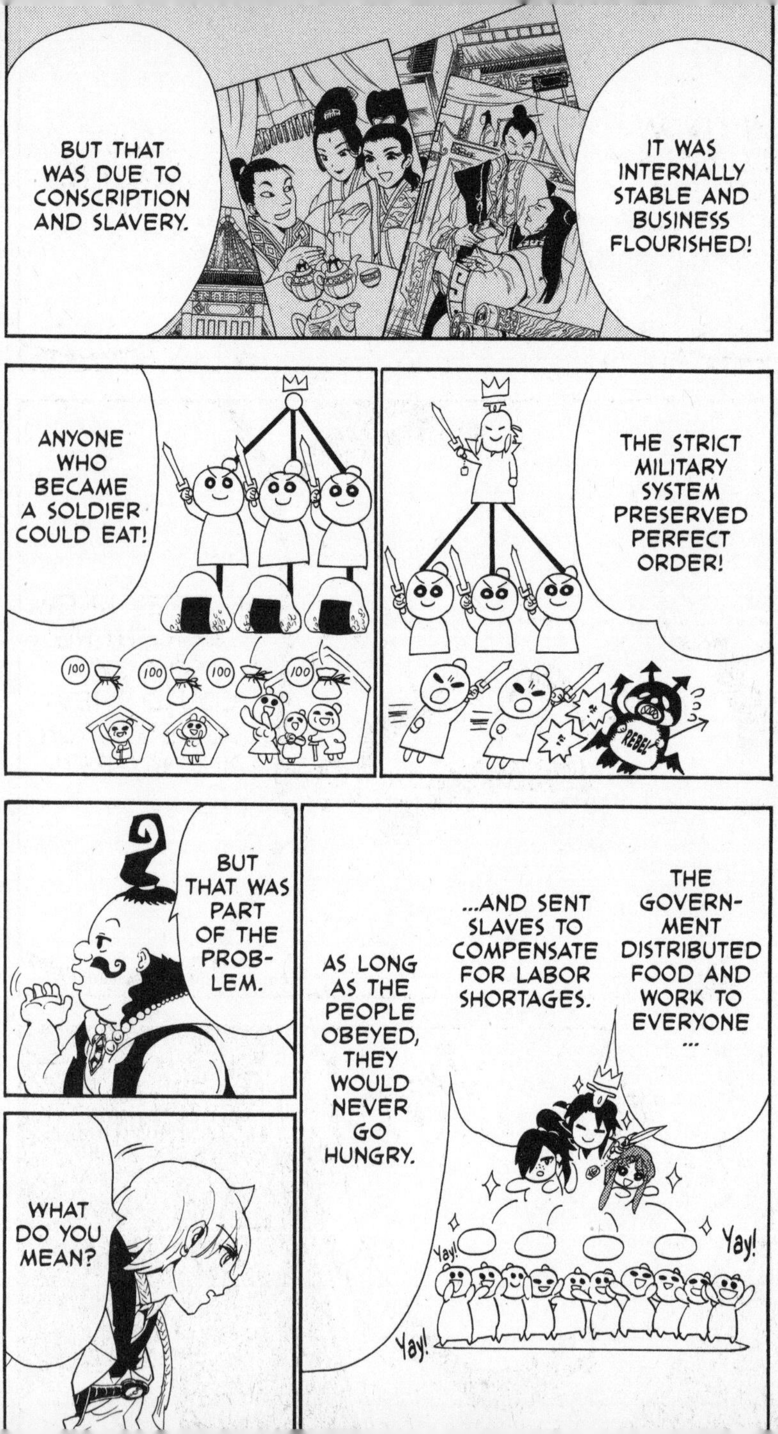
IT WAS INTERNALLY STABLE AND BUSINESS FLOURISHED!
BUT THAT WAS DUE TO CONSCRIPTION AND SLAVERY.
THE STRICT MILITARY SYSTEM PRESERVED PERFECT ORDER!
REBEL!
ANYONE WHO BECAME A SOLDIER COULD EAT!
100
100
100
100
THE GOVERN-MENT DISTRIBUTED FOOD AND WORK TO EVERYONE...
...AND SENT SLAVES TO COMPENSATE FOR LABOR SHORTAGES.
AS LONG AS THE PEOPLE OBEYED, THEY WOULD NEVER GO HUNGRY.
Yay!
Yay!
Yay!
BUT THAT WAS PART OF THE PROB-LEM.
WHAT DO YOU MEAN?

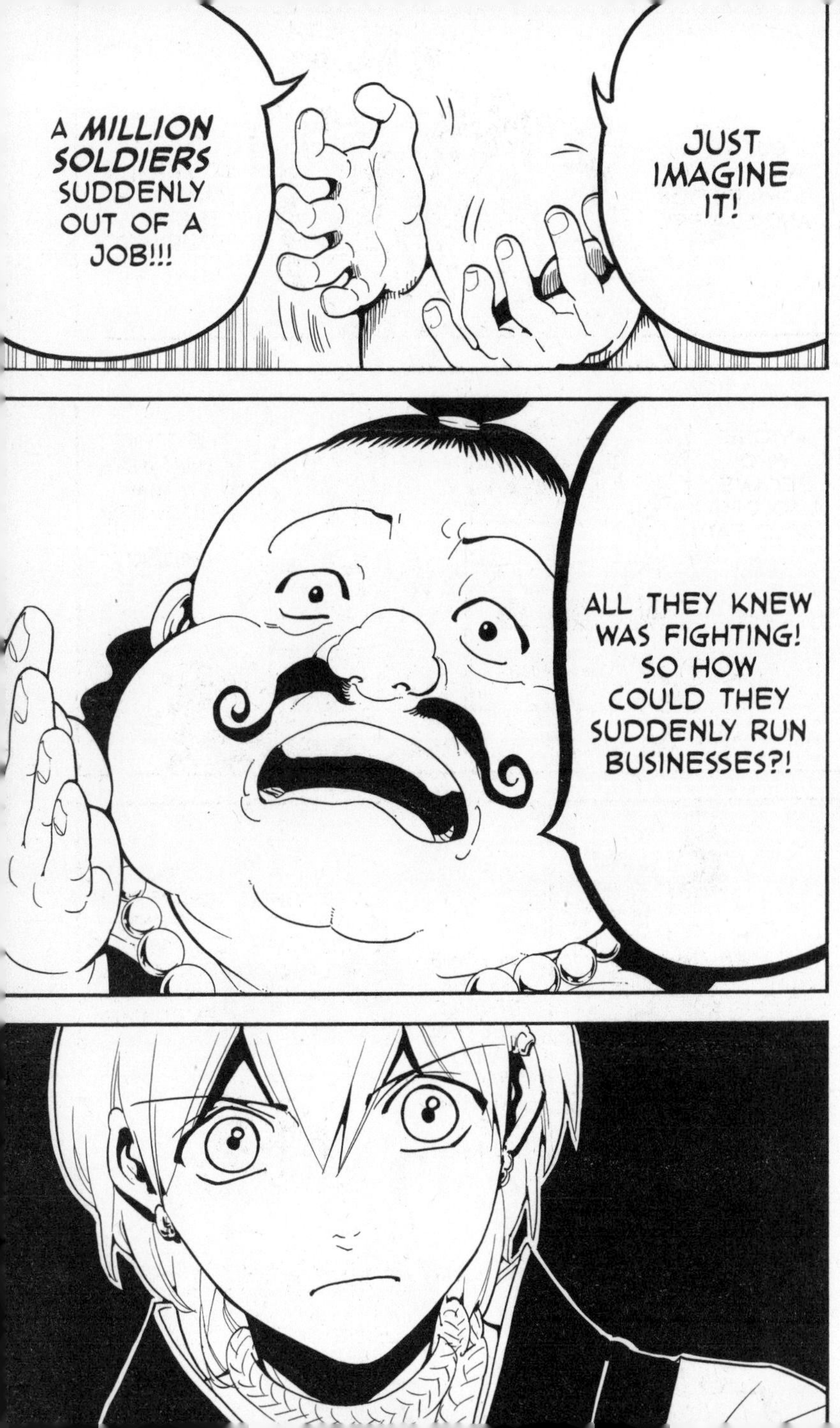
JUST IMAGINE IT!
A MILLION SOLDIERS SUDDENLY OUT OF A JOB!!!
ALL THEY KNEW WAS FIGHTING! SO HOW COULD THEY SUDDENLY RUN BUSINESSES?!

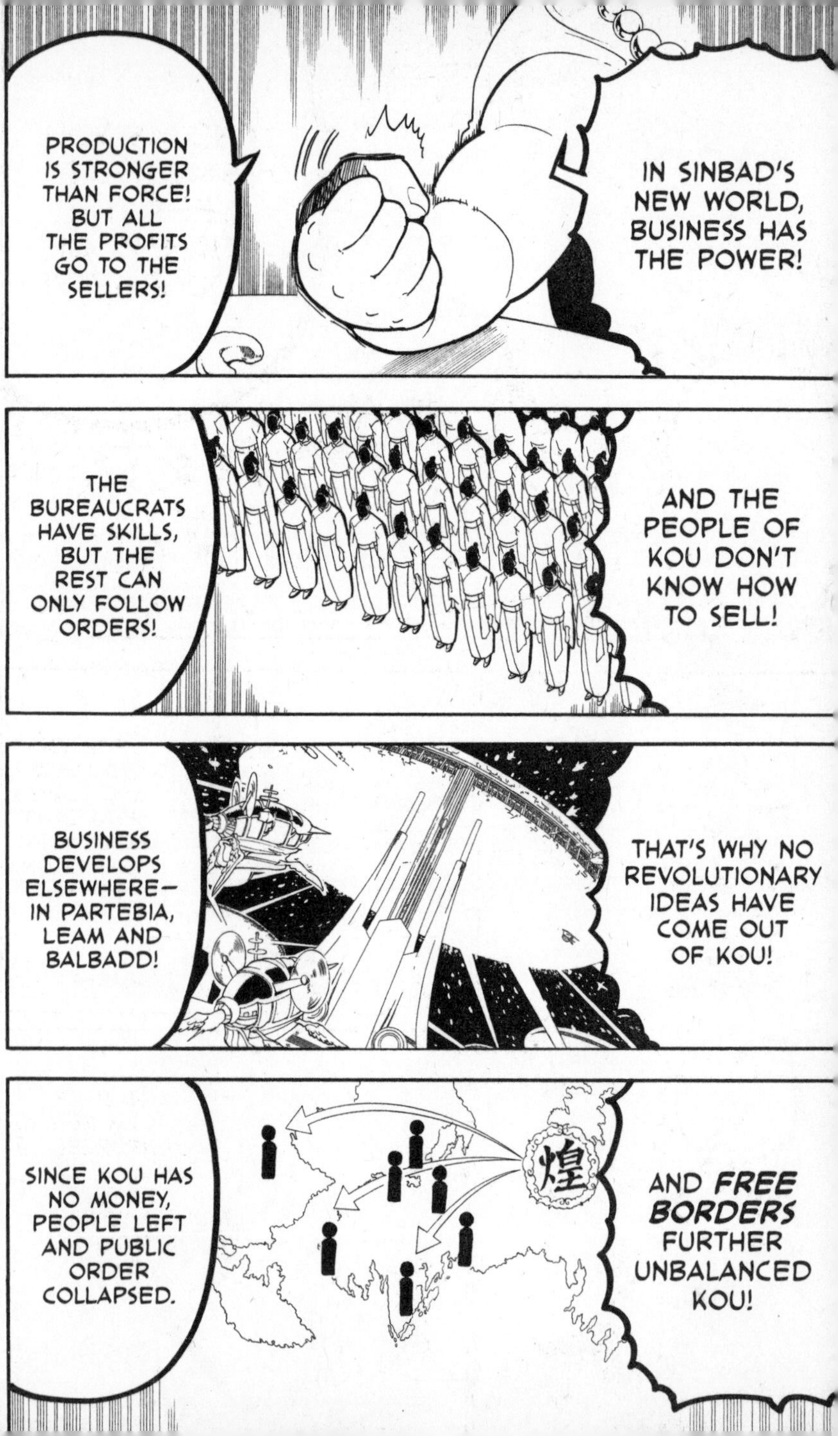
IN SINBAD'S NEW WORLD, BUSINESS HAS THE POWER!
PRODUCTION IS STRONGER THAN FORCE! BUT ALL THE PROFITS GO TO THE SELLERS!
AND THE PEOPLE OF KOU DON'T KNOW HOW TO SELL!
THE BUREAUCRATS HAVE SKILLS, BUT THE REST CAN ONLY FOLLOW ORDERS!
THAT'S WHY NO REVOLUTIONARY IDEAS HAVE COME OUT OF KOU!
BUSINESS DEVELOPS ELSEWHERE—IN PARTEBIA, LEAM AND BALBADD!
AND *FREE BORDERS* FURTHER UNBALANCED KOU!
煌
SINCE KOU HAS NO MONEY, PEOPLE LEFT AND PUBLIC ORDER COLLAPSED.

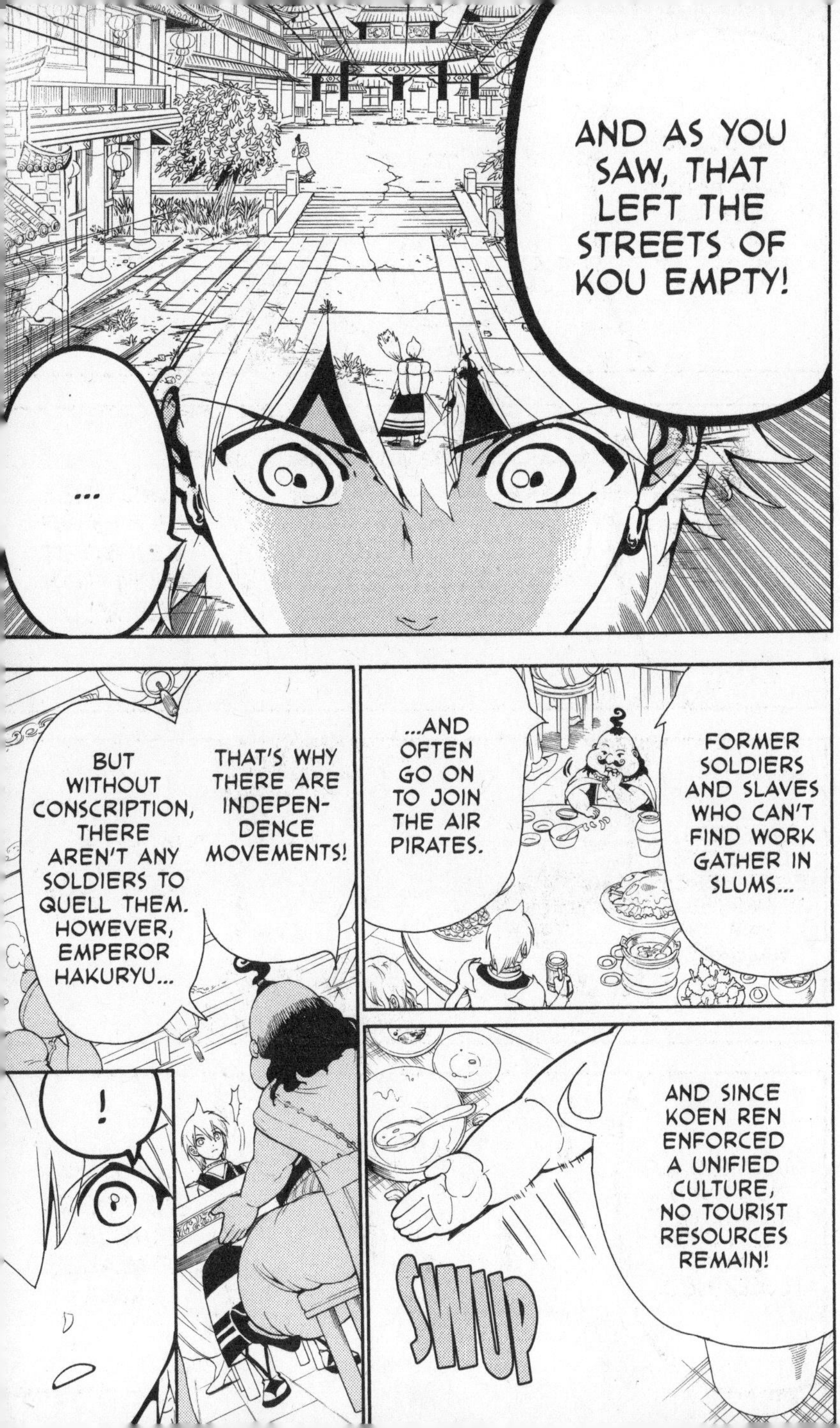
AND AS YOU SAW, THAT LEFT THE STREETS OF KOU EMPTY!
...
FORMER SOLDIERS AND SLAVES WHO CAN'T FIND WORK GATHER IN SLUMS...
...AND OFTEN GO ON TO JOIN THE AIR PIRATES.
THAT'S WHY THERE ARE INDEPEN-DENCE MOVEMENTS!
BUT WITHOUT CONSCRIPTION, THERE AREN'T ANY SOLDIERS TO QUELL THEM. HOWEVER, EMPEROR HAKURYU...
AND SINCE KOEN REN ENFORCED A UNIFIED CULTURE, NO TOURIST RESOURCES REMAIN!
SNUP
!

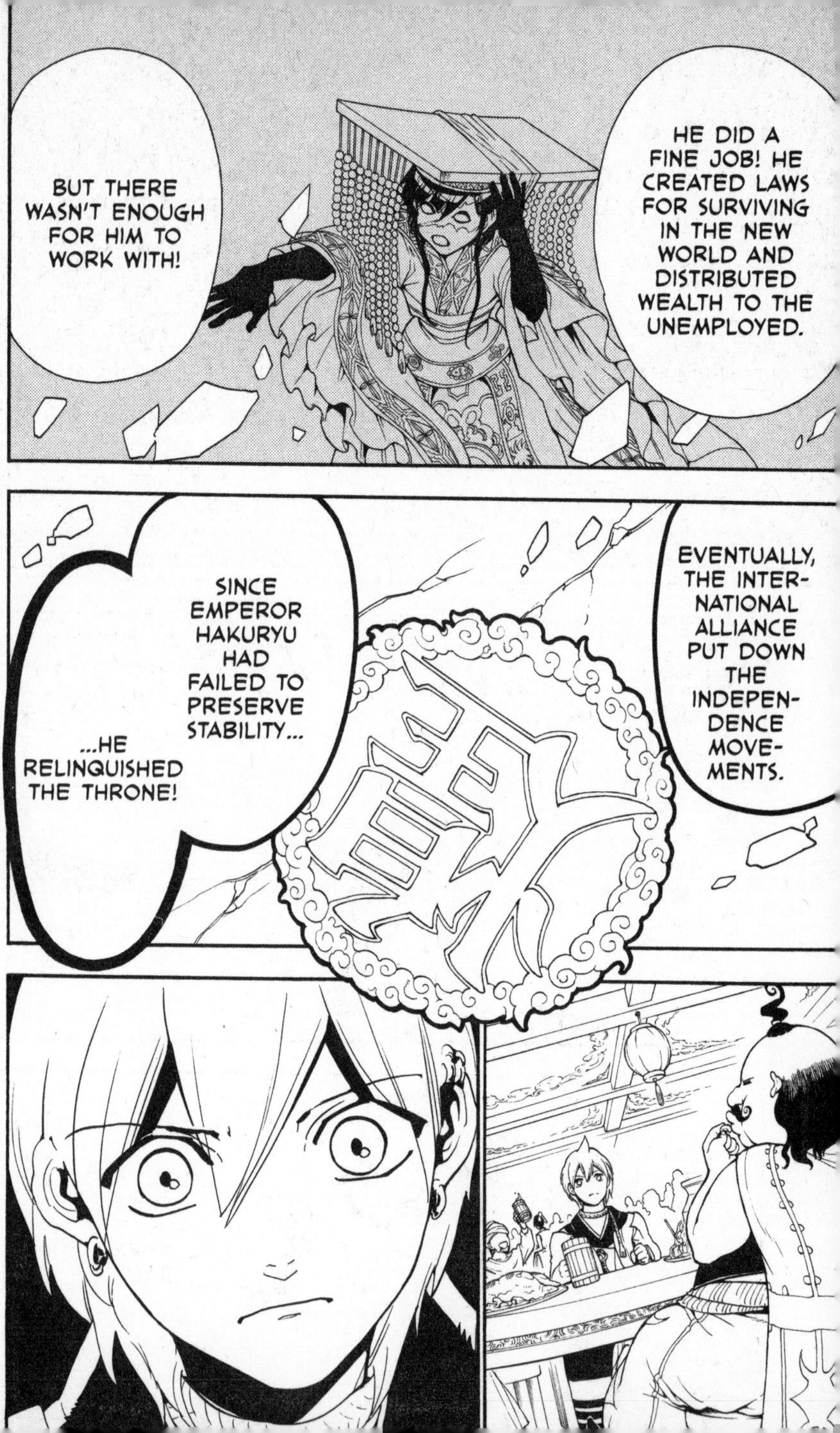
HE DID A FINE JOB! HE CREATED LAWS FOR SURVIVING IN THE NEW WORLD AND DISTRIBUTED WEALTH TO THE UNEMPLOYED.
BUT THERE WASN'T ENOUGH FOR HIM TO WORK WITH!
EVENTUALLY, THE INTER-NATIONAL ALLIANCE PUT DOWN THE INDEPEN-DENCE MOVE-MENTS.
SINCE EMPEROR HAKURYU HAD FAILED TO PRESERVE STABILITY...
...HE RELINQUISHED THE THRONE!

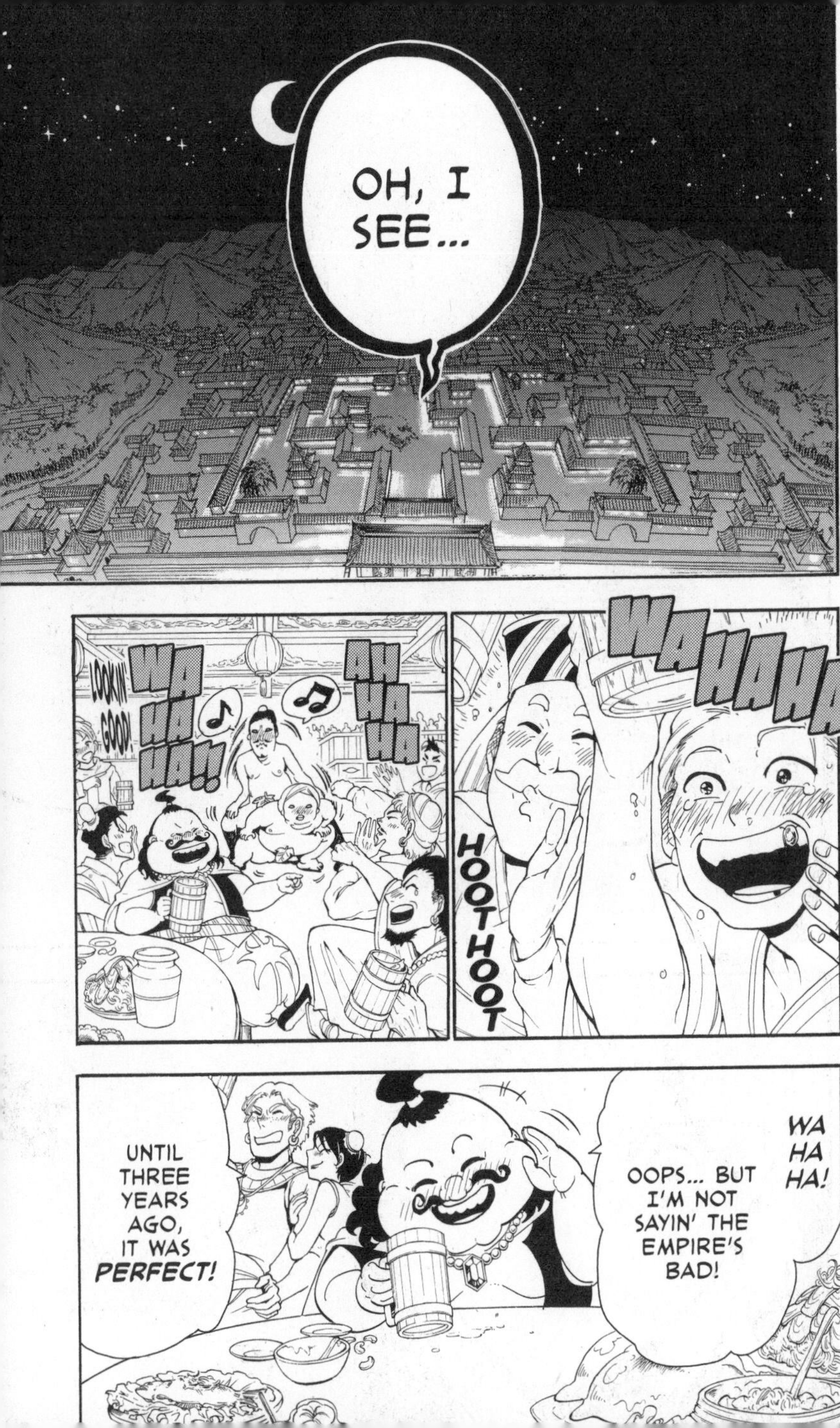
OH, I SEE...
WAHAHAHA
HOOTHOOT
AH HA HA HA
WA HA HA HA!!
LOOKIN' GOOD!
WA HA HA!
OOPS... BUT I'M NOT SAYIN' THE EMPIRE'S BAD!
UNTIL THREE YEARS AGO, IT WAS *PERFECT*!

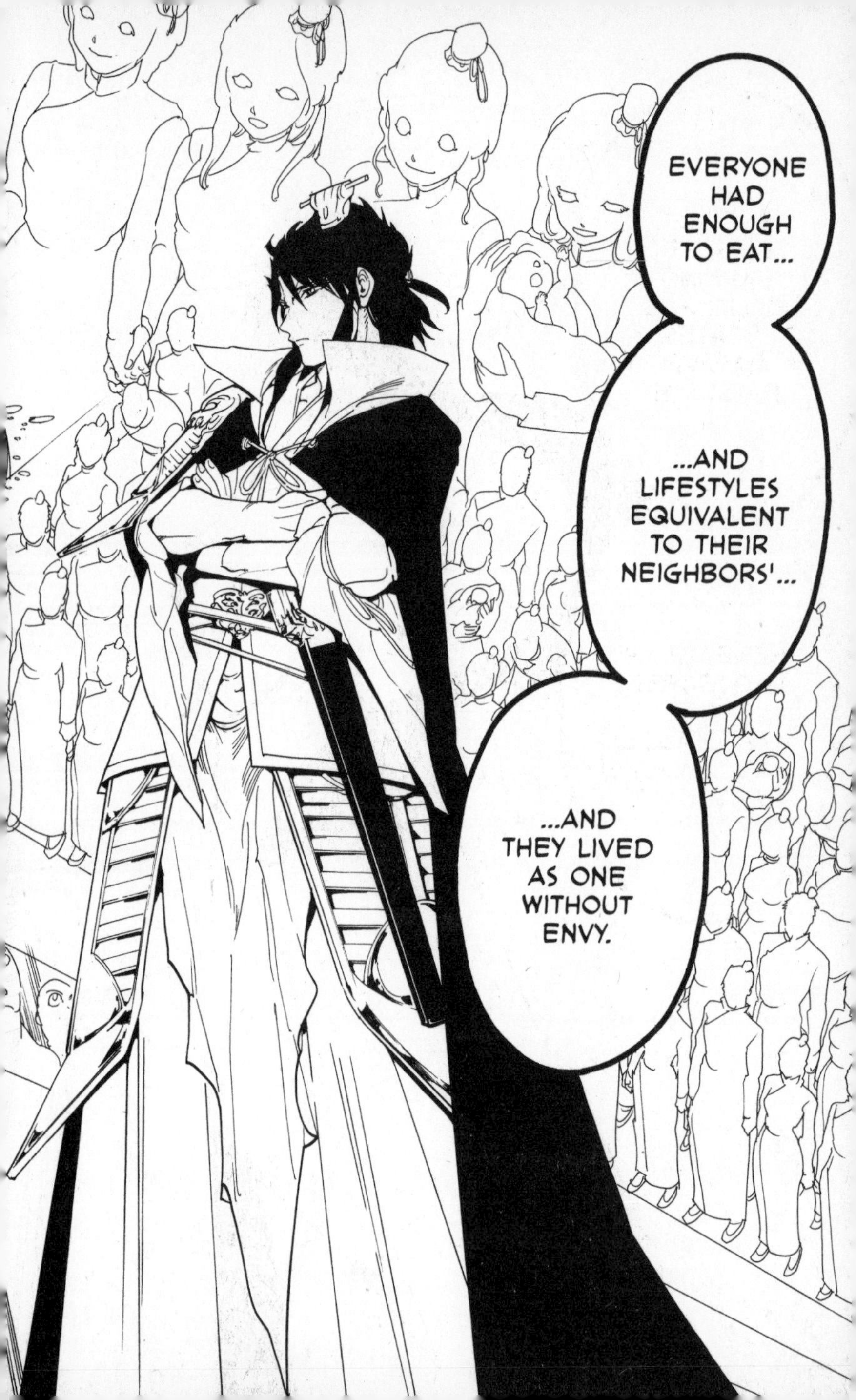
EVERYONE HAD ENOUGH TO EAT...
...AND LIFESTYLES EQUIVALENT TO THEIR NEIGHBORS'...
...AND THEY LIVED AS ONE WITHOUT ENVY.

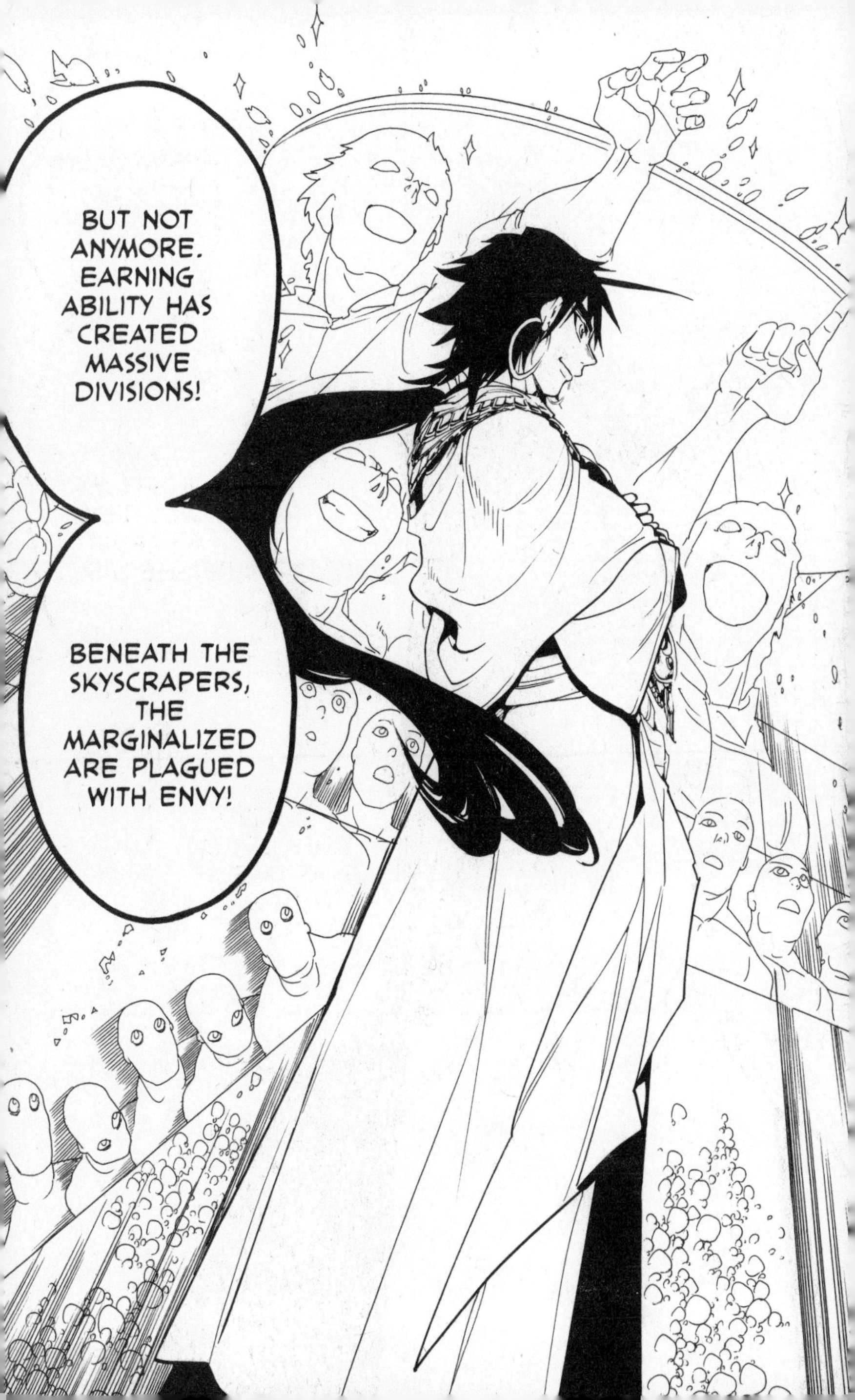
BUT NOT ANYMORE. EARNING ABILITY HAS CREATED MASSIVE DIVISIONS!
BENEATH THE SKYSCRAPERS, THE MARGINALIZED ARE PLAGUED WITH ENVY!

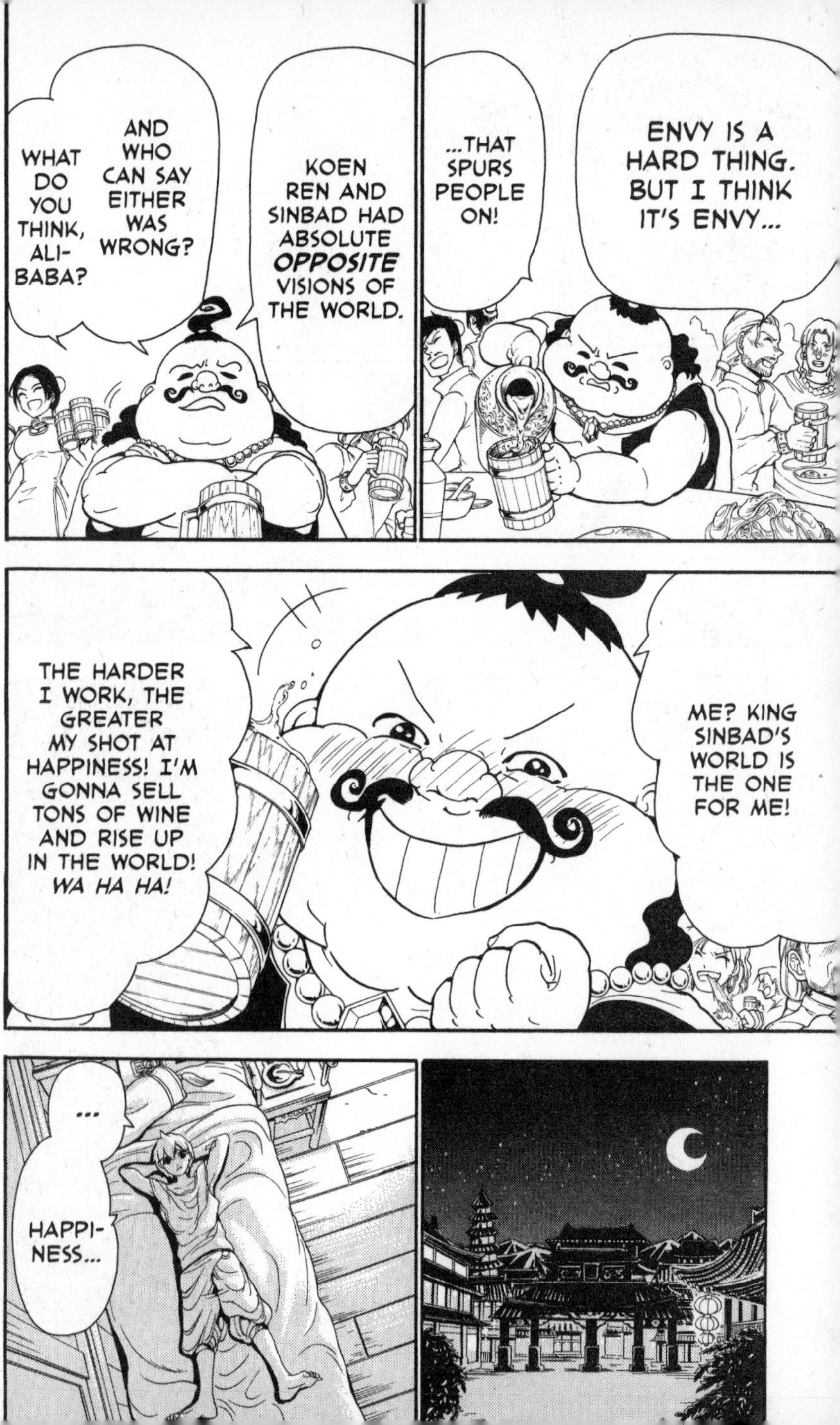
ENVY IS A HARD THING. BUT I THINK IT'S ENVY...
...THAT SPURS PEOPLE ON!
KOEN REN AND SINBAD HAD ABSOLUTE *OPPOSITE* VISIONS OF THE WORLD.
AND WHO CAN SAY EITHER WAS WRONG?
WHAT DO YOU THINK, ALI-BABA?
ME? KING SINBAD'S WORLD IS THE ONE FOR ME!
THE HARDER I WORK, THE GREATER MY SHOT AT HAPPINESS! I'M GONNA SELL TONS OF WINE AND RISE UP IN THE WORLD! *WA HA HA!*
...
HAPPINESS...

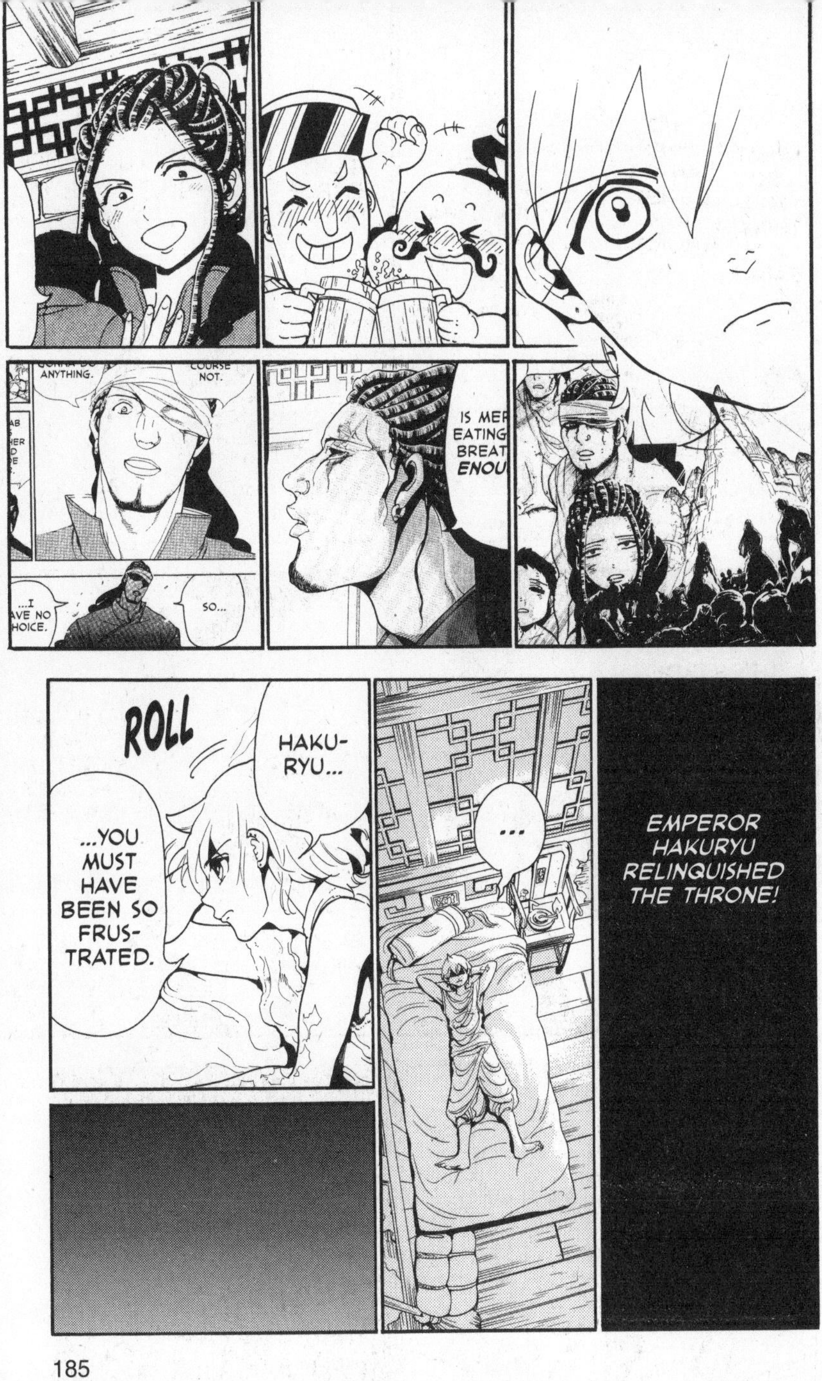

IS MER EATING BREAT ENOU
COURSE NOT.
GONNA DO ANYTHING.
SO...
...I AVE NO HOICE.
EMPEROR HAKURYU RELINQUISHED THE THRONE!
...
HAKU-RYU...
ROLL
...YOU MUST HAVE BEEN SO FRUS-TRATED.

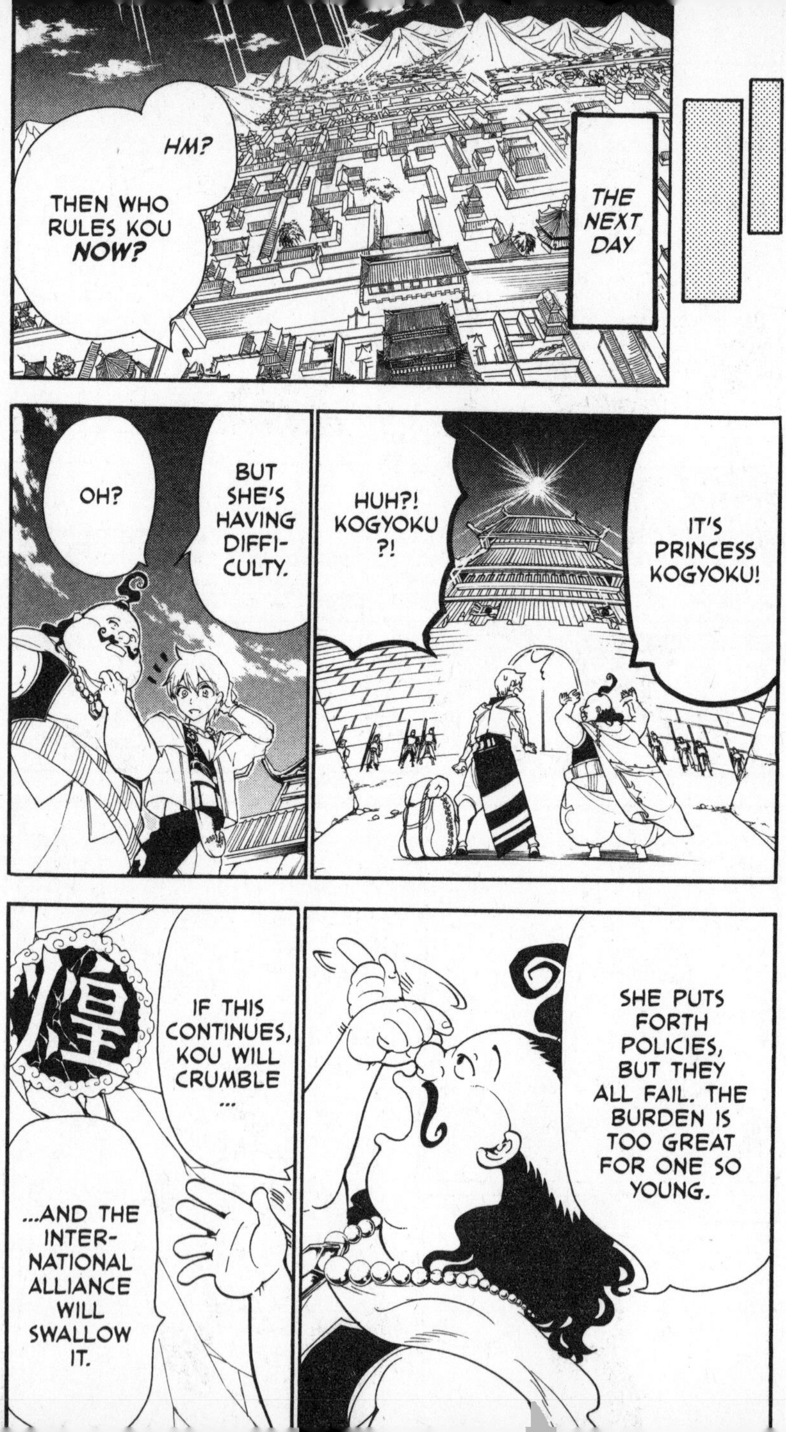
THE NEXT DAY
HM?
THEN WHO RULES KOU NOW?
IT'S PRINCESS KOGYOKU!
HUH?! KOGYOKU ?!
BUT SHE'S HAVING DIFFI-CULTY.
OH?
SHE PUTS FORTH POLICIES, BUT THEY ALL FAIL. THE BURDEN IS TOO GREAT FOR ONE SO YOUNG.
IF THIS CONTINUES, KOU WILL CRUMBLE ...
煌
...AND THE INTER-NATIONAL ALLIANCE WILL SWALLOW IT.

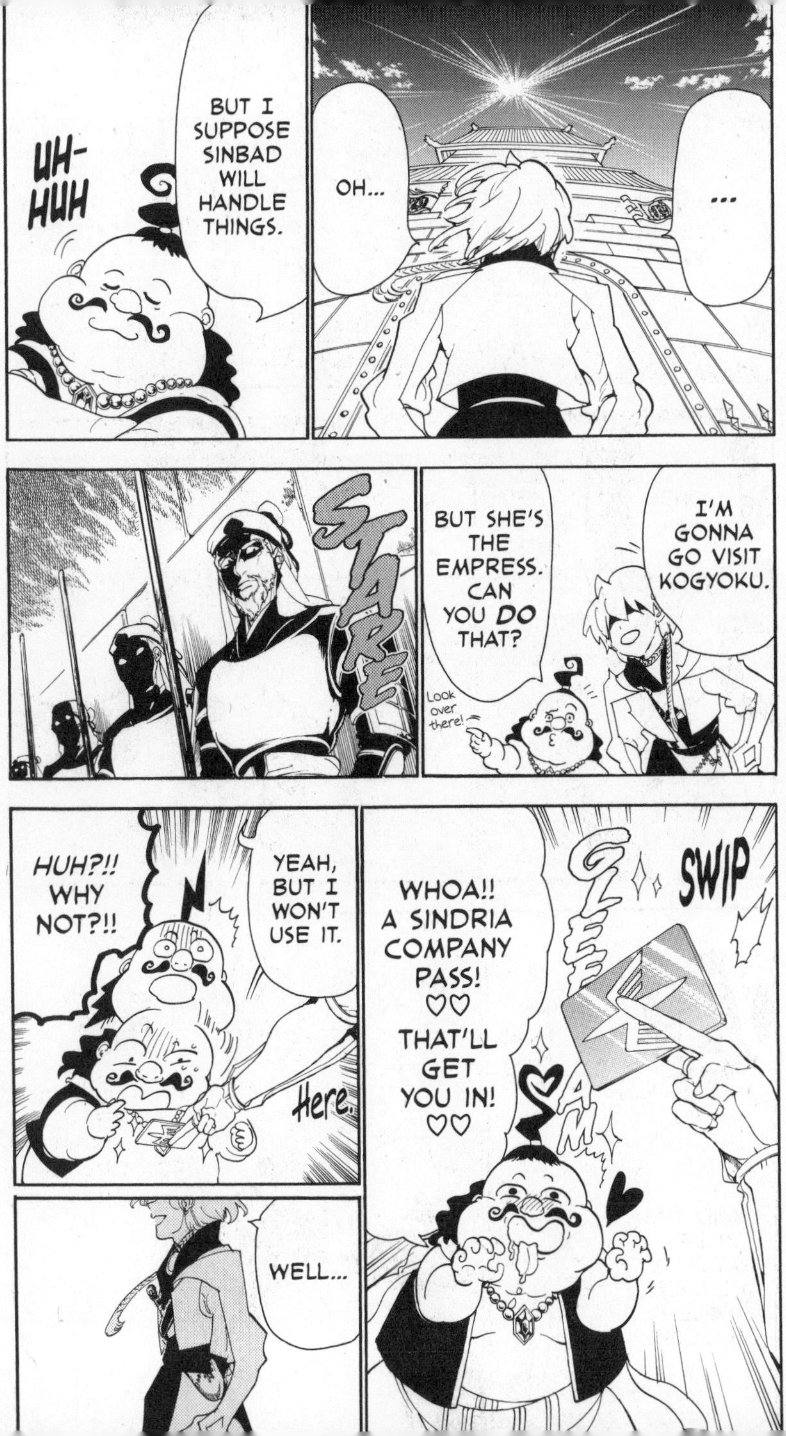
...
OH...
BUT I SUPPOSE SINBAD WILL HANDLE THINGS.
UH-HUH
I'M GONNA GO VISIT KOGYOKU.
BUT SHE'S THE EMPRESS. CAN YOU *DO* THAT?
Look over there!
STARE
SWIP
GLEAM
WHOA!! A SINDRIA COMPANY PASS! ♡♡ THAT'LL GET YOU IN! ♡♡
YEAH, BUT I WON'T USE IT.
HUH?!! WHY NOT?!!
Here.
WELL...

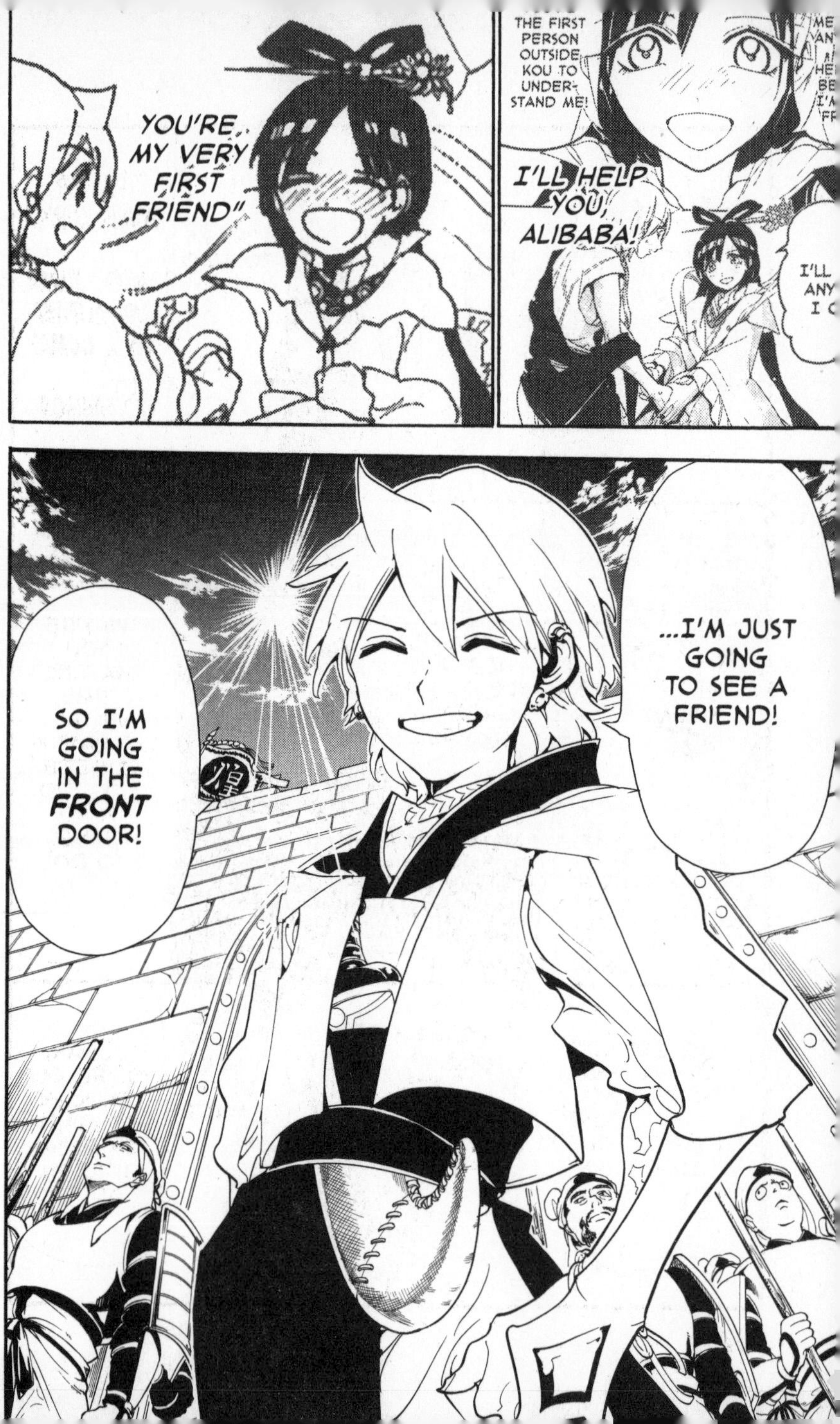
THE FIRST PERSON OUTSIDE KOU TO UNDER-STAND ME!
I'LL HELP YOU, ALIBABA!
YOU'RE MY VERY FIRST FRIEND"
...I'M JUST GOING TO SEE A FRIEND!
SO I'M GOING IN THE FRONT DOOR!

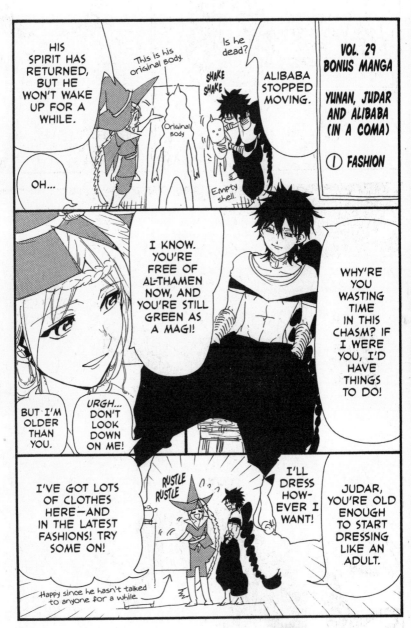

VOL. 29 BONUS MANGA
YUNAN, JUDAR AND ALIBABA (IN A COMA)
① FASHION
ALIBABA STOPPED MOVING.
Is he dead?
SHAKE SHAKE
This is his original body.
Original Body
Empty shell.
HIS SPIRIT HAS RETURNED, BUT HE WON'T WAKE UP FOR A WHILE.
OH...
WHY'RE YOU WASTING TIME IN THIS CHASM? IF I WERE YOU, I'D HAVE THINGS TO DO!
I KNOW. YOU'RE FREE OF AL-THAMEN NOW, AND YOU'RE STILL GREEN AS A MAGI!
URGH... DON'T LOOK DOWN ON ME!
BUT I'M OLDER THAN YOU.
JUDAR, YOU'RE OLD ENOUGH TO START DRESSING LIKE AN ADULT.
I'LL DRESS HOW-EVER I WANT!
RUSTLE RUSTLE
I'VE GOT LOTS OF CLOTHES HERE—AND IN THE LATEST FASHIONS! TRY SOME ON!
Happy since he hasn't talked to anyone for a while.

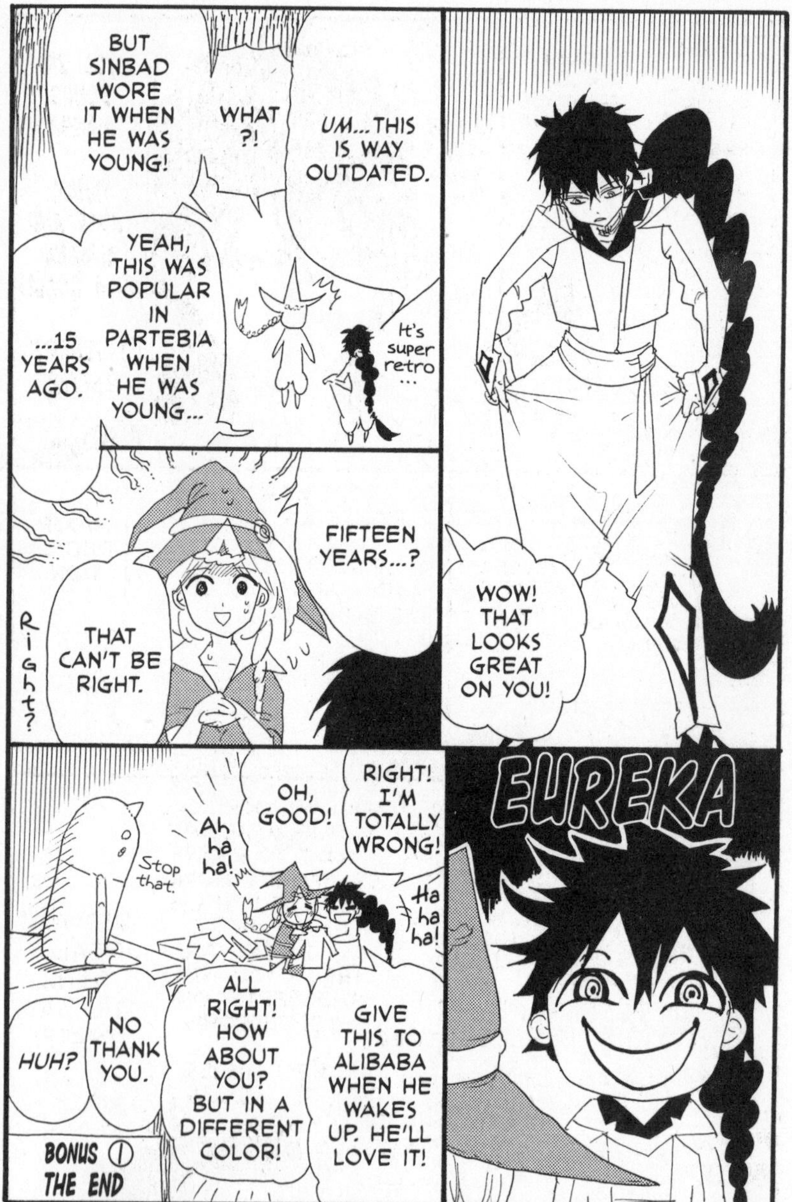

WOW! THAT LOOKS GREAT ON YOU!
UM... THIS IS WAY OUTDATED.
WHAT?!
BUT SINBAD WORE IT WHEN HE WAS YOUNG!
It's super retro...
YEAH, THIS WAS POPULAR IN PARTEBIA WHEN HE WAS YOUNG...
...15 YEARS AGO.
FIFTEEN YEARS...?
THAT CAN'T BE RIGHT.
Right?
EUREKA
RIGHT! I'M TOTALLY WRONG!
OH, GOOD!
Ha ha ha!
Ah ha ha!
Stop that.
GIVE THIS TO ALIBABA WHEN HE WAKES UP. HE'LL LOVE IT!
ALL RIGHT! HOW ABOUT YOU? BUT IN A DIFFERENT COLOR!
NO THANK YOU.
HUH?
BONUS 1 THE END

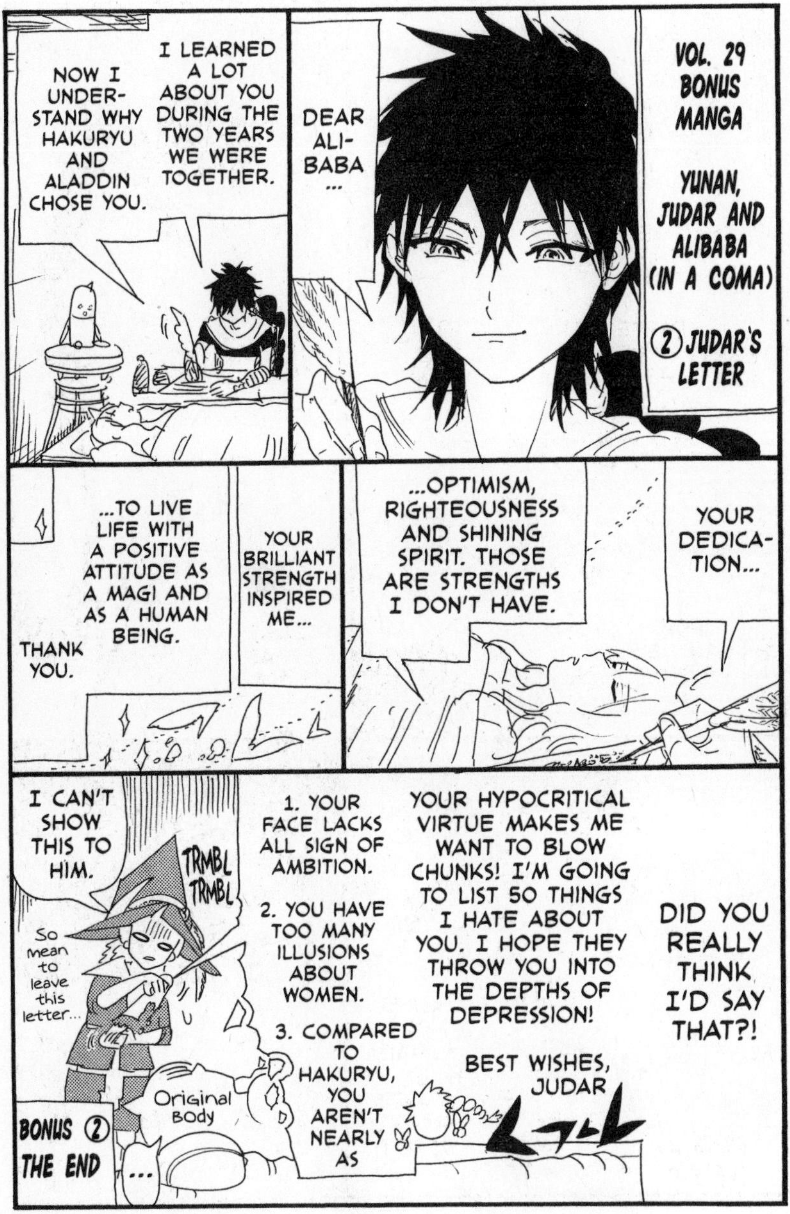
VOL. 29 BONUS MANGA
YUNAN, JUDAR AND ALIBABA (IN A COMA)
② JUDAR'S LETTER
DEAR ALI-BABA...
I LEARNED A LOT ABOUT YOU DURING THE TWO YEARS WE WERE TOGETHER.
NOW I UNDER-STAND WHY HAKURYU AND ALADDIN CHOSE YOU.
YOUR DEDICA-TION...
...OPTIMISM, RIGHTEOUSNESS AND SHINING SPIRIT. THOSE ARE STRENGTHS I DON'T HAVE.
YOUR BRILLIANT STRENGTH INSPIRED ME...
...TO LIVE LIFE WITH A POSITIVE ATTITUDE AS A MAGI AND AS A HUMAN BEING.
THANK YOU.
DID YOU REALLY THINK I'D SAY THAT?!
YOUR HYPOCRITICAL VIRTUE MAKES ME WANT TO BLOW CHUNKS! I'M GOING TO LIST 50 THINGS I HATE ABOUT YOU. I HOPE THEY THROW YOU INTO THE DEPTHS OF DEPRESSION!
BEST WISHES, JUDAR
1. YOUR FACE LACKS ALL SIGN OF AMBITION.
2. YOU HAVE TOO MANY ILLUSIONS ABOUT WOMEN.
3. COMPARED TO HAKURYU, YOU AREN'T NEARLY AS
I CAN'T SHOW THIS TO HIM.
TRMBL TRMBL
So mean to leave this letter...
Original Body
...
BONUS ② THE END

SHINOBU OHTAKA

The Kou Empire Arc ends! And the final chapter of Magi begins!

MAGI

Volume 29
Shonen Sunday Edition

Story and Art by
SHINOBU OHTAKA

MAGI Vol.29
by Shinobu OHTAKA
© 2009 Shinobu OHTAKA
All rights reserved.
Original Japanese edition published by SHOGAKUKAN.
English translation rights in the United States of America, Canada, the United Kingdom,
Ireland, Australia and New Zealand arranged with SHOGAKUKAN.

ORIGINAL COVER DESIGN / Yasuo SHIMURA+Bay Bridge Studio

Translation & English Adaptation ◆ John Werry

Touch-up Art & Lettering ◆ Stephen Dutro

Editor ◆ Mike Montesa

Printed in Canada

Published by VIZ Media, LLC
P.O. Box 77010
San Francisco, CA 94107

10 9 8 7 6 5 4 3 2 1
First printing, April 2018

www.viz.com

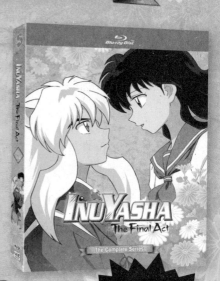

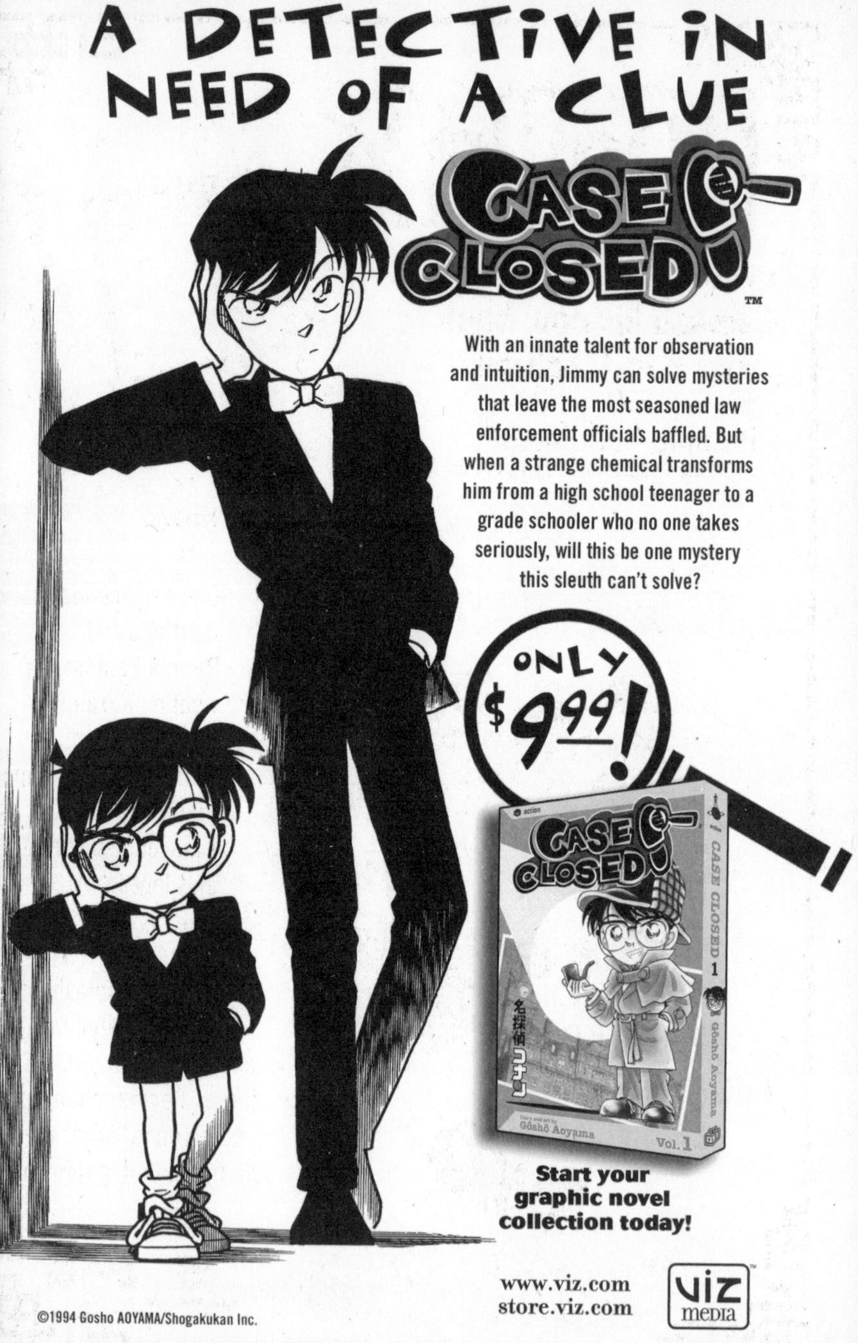
A DETECTIVE IN NEED OF A CLUE
CASE CLOSED™
With an innate talent for observation and intuition, Jimmy can solve mysteries that leave the most seasoned law enforcement officials baffled. But when a strange chemical transforms him from a high school teenager to a grade schooler who no one takes seriously, will this be one mystery this sleuth can't solve?
ONLY $9.99!
CASE CLOSED
Vol. 1
Gôshô Aoyama
Start your graphic novel collection today!
www.viz.com
store.viz.com
VIZ MEDIA
©1994 Gosho AOYAMA/Shogakukan Inc.